DOCTRINE AND DIFFERENCE

Routledge
New York and London

DOCTRINE AND DIFFERENCE

Essays in the Literature of New England

Michael J. Colacurcio

Published in 1997
by Routledge
29 West 35th Street
New York, NY 10001

Published in
Great Britain by
Routledge
11 New Fetter Lane
London EC4P 4EE

Copyright © 1997 by
Routledge
Printed in the
United States of America
on acid-free paper.

Library of Congress Cataloging-in-Publication-Data

Colacurcio, Michael J.
    Doctrine and difference: essays in the literature of
    New England / Michael J. Colacurcio
    p. cm.
Includes bibliographical references and index.
ISBN 0-415-91238-5 (hb.) — ISBN 0-415-91239-3

    1. American literature—New England—History and criticism.
    2. American literature—Puritan authors—History and criticism.
    3. Christianity and literature—New England—History.
    4. Puritan movements in literature.
    5. New England—Intellectual life.
    6. New England—In literature.
I. Title
PS243.C65 1996
810.9'974—dc20

                                                    95-43069

DEDICATION

For
Lisa, Laurie, Valerie
(and Mary and Carol and Jeanette)

ACKNOWLEDGMENTS

AS MOST of the claims in this book were first tried out in the classroom, I should thank my students, particularly those in my graduate classes at UCLA, for treating them as respectfully as possible. Recalling the friendly responses of John Alberti, Geoff Sanborn, Lisa Gordis, Emily Schiller, Eric Selinger, John Lednicky, Laura Arnold, Martin Kevorkian, Will Moddelmog, Maurice Lee, Jayne Devens, Rebecca Humenuk, Stanley Orr, Yair Reiner, Betty Donohoe, Willene Van Blair, Kris Fresonke, Luke Bresky, Joanna Brooks, and Grainne McEvoy, one realizes again how the notion of an "ideal audience" can fairly arise. Let that charmed circle also include Emory Elliott, who sponsored a couple of my attempts; Sacvan Bercovitch, who found a way to praise some other tries; and Barbara Packer and Albert von Frank, who know Emerson well enough to encourage other people's work on that remarkable subject.

More particular thanks are due to Gráinne McEvoy and to that exemplary undergraduate student, Cynthia Bullock, for helping me make my citations more accurate and my footnotes more timely than my own wavering attention could by itself have managed. To David Rahmel and Rick Fagin for (almost) teaching me how to make a computer do literary criticism; to Jeanette Gilkison for typing everything the computer rejected (and helping me remember my name); and to Carol Bensick for postponing her breakdown until after I had had my own.

Finally, my grateful acknowledgment of the publishers of earlier versions of some of my chapters: to the Johns Hopkins University Press, for permission to republish a revision of "The Footsteps of Ann Hutchinson," ELH, 39 (1972), pp. 459–94; to the Board of Trustees of the University of Illinois, for "The Example of Edwards," in Emory Elliot, ed., *Puritan Influences in American Literature* (University of Illinois Press, 1979), pp. 55–106; to the Cambridge University Press, for "The Woman's Own Choice," in Colacurcio, ed., *New Essays on the Scarlet Letter* (1985), pp. 101–35; to the Regents of the University of California, for "The Corn and the Wine," *Nineteenth-Century Literature*, 42 (1987), pp. 1–28; to the Board of Regents of Washington State University, for "Pleasing God," ESQ, 37 (1991), pp. 141–212; and to the University of Notre Dame, for "Puritans in Spite," *Religion and Literature*, 26 (1994), pp. 27–54.

CONTENTS

ACKNOWLEDGMENTS vii

AMERICANIST CRITICISM: 1
AN APOLOGETICAL INTRODUCTION

chapter 1   CHRIST'S REPLY, SAINT'S ASSURANCE:
TAYLOR'S DOUBLE STANDARD 27

chapter 2   THE EXAMPLE OF EDWARDS:
PURITAN IMAGINATION AND THE
METAPHYSICS OF SOVEREIGNTY 61

CODA (1995):
IDEALISM WITHOUT THE SUBJECT 98

chapter 3   "THE CORN AND THE WINE":
EMERSON, THEISM, AND THE
PIETY OF GEORGE HERBERT 109

CONTENTS

chapter 4 PLEASING GOD:
THE LUCID STRIFE OF EMERSON'S "ADDRESS"....................129

chapter 5 FOOTSTEPS OF ANN HUTCHINSON:
A PURITAN CONTEXT FOR *THE SCARLET LETTER* 177

chapter 6 "THE WOMAN'S OWN CHOICE":
SEX, METAPHOR, AND THE PURITAN
"SOURCES" OF *THE SCARLET LETTER*................................205

chapter 7 PURITANS IN SPITE..229

NOTES 251

INDEX 295

AMERICANIST CRITICISM

An Apologetical Introduction

THE MOMENT I let on that the chapters in this book are offered as examples, perhaps even models, of an historical criticism, the alert reader will immediately wish to know whether my history is Old or New. And I confess I'm not entirely sure. I'd like to think that none of these intertextual essays will be confused with the old-time practice of "source study," positivistic in its understanding of evidence and willing to stand off from interpretative consequences. On the other hand, however, I do seem more interested in my authors' religious past than in their political present. And I have almost nothing to say about their "political unconscious," the epistemology of which seems to me even more fragile than the more familiar psychoanalytic sort.[1]

I have tried, of course, not to be naïve about politics in general, or about race, class, and gender in particular, but my focus really is on the sort of religious ideas that always tempt the observer to posit some *conscious* fiction, like "the mind." I think, from time to time, I almost understand what Foucault has meant by "discourse"—and what almost everyone now means by "social construction." Yet I often find myself sneakingly interested in the "author function": it helps me to recall, now and again, that Edward Taylor wrote the *Preparatory Meditations* and not Michael Wigglesworth; and not, in some significant sense, myself.[2] Nor can I quite keep from regarding the construction of texts out of other texts as so many episodes in a *literary* history that is quite as serious and interesting, in its intellectualist way, as other, more material accounts of their social production. Worse yet, I seem constitutionally unable to resist the fatal lure of the rhetoric of dependency. I never can remember to begin a scholastic essay with a dramatic scene, or ever learn to practice what I know about the mode of the multiple or the trope of conjunction. Just when my best arranged juxtapositions threaten to seem positively uncanny, I usually spoil the effect by saying something causal: not just one more exhilarating *and*, but the sure-fire bring-down *thus*. And though I probably could, under extreme pressure, produce an extended account of my personal investment in the texts I talk about from time to time, I find the exercise narcissistic at the outset and boring in the end: they taught religion when I was little, and it seems to me a part of culture still.[3]

Most generally, then, the essays in this volume all flow from the self-protecting wish to keep the academic world safe for the thing I seem to do best— to recover, if possible, and to publish, if permitted, the life and the power of those philosophic and scriptural ideas which make the religious concerns of the past seem not entirely a matter of false consciousness. And, more specifically, to add my voice to the devoted but no longer fashionable chorus of those who think it would be pretty hard to overestimate the interest or the explanatory power of the ideology of the American Puritans.

As interest is almost entirely a personal matter, the best one can do is to enact the terms of one's own: the more the others have recourse to the demon deconstruction, the more angels will I set adance on the head of a pin; perhaps they may come, in the end, to respect my fantasy as soberly as I do theirs. Explanation, on the other hand, is quite another matter, about which we must and do argue as well as we know how. And, in the case of the present volume, it involves more than one significant set of terms. One might wonder, for example, how deeply and formatively the Calvinist premise of sovereignty or the Congregationalist theory of visible sanctity may have penetrated the minds and informed the writings of such Puritans as, for whatever reason, we still do regularly read and teach. Might we miss something interesting, perhaps, if we refuse to let this past conform our minds as fully as possible to its own way of being other? And then—supposing we can discover that such "doctrinal" issues are constitutive for Edward Taylor and Jonathan Edwards as well as for John Cotton and Thomas Hooker—what sort of cultural afterlife can we discover them to have had?

Of course the project is not quite so innocent as it can be made to sound. No one should suppose, for example, that the transplant of church reform from Old England to New is the inevitable and only subject of early American literature; or that, within this Eurocentric preserve, doctrinal recovery and literary differentiation is the only project invited by the writings of the inventors of New England. Nor is it safe to imagine that the construct called "Puritanism" holds the key to all the mythologies of American writing in the nineteenth century. If these sorts of questions have come to seem very familiar, the reason is simply that some scholarly inventions have proven more lively and durable than others.

It remains true, first of all, that the influence of Perry Miller has worked to create one of the most powerfully unified fields of textual study in the history of the modern academy—second only, if at all, to Matthiessen's *"American Renaissance."* Then too, the example of Sacvan Bercovitch's masterful and ongoing account of "Puritan Origins" has served to support and extend rather than to undermine that nearly unique accomplishment.[4] The result of these signal achievements, and of the host of books and articles they have enabled, has been a lively but perhaps disproportionate emphasis on the importance of New England as instance, cause, and model of American moral character. For many, a grateful paradigm: an all but revealed way into and back out of the wilderness of generically peculiar and esthetically unselfconscious texts that flourish in the decades before the various inhabitants of North America became citizens of the United States and began, not incidentally, to be anxious about a belles lettres after the manner of other emergent nation states. For a growing number of others, however, an hegemony: an elitist attempt to ground the literary productions of an early capitalist culture on the ideological efforts of a sect which reified the private self by advertising its vices most unremittingly, and which sanctioned the rule of the socially competent by blurring the line between spiritual and worldly evidences. And there we are.

Probably the worst that can be charged against continuing the effort to elaborate the Puritan meanings of established writers such as Taylor and Edwards is that there are so many other jobs to be done: the Enlightenment and the Revolution as well as the Declension and the Awakening; Virginia and Pennsylvania as well as Massachusetts and Connecticut; women as well as men; blacks as well as whites; a native population as well as their cultural supplanters. Amen. One reads all the new work with a sort of Emersonian joy, that the Soul is alive and well in so many departments of scholarly endeavor; and with a sort of chagrin, also recognizably Emersonian, that one's own gift seems not to lie in those directions. The problem of "Puritan Influences," however, is as much a matter of method as of calling. And—though one is not Prince

3

Hamlet—perhaps it is time to move from the realm of silent assumption to the arena of public explanation.

One may as well come clean at the outset: American literature is a different field from the one we have all been calling "English." The issue may appear to be primarily epistemological, a matter of the generic perceptions that lie behind the invention of our key terms; or literary-historical, as we struggle to say whether British writers or American conditions have more to do with the products of the profession of authorship in the several colonies that go before united states of North America. But the issue is more intelligibly treated as one of commitment or of function, a matter of what those scholars willing to be known as "Americanists" have in fact found themselves to be doing. And also, perhaps, as an issue of ethics and of politics; of the reasons, that is to say, why these Americanists have regularly behaved in some ways and not in others.[5]

The situation would be perfectly clear if we could limit our notice to the activities that have gone on under the label of "American Studies." That academic experiment, once regarded by the proud as a hopelessly undertheorized preserve of amateur sociology, can now be recognized, just as fairly, as an ungainly yet somehow inspired prefiguration of proper academic conscience. For these place-specific Studies were nothing if not Cultural, and one had to begin somewhere.[6] But unless my experience of the profession has been completely warped, most professors of American Literature have been interested in the national literature as an index of national culture all along. Whatever they have written on their office door cards—and whether or not they participated in all those anxious-making conferences on "method"—most specifically trained and consciously professing "Americanists" have stood a step or two aside from the procession of formalisms that have marched through the American Academy in the form or in the footsteps of the New Criticism.[7] Close readings of American texts have abounded, to be sure, yet the simple (if problematic) premise of American-ness was sufficient to belie the posture of political indifference and to announce the inescapable relevance of history.

The claim is not that the New Criticism's defiance of historical conditioning had no full and expressive life in the American academy; indeed it may have flourished more vigorously here than anywhere else. But it worked best—or was trusted most—when faithfully employed by American professors of British literature. And indeed why not? It spoke of the work of literature not as a "criticism of life" but as an "autonomous heterocosm" or else, at all events, as a "world elsewhere"; and what were the lakes, the hedge-rows (hardly hedge-rows), and the pubs of England to us but precisely that? Over *there*, a strong line of staunch citizens of the British Academy—from C.S. Lewis and F.R. Leavis to Raymond Williams and Terry Eagleton—could hardly pretend to a fine disinterestedness.[8] Writing in different critical idioms, yet always as recognized interpreters of the literary product of a once proud and still self-conscious cultural empire, they knew as if by instinct that the task of interpretation could hardly be separated from the duty of defining, judging and, in the worst case, trying to amend the moral and political assumptions that found expression in the literature of a remote island grown used to placing itself at the center. Nor, back across the Atlantic, did culture critics like Leo Marx, Henry Nash Smith, and R.W.B. Lewis set out to make some entirely new departure in Americanist criticism; in fact, the worldly orientation of their critical practice was well prepared by the example of Parrington, Matthiessen, and Feidelson. Differences appear, no doubt, and they can be made to stand out as brightly as anyone's project may require, but it would be impossible to show that American criticism of American literature has ever strayed very far or for very long from the encompassing project of searching out and seeking to estimate the distinguishing marks of American culture.[9]

One might even risk an axiom: whatever else is true—here, there, or any-where—the criticism of the literature of a modern nation state tends to be historico-political whenever it is carried out by the citizens of that same nation state. They may begin, innocently enough, with a sort of instinctive acceptance of the work that lies nearest. But they come in time to see their task as a sort of patriotic duty; a term, so to speak, of their right to eat the bread of the fatherland.

And what else, in all honesty, can we suppose the harried but still leisured class of professional literary scholars is more legitimately *for*? To be sure, a small number of critics based outside of the Academy are free to imagine their life well justified if they have guided some literate remnant of doctors and lawyers through the offerings of their monthly book clubs; or if they have assured those same privileged readers, from time to time, that the scholarship pursued in modern Departments of English is altogether desiccated and jejune. But if so, they are hardly keeping faith with their tradition, which began with a somewhat more vital sense of culture in view.[10] With the much larger contingent of teacher-scholars, the case is complicated enough to permit all sorts of ironies: Americanists cooperate, first of all, with "Britishists," as with professors of many other disciplines, to keep young persons from crowding into the job market as early as they might; and we cultivate, no doubt, a special gift to offer technical instruction and moral support to adolescents in the throes of the best that has been thought and said. But as these functions will be fulfilled whether we advert to them or not, there remains plenty of space in which hard students of the history and present practice of narrative structure and figurative language may bear their own part in keeping watch on the national mythology.

Importantly, the duty is not to praise or recommend the complex and steadily contested model of national identity that seems to rise up from such

5

writings as will attract the notice of the prepared observer, though one can see why this may well have happened in the wake of the two world wars. Neither is it to blame and excoriate, though veterans of the 1960s will notice that acts of national contrition—and even of self-hate—do not come out of nowhere. Nor is the duty to search out, single-mindedly, and then to publicize, once and for all, the precise elements of the national *differentiae* as such, as if in the discovery of America as a biblical antitype or some other end-time essence. It is simply to pay close, continuous, and critical attention to what is always or usually or almost never said in texts that spring up in the American context; to look out for what D.H. Lawrence called "the spirit of place."[11] For readers, as we encounter them, in airports as well in our classes, are no less keenly on the alert for local constructions than for universal forms. And writers, as we seem finally to have understood, are bound to produce the former, even if some may seek the latter with all their human might.

A work of "literature" may still—should anyone care to insist—have power to create a "world" of its very own. But who can forbid the comparing of that construct with any other? Generic precedent may well be the easiest comparison to make: the operation requires historical learning, of course; and there is no reason to assume our author will respect our own sense of canonic importance; but at least the items being compared may be thought to enjoy the same ontological status. Worldly pretext would appear to be much more difficult, even if we should agree that the relevant foreknowledge is always already textual: let literary worlds be as complicated and multiform as we can possibly imagine, they are no match for the model of the superintending world we might construct out of all we know or suspect a given author may have seen, heard, or read. The best we can do, it appears, is to watch out for thematic echoes, distortions, or denials of public argumentation, to listen for the undersong of ideology, and to remember that the discovery of dialogue is as close as criticism may come to the invention of causality.

None of this political unction is meant to smooth over the fact that, at the outset at least, the Americanist persuasion has involved a sense of academic inferiority, as if very much of the writing produced on this side of the Atlantic required the interest of history to compensate for its failure to meet the test of literature "as such." No Chaucer, no Spenser, no Shakespeare, no *thought* of drama in the seventeenth century, only one Metaphysical Poet (and that one looking a little decadent); no Milton, no Swift, no very serious reenactment of classical form and value; no novel to speak of until the very end of the eighteenth century, and no Romantic Poet determined enough to compete with Wordsworth's full scale redaction of Milton's "high argument." Et cetera—as far as one can go before realizing that this alien literary history is glorious without being the least bit normative, and that the most literate parts of North America were founded in conscious dissent from nearly all of Old England's cultural pomps and works. But no wonder, in any event, if most Americanists could sound no braver than Popeye: we yar what we yar.[12]

Or, if this sense of cultural inferiority were less than universal, the fault was certainly not that of the colleagues with whom Americanists have had to live, more or less uneasily, within Departments of English. A wary sort of friendliness prevailed, often enough, but only on certain stern conditions. The embattled minority was never to protest when the Department moved to replace its retiring specialist in Drab Age Prose or Domestic Tragedy with another such, no matter what the tendencies of enrollment seemed to indicate; for the sun must never set on a semester in which the pageant of British literature was not fully reenacted, in Los Angeles, in Lincoln, in Bloomington, and in Chapel Hill, no less than in Princeton and New Haven. Neither must this curious remnant resent their underrepresentation on departmental search committees, even when the target was in fact someone to help satisfy the growing demand for courses in American literature; or raise their eyebrows too far if the successful candidate's interest in American texts turned out to be partial and temporary, a function of a "wider" concern—for some genre, perhaps, or, more recently, for some aspect of theory.

Above all, perhaps, the Americanists were expected to smile at an endless train of (not very) humorous remarks about the clumsy incompetence of most of what was passing for literature in the American canon, and to repress their growing but still inchoate sense that their intrinsically *cultural* study of American literature was coming to constitute a significantly different academic discipline. If one of them ever adventured—in the frustrated aftermath of a general meeting on curriculum or major requirements—to say something like "I don't think we all understand quite the same thing by the word 'literature,'" the answer came back, with a rare mixture of social bafflement and critical scorn, "Why yes, we quite mean it; and you, it seems plain, do not."

Stung repeatedly, but never quite daunted, the Americanist contingent kept on with its daily and yearly business—of locating, explicating, and assessing the texts that grew out from and commented back upon political and social realities of the curious sites where a variously migrant but swiftly assimilating people made strong textual claim to the importance of their experience. Thus occupied, they began to discover, slowly but not surprisingly, that very much of the literature so studied was actually very good. Not as some esthetically pure "thing in itself," such as the intention of absolutely anyone might stand outside itself to contemplate, apart from all possible interests of real life; yet plausibly enough, in all conscience, as a dialogically constructed and memorably formulated response to the questions of belief and action that cannot but arise from an historical world understood and approached as such. Patience, therefore, and resolution: sooner or later somebody else may think to ask why British literature, in all its luminous overdetermination, should continue to

7

seem the inevitable center of literary study in all the universities of the United States. Many students seemed to see the point already. Maybe, in a hundred years or so, English Professors would see it as well. Who knows? In a thousand years we might actually enjoy our very own departments.

But then some curious things began to happen. Theory, for one. A number of different voices began to observe that the special province of "the literary" is not so easy to define as the high priests of high culture had been wont to presume or proclaim; perhaps the notion of "literature as such" was a contestable interest of criticism and not at all a textual fact.[13] So powerfully was this skepticism advanced, and so faintly was it resisted, that for one brief moment it seemed that the Department of the Future would be organized—and also, not incidentally, unified—around the long repressed questions of theory that can be shown to underlie the practice of any criticism whatsoever. Medievalists, drawn back from their strange half-life inside the archive, Restorationists, still squinting from their patient edition of Dryden, Romanticists, refreshed by their annual trip to the Dove Cottage, were duly invited, all and each, to dine and to converse at the high table of Epistemology. Perhaps even Americanists could be lured away from their tiresome and provincial search for the unpardonable sin of national character.[14]

Or perhaps not. For suddenly—interrupting the consummation of this devoutness—other, more concertedly political games moved into town. Sometimes the new interests presented themselves, conservatively, as a needful addition to the canon of literary texts demanding the attention of a truly liberal education; but just as often they rushed in to fill the welcome gap created by the disappearance of "literature" as a stable element in the arts curriculum. In either case, the academy began to be swamped by wave after wave of conscientious protests on behalf of writings by Women, by Gays, Lesbians, and Bisexuals, by African-Americans, Hispanic-Americans, Asian-Americans, and other hyphenated ethnic groups within the ever less homogenetic identity pool of the United States. So that entire "English" Departments have begun to be refit themselves—without any real protest from the social sciences—to serve the interest of Culture Studies.[15] The true project, it appears, is not the problematic relation of literature to culture, but the disqualifying effects of culture itself. And of American culture, primarily, so that old-fashioned Americanists can join right in if they choose. Not with any special authority, to be sure, but as coequal partners in the revolt against cultural hegemony and literariness, if not against literacy itself.

For the lifelong Americanist, the situation can seem just a little unsettling: just when it had begun to seem that sufficient attention to American context and tradition and a careful application of suitably reformed categories of kind were discovering that the United States (and even its colonial forerunners) did indeed possess a literature worthy of the name, the cause of literature began to give up its grip on a very vigorous and dedicated segment of the humanist academy. Or else, quite as painfully, just when it began to appear that Americanists, hemmed in on all sides by the literary empire of Great Britain, might yet secure curricular space sufficient to display a representative portion of the American canon, that canon itself came suddenly to seem but a privileged fraction of the texts that needed the attention of wary cultural watchers. A complex fate, as somebody once said. And even if one suspends, for the moment, all trace of satire, and permits, in all conscience, only so much irony as the situation seems to require, one is no longer sure what cultural duty to perform.

For example: Thoreau's *Walden* had always seemed absolutely of the essence; with an English model no closer in time or genre than the less complete anglings of Isaak Walton, and without compunction about locating the "true west" somewhere in or near America, this astonishing demonstration that Transcendentalists too know how many beans make five seemed redundantly assured of pride and place in any American survey we might care to make. Students, to be sure, have not always known how they are supposed to respond to the merciless encounters with individual nature that come in such profusion after the economical prologue; and few enough ever have caught on to the "I can live on board nails" hyperbole which governs that introductory mixture of saintliness and satire; but we always went right ahead anyway. An authentic American original, we felt bound to insist: a masterpiece of American conscience; love it or leave. Grousing some, they mostly stayed.

Enter, then, Frederick Douglass, with an American lifestory equally sincere in its dedication to human freedom and with a less privileged sense of where and how the battle had to be waged. A short form of this more literal slave narrative can be stuffed, just barely, into an already crowded syllabus in the "*American Renaissance*." The comparison with Thoreau works well enough, though too many students end up preferring the Douglass *Narrative* a little too simply: why can't Thoreau "get real"? We live with that, until it begins to appear that *My Bondage and My Freedom*, a longer and more self-expressive version of the Douglass story, may be the more essential text.[16] Now the seams begin to burst. Maybe we could just leave Thoreau out?—especially as the most elementary concern for context will warn us that, though Douglass and Thoreau may appear to us at about the same moment, the "long foreground" of their life and reading has been sharply, painfully dissimilar. Can we, indeed, teach *any* version of the Douglass text without paying fair attention to an entire tradition of the slave narrative, or to many other voices speaking out otherwise on the subject of New World slavery, or to the inclusive project of African-American literature?

Instances multiply: if Douglass in the 1840s (or 50s), what about Harriet Jacobs in the 60s? And Mrs. Stowe? Does the undeniable sentimentality of her

9

truly epochal book outweigh all other considerations of merit and interest? If not, does not the figure of Uncle Tom imply separate but equal treatment of Babo, his prime opposite number? Will there still be room, then, for *Moby-Dick*, whatever it means by whiteness? Or perhaps *Uncle Tom's Cabin* demands to be read next to *The Blithedale Romance*, an arresting narrative experiment it should be easy to recognize as "nobody's protest novel"? Will *Blithedale* crowd out *The Scarlet Letter*? Or has that cultural work already been accomplished by Susan Warner's *Wide Wide World*, a franker version of the neo-Puritan sermon against loving "the creature" too much? And if Warner and Stowe in the 1850s, why not Child and Sedgwick earlier? Why not, in all honesty, the whole blessed host of novel-writing women? For all of this—and very much more—will come with the territory.[17] Evidently culture watching is going to be somewhat more complicated than anyone had at first supposed.

Faint hearts may wish to turn back, perhaps, to the good old days, when American literature meant the few masterworks students found time to read after confessing the entire literary history of Great Britain. Alternatively, a few brazen souls are suggesting the linguistic high road: given the continuity of the English *language*, the very idea of an American *literature* is unintelligible except as a gross cultural solecism.[18] But other views are possible as well: as the world is under no obligation to conform itself to the space we allot for a major in a college curriculum, we may be discovering that the true extent and interest of American literature is yet to be imagined. Not only Twain, James, Howells, and Dreiser, but DeForest, Garland, Harte, Bierce, Crane, Cable, Chesnutt, London, Norris, and Frederick; not only Dickinson, Jewett, Freeman, Gilman, and Chopin, but Stoddard, Davis, Spofford, Alcott, Phelps, and Hopkins; not only William James and Henry Adams, but Josiah Royce, Chauncey Wright, C.S. Pierce, Henry George, William Graham Sumner, W.E.B. DuBois, and Thorstein Veblen; not just a token recognition of the presence of Amerindians and African-Americans, but a full complement of their vitalizing cultural product. And does each of us really know, in these middle years of the writing of American literary history, what else may be out there waiting?

Detached observers tend to feel that Americanists have always made too much of the slippery premise of Americanness-as-such. Perhaps so; but it seems equally true that we have never really enjoyed the opportunity, institutionally, to teach more than a small part of our democratically expansive canon at any time. In comes one writer, out goes another, in the controlled imaginative (and curricular) space identified as "after" or "in addition to" the masterworks of "English." What might happen if we tried to resist the operating law that American literary space is always at a minimum? What would happen, do we suppose, if someone tried to assemble a faculty which could responsibly teach it all?

• • •

The special case of the Colonialist may serve as a concentrated illustration of the Americanist problem at large. Nowhere has the sense of cultural inferiority and inhibition seemed more endemic than among professors who have taken up the task of teaching the academic field called "*Early American Literature*," in Departments of English, and in comparison and in competition, therefore, with classes in British literature of the seventeenth and eighteenth centuries. Nowhere, accordingly, has the temptation to go aside into history been more compelling. With or without the motive (or even the notion) of belles lettres, rare and remarkable individuals, like William Bradford, Cotton Mather, Jonathan Edwards, John Woolman, and Benjamin Franklin, and powerful groups, like Puritans, Revivalists, Quakers, and Enlightened Citizens, were mastering a world (and one another) by means of tropes; and both the process and the sense of an outcome seemed too important—and too grammatological—to be left exclusively to the historians, especially when their interests had veered off toward the manageably local and the comfortably numerical. And as long as the Dean had no objection, why not? It wasn't hurting anyone.

Quizzed about the nature of his curious interests and procedures, the wary Colonialist could always offer a guarded remark about American Studies. The reply marked him as a second-class citizen of the world of "English," perhaps, but it usually assured him an uneasy concession of his right to continue: Oh, yes, we've heard of that. Or, if left to examine his professional conscience all alone, the meditation usually ended ironically, a step or two short of theory: we all deal with texts, don't we? and what is a "department," anyway, except a convenience for the delivery of mail? So it should come as no surprise if we continue to encounter, now and again, a high-flying advocate of the *really* literary who is altogether convinced that the "literature" of "colonial" America is just another academic oxymoron.

Yet it might also be argued that nowhere has the historical appeal to peculiar conditions of occasion and audience been more signally successful in transforming the balked response of generic dismay into the unalloyed pleasure that comes when we first begin to suspect how a textual thing is supposed to work, and on whom. The works of Edward Taylor might be too easy an example: they seem a little goofy at first, but so does much else indited by the seventeenth century according to the decorum of the metaphysical; and they are written, after all, in verse. But there are many other instances as well, within a process that is still ongoing. And nowhere, therefore, is the choice between long sought and well earned literary recognition and newly discovered and strongly felt social obligation been quite so keen.

As the skepticism of pure theory subsides to the practical reason of politics, the busy world of the multiethnic academy can spare little time to notice that Bradford's first confident and then demoralized history *Of Plymouth Plantation*

11

is one of the most accomplished and moving pieces of extended prose written in English in the seventeenth century. To be sure, it cannot be permitted to do all the things it appears to intend—to discredit the "pastoral" pretense offered by so many explorers and surveyors of the New World, to embarrass the cynicism of John Smith's confessed inability to imagine that "any other motive than wealth will ever erect there a commonwealth," to marginalize when it cannot effectively banish Thomas Morton and other theorists of an alternative and contending American origination, and to reduce the native population to the role of supporting or opposing players in the unfolding plot of Providence. But the primary effect, of thematically sustained observation, survives the fullest force of hostile expose: here was a chance to show the world, Old and New, how a new foundation might be laid, soberly, in "Christian and comfortable fellowship," if not in what zealots might call "holy love"; here was an example to be followed, as it seemed in *fact* to be followed, by a far greater migration of sincere converts to the ways of God set out for the world; and here it seemed to come undone, as the "subtle serpent…slyly wound in himself" under pretense of economic necessity and family convenience. Why should Americans not read this book, even if their major is "English"?

Just less moving—because less fully elaborated—are the plot and theme of Thomas Shepard's remarkable *Autobiography*. Back in print now, along with a number of the confessions of faith given in Shepard's Cambridge Church, it amply provides, with or without its more political supplementation, a revealing account of the public events and private insights that eventually drove even long-time "Nonseparatists" to abandon at last their trust in the politics of gradualism and to reinvent their lives within the Churches of New England. Readers will not fail to notice, of course, that the tale is told for the explicit purpose of mastering the new-world freedom of Thomas Shepard III, born to replace Thomas Shepard, Jr., who died to mark a first, unsuccessful (because impurely motivated) attempt to escape to New England, and that the shame of this oedipal traduction is matched by the bizarre political logic which blames the scourge of the Pequot War on the heresies of Anne Hutchinson. And yet some rare form of sincerity survives, socially heroic if personally hysterical, daring the cynical reader to deny that *this* Puritan father tried his best to put the cause of Reformation first—ahead of sons and lovers, who died into the arms of Christ; and soberly challenging that reader to discover the defections any sooner or sorrier than the sin-conscious writer has detected in advance. A bracing life to read: an original Puritan invention, and not without relation to the construct called the American Self.

Nor do these dramatically compelling texts amount to more than one plausible beginning for the "Puritan" story we might feel some obligation to tell. Sooner or later, we will get a paperback edition of the amazing *Journal* of the omnicompetent John Winthrop, which serves as a running commentary on the fate of the metapolitical ideals outlined in his consciously originary "Model of Christian Charity." Speaking always for the ideal of holy consensus, it rebukes the citizenry of Massachusetts for being more concerned with "charter" rights than with "covenant" obligations; yet it duly records the evolution of a "constitution" made necessary but also possible by the stubborn insistence of subjects who appear to have forgot how they became "freemen" in the first place. Of course it marginalizes the multiform protest of Roger Williams as effectively as it silences the intensifying prophecy of Anne Hutchinson; but it is probably not beyond our ingenuity to represent these more radical voices as part of the necessary conditions of Winthrop's own most masterful text.

And then, as the transplanted orthodoxy begins to speak its own Babel of competing voices, why should we not teach ourselves to think of the sermon as a *genre* like any other, with insights and even pleasures proper to its own habits of thought and expression? Students may think that texts which invoke the big medicine of Christ belong in church and not in school, but they also think that an "s" must never look too much like an "f," and we are paid to help them with all such prejudice. How can we spare them the "holy violence" of the pulpit productions of Thomas Hooker, where the grueling process of preparation spreads out to cover the entire scene of religion on earth? Or the more steady and "systematic" ambition of Thomas Shepard, who falls in love with sanctification only because others would slight or demean this temporal figure of eventual glory? Or the inspired recklessness of John Cotton, who realizes, without help from Emerson, that the Spirit is indeed its own evidence, and dares to fasten on the miracle of faith itself? Together, these painful, searching preachers will persuade even the minimally alert modern reader—student of Donne and Andrewes or not—that the Puritan sermon can be richly imaginative in its arrangement of familiar Biblical texts and topoi; particularly in New England, where a self-selected audience of salvation seekers possessed a hermeneutical skill and interest quite likely unmatched in the history of the world. Someone may even begin to suspect that, in its fertile imagination and strategic deployment of dramatic speakers, the sermon may carry out, in New England, much of the cultural work done elsewhere by the drama.

In any event, a judicious selection from the rich archive of American Puritan preaching—oddly represented in the various Puritan collections of Perry Miller, mightily overproduced in the supplementary gathering of Heimert and Delbanco, and entirely absent from the otherwise wearisome completeness of the Heath Anthology[19]—can make the issues which motivated and divided the Puritan experiment as fascinating to the student of culture as they were vital to the original builders of a new social order. Most students will regret, of course, that Ann Hutchinson contributed no written work of

13

her own, but some may find consolation in the discovery that the Calvinist redaction we know as "Cotton's Rejoinder" is one of the most brilliantly sustained pieces of argumentation in the entire canon of Protestant theology.[20]

And all of this cultural work is accomplished, in writings which only the culpably ignorant or the studiously effete will refuse to call "literature," by 1640—before, so far as we know, anybody in New England had offered the Puritan public a kindly word of poetry, to strengthen by personal meditation what had been handed on as public doctrine. And much is still ahead. It will require decades of puritanic experience before the long view of culture can discover whether Miller or Bercovitch has given the truer account of the Puritan Jeremiad; or whether the remarkable *Narrative* of the captivity of Mary Rowlandson reinscribes or destabilizes the orthodox view of "Savagism and Civilization"; or whether biography can make any sense out of the sequences of Edward Taylor's "Preparatory Meditations"; or whether we can expect to find a text to tell the truth about "What Happened in Salem." More than half a century of historical time must elapse before we are forced to consider whether Mather's *Magnalia* buried the Puritan Fathers in memorial prose or reinvented them as a lively subject for American literature; or whether his *Christian Philosopher* abets the pseudo-theology of Deism or invents the poetic project of natural typology. A full century before we can ask whether the naturalized theology of Jonathan Edwards made him the most or the least modern man in the American eighteenth century; or whether we dare teach, as literature, the difficult texts which cause that problem to arise in the first place. Soon enough, however, the issues do arise; and no wonder if they should appear to demand an academic term, all to themselves.

Or, if any more porous coverage is attempted, the dyed-in-the-wool Puritanist will have to decide whether Edwards' New England successors (Bellamy, Hopkins, Dwight) and his opponents (Chauncy, Mayhew, Barnard, Gay) must give way entirely, so that writers like Franklin, Ashbridge, Woolman, Crevecoeur, and Brockden Brown may have ample room, in the "first" course in American literature, to speak the newly self-conscious Quaker culture of the mid-Atlantic. But this last question will remind even the most zealous ideologue that, unless he or she has thought to launch this regionalist version of *Early American Literature* with the New England advertisements of Captain John Smith, or to compare the rather innocent historical project of Robert Beverley with the complex and encumbered one of Cotton Mather, or to prove the endurance of the Puritan Self by contrasting the periodic piety of Samuel Sewall with the "secret" but altogether worldly concerns of William Byrd, the question of Virginia has been elided altogether. The problem is partly a matter of time, of course, for there has always been far too much colonial material to be crammed into a single course, particularly where the unit in question is defined as everything that comes before the "*American Renaissance*."

But it is also, significantly, a matter of cultural continuity and of what we might call specific literary density.

It may be possible to get "from" the spirited explorations of John Smith "to" the passionate pilgrimages of Washington Irving in a couple of academic quarters, but to attempt that passage in anything less is to play a little loose with the notion of history. But even if we were to solve this problem, theoretically or by inspired curricular coup, we would keep running up against the unsettling fact that we hardly know how to the regard colonial New England and the other colonial regions as part of a credible cultural whole. And we may yet decide, as culture watchers, that "nominal" histories—things we like to teach, a mile a minute, under the inclusive but principle-petitioning category of "American"—are considerably worse than none at all.

New England continues to seem, despite the occasional protest then and now—and despite its own drift toward Liberalism and/or Yankeehood—quite emphatically Puritan in its ordinances, its morale, and even its locus of protest: one way or another, Puritanism is the myth it continues to tell, even in the act of firing the shot which Emerson judged so terribly secular. But other regions appear to have been advertising other projects: in Virginia, a tobacco culture and the "Cavalier" aristocracy it sought to raise and maintain, literate enough, here and there, but confining itself pretty much to a network of gentlemanly epistles; in the mid-regions around Philadelphia, the enlightened appeal of those peaceable kingdoms which fostered both a shopkeeper's millennium and a piety teaching itself when to be quiet and when to make public the protest of the Spirit against the enslavements of the world; and in land of the Yorkers, town and country, a culture so determined to mind the main chance that it would require the fulltime literary efforts of both Irving and Cooper to invent a cultural past ex post facto. God's plenty, and no doubt—a regional pluralism not unfit to run before the multiethnic sort we presently enjoy. As yet, however, it resists convenient assembly into a tale all know the terms to tell.

A distinguished Americanist, in a somewhat mannered yet altogether serious attempt to situate the writings of New England and even perhaps to subsume them into a larger colonial construct, provides a memorable verdict of the (old-style) problem of regional incommensurability. Determined not to begin with Bradford's Plymouth, John Seelye treats first the example of Columbus—who has subsequently come (back) into his own as an originary figure in American letters—and then bravely proceeds to consider Jacques Cartier, Richard Hakluyt, and John Smith, all more or less fully, before saying a word about *The Puritans*. Published today, Seelye's work would be rudely and rashly guilty of omitting the Spanish question altogether. But in 1977, the geographic pluralism of *Prophetic Waters* was well ahead of its multicultural time: first the explorers, mappers, and projectors, then the settlers of Virginia, and only then, in due time (on page 97), the ideologues of New England.

15

Once they are permitted to appear, however, the complexity of their hermeneutics and the density of the literary history it generates threaten to upstage if not to oust all cultural competition, as one more conscientious commentator is lured aside by the same unlikely siren song which made a captive of Perry Miller (and many others) before.

A humorist as well as a critic of culture, the writer can only apologize, 245 Puritan pages later, for his evident departure from suitable comparative form:

> Meanwhile, back in Jamestown, not much had happened since 1624—
> not much, that is, so far as literature was concerned. Something of the dis-
> parity between the cultures of Virginia and Massachusetts is suggested by
> the fact that Mather's *Magnalia* (1702) was the last in a long line of chron-
> icles, while Robert Beverley's *History of the Present State of Virginia*
> (1705)…was the first general history of that colony to appear since John
> Smith's epic effort.[21]

The problem so neatly indicated here is not simply that colonial New Englanders wrote much *more* than their colonial counterparts in Virginia. It is also that they understood the act of writing in a different, more densely relational way.

Occasional and easily satisfied in other sections of colonized North America, the drive toward writing was perfectly relentless in New England, feeding on itself in a pious but competitive effort that is almost always aware of forerunners as well as opponents and which attempts to co-opt the past and pre-empt the future as well as to edify the present. All but impossible to discuss in just a few words, the *ecriture* of Puritan New England is like nothing else—unless it be the segment of American literature it appears to have generated. So thick is the literary plot of New England that, even now, even the studiously skeptical critic seems forced to enter into its ongoing project of writing the Reformation in just the right words. Or else, called away to some other pressing aspect of the Colonialist project, he feels momentarily baffled by the abrupt change of literary pace, like a person asked to compare an apple tree, fully laden with mature fruit, to a couple of tart and tangy citrus products.

Individual commentators will disagree on whether God and history are more likely to produce admirable letters than tobacco and land-based wealth. But the point is simply that the outpouring of texts inspired by the multiform system of covenants in New England provides one of the most continuous and complete models of literary history alive and at issue in the modern academy; nor is it any accident, therefore, that Colonialist prophets like Miller and Bercovitch have built their edifice on the rock of New England. Elsewhere there are *some things*—of moment, if the right person is there to notice and to insist; in New England there is, to our finite faculties, an intimation of plenti-tude. About New England's cherished project, of perfecting the Reformation and thus completing (if not actually ending) the scene of human history, everything that could be said appears indeed to have been said.

Thus the attempt to establish a regional merger, in the form of a single and consistent "history" of New England and *other* departments of *Early American Literature*, produces not only cognitive dissonance (which can be at times cre-ative) but also a bad case of diminishing cultural returns. Puritanism plus Smith, Beverley, and Byrd equals not the full richness of Colonial America but only an awkward attempt to remind ourselves, in the way best known to col-lege textbooks and syllabi, that writing is only one way to take possession of the land; that the triumph of New England is primarily literary; and that in any case the hegemony of Puritanism did not extend very far south.

All of this is, of course, a version of the Colonialist situation as it may have appeared in the days before the present revolution of academic sensibility, best marked, perhaps, by the *Heath Anthology of American Literature* and its ancillary pedagogic productions.[22] Now, besides the question of how, from the first, to honor Virginia, and how soon and how fully to recognize intimations of Enlightenment or to concede the ascendency of the Quaker culture around Philadelphia, we are conscientiously required to decide how to represent not only the folkways and the oral literature of the native populations but also the enormous amount of Spanish language material concerned with the discov-ery, exploration, and settlement of New World territories, within and without the boundaries of what Providence and/or Manifest Destiny would eventual-ly assign to the sovereign power of these federally united American states. Perhaps this new material will, by its sheer bulk, by the challenge of its evi-dent otherness, or by richness of its provoking interest, succeed in finally decentering New England. But not without answering some unusual difficul-ties along the way.

A good many established Americanists, better prepared in French and German than in Spanish and Portuguese, and well accustomed, in any case, to the blissful if naïve task of sponsoring their *own* literature in their *own* lan-guage, may feel a little uncomfortable with the idea of teaching Columbus or Cabeza de Vaca in translation. And more uneasy still, perhaps, in comparing the truly bizarre elaborations of cultural mythology one finds in John Smith and William Bradford with the more nearly elemental belief-stories proper to the peoples we know as Zuni or Navaho, Aztec or Inuit; particularly when these far-off imaginings have been written down, in English, by Intellectuals, a fair-ly long time after the authentic cultural fact. The motives of these friendly and receptive ventures are perfectly irresistible, of course, but the epistemology seems a little funky: surely Columbus opens a passage to much more of "American" literature than that of the United States; and can it really be cor-

17

rect to compare the first impressions of Spanish or English explorers and settlers with whatever Native material happens to be available in anthropologi-
cal transcript?

Nothing is more common—as Americanists working in Departments of
English are in a position to know—than to find cultural bias disguising itself
as professional scruple. So we have to suspect ourselves in repining, "If only
Providence had arranged for the Chickahominies, the Narragansetts, and even
the Pequots to have resisted white conquest in *writing!*" Yet it may really be
true: if the professional corps of Americanist interpreters could find a way to
equalize the cultural conversation between the planters of Virginia or the saints
of New England and the Native population they encountered and resisted,
displaced and dispatched, the substance of the teaching of early American literature would change in a minute. Colonialists may spurn the cultural products of England, from time to time, but they do not for that reason idolize the
notions of the Americans. All they seem to want, really, like everyone else in
the profession, is sufficent curricular space for the cultural story we have the
texts to tell.

Prefatory statements, we know by now, are always written last. No surprise,
therefore, if this one seems to advertise a book yet to be written more properly than to introduce the one now in hand. And yet it was the writing of the
several chapters in this (not entirely inevitable) collection that led to my present (not very theoretical) understanding of the differential aims of (quite a lot
of) Americanist scholarship. And perhaps these convictions—hard-won clarifications, as they seem to me—will make familiar the spirit of the essays which
follow.

"Taylor's Double Standard" was written to supplement (and also to correct)
the argument I made in 1967, that "*Gods Determinations Touching His Elect*" is,
among other things, a complex of poems made up to exemplify the problems
of spiritual assurance and church membership peculiarly experienced by New
Englanders in the latter days of the seventeenth century.[23] No doubt that juve-
nile essay also wanted to communicate something like this: "Hey, this is pretty good stuff, when you discover how to read it back into cultural dialogue
with Wigglesworth, Stoddard, the Mathers, and even Milton and Bunyan; giving the Devil a fair share of his due, it publishes (so to speak) an exceptional-
ly genial explanation for the spiritual diffidence of the much maligned grand-
children of those awesome first-generation Saints, and makes a jolly good case
for bringing even the doubtful into full membership in some particular
church. Nothing else quite like this in the whole history of words living off
The Word. To be sure, no man ever wished it more eccentric; but hell, if we
take the matter of Puritanism seriously at all—not as "background," evoked in
pious historical wish and disappearing in a cloud of close-textual observation,

but as the life-stuff out of which seventeenth-century literature was made—
this is a real high point, a full-scale translation of a prime doctrinal difficulty
into the give-and-take of a dialectic which admits the limits of its language
but loves it just the same."

Or so it seems to me now. Evidence that my enthusiasm was insufficiently
infectious, however, came almost at once, when a *very* sympathetic senior col-
league said he liked my essay on Taylor's Puritanism but wondered what I
thought of his poetry. I spluttered some reply, then went home and fumed:
what was I supposed to say?—seven on a scale of nine; or, I'd give it about an
eighty-five, the kids can dance to it. Wasn't it obvious that my appreciation of
Taylor's literature was exactly the same as my perfect willingness to inhabit his
premises and to revel in the prose his poem had put me in the place to write?
Had I really needed to say it, in so many words? "Taylor's conservative Puritan
doctrine is precisely so-and-so, opposite and not quite equal to that of
Solomon Stoddard, who seems to win the argument, in The Valley, at least. But
don't forget that other little difference: Stoddard's logic predicts the future of
the Congregational Church in New England, right down to a certain
Emerson sermon on the meaning of the Lord's Supper;[24] but Taylor gathers
in the loose ends of Everysaint's anxiety, refuses to tie them all up, and weaves
them instead into a conversational story made up to stand for it all." Consider
it said, even if the newer essay does more to revel than to proclaim.

The case—or the "example," as one acquires the mannerism to say—of
Edwards is a little different. One's generic prejudice is all in favor of Taylor
going in, and only the readerly discovery that his poems are full of strange
dialectical words and hard theological sayings begins to edge his work toward
the province of history. But Edwards is a "poet" only so long as some really
Big Dog like Perry Miller is around to issue the challenge of that ultimate special plea; so that his place in the canon that is the special creation of
Americanist critical practice is both better established and harder to describe
than that of Taylor.[25] It is thus a crucial and revealing instance; the most so,
perhaps, before Emerson, who has mattered to us more as a thinker let loose
by God than as a singer with a husky voice.

Supposing the need to call it anything at all, the brief but moving tribute
to "Sarah Pierrepont" is easily recognizable as a sort of prose poem, as are a
number of sustained passages of image and symbol in Edwards' own "Personal
Narrative"; so too, though somewhat ironically, are the more frightfully memorable paragraphs of the widely advertised yet never trite "Sinners in the
Hands of an Angry God." And no doubt the multivolume publication of
Edwards' *Miscellanies* will do much to revive Miller's lively sense that, to a truly
remarkable degree, Edwards was a thinker who dwelt always among "Images,"
some of them biblical commonplaces, to be sure, but many others the result
of nothing more than his own most poetic notice. Such a return to origins

19

might provide a fitting conclusion to the long-standing Edwards revival which Miller began, but it would not perfectly summarize the intellectual, moral, and political interests that have driven it along. With or without his eccentric and unsteady claims on our interest in the fate of the poetic figure in the age of the cultural critic, Edwards has demanded attention as a luminous example of the possibilities of the culture of the mind—including the affections or sensibilities—in a society finding itself increasingly forced to choose between Awakening and Enlightenment.

Nor has it helped us much to think of Edwards as a prolific and skillful writer of narrative—of himself, of his wife, of the ailing Abigail Hutchinson, of the precocious little Phoebe Bartlett, or of many other nameless persons whose individualized stories went into the formation of the newer, less formalized, more empirical morphology of conversion that appears to distinguish Edwards from the New England Fathers.[26] Perhaps we will yet come to understand the genre of the "personal narrative" as a significant influence on the kind of fiction American writers would learn to write in the long years after the surprising conversions; and even now we might ask ourselves what epistemology or what politics makes us tend to elevate "self-writing" to the honorable station of a fourth literary genre, just below those of poetry, fiction, and drama. In any event, however, the "novelistic" claim reveals far less about Edwards than about the anxieties of Americanists within their departments of English. And, even more than the "poetic" claim, it attempts to gather privilege from a system whose credit Edwards himself might in no way honor. For as he clearly expected his "Images" to ground a rational account of the universe rather than to generate a number of lyrical ballads, so he meant *The Nature of True Virtue* to deconstruct the precise moral system which made most eighteenth-century fiction possible.

Not quite an Americanist himself, Edwards unfailingly provokes a prime version of the problem: what are we supposed to say about a writer passionately committed to the cause of religion as an unavoidable form of "ultimate concern," but whose interest is never quite used up by the articles that appear in *Church History* or the *Harvard Theological Review*? A writer all but consumed by the fatal attraction of dialectics, but also committed to the more poetic truth of Scripture, so that our "analytical" philosophers tend to read him out of their foundational story? A writer whose multiform intertext continues to underwrite academic conferences which attract critics who do their writing across the curriculum, and who may come to conclude, in the end, they can't quite say why he continues to fix and fascinate, except that he remains "somehow a great man"?[27] And what, therefore, are we supposed to say about a writer who tends both to raise and to embarrass and even to illegitimate the otherwise unavoidable "disciplinary" question of who we are when we talk and write about him, one way or another?

Perhaps we should use Edwards as the appropriate occasion to take the exasperated advice of William Spengemann—to encourage all licensed and well motivated professors to study and write about whatever texts have captured their multifarious fancy, but realize that *literature* no longer has any stable meaning and stop using it altogether.[28] Yet the word has an important if relatively brief history; and even now, well shorn of its immense New Critical valeur, it continues to point to a region of textual insistence, and even of duty, that is quite different from ordinary academic whimsy. *Other* Professors go on claiming the right to assign or withhold Edwards' place in the factitious and shifty canon of "philosophical literature." We wince at the painful mannerism of trying to validate the study of Edwards by representing him as a poet or novelist; we readily grant everyone's perfect right *not* to teach the *True Virtue* side-by-side with *Tom Jones*; and we doubt that works like "A Divine and Supernatural Light" or *A Treatise Concerning Religious Affections* belong to any of the "kinds" which Comparative Literature will wish to study on a worldwide basis. Yet it still seems both intelligible and necessary to say that many of Edwards' self-consciously genre-breaking texts are and will remain an essential part of "the literature of America."

The present chapter on Edwards restates, with significant revision, my old argument about the exemplary importance of Edwards' translation of the Calvinist idiom of "dependency" into its inevitable and perfect philosophical apotheosis, an "idealism" which naturalizes Berkeley, prefigures Emerson, and suggests, with both Hume and Derrida, that human beings may have to get along without the comforting construct of a noumenal self.[29] But it isn't all a question of metaphysics, for Edwards bears an important part in the writing project of colonies whose union in prayer and revival gave powerful notice of what a little correspondence could do. And he bears that part *better*—more memorably, with more subtlety of intelligence and more genuine fascination of style—than anyone we could possibly put in his place. It may be objected that this estimate moves the definition of literature a little closer to that of intellectual history than is quite customary. To which the answer ought to be: Ah, yes, thanks for noticing, for we may not spare ourselves the difficulty of this worldly connection.

Certainly we require it in the case of Emerson—not in the form of a boost to a writer of ambiguous literariness, but to account for the full range of interest which readers, in and out of survey classes in American literature, seem altogether unwilling to give up. Unlike Edwards, Emerson is a very considerable poet, in the perfectly ordinary comprehension of that term; and no doubt it is only the sense of having an already overcrowded syllabus that has held us back from a steady representation and an evolving estimate of his remarkable output in verse. Further, his more firmly reputed cultural product is a prose form we may choose to call the "essay," compare to Bacon or Coleridge or even to Montaigne, and then die defending its established formal integrity. But these are scarcely the terms which has made Emerson the most variously influential writer in the American nineteenth century, the figure who predicts, so to speak, the rest of the canon. The interest, rather, is in a writer who openly proclaims his hope or dramatically implies his disturbance in a form which philosophers do not quite recognize as argumentative reasoning, which literary types have yet to reduce to some repeatable rhetorical rule, but which an emergent culture recognizes as representing, even as constituting, in letters, its own remarkable case.

That this auto-cultural definition of literature is not necessarily self-congratulatory—that it needs in fact to be as "comparative" as possible—might be taken as the lesson, if not quite the announced subject, of the Emerson chapters in this volume. The first observes Emerson writing himself into dialogue with George Herbert: aware that he is approaching his own *beau ideal* of the poet-priest, he yet resists the old religious magic wherever he can, working instead toward his own latter-day sense of what worship might mean in a world where God no longer figures as a person and where veneration of the state (or any other figment of collectivity) is simply unthinkable. The second begins by noticing that American religious culture installs, for Emerson, a set of troublesome precursors who never do make it onto the "strong poet" list of Harold Bloom;[30] but it does eventually range far enough beyond the provinces to observe that the ultimate source of Emerson's New English anxiety is the Old World Jesus.

And then there is the complex and in a sense climactic case—of that most emphatically American writer whose canonicity has almost never been doubted, who would be taught even if he were English. Too literary by half, in the long history of his critical reception, and too easily stereotyped as a "Capital Son of the Puritans" who fled his own age to take up "imaginative" residence in the seventeenth century, Hawthorne is only now coming into sharp cultural focus: shrewd critic rather than hapless heir of the New England orthodoxy, he may serve to suggest that self-conscious and, in the outcome, successful craft need not be set in opposition to the motive or the accomplishment of national critique. Indeed, as I have made the argument at large elsewhere, we do well to think of Hawthorne as our "Americanist" ancestor. At the same time, however, in the cogent work of the newer and more frankly secular historians of American literature, his political uncertainties and incautious overbeliefs can suitably appear as a index to some of the most vexing questions at issue in his own antebellum world.[31]

Accordingly, therefore, I have annotated my two essays on *The Scarlet Letter* in ways that take account of this more presentist perspective. But their original (and mutually supporting) claims remain intact. Refracted in the rhetoric of this frank and full-scale emplotment of the Puritan world is the painful attempt to deal with the challenge of Ann Hutchinson and her supporters, in which New Englanders had found it all too easy to discredit their first intimation of "female language" with the verbal and psychological implication of sexual irregularity. And, when this episode is placed in its larger context, of a surprisingly fluent reliance on sexual metaphor, to cover an entire range of theo-political ideology, we are forced to notice that a crucial function of Hawthorne's most competent literary text has been to push the Puritan mind to the limits of a founding symbol system. From this one point of view at least, it really was all about sex.

More generally, however, *The Scarlet Letter* may stand as the limit case of an American literature which refuses to disavow its concern with regional culture just because it has been assumed into the heaven of the art-texts of the nations. Here, signally—as to some degree in all the texts discussed in this volume—the consideration of *theme* calls our attention to questions of intellectual and behavioral commonality that are not quite "universal," but only general enough to stand for the ways of a group we know to name and decide to remember. And the quest for *form* answers to our sense that the representation in question, whether mature and consciously critical, or naïve and simply indexical, must make real world issues seem about as complicated as our extra-literary experience discovers them to be. In this light, we might re-understand the New Critical passion for form not as an inherent condition of disinterested esthetic pleasure but as the criterion we impose on texts we mean to sponsor, in class or in print, with the authority of our own never-quite-neutral voice: the answer we find in a literary text may be "correct" or not, but its placement of the question had better not be too simple. And who knows?— where meaning itself is said to be indeterminate, the politics of certain texts might indeed turn out to be "ambiguous."

Implied in this view, clearly, is a sense of why many of the texts judged to be literary by the older formal/esthetic criteria may migrate so easily to the canon of the cultural. An available cynicism would suggest that Americanists, especially Colonialists, make a special plea for the relevance of "literature" in their extended sense only until—with the advent of Irving and Poe, or is it Tyler, Dwight, and Brockden Brown?—the real thing comes along. Also plausible, a priori, might be the claim that certain Colonialists (though not the same ones just imagined) get started one way and simply forget to change their habits, sitting down at the wedding feast of literature without remembering to remove the dusty clothes of culture. But if the assumptions of this essay have been at all correct, something less awkward may also be true.

Like every other sort, Americanist criticism always does the best it can with what it has. Less obviously, however, it does what it does with the best it can find. Accordingly, it seldom honors inept attempts within the genres some other culture has declared to constitute the literary-as-such; given the choice, it usually prefers luminous expression in didactic prose to the tiresome iteration of stanza or scene. But it seems to know—not exclusively, but along with the entire ambient academy—that the "literary" kinds, honestly regarded, have a tendency to impose an epistemology of their own. Meditative poetry can scarcely force a dolt to provide an insightful and moving account of his inner states, but the ongoing life of the genre appears to make precisely that demand; so that, if one extreme of culture is the factitious but naturalized content of "privacy," we don't ask a rocket scientist where to go looking for the more "personal" evidence. And the multiform devices of fiction, supplementing and often supplanting the ways of drama, take up where the convention of self-expression ends, loosing the tongue of a heteroglossia that not only subverts the One Speech which pretends to The Truth but also makes it clear that neither Nature nor Culture can have a single voice.

Americanists may be a little uncouth, but for the most part they know where they live. Respectful of private fantasy as well as of sociological fact, they do not reject the story of Hester and Dimmesdale just because they know it as fiction. And they may yet blunder their way to a grown-up definition of literature—which honors the motive of creative self-expression in the artist and respects the interest of pleasure in the ordinary reader, but which names culture as the proper interest of the scholar. To do so would be to replace the old distinction between a "literature of beauty" and a "literature of power" with the sober recognition that textual beauty, which has more than a couple of kinds, commands a power of its own; which someone needs to watch. Americanists merely bring the lesson home.

A final chapter attempts—survey fashion, as if to advertise another unwritten book—to represent the vitality of Puritanic themes in the nineteenth century. By then, however, an equally important point has already been made, or at least suggested: a significant variety of "kinds" of texts have all been referred to a history of "strong values" in an important sector of the "native land."[32] The result, I trust, is less a dogmatic monolith than a tentative display of the interest and the explanatory power of intellectual religion within the developing culture of New England.

Taylor's poems are different from Edwards' sermons and treatises: the first are all but ironical exercises in the play of metaphor across the (hidden) face of the divine; the others are desperately earnest attempts to make the Images refer. Both these religious ways differ widely, no doubt, from the ones preached in the pulpit or believed in the heart of New England's average spiritual man. Even more obviously, perhaps, the lengthening shadow of Reason and of Criticism separates this most biblical religion from the possible passions of Emerson and Hawthorne. The one, well protected by the moral arguments of an altogether enlightened Christianity, seems nevertheless to have become possessed with the idea of planting himself ever more firmly on the Antinomian (or, more properly, Spiritist) road not taken; and the other, who tried *very* hard to be a nonbeliever, seems to have offered his learned faculty so repeatedly to the matter of the Puritans that even he began to have trouble deciding where liberal imagination ended and orthodox belief began. A various story: nothing stands for anything else: the history expressed is the history intended. Yet all these differences appear to imply a common standard which refuses to be left out of account.

Perry Miller called it "The Augustan Strain of Piety."[33] Significantly less catholic, the seventeenth-century Puritans probably thought of it as, simply, *piety.* And so may we, who do not like to let other people's ideologies multiply our own distinctions of reason. And yet it seems worth insisting: other worlds are not exactly like our own; some differ so far as to insist that duties beneath the surface and ends beyond the limit of the economic arena and the political forum are transcendentally important, are in fact at the center of consciousness and the root of intention. We need not accept such claims at face value, of course, as if Marx and Freud had never been; but we need to be able to hear them when they are made. And—unless we are content to allow all studied and genre-specific expression to lapse to the condition of document or of discourse—we need to follow them as far as they will lead.

My own claims, therefore, are simple enough to specify. It is next to impossible, first of all, to overstate the "Puritanism" of writers such as Taylor and Edwards: they wrote their creed, which is alien but in part recoverable and of wondrous complexity; if we prefer them in other terms, we had better be pretty sure of our premises, or at least our audience. And secondly, the creed they wrote cannot be got to go entirely away, not all at once, in the manner of the Deacon's one-hoss shay, nor little-by-little, by some process of finite cultural subtraction. It proves a little hard to say if Melville, Dickinson, and perhaps even Hawthorne are *suffering* the burden of the Puritan past, but they certainly are *writing* it, which is more significant still. And even Emerson—"no Puritan," as I say in so many words—is aware of standing, for conscience' sake, in just the place the old-time creed had stood. He could do, it appears, no other. And we at least should notice, if only for the sake of culture.

25

CHRIST'S REPLY, SAINT'S ASSURANCE

Taylor's Double Standard

ONCE, LONGER ago than one cares to remember, it seemed quite necessary to insist that Edward Taylor's most localized allegory—of the Soul's salvation in latter-day New England—is possessed by a single-minded interest in the question of presumption and despair. Always a problem in a theology which can only ambiguously say "It's not over till it's over," the private uncertainty is advanced to social crisis when the conscientious Congregationalist must go public with the grounds of his assurance, in time, of his election from all eternity. For just how, as a later, "moral" argument would indignantly inquire, could the claim of visible sainthood fail to "end in pride"?[1] Clearly Taylor knows, no less than his own Satan, that the ways of Calvin's God make no sense till one has mastered this outsetting difficulty. And so, in the dramatic disposition of *Gods Determinations Touching His Elect*, the teacherly sameness of this crucial argument tends to overshadow whatever empirical differences may have shown up in the region of Taylor's pastoral care.[2]

Still, as other scholars have aptly observed, there is *some* variety in the religious experience, and hence in the implied audience, of this remarkable poem: the would-be saints Taylor identifies as Ranks Two and Three in his home-made *ordo salutis* are indeed "half-way members," needing to learn to interpret their sorrows and fears as "blessed motions" (432); Rank One, by contrast, appears to be a Church Member already, having scruples now, about the ease of his conversion and admission, and falling prey to what we might call the Supper Panic. In that preliminary and simpler case, the issue is some sort of *re-assurance*, of the Soul's right to continue taking the "Children's Bread" (407) when offered: one's conversion experience has *not* been illusory.[3] In the eventual and more highly elaborated one, however, the problem is present and future—the confidence to claim the rights of full church membership in the first place. And no one familiar with Taylor's relation to the formal history of New England religion can regard this as a merely trivial difference.[4]

Yet the general term of anxiety is the same in both cases: have I been, or am I about to be, guilty of "presum[ing] on Grace" (409)? So the difference comes to matter less than we might expect, which is one reason why it was so easy to miss. But there is another reason as well: when faced with the fact of radically different sorts of religious experience, the poem goes on at energetic lengths to suggest that the one crucial distinction which can fairly be made between the kinds of assurance of salvation that might be enjoyed by the Puritan "Saint" does not matter that much. Not everyone had thought so. And Taylor's argument could have been otherwise. For surely it would have made recognizable theological sense to *emphasize* the important distinction between Rank One, on the one hand, and the conflated Ranks Two and Three on the other. Indeed, the failure to *insist* on this difference must be counted as no less important than the difference itself.

The problem begins when Taylor reduces his original distinction among three separate sorts, or "Ranks"—of those whom God has determined to save—to a simple dichotomy. Initially we were instructed to believe it made fair theological sense to imagine three separate stories or "morphologies" of conversion: some souls would be saved by "Justice," well (and humorously) characterized in "A Dialogue between Justice and Mercy" as both a "Rampant Lyon" (391) and the sort of father who believes in retributive justice; some would be saved by "Mercy," characterized in that same poem as intercessor and protective mother; and some would be saved by Justice and Mercy together.[5] The tripartite scheme seems plausible enough: not "Trinitarian," by any means, as Taylor's theosophic "Dialogue" in heaven, like Milton's, gives no human voice to the bird or tongue or wind of the Spirit; but workable enough for a sequence of dramatic poems. And consistent with the arithmetic of the

Covenants: two things taken one or two at a time: three possibilities; each with a minor variation, perhaps, on the logic of the true sight of sin, without despair, and the fair hope of grace, without an inane sense of moral safety.

But then the threefold plan is scrubbed without explanation. Or rather, it is maintained in formality and in name, but ignored as a dramatic opportunity—to give three separate feelings to the process of conversion; or, more practically, to outline three stories that will satisfy the Church's "Watchmen," "Porters," and "Centinalls" who "of all demand/ The Word to shew" (330–31). After Rank One has been appropriately and, for the sake of the fiction at least, finally reassured (in a second poem entitled "Christs Reply"), we suddenly find that Ranks Two and Three are being treated *together*—accused together and then reassured together. The long morphological "middle" of Taylor's sequence retains a three-part structure, but its outline is not the one we anticipated: not Rank One, Rank Two, and Rank Three; but Rank One, Accused and Assured; Ranks Two and Three Accused; and Ranks Two and Three Assured. Suddenly, it appears, no nice distinction need be made between those saved by Justice alone and those saved by Justice and Mercy together.

The effect is curious and might be worth some exploration in its own right. First of all, certainly, it allows Ranks Two and Three to compare notes: competing to bemoan their hapless condition in a "Threnodiall Dialogue" (426–28), whose comic decorum is easier to appreciate than that of the earlier "Contest" (398) between Justice and Mercy, they clearly establish a commonality of confusion that justifies the need for an intrusion of moral intelligence, from somewhere; they simply *cannot* work it out for themselves. Then too, arguably, it relieves Taylor of the tricky task of dramatizing what the exact cooperation of Justice and Mercy would look like; for the skeptical reader suspects that wherever they appear together, Justice will be, in human impression, altogether dominant, and Mercy so recessive as to fail of significant impression. Perhaps Taylor changed his plan when he realized the schema worked better than the scenes. Or perhaps, most drastically, he asked himself what it would mean for a New England man to be saved by Justice *alone*. The thing might appear to happen psychologically, as the out-and-out preparationism of Thomas Hooker seemed to suggest. But not all Puritans had been edified by that model, and perhaps its theory began to look insufficiently Protestant.[6]

But the point here is simply that Taylor appears to have changed his plan without telling us why. And in doing so, he has reduced the varieties of Puritan assurance from three to two. The first is, let us say, an experience of Mercy; but is also, and more memorably, an experience of divine assurance in the positive. The other is an experience of Justice, or of Justice and Mercy together, however one imagines the outcome of Taylor's theological collapse; but it is better characterized in terms of the kind or quality of its assurance, which is negative, inferential, and anxious. So reduced, the varieties do indeed appear.

29

Taylor's norm of saving experience is not triple, but it is double; and the difference needs to be noticed.[7] But so—and perhaps more so—do the implications of the fact that this remaining difference does not take the form of an emphatic either/or. What are we to make of the fact that, in the lengthy discussions between Saint and Second- and Third-Rank Soul, a distinction that might have been presented as all-important is all but effaced? And how do we suppose Taylor regarded the difference between his two stories of saintly assurance?

Rank One, we notice, has had a relatively easy time of it. Though young, he appears already converted. "Always already," we are tempted to say; as if, grown up in the bosom of the Church, he cannot remember a time when he did not take the timeless decree of election as the constituting fact of his identity. Until the urgent "now," that is, of "Satan's Assault against those that first Came up to Mercy's terms." The assault begins, vigorously enough, with Satan's folksy prediction of "Soon ripe, soon rot; Young Saint, Old Divell" (407); and it settles into a technical and searching charge that *this* putative Saint never experienced the crucifixion of his own sins; that he is "presuming" a salvation for which there was no significant preparation, trying to grasp the salvation of the Gospel without facing first the doom of Law, the good news without the bad. And now, at any rate, he cannot get away without undergoing Satan's justice-oriented and quasi-conscientious inventory of his "Inward" (409–10), "Outward" (411), and formally religious (412–13) behaviors.[8]

The ultimate effect of all this is happy, of course, and even in a "systematic" sense predictable; for the terms of Rank's One's "Groan to Christ for Succor" are as subtle as those of the knowing attack: I'm a hellish sinner, to be sure, but Satan is no true Protestant, striving "to mount my sins.../ Above thy Merits, Pardons, or Good Will"—accusing not so much me as "thy rich Grace" (413). Part of the plea, then, is for renewed endorsement of the Reformation's rare theodicy of grace. And from its ready sophistication we easily infer that we are not yet exposed to Puritan anxiety in extremis.

Less predictable, however, is the tone and tenor of Christ's reply. That the heavenly Christ should speak *at all*, on earth, in the latter days, might itself seem a significant fact, particularly in a world that still recalled the bizarre self-justification of Ann Hutchinson.[9] But we come to accept the convention, naturalize the trope: everybody here is speaking human, indeed vernacular language; Satan knows the soft points of Protestant soteriology as well as Cardinal Bellarmine; and Christ made "Reply" to our "Address" several poems ago, so why not now? There, however, he was still talking rather stiffly, like a schoolman: "I am a Captain to your Will./ You found me gracious, so shall still,/ Whilst that my will is your design" (405). But now, as if moved by Soul's distress to further condescensions of love and language, his "Reply" takes the tone of husband to wife; or father to child; or else, to admit the worst, of husband turning wife into child with tone:

> Peace, Peace, my Hony, do not Cry,
> My Little Darling, wipe thine eye,
> Oh Cheer, Cheer up, come see.
> Is anything too deare, my Dove,
> Is anything too good, my love
> To get or give for thee?

What follows, in this relatively long speech, tells too much, perhaps, about how and why Satan is permitted to trouble the saints, for their own good, much as a sheepdog is used to keep a flock assembled in good order. But the intimacy of its explanations, assurances, and promises are more than sufficient to bring forth "An Extasy of Joy" (418).

Particularly as it ends with a frank declaration of divine satisfaction in the very person of the sinful, fearful, saintly Soul. "Oh! fight my field," begins the enthusiastic peroration of this long and personal enactment of divine assurance; fear nothing, when you "my Battels fight"; "Anchor thy heart on mee thy Rock"—because, well, because "I do in thee delight" (418). Only a more clouded sequel can make this resolution fully emphatic, perhaps. And it would be hard to say if the Imaginary Puritan Audience is supposed to keep the unalloyed delight of this most happy outcome clearly in mind; or whether some purpose requires that it actually be forgotten. Taking due note, however, of this first resolution, the ordinary critical reader may well be shocked by the extent and implication of its difference from the alternative later proposed.

Ranks Two and Three are, we recall, a cruder sort, first approached by Satan with a crasser set of spiritual considerations; and no doubt this has some connection with the fact that they are, at the outset, only half-way members. On the other hand, they are led, and quickly enough, to exactly the same point of doctrine and doubt—the fear that the faintest imagining that *they* may somehow be elect is not only empty and vain but sinful itself in the unpardonable extreme. Satan says it for them: "Hence sprouts Presumption making much too bold/ To catch such Shaddows which no hand can hold" (425); and in their "Call…for Mercy," they learn to say it of themselves: the minute we think to claim Grace ours, "she'l surely smite/ Us, for presuming on an others right" (429). About the significance of this range of sameness and difference, the individual appetite for doctrine or the private relish for tone may well decide. In the end, however, Ranks Two and Three must themselves call on *some* name or aspect of God for help against Satan's racy but unsettling abuses of salvation theory in the name of honest conscience. And the crucial difference comes not before this fateful moment, but after.

31

Sounding as much like Rank One as they ever do, Ranks Two and Three end their own distressed "Call" on a fairly high note:

> We've none to trust; but on thy Grace we ly,
> If dy we must, in mercy's arms wee'l dy.
> Then pardon, Lord, and put away our guilt.
> So we be thine, deale with us as thou wilt. (430)

Given this powerful mixture of evident good faith with hard-won Protestant sophistication—this working through to the domain of Mercy, after a long and losing bout with Satan in the arena of Justice—we can easily imagine them actually receiving some hopeful, if perhaps less personalized assurance from God. Less, we imagine, might seem cruel: "Of course I prayed/ But did God care?" Or, at very least, not very consistent with the poem's evident goal of filling the third-generation New England Church with visible saints.[10] But nothing happens. Indeed a most meaningful silence must be read into the blank spaces that separate the end of their call for encouragement and next morphological moment: "pardon, Lord": Lord? Mercy? Grace? God? Somebody? But only a silence.

The point of the earlier episode seems suddenly clear beyond mistake: in a rare and powerful trope, at least, God has actually spoken, to somebody, unmistakable words of love and assurance; but now, at the very same point, structurally and indeed doctrinally, where Christ had coddled and petted his little "Sweetums" of a Rank One, He tells everybody else just nothing at all. Students of poetic convention may still feel called upon to identify the language in which Christ responded to Rank One as "homely"; and feminists too protest that Taylor's gendering of the Soul is no favor to the image and status of women. But for the old-time Puritan watcher, the overwhelming point is that this time there is just no "Reply." Only a pregnant pause. And then the poem's own pressing rhetorical energy, its determination to take the next step *anyway*.

When the talk takes up again, the sound is pretty gloomy. In a poem implausibly titled "The Soule Bemoaning Sorrow rowling upon a resolution to seek Advice of Gods people," that balked and baffled second- or third-rank spiritual personage seems driven back to square one—lamenting first, Dickinson fashion, the "smart misery" of having a soul at all, "to illuminate a Lump of Slime" (430); and then, more conventionally, a body with "sensual Appetite to satisfy" (431). But this doubly composite speaker soon comes back to the main point: the evident need, against all hope, to find some hope, to "force Hope's Faculty, till Hope I finde" (432). Reduced to a place where the "nice" rules of presumption and despair seem no longer significantly to apply,

Ranks Two and Three express a thought which, temporarily at least, stands in painful place of Rank One's "Extasy of Joy":

> Perhaps these thoughts are blessed motions, though
> From whence they are, as yet I do not know.
> And if from Christ, Oh! then thrice Happy mee.
> If not, I'st not be worser than I bee.

Evidently, you're damned if you don't discover sainthood, Soul; and in a case like this you seem damned also if you (presumptuously) do; but as you can be, at last, only so damned, why not go with it?

Not quite "just do it"—just profess Sainthood, take the Supper, and let the chips of Judgment fall where they may. But why not allow the best possible interpretation to the present evidence? Perhaps a heightened sense not only of guilt but of alienation from God is itself a hopeful sign; a step perhaps, in a process that will yet lead to some positive, or at least noticeable, assurance from God. Or perhaps this is as good as it gets, for *some* garden-variety Saints. Who knows but some faithful shepherd will yet infer from anxious cases like these that lifelong anxiety must somehow be "made to tell positively on behalf of assurance itself."[11]

What follows first from this consciously forced hope, in any case, is nothing but a six-poem-long conversation with character named "Saint." And, so far as we can learn from Taylor's structure and his actual inclusions, this saintly good conversation is all that Ranks Two and Three are to get in the place of Rank One's little pillow talk with Christ. Never God's own "Peace, my Hony," so far as we know, but only a sociable townsman's cheerfully irritating "methinks I find there dart/ Some pleasant Hopes of you within my heart" (433). For which relief, one is tempted to say, not *much* thanks. Except that— apart from Satan in the forest, perhaps—there really is no place else to turn. Then too, this Saint seems eager to assure Ranks Two and Three that he can remember a time when his case seemed pretty much like their own. So maybe *not* hearing back from God is just no sign.

Maybe; but as the talk progresses, the reader may begin to wonder if the cordial and helpful Saint is telling all he knows. And just here we may want to settle our doubts about the exact identity of this character. Is he an altogether new voice and personality, with a religious experience uniquely his own, full formed in its own right but entirely hidden from us, except for his generalized statements that he too knows, first hand, all the sins and sorrows, doubts and fears which Ranks Two and Three continue to confess and bemoan? Might he be, for example, and as Norman Grabo long ago suspected, a singular embodiment of those Saints who surrendered to Grace "at once" and who entered the Coach prior to Taylor's division of the savable remnant

33

into three ranks?[12] Or might he be none other than Rank One Soul, reappearing here not as theological subject but only as religious enabler, and bearing now his once challenged but now established social alias? It appears to make a difference.

On one set of assumptions, we conclude only (what we may have been suspecting) that Ranks Two and Three are not, just as they stand, so very different from many others who already find themselves full members in good standing. Perhaps a certain level of a certain kind of "anxiety"—sorrow for the inevitability, the extent, and the enormity of sin, together with a pretty clear sense that there's nothing the human being can say or do to cover, assuage, or redeem the case—has been sufficient all along, even in "conservative" churches, to justify admission to the Lord's Table. Not *much* of a "wedden garment," perhaps, but a higher standard still than the one set by Stoddard and the majority of Valley Presbyterians who followed him into the way of "open communion."[13] It might even be fair to surmise that Taylor regards this "negative" sort of assurance as altogether normative. He offers us, after all, only one character with the public name of "Saint"; and, as it's hard to install and deconstruct an allegory in a single gesture, how can we assume that this strategic figure does not aptly epitomize the group whose class-name he bears? It would be like suspecting Bunyan meant his protagonist to suggest merely "a certain sort of Christian." And would it be *so* shocking, after all, if Taylor knew perfectly well that fewer people were holding personal converse with a Bridegroom/Redeemer in the 1680s than in the 1630s? And that no church could afford *that* test as a single standard?[14]

On the other hand, however, if Saint is merely Soul Rank One Redivivus, our analysis, perhaps even our response, might change somewhat. For on that account Saint would indeed be holding back something very important in his otherwise plausible and in the end reassuring dialogue with those not-first-rank Souls who seem doomed to know their sainthood in some *via negativa* merely. Having experienced, in a direct and loving way, God's "personal" assurance of spiritual safety, he now finds himself in the odd position of offering spiritual (and quasi-authoritative) counsel to some type of those would-be saints who have desired and been denied precisely that ultimate and undoubtable comfort—besides which, everything else is "as a candle to the sun."[15] The scene could be a little delicate, for the cases really are quite different: "Oh, by the way, on the score of our differences, I talked to God the other night." "Checkerwork of Providence" (450) indeed.

To reveal this master difference would be, of course, to seal despair, to crush at a stroke the budding Hope that dare not name itself as such: "What, a pardon from Mercy's person? Then doom itself is surely mine." Or else, in a comedy Taylor himself came very close to creating: "Well, Mom always did like you best." But the poem must proceed, with as much sobriety as is possible in a world where Glory shines but tropes are a little dull. And whether we think of the counsellor as Pastor Taylor or not,[16] it must say only what can, fairly, be said—in the cause of saving for the visible church those Souls who hear not the love words of Christ but only the school sentences of a smiling public man, doing what he can to make a cluster of negative similarities seem more important than the enormous, unspoken positive difference. To a sensibility like that of Edwards, or even of John Cotton, the whole sequence could seem like a sighted man talking earnestly to a blind one, avoiding the subject of color. But it does what it can.

Your sins are taller than the tide of grace can rise?—"I thought as you" (434). You seem withall to love your sin?—So I, when first "God powred out his Spirit sweet on mee" (435). You wish there were no heaven or hell?—"I often thought,/ Oh! that there were no God; or God was Naught" (436). And many more of these same specifics of comparative confusion, though Saint seeks also to identify the premise of the via negativa: Satan's *own* "He troubles not with such a thought as this./ But Wicked thoughts he in the Saints doth fling" (437). Consider, that is to say, that an anxious awareness of one's sin is itself a powerful hint of grace, somewhere. So give it a rest. Leave off this earnest but endless (and self-emphatic) need for self-critique. But talk breeds talk; and as no one intervenes to stop their mouths, Saintly Mentor goes right on trying to assure Spiritual Novice that their experiences have been perfectly similar.

You notice your evident "Want of Grace" (438)?—And did you *want* it all at once? You're all bewildered by the myriad of "Satans Temptations"?—"I once was thus" (442). You fear a secret selfishness is marring all your best attempts?—Of course you do, but note how Satan *will* try to work it both ways: in worldly minds, "He makes Civility to pass for Grace"; to bidden Saints, "he doth reply/ That all their Grace is but Hypocrisy" (443). So go on doing your duty, with all your moral might, without trusting to the results: "Do all good works," then "on a naked Christ rely" (444). That manly resolution—"and adherence to the multiplication table," as Emerson might think to add—will get you out of any labyrinth. Or else, if a little more theory really is in order, let's expose this "Sophestry" outright. Your sins are small, Satan will say, until you get some grace; but then the "scales are turned": "Though just before mans mountain sins were mites,/ ...His mites are mountains now" (445). His other case is much the same:

So Faith is easy till the Soule resolves
To live to Christ, and upon Christ rely,
Then saving Faith he bold presumption Calls. (446)

35

So learn, from my experience, to notice all these wily turns of thought; and end this "ambling work within a Ring" (437).

Not only Satan works this way, to be sure, for the poem itself has shown its own resource of stark inversion: by a simple turning of expectation, the same evidence is desperate or hopeful. Bound to see and say the worst, Soul can by no means accomplish this reversal for himself; but Saint accomplishes it for him, with noticeable ease. Surely rhetoric can do no more, in any cause. But all the while that Taylor's Saint pursues his troping art, the reader continues to wonder if allowance is to be made, ever, for the fact that Ranks Two and Three are being instructed to pass the second and easier (presumably) of two possible tests of assurance. Does Saint *know* this is the case? If so, does he know it from his own experience, as Rank One? Will he manage to intimate, somehow, when the time seems right, that not *all* cases are so exactly alike as his instant and repeated "me too's" have been leading this poor bedeviled latter-rank of a Soul to believe?

Will he—or anyone else, for that matter—ever say anything comparative and cautionary? Something like: "Finally, my dear Soul, one last consideration, delicate but necessary: don't be at all put off in your strivings by the rumor that there are persons, right here in New England, who tell of an assurance direct from God; who still have the problem of presumption, to be sure, and hence of despair as well, but who have, in the midst of their bouts with both conscience and Satan, the memory of God's own plighted love to cheer their struggle to endure. Such persons there well may be, and blessed they are, if all they claim is God's own truth and no delusion. But such are not the norm for other men, whom God is free to call in other ways. Nor will it ever be the way, in Churches made by men of old New England, to ask a man to say he knows the voice of God." The (finally alerted) reader would certainly *like* to hear Saint's version of that "don't make the wrong comparison" speech, whether Soul could make good use of it or not; and Taylor's version too, if he means to know the full post-1662 and anti-Stoddard statement of *Gods Determinations.* When nothing even faintly like this happens, however, the reader comes to the verge of concluding that Taylor has decided to exclude all comparison between the quasi-mystical experience of the privileged Rank One and the mundane struggles of the ragged remainder.

But then, suddenly, in a brief, last-second formulation, the poem suddenly remembers. A single couplet, altogether overshadowed—perhaps deliberately upstaged—by Saint's moral pontifications, becomes all at once more emphatic than a versified treatise on the difference between the sweetness morphology of Cotton and the anxiety model of Hooker. A rare device, if design should govern in a thing so small.

In one reading, fair but too generalized, the logic of Taylor's argument for braving Satan's eveready challenge and risking the duties of Sainthood and

Supper comes in the final couplet of Saint's final speech. One last attempt to turn the force of Satan's cruel inversions and name the poem's single overriding theme: "Presumption lies in Backward Bashfulness,/ When one is backward though a bidden guest." On the premise of "varieties," however, the couplet just before this final thrust deserves concluding emphasis. We doubt if Soul can take the subtle, "comparative" point; and we never learn if Saint himself knows all his lines may mean. But only to *someone's* memory of "Christ's Reply"—of God's own professed "delight" in the beloved Soul of Rank One—can Taylor address Saint's most pointed advice to the Soul at pains to know the love of God:

> Call not in Question whether he delights
> In thee, but make him thy delight and all. (450)

Somewhere, no doubt, the literature of religion in New England propounds a harder thought; but never, that I know, with quite the same effect. Long withheld, all but obscured, then dropped like a small but powerful explosive: a Saint is one to whom the very God has spoken words of love; or else, at all events, a man who comes to speak the very words himself.

Of course it need not seem a hard thought at all. To the dramatized understanding of Ranks Two and Three it means simply that the local church has decided to regard holy seeking—elsewhere thought to be a cause of divine favor—as itself a prime effect: (truly) seek and you have found; knock (with the main strength of full sincerity) and it has been opened unto you. Who could ask for anything less? So off he goes in a rapture, duly convinced by no less a saint than Saint himself, that his story, of "anxiety as assurance," is just the stuff of saintly life.

He tries to get too far too fast, of course. Wishing to "sing Praise" at once but also "to soar/ Above the stars, and stand at Heavens Door" (451), he needs to be reminded—by the structure of the episodes now, for Saint has been withdrawn from the drama—that we don't sing (i.e., praise) very well in this world and, besides, as singing is a social act, he has to join the local church. And since "Corruptors" are kept out by "Watchmen" on the "Towers" of the "Walls" that surround this "Curious Garden" (454), he'll have to tell his whole story. He's wracked by a new round of anxieties, to be sure, but this time they're mostly social; and there's nothing to indicate he has any real rejection to fear, even though the Elders and the Congregation will hear little more than the doubts and fears expressed to Saint put into a narrative form. While Taylor turns aside to praise the Congregational Church—outside of which there is (almost) no salvation, and to pick a quarrel with Bunyan (who thinks you get there *walking* rather than riding in the Coach)[17]—lower-ranked Soul

37

will be admitted as is: with no account, that is, of a "Reply" to his earnest plea for mercy. Once again, the quality of the plea itself will have to carry the day.

What this Soul's story will lack, in terms that verge on the technical, is any account of the time when, in "faith," his justification, his adoption, his personal acceptation came clear to him in a memorable moment of heightened security and luminous joy. His assurance has had to do without any special illumination, and his spiritual judges will hear nothing of what a Founding Father of New England Congregationalism had called, scornfully, an "immediate revelation in an absolute promise."[18] This would mean, for one thing, that unlike Rank One, Second and Third Rank Soul might have difficulty getting into John Cotton's church—when he managed at last to have one of his own, apart from the pastorate of John Wilson, and were he not dead these thirty or forty years, depending on when we think *Gods Determinations* got itself written. But it would also mean—to continue this anachronistic minimalism—that he would fare well enough with the admission standards erected by most of the other ministers in the founding generation. With Hooker, pretty clearly, as his "*Poor Doubting Christian*" seems to have invented not only the protagonist but even the genre of Taylor's latter-day poetic effort; and equally well, perhaps, with Thomas Shepard, who opposed Cotton's position in the 1630s more effectively than did the absent Hooker, and who authored the scornful phrase about "absolute promise."[19]

For these men—and others as well, who also misliked the "immediate" standard of assurance Cotton propounded in the sermons that made up his *Treatise of the Covenant of Grace* and defended, brilliantly but without entire success, in his famous "Rejoynder" to the "Sixteen Questions"—the problem had been, from the outset, to find a way to include in their churches that significant number of persons who seemed vitally interested in, perhaps even obsessed with, the project of assurance of salvation in a Calvinist world, but who could not say they had experienced acceptance by God. What they stressed, instead of a central moment of conversion, was a whole life of turning, away from sin and toward the God whose written Word they knew, if not his very voice. Taking their cue from the churchly persons they served—and perhaps from their own religious experience—they established at the outset a norm of saintly life that stressed preparation and sanctification and said as little as possible, authoritatively, about the moment of justification, by and in faith, that was supposed to come in between.[20]

Cotton protested, in the name of Calvin, that all this moral stress seemed *very* like a way of works: that to be truly itself Protestantism had to stress faith psychologically as in every other way; that no one could, logically, call on works to witness their faith without a prior experience of faith for them to witness and be witnessed by; and also, most cogently, perhaps, it was nowhere promised that "all those who hunger and thirst" for God should come and be made more keenly aware of their gnawing hunger and parching thirst. Somewhere, he kept saying, until his attention was taken up with numbering the days until the end of world, gracious experience had to be different from the merely natural; there had to be some positive something to point to; some experience of faith, in which something new happened or was seen or known or given or experienced. Deploying the love poetry of Canticles, Cotton once thought to call it a "kiss." A remote and most academic successor (who used Shepard as a very effective smokescreen) would call it first a "Divine and Supernatural Light" and then, in growing epistemological desperation, a "new simple idea."[21] But if, in the mean time, someone else should express it as a word of love, well that would be all right too, provided only the context made clear that the expression was once again altogether figurative. (Unless, of course, that poet should then turn around and approve the *other* way as well.)

And that, I am suggesting, is the appropriate intellectual setting for *Gods Determinations* read not globally, for its telling placement of the conundrum of presumption and despair, and not quite locally, for its energetic opposition to the ready and easy way of open communion, but in a surprising and significant way, historically, as an apt but also humorous reversion to the morphological controversies of the first New England generation. For there—and not to Calvin or Stoddard—is where we go to explain the problem of the Ranks: two and not three; separate, whatever we decide about the agreement between Saint and latter-rank Soul, but also, before the church at least, entirely equal.

At issue between Stoddard and Taylor—and entirely familiar it is to the reader who has pursued the poet's doctrine in the appropriate sources of prose argumentation—is a very complex and evolving set of ecclesiological problems. What *exactly* are we supposed to mean by a "visible saint"? One who possesses a sound "historical" faith in Christian teaching and leads an outwardly virtuously life? Or something *more*? One who has had, and will declare in a suitably public way, the content of some specific Christian experience? Are these latter "professed" saints the only proper "matter" for the Lord's Supper? Or may that sacrament be opened to the former as well, even though they be, according to the canons of 1662, but Half-Way Members? And, as positions unfolded themselves, may it be proper to think of that sacrament not as a "seal" but only as a "means" (among many) to realizing divine grace in a human way? There is no denying, of course, that Taylor's poem sets itself in some relation to all these problems, as Taylor tries to convince some (hypothetical) audience that sainthood is not a category of presumption and that sincerely religious persons should press beyond the status of half-way membership. But it is a distinguishing mark of *Gods Determinations*—not to say one of its great beauties—that it leaves the details of this Scriptural (often technical) argument largely out of account.

What it concentrates on, instead, is the prior, more "personal" problem, thoroughly debated in earlier generations, but often passed over or assumed in the works of this latter-day "sacramental controversy," of what a *visible* saint might look like.[22] What the poem concludes, from this point of view, is that a *visible* saint may be thought to look—or to sound, for it came down in the end to one's story—more than just one way. Not really three, as it had been tempted to think. But certainly two; and these as different as the mind of Calvinistic Congregationalism could imagine.

Not that Taylor was trying to renew the originary debate about styles of gracious experience. Far from it. That, indeed, is the point observing that the poem lets the (once devisive) difference between Rank One and Ranks Two–Three pass without emphatic marking. Showing himself once again a staunch and reverent traditionalist, Taylor tries only to recall and represent the best he can grasp and endorse from the Congregational Fathers. In doing so he is of course guilty of raising the folkways of the founding generation to the level of divine plan; but by the time he does so it is pretty late in the Christian history to begin complaining of that. What is more remarkable about the morphological gesture of *Gods Determinations* is its tolerance—indeed its frank endorsement—of styles of saintly psychology that had once seemed diametrically opposed. For Taylor's plan will admit, without prejudice, *both* the not very severely distressed who can yet confess a work of the Spirit *and also* those whose only knowledge is, searchingly, of their own unworthiness. It is as if Cotton and Hooker were to kiss, like Moses and Aaron, and make up, as the two sides of the more-than-antinomian controversy never really did.[23]

The collapse of Ranks Two and Three may well proceed from Taylor's gradual realization that there is, in the end, not much reason to maintain a strong distinction between the morphologies of Hooker and Shepard. Both are "preparationists" of a sort and to a degree Cotton never was. And though Shepard's system—elaborated over the pages of separate but continuous works—has the look of a greater completeness and balance than Hooker's single-minded interest in humiliation and contrition, it proves in the end to be as anxious and indirect as Hooker's own. The two might find ways to quarrel with one another (though there is no real evidence that they did); but their differences disappear when they get in the same room with Cotton, whether Hutchinson is there or not.

Hooker's system we remember as the one which never could write the Soul all the way to a positive realization of the state of grace. The monumental *Application of Redemption* elaborates the doctrine and experience of preparation for almost a thousand pages and then breaks off before we get to the Soul's actual "Implantation" in Christ; not much urgency in that direction, we fairly conclude. And when we turn to an earlier work on "The Soules Ingrafting into Christ," we learn the open secret of the unfinished summa. A

Soul in the evident distress of an advanced preparation asks a version of the question that threatens to deconstruct Hooker's system: if I build it, will He come? *Yes* means man's efforts bind God, and so goodbye Calvin; *no* means a little more than the audience can bear. And so a turn, to the premise itself: have you *indeed* undergone a full and perfect preparation? If so, then "the Lord Jesus Christ is come, and hath come many a day though thou perceive it not." Expect no "extraordinary sweetness and joy," no "hug" from the "King."[24] Sainthood—in this life, all of which is a preparation—is nothing but the power to hate sin with a truly Godly hatred.

Shepard is also a significant "Preparationist," of course, as the bulk of *The Sound Believer* makes perfectly clear. But rather than lingering in the supposedly preliminary phase—and redefining the threshold as the top of the relevant scale—he moves on to, and quickly through, the "faithful" center of his system, at the end of this still developmental work. Then, past this moment of great uncertainty, he goes straight on to a six-hundred-page account of sanctification, in *The Parable of the Ten Virgins*, to counter the influence of Hutchinson, who is said to have denied its relevance, and of Cotton, who most certainly did declare it not only useless but finally unintelligible without a central and informing experience of justification received as faith. And there, we feel, he hits both his stride and his mature, definitive theme: saints are those who keep both their moral and ceremonious lamps burning bright, against the moment of the Bridegroom's sudden appearance. Furthermore, as he defines the moment of faithful conversion as "espousal" rather than "marriage," he leaves his first-generation full members still, again, indeed always "preparing" for the consummation hereafter.[25] Another anxiety system, one fairly concludes. Another way to do without a *positive* sense of loving assurance.

What this leaves—for Taylor, as for anyone else interested in differences which matter—is Cotton's way versus other ways: the way of immediacy, in which Soul's longings really find an object; and the way of inference, in which the Soul's anxious doubts and questions must themselves be taken as evidence. Two ways, which once divided the world as diametric opposites, now seem merely complementary. Both enjoy good authority in the vigorous intellectual history of original New England, a powerful recommendation to anyone who, like Taylor, continued to regard that provincial episode as indeed a turning point in the history of salvation. New England saints having given voice to both, might not both be regarded as part of God's determinations? Why not say, in all latter-day conscience, that both had the look of a divine calling and that either one was sufficient to establish the quality of sainthood, so far as that quality may ever be visible?

Consenting to that degree of variety, Churches might yet agree to retain the test of public profession. Some saints will express salvation as a confirmed sense of the Lord's delight in the soul of a saved sinner; others as the piercing sorrow for sin and the delight they *long* to take in the things of the Spirit. But all will express it, whether we take Taylor's Soul as a hidden precursor of Emerson's Poet or not.[26] It is, after all, only a rare form of language game, this trying to say the things of God in words—that translate words that translate words, and so on, in a system where the only "transcendental referent" is a God as transcendent as any conceived in the Christian West. Such a game entails parody by very definition. Yet it is, the strong-and-silent theory of Mr. Stoddard notwithstanding, a game which reverence itself requires us to play.[27]

Beyond these historical speculations, there is at least one other way to explore Taylor's investment in his (only) two distinct Ranks. For a similar—tolerant, demystified, and very nearly ironic—sense of the double standard of visible sanctity to which he found himself the spiritual and literary heir shows up in the *Preparatory Meditations*. The "comparative" effect is particularly evident in the early numbers of the First Series, where Taylor seems still to be experimenting with the possibilities of his chosen materials and the implications of his own religious sensibility.

Before settling down to the relatively systematic exploration of typological matters, particularly those dealing with the Lord's Supper, and before fully establishing his familiar tone of poetic self-deprecation, for the failure of his works to realize the glory of these types in any but the most primitive and amateurish way, Taylor gives a fairly clear (and often agreeably humorous) sense that he is telling us a version of his own saintly story.[28] And wondering to which "Rank" he himself really belongs. He can pass, he feels pretty sure, the test applied to Ranks Two and Three: vigorously effective language is always there whenever he needs to express his own sight of self under the aspect of sin. But can he really convey what he calls, with bland morphological understatement, "The Experience"? Can he, for that matter, even *recall* it? Can he say what it has been like to know God once, but not again? Can he say what it means? Does it mean *enough*, spiritually, or must he rest his case with those other facts?—his sin, his sorrow, and his (now heightened) sense of lack? Perhaps there were personal reasons inclining him to accept both salvation stories.

The sequence begins in a way that only faintly suggests the problems which will quickly develop. The first "Meditation" concerns not the precise sacramental nature of or the appropriate human response to the Lord's Supper, but the prior theological fact which makes it possible: saintly men may commune with God in the Supper only because a personal member of that triune divinity has made himself communicable in human flesh; men may, in another idiom, marry with the Heavenly Bridegroom because He has, by assuming its flesh, espoused the human kind. The speaker finds this divine *donnée* so astonishing that, from the outset, the ordinary meditative task of effective comprehension seems just about impossible; the speaker's agitation may come simply from his sense of the mind-boggling enormity of the matter he has set out to consider. His affections are powerfully moved, to be sure, but the reason may be that his already faithful understanding is balked and affronted rather than suitably instructed.[29]

Appropriately, therefore, it takes a while before the speaker can say any words that are truly his own: he's just trying to be sure he can handle what seems implied in the language already well received. By the second stanza he has settled down to a couple of affective Oh's; but his first response, to his self-proposed but familiar formulations of revelation's prime mystery, is a pair of astonished *What*'s: "What love is this" that cannot be confined, paradoxically, in infinity, but must join itself with human finitude? And "What! hath thy Godhead, as not satisfied,/ Marri'de our Manhood, making it its Bride?" (5). This second, grammatically independent "What" has some of the force of our vernacular "Say what?" "Let me see if I've got this straight," the speaker seems to be asking: "you're telling me that God actually became man, that He wedded his nature to our own in a way the sexual and legal union of persons in marriage only dimly suggests? How *could* a person respond to that?" The cognitive and linguistic shock stops short of some comic "Well, if that don't beat all." But just barely, we sense; and only because the speaker goes on to discover a second mystery more surprising than the first. For the effect of this "Matchless Love"—overrunning heaven, this world, and hell itself—has been to create the wondrous Anselmian hybrid, "that there our Veans might through thy Person bleed."[30]

43

Evidently we respond to the sight of blood a little more immediately than to the thought of "hypostatic union." And so, as the moral outrage of substitute sacrifice both exaggerates and supplants the metaphysical paradox of God-man, the speaker gradually recovers his own voice. Understandably enough, however, what he can manage to say is scarcely a match for what he has just heard, from the authority of received theology.

The ardor of the "Oh" that marks his response to the "Matchless Love!" of the atonement informs his prayer that "Oh!" God's "Love might overflow" his own heart. But then it drops away—as a quite another *Oh* makes clear: "But oh! my streight'ned Breast! my Lifeless Sparke!/ My Fireless Flame." As fervent as poet can write, the wish has simply not been granted. And the poetic signs of failure are unmistakeable. With the final exclamation of this essentially exclamatory poem, the mood turns from one of an aroused desire to grasp the incomprehensible—and so respond with feelings on the same scale, if not with language in the same decorum—to the inevitable sense of emotional and expressive inadequacy. Then too, the whole image system of the response seems left over and borrowed from an earlier poem, in which the "Ebb" of affect already seemed a settled fact. There the "bellows of [the] Spirit did occasionally "blow away [the] ashes" (470). Here, however, we end not with fact but with prayer: "Lord blow the Coal: Thy Love Enflame in mee." And so we find, here at the outset, an inspired seeker, but not a finder, of experiences to confirm the doctrines wrought by love. The speaker loves, to be sure, but not enough; and the love he *would* feel, he knows, comes only as a gift, of better mind and will.

We can, of course, intervene on the poet's behalf, in much the way that Saint came in to rescue Soul: you're asking too much of yourself, surely; for what response can possibly compete with so immense a stimulus? And besides, we could say, continuing the dialogue into the discourse of literary criticism, look at what your poem has accomplished: the entire matter of Christian redemption, on the side of "purchase," at least, has been knowingly and feelingly compressed into two brief stanzas. Your problem in this meditation, surely, was less to compose the perfect state of affective response than simply to put the case of Redemption without being astonished into silence—or flat incredulity—from the very first word. Tell the truth: Can you imagine an equal effect, anywhere else in the history of Christian poetry? Edward, "you understand enough...why don't you let it out then?"

Better repressed than some others, however, Taylor will not *simply* let it out, not without scruple, nor outside a formula for failure which criticism has been remarking ever since the work of Roy Harvey Pearce. From the effect of this poem, we know he knows enough; and, from the tolerant, "double" outcome of *Gods Determinations*, we know he knows he knows. Enough to have entered the church, obviously, since on that Foundation Day in 1679 his own Public Relation had preceded all the others; and enough to go on serving as guide in all spiritual matters.[31] Yet not enough to satisfy himself, apparently; and not as well as he imagines it is possible to know. So on he goes, after this preliminary and rather doctrinal effort, to apply the test that cannot fail to embarrass his powers of spiritual discernment.

On he goes, from a "textless" epitome of the orthodox Christian system to the text of Canticles, that rich embroidery of oriental love poetry turned by a different sort of fantasy into a highly figurative account of Christ's love for both the soul and the Church. Most of the original Puritans had steered wide of this provocative but unstable allegory; John Cotton, however, had loved the text and had managed to provide his own line-by-line explication. Taylor too would explore, though much later, the whole book, in full and quasi-systematic detail.[32] Here, however, are merely four meditations (I.2, I.3, I.4, and I.5) that try to make response to a couple of lines from the first and second chapter: "Thy name is as an ointment poured out" and the familiar figures of "Rose of Sharon" and "Lilly of the Vallies." Nor is there as much continuity as the orderly numbers suggest: in a anomaly peculiar to the beginning of the *Meditations*, the short series is interrupted by three poems that have no sequential numbering, no date, and no announced text to set the subject. We need to know, of course, exactly what "Experience" interrupts the tidy little exegetical plan, but also, and perhaps more so, the sense of what it interrupts.[33]

Meditation I.2 takes its own sweet time arriving at the problem of the "Ointment" announced in the text, dallying on its typological way with the attractions of a certain Pearl and an assortment of associated Rubies, all of great price and all better appreciated by the self-deprecating speaker in the tiresome, materialistic literal than in the wondrous figure of salvation. Eventually, however, these random reflections arrive at the realization that, as ointments are rare and precious, the speaker might like to have his heart made into the lovely porous "Pomander" box in which this gracious gift, expressing God himself, might be kept. But no: could his "poore eggshell ever be an Hoard,/ Of excellence enough for thee?" (6). The speaker is a visible saint, we continue (biographically) to assume, so something like this had better be the case. But nothing half so poetic: only the bourgeois hope that I'm thy "Purse, and thou my Mony bee." And so we escape, without facing the fact that, as ointment is perfume as well as salve and magic potion, part of the value is the marvellous sense of scent.

Inevitably, then, and with an outcome all but predicted in advance, Meditation I.3 takes up the challenge: the Canticles poet has said, whether he knew his meaning or not, that the name of God is sweeter to the saint than the anointed desert lover; sweeter, in fact, than all the perfumes of, well, wherever they make and keep that typic stuff. Easy for him to say. But what about me? Oh, I *believe* it's so, right enough; and I can *say* it's so, in lots of metrical ways. Just watch me do my sweetness tropes:

> A Box of Ointments, broke; sweetness most sweet.
> A surge of spices: Odors Common Wealth,
> A Pillar of Perfume: a steaming Reech
> Of Aromatic Clouds: All Saving Health.
> Sweetness itself thou art: And I presume
> In Calling of thee Sweet, who art Perfume. (7)

All very fine as talk, but it doesn't take an empirical philosopher to know there's a wide difference between discoursing on and actually tasting of the pineapple—I mean, smelling the heavenly perfume. Other things, indeed most worldly or natural things, I smell right off, "And yet thy sweet perfume doth seldom latch/ My Lord, within my Mamulary Catch."

The reader wants to stop here, no doubt, to wonder about the anatomy and/or the imagery: does Taylor's physiology suppose that nipples have some olfactory power, or is he merely thinking of the nose as a kind of teat?[34] But the quasi-medical inquiry goes right on, manicly ignoring its rare talent for low comedy on the highest of subjects: "Am I denos'de? or doth the Worlds ill sents/ Engarison my nostrills narrow bore?" The second alternative makes sense immediately, though it turns man's enduringly sinful nature into a case of "snotty nose." The first seems to require a knowing (if baroque) anticipation of Edwards: do I lack in fact that spiritual "sense" which alone makes the things of God and salvation into objects of wonder and delight?[35] Then, while the reader is wondering how seriously Taylor will consider the drastic case— that, failing to evince a sense of divine things, he is not really a saint at all—a third possibility is added: "Or is my smell lost in these Damps it Vents?" Why he's turning the whole thing into a *romp*, the reader may well suppose; for what (the hell) is the typic meaning of mucus?

Very quickly, however, in the midst of a stanza, in fact, the decorum recovers itself, as the speaker finds a way to think of his sinful sense that is apt enough to seem not entirely comic:

> Or is it like the Hawks, or Hownds whose breed
> Take stinking Carrion for Perfume indeed?
>
> This is my case. All things smell sweet to mee;
> Except thy sweetness, Lord. (7–8)

We still have to face the prospect of some mighty spiritual sneeze, to "Expell these damps," or some gracious nose drops, perhaps, to "Breake up [the] Garison" of sin's congestion; and we may puzzle yet a while over the speaker's prayer that God will "both [his] Mamularies Circumcise." But we know where we are: "reverent" still, the "parody" is directed at the speaker's own lack of spiritual discernment—to heighten the sense, without overstating the meaning; and the case of saintly conscience is one we have *almost* seen before.[36]

The speaker cannot "sense" God. He knows quite well his own insensitivity and correctly identifies his sin as the cause. Further, he knows enough to know that though sin and grace are perfectly opposite in their nature, they often live a long time together in the hapless human case. And so he knows to refrain from resigning all claims to election just because he cannot register the divine as an overwhelming sensation. But neither will he, on the other hand, renounce that standard altogether: texts there be, and saints there have been, to tell us the possibility—and the joy—of passing out of the world of sin and sorrow and doubtful hope and into a heaven of grace and pleasure and knowledge as sure and sweet as the smell of perfume. There is, perhaps, no other way to be *really* sure. Nor are there occasions more appropriate than the Supper's "Days of Comfort" for experience to confirm what desire has implied.[37] And so—as if Ranks Two and Three were to press on, toward a most particularly *sensuous* version of the experience of Rank One—the sacramental meditator laments his sin and prays for a scent that will confer and then cloy the new olfactory sense.

He prays, that is, for an experience more sensual than anything Edwards would dare imagine, more nearly sexual, in fact, than Cotton's denatured (textual) "kiss." But he prays for this ravishment as an accomplished and all but confirmed Hookerite. There is, in fact, more than a touch of Hooker in the rough comedy of the final stanza. When the speaker prays his Lord to "breake thy box of ointment on my Head" (8), some readers will recall the modern joke about the donkey sold as willing and *so* tractable, who needed nevertheless to be cracked across the brow with a two-by-four: sometimes you need to get his attention. Others, more reverent or better read in scripture, will remember the bible scene, of the box of perfume broken over the head of Jesus. But the idea of what it might take for God to make an impression on the comically insensitive sinner has all the force of what Hooker called "holy violence," as he theorized the usual manner of God's workings in (life-long) preparation.[38] The result of *this* holy violence would be a delicious running down of soothing sweet and healing stuff on all the speaker's hair and face. Then he'll *know*, perforce, "How sweet a Lord" is his. But you do have to get his attention. And it is, all the while, a prayer and not a fact.

Nor is it a prayer we particularly expect to see answered. The first three poems have all been praying for much *more* insight and ardor, knowledge and assurance, but they have also arranged themselves to do without. Once again, by an irony it seems friendly to call self-preserving, a heightened awareness of the blockage of sin and a keenness of desire in spite of that have been made to do the work of providing *sufficient* assurance. More is rumored to be available, in the mode perhaps of exquisite favor, but it will probably not be offered in the present clumsy case. We will, in all likelihood, have to go on as we have been, giving, taking, and preaching about the sacrament, and writing poems about the text of the preaching, at the customary interval. They also serve. And, where the literature of latter-day Puritanism is concerned, the reader will take whatever is sincerely offered.

But then something happens, something in fact not expected and in form very peculiar: an experience—significant enough to be called, simply, "The Experience," and authoritative enough not to need a text for name and warranty—but not at all the sort just prayed about. Not a cloyingly sensuous experience of perfume, but only "an aire" and at the same time a "Beam of Light" (8). Pretty surprising, in context, no doubt: much more agreeable, amid a landscape of constructed absence, than just nothing at all; and much better, on the whole, than another poke in the conscience with the sharp stick of conviction. But a little too abstract to read like a gloss on Canticles.

We can hear about it, of course, only after the fact. Even those who doubt Thoreau's remark that "writing is not what interests us" may concede that no one writes while caught up into the seventh heaven; so we're necessarily dealing with a sort of afterglow. Still, literary strategy might have arranged for the poem to imitate the moment of ecstasy itself. Settling, instead, for a more tranquil recollection of powerful emotion, it insists on its own past tense, for reasons and with consequences that turn out to matter. Absence, for the first three poems, has been a fact of the present; presence, a hope for the future. But then, when it did in fact present itself, the experience fell at once into the past: "Oh! that I always" felt what I felt at the "last Sacrament."

Theorists may go on torturing the grammatical puns, but the student of Puritanism will wonder why Taylor's "For Once Then Something" turns so quickly into a "Once Is Never Enough" and even a "Door Marked Nevermore." Certainly the actual experience would have seemed all too fleeting. Inserting itself into a sequence of pious but prejudicial wishes, was it also just *too* pale a simulacrum of the one made famous in the literary model? Or were there reasons why Taylor needed to remain perched on the edge of certainty, expressly unhappy with his second-rank status, but never willing to admit to anything more? Would more have seemed to him presumptuous? (As it did not, apparently, to Cotton.) Is full assurance the sort of case we can imagine as an abstract possibility, can "imitate" as a possibility for others, but not really confess of ourselves? Or would it simply have taken Taylor too far beyond the standard of the audience he regularly addressed in sermons and continuously imagined in private? Would it have deprived him, that is to say, of a "sincere" relation to his needful persona?

A curious problem of literary history suggests itself as well: when exactly do we imagine the experience of the (undated) "Experience" to have taken place? On the sacramental occasion we can posit between the recording of I.3 (11 Feb. 1683) and I.4 (22 Apr. 1683)? Or might this rare but thin surprise have occurred, ironically, on the Sunday in advance of which Taylor had written of his desire for the divine "Odours" to become his "nostrills fare" (8)? Or at some other time altogether? We could also take this opportunity to remind ourselves that it need not "really" have occurred at all: we may suppose these poems all "correspond to" real sermons really delivered to a real audience, but the laws of their making are entirely their own, and we have no way to know when Taylor may be inventing more properly than recording.[39] But even the less radical alternative is sufficient to raise the important question.

Are we to think of a sequence on Canticles as having been interrupted, all of a sudden, by an experience most unlike the one the laws of prayer and poems both require we hold in mind? And did he preach a sermon on the personal text? Trying conscientiously to experience God in the language of oriental sexuality, I suddenly found Him—quite beside my own meditative will—in a breath of air, a beam of light and, more cerebrally still, in an idea of unity. Or might we be justified in thinking of the interruption as itself a planned thing? What would be the effect of inserting an "Experience" into the meditations of a second-class saint busily preparing himself to do without such things? And what if the experience were to be, though quite wonderful in its way, most unlike the thing suggested by the nearest provoking text? (Then I think I'll write a poem about a man who's awakened from a dream about a stately pleasure dome.) Or, if that hypothesis would betray our settled theories of Taylor's literary amateurism, might we think of Taylor as beginning the entire sequence, with a certain short-range plan in mind, only *after* the experience of "The Experience" had already occurred? Of planning things, that is, with that early but unlooked-for climax already on the record?

Certainly "The Experience" answers the need of "Meditation 1" almost as pointedly as it defies the agitated request of the poems on Canticles. And the point of the "plan," on this hypothesis, would be to confirm, for the meditating speaker, the fundamental fact of the Christian economy of salvation without offering a magic clue to the speaker's own status. A high Calvinist might tease (first) assurance out of just this much.[40] But it might leave the average sensual Puritan still praying for his taste of honey. It might be—supposing one dared to care about such things—a very nice poetic effect.

A single word, in any case, is all we have to connect this chaste, almost doctrinal experience to the sensuous prayer it all but declines to answer: nothing like a drowning in heavy perfume or a soaring in delicious divine odors, it was nevertheless somehow "sweet." Encouraged by later example, we might persuade ourselves that Taylor's "aire" is itself a sort of zero-degree perfume: "it has no taste of the distillation...it is odorless"; and yet might not a man be "mad for it to be in contact"[41] with him? Except that in the Puritanic version it's not perfectly clear where the sweetness may lie. Indeed the sequence or causal mechanism of the experience seems a pretty complicated affair:

> Oh! that I always breath'd in such an aire,
> As I suck'd in, feeding on sweet content!
> Dished up into my Soul ev'n in that pray're
> Pour'de out to God over last Sacrament. (8)

Praying to God, in thanksgiving, no doubt, for the sacrament that unifies the soul of the professed saint with the life of living God—and hoping, once again, for sensory confirmation of the status still too personally at issue—I suddenly drew a breath that canceled all such anxiety. Just a breath, such as any man might take at any time, but somehow, without thought of "any occurrence of special good fortune," it solved the whole sense of existence. I guess you could call that "sweet."

Sweet, but also "strange," like that "Beam of Light" which revealed to my enraptured sight a closer proximity to God "than ere Came in my minde."[42]

And not an illumination, merely, but more strangely still, a shining, "Which filled my Soul then to the brim," as I really *saw* what formerly I only believed—and stammered when I tried to say:

> My nature with thy Nature all Divine
> Together joyn'd in Him thats Thou, and I.
> Flesh of my Flesh, Bone of My Bone. There's run
> Thy Godhead, and my Manhood in thy Son. (8–9)

An inspiration, surely, given that strange breath, but only to reveal the truth of incarnation. Enough, however, to "enflame" as well as to enlighten, as the balked intelligence and clumsy desire of Taylor's first sacramental exercise is turned—by ecstasy, as it appears—to the instructed personal affect of meditation as such.

No longer present, but not (now) simply absent, the reality of the experience endures with sufficient strength to turn the "Oh!" of the barely possible to the quite different "Oh!" of the scarcely departed—not "Oh that I could" but "Oh that I might *always*." The turn to the negative is clear from the third (of five) stanzas, to be sure; but the spirited moment lasts just long enough for the recovering mystic to make a very surprising claim: not confirmed or renewed knowledge of sainthood for himself, but a supra-angelic place for his kind in the scale of being; for where is it written that God ever became an angel?[43] And what tunes might that theme not inspire? The "sweetest," no doubt; if only "what I had, my heart might ever hold" (9). He cannot do that, of course; but neither can he, we imagine, go on as if nothing extraordinary had happened. For how could the saintly person *not* take comfort in an experience so wondrously revelatory, though brief? In a prayer so powerfully, if also so unexpectedly answered?

It comes as no surprise that the next poem—also without a number or a text—is titled "The Return": having been somewhere else, the speaker is now back. Interrupted by an experience some might call "mystical," how could the planned, or at least the more routine sequence begin again without noticing that something unusual had happened? And so, in the aftermath of ecstasy, a series of images of divine things, punctuated by the true sight of "Thy Human Frame.../ Lockt to thy Holy Essence by thy Hand," are all greeted by the repeated wish "that thou Wast on Earth below with mee!/ Or that I was in Heaven above with thee" (9). A new thought in the sequence, but an altogether plausible response to the "heavenly" experience just recounted; for it has given the speaker an even keener appreciation of the present deprivation, to which he must now return.

Less predictable, however, are the terms of the poem's turn to comfort, as the wishful refrain is varied at the end. Taking the recent soul-filling "shine" for a sort of down payment on the bliss of eventual union with God, common sense might expect something like this: "As I was once with thee in Heaven above/ So guard Me here till I rejoin thee there." The speaker, however, makes just the opposite declaration: "That thou hast been on Earth below with mee/ And I shall be in Heaven above with thee" (11). The implication is definitely *not* that the experience of "The Experience" took place "on earth below" but, more astonishingly, that the speaker is not now thinking of that experience at all.[44] His spiritual confidence seems unusually calm and unclouded; and it may in fact have been increased by his recent "vision"; but he is taking comfort from a completely different set of life events. As if a transcendent experience never could inform the ordinary.

Wishing still for more intimacy with God, either here or there, the speaker reminds himself of the sufficiency of all his more regular grounds of settled hope:

> But I've thy Pleasant Pleasant Presence had
> In Word, Pray're, Ordinances, Duties; nay,
> And in Graces, making me full Glad,
> In Faith, Hope, Charity…

These ordinary matters—quotidian, by some accounts, specifically "Christian" by others—constitute, he says, a very real kind of divine presence, "on earth below"; and it is this familiarity which warrants his predicting his own eventual presence "in Heaven above." An admirable line for assuring the latter days of some well encovenanted but now dispirited second-rank Saint, no doubt; but a little surprising from the man who saw Incarnate God the other night. As if the "Pleasant" were more persuasive, at last, than the rapturous. Or as if the speaker were deliberately refusing, once again, to do more than *recognize* anything at all above the norm.

And then, while the reader is wondering what to make of this latest deadpan refusal to notice the elephant in the room, the sequence executes a second "return"—to the project, this time, of meditating over the matter of Canticles. An inflation of standards, in one sense, as the speaker will once again be begging for the assurance of religious experiences "slickt up" in types of the explicitly gorgeous and implicitly sexual. But also another letdown, as he will (we somehow know) once again be failing to get what he says he needs, and hectoring himself for that reason; and also because he will be returning to the thing he was doing when he got the thing he no way expected. And biographically, of course, Pastor Taylor will be going back to the dutiful (if "Pleasant") task of writing poems about the texts of his sermons.

Glad to be back, perhaps, if our inferences about his uneasiness with the paranormal have been anything like correct: meanwhile, back to the text; and back to the problem of worrying the signifier into a credible sign of the real. But as the text is going to be Canticles, the secular reader, who cloys more easily than the religious poet, may be less pleased: the "atmosphere is *not* a perfume," Edward; go try the experiment of "crossing a bare common."[45] Soon enough, however, even *that* reader is repersuaded: the drama of the speaker's trying to experience God as "the Rose of Sharon" and then, at a discount, as "The Lilly of the Vallies" is less broadly humorous than the case of the "Ointment"; and it takes several poems for the comedy to unfold; but the "story," of deriving comfort from honest failure to meet the highest possible test, is as sure as ever. Somewhere Taylor really has got a life.

Taylor's meditative persona seems everywhere to know a lot more than he can well convert to affective capital, and it requires several readings of "Meditation I.4" to get past the sense that he can offer us nothing a but crisscross of secular and typological learning about roses.[46] Eventually, however, the sense of a plot appears. The speaker would like to turn from the false shows of the world to regard Christ in the matchless beauty of the Rose and the marvellous efficacy of its byproducts. But something distracts him: his sinful incapacity, as always, but also his realization that the rose in question is not *red* for nothing; that its full efficacy appears only in the shedding of its rosy blood. Suitably chastened, the speaker wants less at the end than at the beginning.

His first metaphoric wishes seem quite graphic, if a little mixed: first, "lead me into this sweet Rosy Bower" and "Lodge my Soul in this Sweet Rosy Bed"; then, changing to a less suggestive figure, "Array my Soul with this sweet Sharon flower"; and also, in any horticultural event, "Perfume me with the Odours it doth shed" (12). We've been in that sensuous place before, of course; but while we're again wondering how sexual may be Taylor's own understanding of the Rose, the poem races on to the healing or soothing powers of various rosy extracts, all richly available in the "dayly Bread" of the Supper, and all desired by the speaker in slathering abundance:

> Oyle, Syrup, Sugar, and Rose Water such.
> Lord, give, give, give; I cannot have too much.

But then, at just this point in the speaker's prayer for the lavish and delightful assurance he *knows* Christ has made available, the memory of Redemption's price:

> But, oh! alas! that such should be my need
> That this Brave Flower must Pluckt, stampt, squeezed be,
> And boyled up in its blood, its Spirits sheed.
> To make a Physick sweet, sure, safe for mee. (13)

The meta-physical wit continues unabated, in the turn from desire to pain, but the latest "oh!"—another variant still, in Taylor's ample repertoire of exclamatory tone—makes the transition safe: I was being a little selfish, wasn't I? Goofy, even.

Still, "This mangled Rose rose up again," as part of the same well made plan. And as the cause of assurance is hardly separate from that of redemption itself, it cannot be *entirely* selfish to seek the full fruit of its application; indeed it would seem ungrateful, from another legitimate point of view, to seek less than perfect love has made available. So he tries again, with yet another version of the terms provided for the purpose: not just a rose in my lapel, or my rest among a bed of flowers; but "Open thy Rosie Leaves, and lodge me there." A bold request, the speaker cannot help but know; but then it is a holy type and no mere carnal trope.[47] And it is, after all, only a prayer—an outside chance and not a fact: "*shall* I thy glory meet/ Lodged in a Rose"[?] (13, Emphasis added). Possibly, given the terms of our redemption; yet given my sin, not bloody likely.

Or if indeed a fact, a fact of typic mystery and not of present affect: "What[!] *is* my way to Glory made thus sweet"[?] (13, Emphasis added). Yes, I suppose so. A wondrous fact, and me not knowing. But what *is* the odor of a rose I cannot smell? Is it anything like what some Romantic fellow will be calling "ditties of no tone"? Well, no matter: suitably sentient or not, I'll do my own level best, in any event. Like the Saint said to the (Poor Doubting) Soul, not easeful assurance but perfect committment: ask not what the Rose can do for you.

> I'le walk this Rosy Path: World fawn, or frown
> And Sharon's Rose shall be my Rose, and Crown. (13)

Eventually, that is, as the future tense makes clear: a rosy crown at last, but a thorny one for now: "To learn the transport by the pain."[48]

A venerable and necessary "way," no doubt. Why not assume, at last, that one is indeed walking in the rosy way of genuine Christian sanctification? Or if it's really just the primrose path of "splendid sins," then better the sins of virtue than of vice: His way, though He slay me. A "definite belief," by most later standards of measure, but one that leaves the speaker "wandering to and fro over [the] deserts" of that sort of faith which, though entirely persuaded of Calvinist soteriology, must take its assurance from that fact alone; which knows what an oasis of personal assurance is supposed to look like, but whose only moment of visionary refreshment was strangely arid.[49] And so—in "The Reflection," the third of Taylor's extranumerary insertions—a return to the true if repressed matter of "The Return": why only once? and why so doctrinal? Concede my Christic faith had need of visionary confirmation: does not my soul—my sense—require its own supply of food?

Here I am at the table reserved for Visible Saints, wondering, Lord, if thou art in fact, "at the Table Head above/ Meat, Med'cine, sweetness," and whatever else it takes to "Enamour Souls with Flaming Flakes of Love." If so, then why will "not my Trencher, nor my Cup overflow?" Well I remember the teaching of your prophet, Cotton, that many mistake their estates by confusing strength of appetite with quality of satisfaction: "Be n't I a bidden Guest?" And if not there, then why here? Does "visible" mean "false"? What is my story?—"Shall I not smell thy sweet, oh! Sharon's Rose?/...Shall thy sweet leaves their Beautious sweets upclose?" (14).[50] Of course I remember sin, whose "mud" has stopped our spiritual conduit pipes, and for which the glory's locked away that else would ravish every soul with earthly sight. But grace's key, we know, has thought to open up a "Doore" and make for saints "a golden day." As even I can testify, from my one, singular but too brief "Experience":

> Once at thy Feast, I saw thee Pearl-like stand
> 'Tween Heaven, and Earth where Heaven's Bright glory all
> In streams fell on thee, as a floodgate and,
> Like Sun Beams through thee on the world to Fall. (14–15)

Well, all right, that "Beam of Light" was somewhat more graphic than I had been willing to express. And perhaps my sense of the contrast made me say too little about its sweetness. But not now:

> Oh! sugar sweet then! my Deare sweet Lord, I see
> Saints Heavens–lost Happiness restored by thee.

In further retrospect, and by later comparison, "So much before, so little now!" Yet the experience was in fact about the glory of redemption by an incarnated divine mediator and not about my own place in the scheme. Besides, that was then and this is now. Why now this starvation diet, this Sunday Supper without the honest sense of food? "Dost thou sit at Table Head, where I/ Do sit, and Carv'st no morsel sweet for mee?" (15). But let me beg, once again, and at the typic risk of mixing the human figure, the grandest favor of all: "Springe, Lord/ Thy Rosie Leaves, and me their Glee afford."

The monologue format permits no answer of course, but the rhetoric of the one-sided discourse makes the logic clear. No answer, so the lesser question: shall not even "thy Rose my garden fresh perfume?" Probably not, even if I *am* a bidden guest to the banquet above. If not, then, the "Glee" of communion with the God who was a man, at least the gift to apprehend the world through Christ-colored lenses: "Enthrone thy Rosy-self within mine Eyes" (15). Not the last gift of personal assurance but proper thoughts and wishes. Christian perception, if not quite mystical experience.

Or, as the now familiar reduction carries over into the next meditation (I.5), maybe the whole thing will work better with the chaste Lily than with the sexual Rose. The facts should be the same in either case, but maybe it's also a matter of sensibility: *art* thou, Lord, "a Lilly Flower?" Then "Oh! that my Soul thy Garden were." No need for you, as female, to take me up inside this time; but plant your self at least in me: "Thy bowing Head root in my Heart, and poure/…of its seeds…" (15). Too much still? Too Melvillean and withall too grand? What then, in view of present insensitivity, is the least the sacred figure will permit?

> Be thou my Lilly, make me thy knot:
> Be thou my Flowers, I'le be thy Flower Pot.

With that final characterization—of the speaker himself as "potty" or trifling—the art of sinking in poetry has done about all it can to aid the cause of rising in assurance.

Broadly humorous or not, it comes as the climax to an extended and deliberate structure of reduction, designed not to flatter the modern reader's impatience with a wit that seems not to know its own name, but to enhance the speaker's nearly ironic understanding of what he's asking of himself. Not "who *wrote* these lines"; but "can they possibly apply to *me*?" First a Rose: is it that I may be inside the petals? or bide at least within a rosy bed or bower? Or is it merely that the Rose must grow within the garden of my heart?—which the "Golden Spade" of "Grace" (or the holy violence of Thomas Hooker) must first "dig till the Spring/ Of tears arise" (14). And then a Lily, equal in Scripture type, perhaps, but hardly so in poetry's flourishing language of flowers. And no thought, now, to be inside of it: plant the "Lilly Flower" within the garden of my heart, even if that bed or bower be reduced to the lowest possible figure. Now it might be true. Or now at least a mind like mine could dare to think it so. But if indeed the Lily should be planted thus, may it not seed and spread, turning the pot-sized heart *into* a "Fruitfull Vally" (15) in the process? Then, of course, what "Spangling Glory" may not my grace-transmuted heart reveal?—the Lily of the Valleys "being mine," "My Vally *then* with Blissful Beams shall shine" (Emphasis added, 16).

And there, for once, he seems to have it. Not quite as well as he will in the very next poem—where the figure system changes, unaccountably, from flowers to money—but as well as ever in a poem that deploys the matter of Canticles in the name of personal assurance rather than typological education.[51] Multiply reduced, rendered all but ironic by self-effacing humor, and deferred by a conditional impossible to distinguish from a (perfect) future, the figure system works well enough that the speaker can almost say something; can do more, in any event, than deny or anxiously question. If my earthy heart is, at the same time, no *less* than God's flower pot, then who's to say I may not yet know it as a site of "Spangling Glory." Only "hereafter," perhaps, but may not that regime of time be at its first inception now?

But then the terms change once again. Very noticeably, in fact, in the very next poem, the last of those textless and undated insertions into what appears an otherwise orderly Supper sequence. Falling out of Canticles altogether, and into a realm of experience—and a figure system—most unlike anything we have seen so far, the speaker demonstrates quite amply, if unwittingly, that he can do much better with figures less intimate than those furnished by the oriental sublime. An extended reading of the "economy" of the remarkable Meditation I.6 lies beyond the scope of this essay; but it is worth suggesting that this elaborate and subtle but not at all forced attempt to make the system of minted currency express the problem of apparent and real value within the system of strict Protestant theology represents a singular success in the section of the first series of the *Preparatory Meditations*, and that its success throws further light on the problem of trying to make the erotic say grace.

Embarrassed, before the middle of the very first line, by the notion of himself as God's "Gold," the speaker immediately hedges his theological bet: "Or Purse, Lord, for *thy* wealth" (16, Emphasis added). The problem is evident at once. Or, rather, the *two* problems. First, as always, is the presumptive saint being merely presumptuous in imagining he might be a thing of value in the sight of God? But second, and a little more strictly, could that value ever be thought of as "inherent"? Is grace the kind of thing which transforms the human personality so as to make it, now, valuable in itself? Or does the transaction of "justification" remain entirely fictional ("forensic"), leaving God to value saints "just because He does" or, at most, to value not (re)created beings so much as his own gracious presence within them? A lot of ink has been spilled.[52] But not here. In three workmanlike stanzas—all marked by the entire absence of the exclamatory "Oh!" and the incredulous "What!"—the speaker moves his images surely and steadily toward his own satisfactory solution.

Raising, for the sake of the scruple, but then declining to pursue, in the name of ordinary good sense, the originary Protestant quibble, he gives all his explicit attention to the fact and not the definition of value; namely, his. Help me—as spectacles, not appearing as particularly "rosy"—to read "Thine

Image, and Inscription stampt on mee," and we'll call it…not even, God knows, but close enough for tropes. The tenses say future, but the tone this time says fact. Or else, at very least, a condition not so hard to find fulfilled: write on me

> Thy superscription in an Holy style.
> Then I shall be thy Money, thou my Hord:
> Let me thy Angell bee, bee thou my Lord. (16)

The manner is calm, jaunty, almost, as if the speaker were taking spiritual comfort from his own evident ease with the familiar system of terms. Further, the tendency to deflation, elsewhere uniform and indeed self-parodic, is here convincingly reversed: show me your markings, and I'll drop that neo-scholastic nicety about being a container of value merely; show me your mark—in language I can read—and I'll call myself as good as gold. And get on with the project.

There is No "Glee" here, to be sure; no ecstatic absorption into the Godhead or its figures; but no self-generated hysteria either; no self-exacerbated emphasis on the failure of the types to reveal their *sense* to the metrical meditations of a latter-day New England saint. And the imagistic let-down—from the types of perfume and flowers to trope of money—does not at all announce itself as such. Elsewhere, Lilies reduce the Rose, food must parody perfume, and flower pots make fun of flower beds. But money stands up staunchly by itself: here I count; I can do no other. A friendly little climax for the reader. And not without instruction for the saint.

Perfect, actual, applied, personal assurance remains as far off as ever, perhaps, but the speaker seems here convinced he'd recognize the thing in just these terms. And that confidence seems to help: having solved or elided one problem—*all* value is at last subjective, a matter of value to or credit in *somebody*—and having worked it out in a poem that has no need to prevent or unsay its own effect, the speaker seems to find a moment's rest. The wicked man could charge that he has put doctrinal resolution and/or poetic closure in the place of spiritual certainty, and that, even in its own terms, his tidy little argument is entirely tautological: "Am I *really* valuable? To You, I mean, as other standards all collapse to that at last? Well, show me that I am, and then I'll really know." But then the wicked man would have to prove that the speaker is no way privy to his own deconstruction. More friendly, and not less plausible, would be the suggestion that Taylor (himself) has made, from a suitable play of words, not a flawed profession of Christian comfort, but perfect Calvinist prayer about its form and meaning. A petition of grace and not a begging of principle.

57

• • •

And then the sequence does go on, as we sense it must, with the private poet's quasi-public task of testing out the text. The poems continue to be, essentially, sermons to himself; and successful apprehension of Scripture doctrine continues to serve as a sign of grace; so the problem of the speaker's own spiritual style—his morphological identity, so to speak—can never be very far from the surface of the poems which follow. But we never hear it again, I think, with quite the same urgency.[53]

The very next, famous poem (I.8), on the "Living Bread" of John 6.51, has its own self-agitating "What," but the sense of paralyzing personal astonishment is overwhelmed by the bravura effect of "streams of Grace" from "God's Tender Bowells"; and when the artifact called "Heaven's Sugar Cake" (19) is made to call for its own consumption, discussion usually shifts from the speaker's spiritual competence to his taste. Meditation I.23 takes a turn with "My Spouse" (of Canticles 4.8), but the speaker emphasizes not his erotic failures but his ontological surprise—as if a "Prince" should spouse "a snake or Fly" (39). And as the sequence settles into its groove of pursuing and relating all sorts of texts to the master signifier of the Supper—Psalms, John, Isaiah, Colossians, Hebrews, Luke, Revelations—the speaker seems to become less obsessed with his own assurance and more devoted to the proper interpretation of the gospel his duty gives him need to preach. His own responses continue to seem inadequate, but his problem of affect comes to appear as much structural as personal. And his expressions, or at all events our responses, turn formulaic rather soon: he never can have *sufficiently* moved affections; but who, aware of the mystery, really could?

The effect of this shift—gradual and never complete—is somewhat mixed and might strike different readers differently. Repetition of tones and strategies lessens the sense of an "original relation," no doubt, but the evident determination to go on in a system whose end is known but never reached may also heighten our appreciation of Taylor's public dedication: a convicted preparationist and a convinced sanctificationist, who kept holding out for the sweetness of God's kiss, for himself no more and no less than for his audience; an arch defender of New England's first ways, doing his Suppertime thing, with learning and with wit that tried to bring it home. Or so it seems in light of the present account.

Someone may yet attempt the truly daunting task of trying to show that the whole body of the *Meditations* specifies the full "progress of [Taylor's] faith from conversion forward"; that the entire double sequence, of 220 (or so) private poems that meditate the texts of public sermons, really do add up to a personally faithful and at the same time morphologically correct account of Taylor's spiritual life, from conversion to the brink of glory.[54] And within that account, perhaps, the final extended sequence on Canticles (from II.115 to II.165) might redeem the present impression—that the proximate prospect of perfume, roses, and other signs of divine intimacy sends Taylor scurrying. Back towards Ranks Two and Three, towards Hooker, and towards the comedy of holy violence against the head and heart of the spiritually obtuse. We would, of course, all read that redemptive account with anticipation as of a new revelation. Somebody might even try to teach it, occasionally, to a small seminar of graduate students already past their Qualifying Exams.

Meanwhile, perhaps we can settle for a shorter version: the Taylor we see at work in *Gods Determinations* and also, equally, in the beginnings of the *Preparatory Meditations* presents us with a curious and dramatically effective case of the limited varieties of Puritan experience; he indicates the area where some fully positive assurance might lie but, far from insisting on it, emphasizes instead, as more nearly normative, the *via negativa*, the argument from instructed absence. He knows about Cotton, that is to say; he even uses the norms of that departed prophet of positive assurance to test and to pique his own living lack. But, as if to "open" the church to the widest circle of *professed* saints, his deepest sympathies are with those who do not yet find that The Highest is present to their soul. Among whose number he works hard to place and hold himself.

What the telling of this short story implies—at least as well as would the novel form—is an appreciation for the value of Taylor's poetry as *narrative*. In the interest of which it has been my strategy to go right on from the obvious, public tale of *Gods Determinations* to a more private account of similar questions in the early poems of the *Preparatory Meditations*; and to insist, once I got there, on imagining the terms of an argument, or plot, to connect one poem with the next. The effect, I readily concede, is somewhat artificial and could not be continued indefinitely. But I have tried to do these things, responsibly, because I am not persuaded that our interest picks up when the drama of assurance lapses to established pattern; or when we decide to tool up for a technical explication of Taylor's rendition of the types he wishes to love even better than he does. Tastes vary, of course, but some, it appears, are harder to acquire than others.[55]

Most simply, I *still* think there are strong reasons to teach *Gods Determinations*, all of it, for its compressed and most agreeable version of the whole Puritan story.[56] It may be a little harder to read, line by line, than Milton's grand religious epic; but it's also a lot shorter; and funnier; and more ironically aware of the unsolvable problems implied by its own (necessarily parodic) undertaking. And it bears about the same relation to the religious culture of New England in the seventeenth century as *Paradise Lost* does to that of the Old. As new texts and new interests press daily in among the old, and worries about the problems of "representation" force a return to the "survey" method, of sampling a small bit of any writing that may possibly have or generate an interest, would it be so bad to look closely at a "whole" text that man-

59

ages to include so much? William Bradford endures, from the age of the founders, to tell the story of population, land, and inflation as a threat to the ideal of the single, small, close-knit community. *Gods Determinations* raises, I think, the "other" Puritan story to a similar level of coherence and interest: Church, Sacrament, Saint: a poor agenda, it may be, but a needful form of historical explanation.

And surely the opening of the *Preparatory Meditations* tells its own vital story—of the presumptive but not presumptuous Saint who would be more, the Visible Saint who would be a Mystic—with similar cogency and effect. A speaker with knowledge and sensibility enough to want *it all* is sensitive to his own want of sensory experience in the area of images and shadows; but sensible enough, it turns out, to hold this unhappy fact as one among many. He knows there's more, somewhere, than Saint let on to Soul. They're writing songs of love but not it seems for him. *He* loves, he knows; or *would* love, if the censorsious will forgive this modest start on an infinite regress. But where's the sweet requite? And then a vision intrudes upon this studied learning to do without. And whatever we decide or may yet discover about the source of this intrusion, from literary plan or by the serendipity called grace, the unnumbered poems which "interrupt" the early course of commentary and aspiration really do interrupt it.

We probably can find categories to regularize (if not quite to naturalize) what happens next, and from then on, perhaps. We can even imagine how, in a different format, another character would be brought in to explain how it's all supposed to work. But here the fun is in the speaker's unsettled, and repeated, attempts to sort it out for himself—from stanza to stanza and in the conversation of one poem with another. Before the Pastor settles down to deliver all he knows about the significance of the Supper, the Visible Saint has to work out a few things with himself; to play out his own part in the provincial drama of the sorting of the Souls. Three Ranks there are not, as *Gods Determinations* as good as shows: you've either got or you haven't got "experience." But what if it's not a rose? Maybe there should be two and a half Ranks? It makes a nice story.

THE EXAMPLE OF EDWARDS

Puritan Imagination and the Metaphysics of Sovereignty

chapter 2

THE REACTION to Perry Miller's surprising claims about Jonathan Edwards'
"modernity"—first furious and then quiet but steady—has established at least
two propositions beyond the need of further academic quibbling: first,
Edwards' thought bears strong and evident relations to many systems, Puritan
and otherwise, that flourish and seek to prevail in the centuries between the
triumph of the Reformation and the first failings of the Enlightenment; and
second, that the overall orientation of his thought is actually "medieval," in
the special sense that he allowed his philosophical speculations to be guided,
always, by what his training and tradition persuaded him were the uncon-
testable teachings of Christian Scripture.[1] A "Late Medieval," we might risk
calling him, in the light of his method and program; an "Early Modern" (as
that phrase is now used) in light of the similarity between his arguments and

those of the classic philosophers of the British Empiricist and Continental Rationalist traditions. And so much for the names.

No doubt some very strict academic watchdog might want to insist that the question Miller really meant to raise was never properly settled because it was, from the first, a question *mal posé*; that Miller's habit of always saying more or less than he meant touched off, in this instance, a great deal of misplaced precision about "medieval" and "modern," even as the paragraph above may suggest. From such a premise such a person would go on to a process of careful and sympathetic reassessment, hoping to suggest that it is a mistake to allow the special character of Edwards' thought—and the genius or difference of his way of writing—to lose its distinction amid a welter of claims about his contemporary analogues and influences; that, even historically, we have more to learn from Edwards, still, than from Malebranche, Locke, Berkeley, and Hutcheson, separately or together.[2] A thankless task, however, and better left as the subtext of an essay on Edwards' status as a "Christian Philosopher": as powerful an apologist as the Puritan Tradition has to show, he is also (if this is indeed different) an authentic thinker who meant to be, at the same time, as devout as humanly possible in his approach to the problem of Being.

Past the moment of hysterical response to Miller's challenge, we need to remind ourselves that it is no particular shame to be the sort of philosopher who places oneself "at the service of Scripture and [is] willing to take orders from it."[3] Materially, first of all, certain teachings of Scripture might well be, in some relevant sense, true. Then too, more formally, the "genre" of philosophy might not be quite so pure as it once seemed possible to suppose.

It will not quite do to insist that a number of very powerful thinkers did, once upon a time, take marching orders from some unified reading of the two Testaments, because by Edwards' own time quite a few appeared to feel no such obligation; and a number of others managed, in the name of generic good taste, not to obtrude upon our notice the fact that their skeptical and free-ranging inquiries were inspired if not constantly guided by some quietly faithful agenda. The point is simply that the myth of motiveless inquiry, of perfect originary neutrality, is quite false to the history of actual philosophy, and that Edwards seems to have known this no less well that did William James. Everybody has to start somewhere, with first premise or founding assumption that cannot be thought to announce or to posit itself. It might be too much to claim that *most* philosophers are really more like Emerson and Nietzsche than they (or we) care to admit, that they intuit their conclusions and then argue for them, if at all, after the founding fact of pure personal conviction. But it seems plainly the case, as Anthony Kenny has argued in defense of his book-length study of Aquinas, that odd motive is no bar to valid conclusion.[4] Thought is thought—and writing merely "writing"—whatever secular bias or disciplinary pride might wish to the contrary.

Of course it *matters* that Edwards is explicitly committed to the project of a "Christian Philosophy": this prime fact determines not only his intellectual sense of what is and what is not a problem, it also controls his more public understanding of whom he is trying to persuade of what.[5] Occasionally—as in the *True Virtue* and the first, "analytic" sections of the *Freedom*—Edwards appears to be arguing *contra Gentiles*, so to speak; to be trying to persuade an entirely secular audience, one with no Christian interest or program whatsoever. In these pure but rare cases his arguments are drawn, as they must be, from "natural reason" alone; alert readers may hear echoes of Scripture teaching or detect the bending pressure of exegetical or apologetic context, but the jury of philosophical observers must work to make themselves immune to the force of all such suspicion. Impossible in practice, perhaps, yet not less meaningful than many another premise in the epistemological constitution of genre. More often, however, Edwards is frankly trying to persuade other avowed Christians that a sufficiently clear-sighted reading of the findings of natural and human science provides a powerful but in the end not really surprising confirmation of the wisdom and insight of orthodox Christian tradition. And no doubt such arguments may have an elegance and power of their own.

The hostile reader will tend to suspect that the autonomous and noble art of philosophic reasoning is being reduced to the status of "handmaiden of religion," and may object, from time to time, that wondrous rationalizations are being brought in to "prove" a proposition to which the reasoner has long ago offered complete assent. But the problem of the Christian Philosopher is more complicated than that.[6] Most instances of such transparent sleight of mind pass rather quickly from the history of thought. And the real situation, well back behind the moment of writing, perhaps, but not inauthentic for that reason, is that traditional belief and novel discovery have encountered one another in a powerful moment of epistemological challenge. Historically speaking, all sorts of outcomes are at all times possible: Faith may or may not seek a Reason; seeking, it may or may not find; finding confirmation—here, there, or anywhere in the long life of reflection—it may publish its discovery or not; and publishing, it may explain itself a little or a lot, and well or ill. To suppose anything less subtle, at the outset, is not to reject the Edwardsian example but to fail to notice it altogether.

It is to miss the Edwardsian difference—the reason which history, literary and otherwise, can fairly give for setting Edwards aside from a host of other late-come Puritan ideologues who also wished to safeguard the cause of Doctrine within the episteme of Reason. Edwards has, of course, his own version of the play and the place of preparation, the sound and the sense of a story that proves a conversion true, and even an articulate conviction of why such matters remain essential to the corporate life of Faith in the ongoing task of

63

Reformation. But these were not the issues that drew him beyond the known orbit of thought and expression in provincial New England. Where Taylor reveled in the comedy which transcendent demands make upon local conditions of assembly and communication, Edwards drove himself to show that those same demands find echoes in languages men have never used in church. Reason supports Faith because thought is thought and because all signs were made to agree.

Yet the special quality of this latter-day difference remains a little hard to come at fairly. Any strictly *philosophical* approach to Edwards' thought has to face the problem of abstracting the purely rational elements away—not only from poetically given teachings of Scripture, but also from the total system, whose primary impulse or rationale may not have been philosophical at all. Any larger sort of address will have to address the touchy problem of discovering the laws by which his total system assimilates philosophical strategies to the idioms of Scripture or the founding assumptions of selfhood, and the cogency, or at least the coherence, of that assimilation would surely provide an important index to Edwards' value, or at least his elegance, as a thinker.[7] This last operation is by no means an easy one. But it remains, in my view, the continuing and essential task of Edwards criticism.

There are, of course, too many Edwards texts, even excluding a long and steady encounter with the "Miscellanies."[8] Potentially at least, each of these texts could present a different configuration or model of the cooperation between reformed certitude and rational analysis; potentially, at least, there are as many variations as there are problems and occasions. But the situation is far from hopeless. One very important continuity seems assured by the nature of Edwards' audience, largely defined. We might think of it as American latter-day (and perhaps backslidden) Puritan; or American, Scottish, and English (Low Church) Calvinist; or Atlantic Community Protestant. It is each or all of these at various times. But in every case Edwards can legitimately imagine that many pious souls want or need to hear what he has to say against those backsliding Arminians or other "supernatural rationalists" who, having agreed with John Locke that reason must sit in judgment on any supposed revelation, are in fact corrupting the Pauline-Augustinian-Calvinist-Reformed-Puritan reading of the Scriptural economy of salvation.[9] Towards them Edwards' task is always to show that a sound philosophy supports or ratifies the "orthodox" religious teaching as surely as an unsound one perverts or revises it. Those who can both *read* and *think*, he argues, have no trouble—not with the Calvinism of the Founders and not with the Unity of Truth.

And if the rhetorical task does (undeniably) change somewhat in the course of his career, it does so intelligibly and in ways that are both limited and predictable. Edwards' dismissal from Northampton in 1750 would mark an almost-clear division of his career into two phases. Before that date Edwards' philosophy almost always has a pastoral context: we find it—passim, as needed, and largely by implication—in works basically designed toward the conversion of souls, for whom bad reasoning could only be a sign of bad faith. This is so whether the souls are those of Northampton or of some wider evangelical world, interested and perhaps participating in a season of grace; and whether they are, as events develop, likely to be on the side of Davenport's enthusiasm or of Chauncy's rationalism. After 1750, however, the philosophical problem becomes more prominent and direct. As Edwards goes to work, one by one, on the various parts of his projected summa, the philosophy can no longer remain implicit. His audience must now be thought to include not only the unwary and the perplexed but also the rationalistically and determinedly hostile: Davenport and Chauncy may be supposed to regard themselves as good Calvinists but Taylor and Whitby may not. Still, even these men imagine themselves to be within the pale of Protestant consensus. And so their doctrines of freedom and of original sin can (indeed from Edwards' point of view *must*) be met on the complicated ground of what the orthodox inheritance and the best rational analysis conspire to teach the mind about the divine economy.

The pages that follow, then, will survey a number of the major Edwards texts, including some from the earlier period which are not on the surface very metaphysical. Acquiring, thus, a sense of Edwards' situation, problems, strategies, and "style" as a Puritanic sort of Christian Philosopher, we may conclude with special emphasis on Edwards' treatise of *The Great Christian Doctrine of Original Sin Defended.* Whatever Edwards believed about the strategic importance of his *Freedom of Will*, a fair number of interpreters have sensed that it is the *Original Sin* which "leads us to the very secret of Jonathan Edwards" himself.[10] Here is where the whole intellectual system of New England comes to a sort of vexed completion—at a point which is, theologically, fairly appropriate for a latter-day Calvinist trying to rescue the *rational* validity of God's sovereign decision to treat with all men in Adam, and at a point which, philosophically, is fairly predictable for an idealist who had begun by discovering that God is the only substance and that His stable ideas and efficient will are all we can ever know our "world" to be.

The first problem concerning philosophical speculation and theological tradition in Edwards' early publications has been to discover that philosophy matters *at all.* Herbert Schneider, himself a professional historian of philosophy, long since concluded that it does not. More convincingly than any commentator prior to the Yale Edition of the *Scientific and Philosophical Writings*, Schneider traced Edwards' early discovery that Locke's "power" and Newton's "atom" both lead the mind to the same immaterialist "point"; and that whether we start with Locke's "substance" or Newton's "space" we always end up with the idealist discovery that the world exists "no where but in the [Divine] mind." But then, according to his view, Edwards "practically discarded" his early insights "in his later and maturer thought." Thus Schneider read Edwards' career from 1731 to 1750 without reference to his early idealism; and when he came to the later, explicitly philosophical works, he proceeded on the understanding that these "are based on an entirely different set of categories." And the power of this model has been considerable.[11]

Moreover, contradictory assumptions have managed to produce similar embarrassments. Many critics have felt that Perry Miller vastly overemphasized Edwards' early philosophical debt to Locke and Newton, as opposed to his reliance on ideas more readily available within an established theological tradition. And Miller himself—separating things that may ultimately belong together—concluded that nineteenth-century commentators had made entirely too much of Edwards' similarity to the peculiar (idealist) theism of Berkeley. And this verdict has also received a fairly widespread endorsement.[12]

All of this is a way of saying that the figure of Edwards' philosophy—within, around, or behind his Puritanic doctrines—had been for a long time difficult to discern. A Calvinist theory of sovereignty there is, abundantly and from the first: to begin with the familiar sermon on "God Glorified," the first published utterance, is to confront at once the premise that man depends on God *absolutely*, for all his being and all his good, both material and spiritual, both before and after the gracious work of redemption. And then, once the Awakening is fairly under way, a "pietist theory of love" forces itself on our attention, as does a sensationist/affective theory of virtue: implicit in the experiences recorded in the various versions of the *Narrative of Surprising Conversions*, and well worked out in the psychological distinctions which make up the first part of the *Treatise Concerning Religious Affections*, is Edwards' constant and controlled theory that our willings can be only as our experiences have been.[13] But a theory of Being equal or appropriate to these forms of piety does not immediately announce itself, explicitly and as such. At first glance one is indeed tempted to conclude, even as Edwards and Berkeley both suggest, that after the idealist has made his critical reduction of the world from substance to phenomena, everything really does go on just as before,[14] including the principal plot of human history, the application of redemption.

And yet the double premise—that everything human depends *absolutely* on God, and that man can (and must) have a profoundly affective *sense* of this state of affairs as the highest reality—seems powerfully indicative of a reality principle lurking somewhere. And hard students of Edwards, now able to follow the progress of Edwards' thought from his early "Notes" on to his "Miscellanies," find themselves more and more uncomfortable with the premise of a divorce between philosophy and theology in Edwards' early career. For in those seminal but (in Edwards' own day) unpublished works new insights confirming the ideal status of the world are constantly being correlated with biblical discovery that it is only in God that we "live, move, and have our Being."[15]

Perhaps the real problem has been in knowing exactly what to look for. It may be that the essential task is not to discover rational extensions of biblical knowledge; in fact we find very little of this. Nor even to locate specific philosophical supports for embattled theological doctrines, though here Perry Miller's tendentious sense of the occasional loaded word may well be accurate. But the simpler and more pervasive question may be more revealing: can we identify an encompassing "metaphysic" which needs to be true for Edwards if the theology he is espousing is to be coherent? What view of the world does the rhetoric of Edwards' Puritanism seem to be taking for granted? What, given his special religious emphasis, might his principal philosophical insight be?

It might well have something to do with a specialized understanding of "cause." Surely Miller was right to see that a radically Protestant economy of salvation must sooner or later develop some "nonefficient" theory of the relation between man's faith and God's gracious gifts; and certainly this occurs in his early but efficacious sermon sequence on "Justification by Faith Alone." Obviously faith and justification go together, but the problem is not one of mechanics; and, more subtly, faith cannot be the cause or even the "condition" of salvation in any sense implying that man forces God. The terms of Edwards' solution could indeed have been suggested, even as Miller proposed, by one peculiar, nonmechanist sentence in Newton. Or, less deliriously, they may have been influenced by the parallelist "occasionalism" of Malebranche; or they might be powerfully proleptic of Hume's radically empiricist theory of cause as repeatedly observed sequence. But in any event, Edwards wants to say (among many other things, of course) that, in general, "cause" is a very tricky notion; and that, in particular, there is plenty of "reason" to deny that man's choices compel God's responses in a mechanical chain of events.[16]

To be sure, it is hard to feel that Edwards ever does solve his basic problem of showing how (in the formulation of Conrad Cherry) faith can be at once a completely free gift and a fully human act—not in this attempt at least. In terms of perception alone, as we shall see, he does very well. But in terms of cause or condition, no matter how subtly conceived, his argument seems to imply the familiar but finally inelegant reduplication of the orders of grace: grace has to mean *both* the (Biblical) offer of salvation freely made and the (psychological or moral) power of acceptance, also given with equal freedom. In short, the totalizing ("Puritanic") problem of God as the Giver, the Gift, and the Power to Receive remains a problem.[17] Nevertheless, the moves Edwards makes in this compound treatise are philosophically revealing. At the very least we see him assuming and operating according to some subtle "way of ideas" in which the nexus between any event and any other is more arcane and rather more perceptual than we ordinarily imagine.

Or perhaps we sense that Edwards' root problem involves the competition (not to say the contradiction) between the Lockean and other, less empirical, more illuminist epistemologies in his early theories of grace. According to what philosophical scheme, we might wonder, can grace be called both a "sense" and a "light"? The problem exists not only between "God Glorified" and later works, but within most of these later works themselves. "A Divine and Supernatural Light," which Miller's love of the portentous singled out as containing the whole of Edwards' system in a kernel, is a particularly revealing instance. The title points one way, and scholarship can easily find its way to the Cambridge Platonism behind it. But the emotionally crucial passages point quite another: identifying idea with sense, and epitomizing sense as the peculiarities of *taste*, they lead just as directly to the noetic revolution of John Locke.[18]

Evidently all sorts of roughly approximate psychologies and systems of metaphors can be reconciled if one's metaphysics is large enough. Granted that something not unlike Edwards' movement of thought may occur in Thomas Shepard—or elsewhere, at large, in the Puritan emphasis on "experimental" religion—still the precise model for his doubly sensationist reduction occurs in a famous section of Book II of the *Essay Concerning Human Understanding*. And when all the dust of "source" and "influence" has settled, surely this fact counts for something.[19] Evidently Locke himself is not impossible to reconcile with Plato if one has already interpreted him as the thoroughgoing idealist which his preliminary definitions threaten to make him, rather than as the stubbornly dogmatic believer in objective "qualities" and hidden "substrates" his later conclusions insist. And evidently Puritans, Platonists, and Really Radical Empiricists can all help one say that grace must be nothing but an idea if he has already demonstrated that, between God and man, ideas are all that ever *can* be.[20] Biblical precedent would not be insignificant, of course; but even there the tolerance of diverse idioms might have to be accounted for in terms of the nature of things. And evidently some form of idealism has, all along, provided Edwards with just such an account.

What we seem to sense, therefore, at least in a general way, is that when Edwards writes about the Calvinist (and pietist) theory (and experience) of grace, he is keeping the terms of his early idealist speculations steadily before him; that they provide him, quite simply, with the rational support and even the philosophical counterpart of the theology of grace. He never makes the parallelism explicit, of course. And the reason surely has less to do with any growing speculative timidity than with a perfectly just perception that such a comparison or translation of idioms would be confusing or irrelevant to his local audience of anxious souls. Spared the reverent parody of Taylor's little games of holy language, the problematic saint—still having trouble learning to put aside all causal reliance on his own moral works, and sensuously to apprehend the perfect omnipotence of God as *the* saving psychological truth—will probably not be helped by being told that, after all, his entire world exists nowhere but in God's "determination, His care, and His design."[21]

Academically, of course, the insight might be very helpful indeed. If God is, in the last analysis of *reality*, not only the "*ens entium*" but the only "real existence," then how can the first moral quibble fairly arise? If philosophy is always running up against the discovery—in perfect validation of the Divine Name—that "God and real existence are the same"; and that "in metaphysical strictness and propriety, He is as there is none else"; then why should we expect the situation to be any different in piety?[22] If God is, properly speaking, the only true substance and the only truly efficient cause in the history of that lively process we call the universe, then why should anything *but* God be supposed to matter in the history of the process of salvation? Why should God's determinations touching his elect be any less spiritual than the prime disposition of His Sole True Being? It seems possible, for example, that this idealist version of sovereignty came to Edwards himself, as a sort of philosophical "preparation for salvation," just before the transforming spiritual experiences recorded in the "Personal Narrative." Indeed, the cynic might argue that the philosophical insights *were* that salvation, and that—reversing the customary, parodic order of Faith and Reason—the doctrines and piety came later, only as a sort of psychological corollary.[23]

But however that case might be, it is well to remember that, even in the eighteenth century, Every Christian is not necessarily his own philosopher; and no more so, certainly, in the Northampton of the Williamses and the Hawleys, the Bartlets and the Hutchinsons than elsewhere. If, philosophically, as we may already begin to sense, the problem with the correspondence between Idealism and Really High Calvinism is that it is altogether too close; that the two are, essentially, too nondifferent to be truly useful as explanation, the one of the other; still, practically, the matter is much simpler: the Evangelical Christian regards Pauline (and not quasi-Berkeleyan) language as normative; and the eighteenth-century inhabitant of the Connecticut Valley would probably find the terms of the philosophical solution more difficult than the religious problem itself. And with intellectual frustrations added to his already desperate moral and psychological ones, he might well learn the Enlightenment cry of "metaphysics!"

And so—as one may read the documents of this first public period—Edwards goes on, never *explicitly* referring to the intellectual work done in his early "Scientific and *Philosophical Writings*," never *overtly* invoking his radically idealist insight, and yet never for a moment ceasing to think of the world exactly as he had in his early "Notes" and in his essay "Of Being." What we see, quite plausibly enough, is the figure of a man who can easily swallow the gnat of sovereignty because he has already fairly devoured not only the camel of idealism but indeed the dinosaur of "panentheism": God is the only efficacious cause in the process of salvation because God is the real being of all that exists. Surely Edwards needed to be *at least* an idealist to assure himself that his theory of sovereignty was more than a pious fiction or feeling, that the totality of man's dependence on God was as direct and unmediated as it was absolute. Would not some material substance be just as much a troublesome intermediary in a psychological theory of grace as it was a needless and operose hypothesis in the theory of being? And, even more fundamentally, how could God really be ALL IN ALL if it were necessary to ascribe fully real being to anything else? This cluster of ideas might threaten to have serious consequences, of which both the Christian and the Philosopher might need to keep track. But surely the literary critic, looking for the implications of structure and listening for the confirmations of tone, may fairly point to the perfect congruence between a theology of sovereignty and a metaphysics of idealism in even Edwards' *least* philosophical works.

If anything, those works tend to be even less philosophical after the "surprising" events of 1734–35 than before. The successive versions of the *Faithful Narrative* give us very little more explicitly to go on, as Edwards becomes less and less a framer of theses about salvation and more and more a psychological sociologist, not to say (with Miller) a "novelist." Yet even when he is being most intensely particular, Edwards never lets us lose sight of the kind of universe we are in.

The four-year-old Phebe Bartlet retires into the "closet" of her own mind and speaks directly to God. She speaks of heaven and prefers it to earth—preferring God to mother, father, and "little sister Rachel." But she has not "been in heaven," and it is not "any imagination of any thing seen with bodily eyes that she called God"; her experience is not memory or fancy of anything earthly, but a direct idea or sense of the divine order. And after her remarkable experiences she cares for the "plums" of this world not at all; her true satisfactions is merely "to sup with God." Surely no human writing has ever intimated to her that the deepest reason of the world is a "typological" reason, that all human and natural "things" appear as they do on the sole purpose of providing "Images or Shadows" of a divine and supernatural order which alone is true and lasting; and yet what most people would call a metaphor is to her more real than what most people would call substantive nourishment. Accordingly, Scripture and catechism become more real to her than anything else, and she is well prepared for death.[24] She is already living out of time and in that true space which Saints—of whatever age, and with or without the aid of Sir Isaac—know as God's body.

• • •

Metaphysics may be a grown-up pastime, but evidently the sense of the really real can come to anybody, so that Edwards' adult accounts add scarcely anything at all to the childish paradigm. Abigail Hutchinson is not a well woman. But she is no enthusiast of wild and diseased (Poe-etic) imagination; the only effect of her "direct intercourse" with God is that the healthy wish to become "meek and lowly in heart" replaces her sickly tendency always to be "murmuring at God's providence"; and that she now has a "sense of glory of God in the trees." She dies "without any struggling."[25] Sarah Pierrepont Edwards does not die but lives, gloriously, in a crescendo of "extraordinary transports" and as the crowning literary glory of Edwards' *Thoughts Concerning the Revival*. By now Edwards is distinguishing his truly spiritual cases from those involving "distempers catched from Mr. Whitefield and Mr. Tennent"; and, among other things, one catches the merest hints of metaphysical distinctions. Mrs. Edwards' experiences are not those of an "enthusiastical season" but of "the eternal world." For a time, indeed, our own shadowworld entirely disappears: "All that is pleasant and glorious, and all that is terrible in this world, seemed perfectly to vanish into nothing, and nothing to be left but God." She does not become "antinomian" in after-moments, of course, but the essence of her experience is that a sense of "the awful majesty of God" serves not only "to take away her bodily strength" but also, at times, to "overwhelm body and soul." She knows she is nothing, and the corresponding all-sufficiency of God comes to her in remembering the divine definition and name: "I AM THAT I AM."[26]

This is piety, of course, and not philosophy; experience and not metaphysics. Sarah can scarcely be thought to have reflected on the implications of Locke and Newton any more than can Phebe Bartlet. But Edwards' idealist imagination shines through the experiences of all his literary creations: in grace God is perceived to be ALL IN ALL because in metaphysics it is only to him that real being can be ascribed.

Edwards' own experiences, recorded so passionately in the "Personal Narrative," could easily be made to yield the same "philosophical" conclusions. The ardent man who, unlike Ahab, learned not to resent Arbitrary Power but to worship Sovereign Authority in the awful voice of the thunder, and who prayed for a complete self-abasement so "that God might be ALL," is clearly related—whatever Edwards' later theory of identity might imply—to the "advanced" but still adolescent student who intuitively knew that Newton's occult atoms and Locke's occult substance could be nothing *but* the omnipresent, regular, and powerful will of God. And no doubt the two descend in about equal parts from some precocious boy who once only watched the spiders, spinning and being blown out to sea, and dared proclaim design to govern in a thing so small.[27] Spiders, material substance, and even (as the self-abnegating piety of the "Personal Narrative" spiritually forecasts the literally self-destructive philosophy of the *Original Sin*) the substantial self: all must be sacrificed to what some Narrator, meditating Pierre, would instructedly call "the ever-encroaching appetite for God."

But before creating for ourselves the impression that Edwards' Puritanism and his idealism are *nothing but* the (perfectly interchangeable) theological and philosophical counterparts of one another, and that there is in his career neither chronological development nor any meaningful disposition of aboriginal convictions or basic insights or root metaphors into philosophical discourse, we should remind ourselves that the pious narratives of the Awakening lead us directly into the rational distinctions of the *Religious Affections* and, indirectly, across our one firm line of periodization, to the strenuous argumentations of *The Freedom of the Will*. It is one thing to doubt that Edwards' "conversion" to sovereignty actually constituted so radical a change of mind as the "Personal Narrative" would have us believe. But it is quite another to imply that nothing new ever happens to Edwards. There may well be, even as Perry Miller insisted, only one fundamental perception in Edwards, repeated over and over again, in a variety of idiomatic approximations and with various degrees of indirection.[28] But it is impossible to deny that, after the public challenge offered by the writings of Chauncy (and others) in the 1740s, Edwards began a process of more and more careful, more properly "philosophical" explanation.

The *Religious Affections* is, clearly, the transitional work: by the time Edwards has got down to actual "cases" (in Parts II and III), we are back in the sociological world of the Awakening and back to that once flourishing metapsychological project known as "the distinguishing of spirits"; but before we get there, we must pass through simplified yet still moderately technical discussion of the human "faculties." And it is here, precisely, that we have to begin to take account of Herbert Schneider's second large assertion about the presence of philosophy in Edwards—namely, that the later works introduce us not only to a philosophical terminology but also to a set of problems entirely different from those of his early idealist deductions.

Once again, it is easy to see what this would mean. What we have now, in place of bold speculations about the ultimately mental character of reality and the logical primacy of the divine mind within that system (in place even of pious echoes or analogues of such theories), is a set of argumentative observations about the relation of affectivity and action, or, equally, the nonrelation of speculation and action. The shift seems radical indeed, but we do well to resist the conclusion that Edwards has altered his basic views. On the one hand, he is taking up a problem as posed by the scholastic or relatively rationalistic challenge of Chauncy; at this level of debate, all he feels called upon to show is that, within the very "world" supposed by Chauncy's common sense, a better

case can be made for the religious use of affection or will rather than of reason. And, on the other hand, the explicit "faculty psychology" of Part I does
eventually lead us on, later in the work, to the same sort of "ideal" hints we
have heard before.

At issue, initially, is not the absolute problem of BEING, in which *of course*
everything threatens to fall back upon God—and on which, incidentally,
Edwards might be, for different reasons, as hesitant to instruct Chauncy as he
would his own Northampton parish. At issue, rather, are the relative problems
of human perception and motivation which must, on premise, presume a certain reality for human affections and motions. Challenged by a rationalist on
his "pietist theory of love," Edwards responds with an "affective theory of
will": to will means no more than to be affected or attracted or inclined; to be
free (as he will repeat with greater force and clarity later) is merely to have the
power to execute inclinations, whatever they may be, and however they may
be thought all complicatedly to have come about. Philosophy, in his view, can
tell us no more. So that what remains to be said is, theoretically at least, very
simple—as evident to common sense as it is patently the sense of the poetry
of Scripture: true religion consists in having and executing holy inclinations.
Chauncy, therefore, will please desist from embarrassing the work of God's
powerfully inclining Word on the basis of either his attenuated scholastic sensibility or his tediously reiterated philosophical misapprehensions. For his own
part, Edwards will get on with the main theological business of providing a
detailed explication and elaboration of the affections or inclinations which
Scripture teaches are the direct and proper work of the Spirit in conversion.

73

And yet if Edwards is impatient here, dealing with the preliminaries of
philosophical psychology, and using tools which touch only the structure of
human motivation as it may be observed by anybody who will pay close and
unbiased attention to what consciously occurs, he is nevertheless very expansively and lovingly detailed when he arrives, in his first "distinguishing sign,"
at his own peculiar, Lockean definition of grace. After he has dismissed certain
affective states as inconclusive, as not-signs of saving spiritual influence, and
before he is well launched into his lengthy and sensitive (but finally circular)
excursion into the true science of spiritual semiology (which may also be read,
more simply, as his phenomenology of the Christian life),[29] he once again
reminds us that grace can be, after all, nothing but an idea.

Some have called grace a "light," and though this may confuse "the common and less considerate and understanding sort of people," such a usage is
perfectly proper; in speaking of spiritual things "we are forced to use figurative expressions" and, of course, "scripture itself abounds with such like figurative expressions." But if we may usefully think of grace coming to us as,
metaphorically, a light to illuminate our darkened spiritual perceptions, still in
strict philosophical propriety we receive it as an *idea*—once again identified

with a *sense*, and once again epitomized as a *taste*. Locke's revolutionary paradigm reappears unchanged from the "Divine and Supernatural Light," and Edwards now publicly signals this context by suggesting that grace might most properly be defined (generically, at least) as a "new simple idea"; it is a "nucleus" or "kernel" of experience, unitary and indivisible, a cornerstone and building block of consciousness which is not to be had by what Locke and Edwards both call "composition."[30] And once again we are tempted, perhaps invited, to ask why—according to what ultimate scheme of things—this must be so.

Indeed this may be the only really useful direction our analysis can take. For, on the one hand, all our explicitly theological questions are answered in advance. Edwards has already taken great pains to explain that a "spiritual" idea is not an idea of the soul as opposed to the body; that it is a special rather than a common communication from the Spirit; that having this utterly simple but remarkably new idea is equivalent to an actual indwelling of the Spirit; and that (accordingly) it makes possible a whole new range of affections or inclinations, even as the *new* simple idea joins with other (old) simple ideas in an endlessly rich "composition" of complex ideas, themselves all made now apocalyptically new by that very composition.[31] And on the other hand, we are shut off from asking modern ("experimental") questions about the sensory mechanisms by which all this comes about, as effectively as we were in the "Supernatural Light." Edwards is appropriating Locke to his own purposes, of course, and we can argue—with Hartley and Priestley, perhaps—about the legitimacy of his procedure. But clearer than anything else is the fact that he is taking Locke in an idealist rather than a behaviorist direction. He simply declines to ask whether the Spirit-as-Idea can more properly be said to enter at the eyes, the ears, the taste, or the touch, and leaving to others all mechanistic attempts "to explain soul out of sense," he offers no word about what physiological motions—vibrations and vibratiuncles—might be thought thereafter to occur.[32]

All we can say for sure, apparently, is that the experience is *like* that of a person seeing color for the first time; or even more appropriately, tasting honey for the first time. Though Edwards seems to fuss inordinately (and even to contradict himself) about whether the persons in his analogies are supposed to be equipped with the general power of sight or taste before their new experience, he nevertheless makes it quite clear that in his primary, theological case no new "faculty" is given; there is, physiologically, no "sixth sense" which might be described by analogy with the other five. It is merely that, experimentally, the saint has a new subjective awareness of divine things, sensory and affective in kind.[33] It is simply that—by a process we cannot begin to understand, but with effects which the person so affected (the Saint) cannot fail gloriously to confess and which the impartial observer is constrained however reluctantly to admit—an entirely new relation to reality has been produced.

THE EXAMPLE OF EDWARDS

Some powerfully regenerating experience has changed everything. Some radically simple insight into the way things are has made reality secure and the economy of salvation intelligible—and both lovable, as God's stable idea and sovereign will.

As the furious swirl of Edwards rhetoric may suggest, we are at a crucial chapter in the story of Edwards' performance as Puritan Philosopher. If we are willing to take him seriously here, we can, I think, grasp and perhaps admire the insight that holds his whole world view together. And unless we are willing to take him this way, the various arguments of the *Religious Affections* must always seem, despite their modern defenders, a little factitious—less a primary "vision" than a congeries of separate propositions, got up on the ground, ad hoc and *ex parte*, for the essentially reactionary and arguably obscurantist purpose of rescuing a deeply embattled orthodoxy. At issue is not only Edwards' philosophical elegance but also his spiritual coherence.

To pursue Edwards in the direction he would consider most legitimate is to ask why grace can be explained entirely according to a "way of ideas" and in no other way. Grace has always been, after all, a double sort of divine influence, which enlightened the mind *and* strengthened the will; a special infusion of knowledge *and also* a special aid in the will's somewhat separate struggle to love and enact the good and to hate and avoid the evil. Here, however, there is only one influence: a new sense of reality, from which everything else immediately and automatically flows. According to the new and simplified paradigm, all God has to do to convert (and then, progressively, to sanctify) a man is to grant him, by his Spirit, some sense, some sight or taste—by the now famous Lockean conflation, some *idea*—of the way He truly is. To know BEING at all, it appears, is to know enough.

In one respect, internally, Edwards' elegant simplification of the logistics of grace is accomplished, obviously, by means of the very relationship he has posited between intellect and will; or, more precisely, between consciousness and affectivity. An operation or a fact or an outcome and not a "faculty," the will does not follow but "*is* as the last dictate of the understanding"; or else, more simply still, we love according as our important experiences have been. And it is toward this radical simplification and psychologizing of grace that Edwards' much discussed and celebrated unification of the "faculties" ultimately points.[34] But this is hardly Edwards' ultimate consideration. With REAL BEING always before him, how can he be other than impatient with the question of whether epiphenomenal man needs only light or both light and heat in order to love the essential God? What concerns Edwards far more deeply, it seems to me, is the "objective" status of grace as a consituent principle in an essentially "ideal" world. What kind of "thing," after all, could grace be in the subtle world Locke and Newton have (for Berkeley and others) implied?

To admit the legitimacy of this placement of the question is to see the answer at once. If "nature," as we ordinarily understand it, has no true existence anywhere "but in the divine mind"; and if it comes to us as a communication of "His determination, His care, and His design that ideas shall be united forever, just so and such a manner as is agreeable to such a series";[35] then how can that "grace" which theologians all know to be its counterpart be thought of as any less simple? If nature is nothing but so many of God's ideas regularly communicated to all men's minds, then what could grace *conceivably* be but one very special idea communicated to the saints alone? If all God does in his ordinary work is to maintain a stable sequence of simple ideas, then surely it is philosophically retrograde to suppose that his extraordinary or supernatural or gracious activity involves anything more than the unique communication of his Spirit as a "new simple idea." Any separate form of spiritual "strengthening" would be as quaint a premise in divinity as that of material substance in metaphysics. Entities are not to be multiplied—of reason or otherwise. And as the so-called "corporeal" world "is to no advantage but to the spiritual,"[36] so the spiritual world itself need turn back for no help any more corporeal than a mere image.

This insight takes us, then, close to the heart not only of Edwards' system but also to his sense of life in the world. Taken all by itself, the premise that God obtrudes Himself, as a simple idea, into the normal order of human consciousness and affectivity seems merely odd, a strangely pious guess at what Shepard (or Poe) would call the "Plot of God." By itself, it suggests the magical rescue of a bad romance rather than the inevitable effect of a well-made tale or of a really elegant proof in the higher geometry. But taken together with an idealist epistemology and metaphysics, it comes to seem not only sleek and efficient but really inevitable. All God does in grace is all God does in nature—furnish ideas to other minds. If the move were not there in Edwards, it would surely have been invented by Emerson, just before that latter-day Idealist went on to discover that, where mind is concerned, there can be none truly "other."[37]

To be sure, this insight takes us to the precarious edge of intelligibility. And it leaves us, for the moment, with some very nasty problems. Granted, now that grace is only a special idea in the midst of a nature which is, as it were, "already" ideal. And granted that the prime effect of this very special idea is to give any man or woman (or child) who receives it the sense of a direct and absolute dependence on God's continuous activity at least as compelling as any philosopher's reasoning. Still we may want to ask where all this really does leave the human creature, considered (so to speak) in himself. A man may know, from the virtual conversion afforded by the idealist revolution in metaphysics, that his world is God's will and idea. And he may come to sense, from the conversion effected by one very special idea, that God is just what

Scripture says, BEING ITSELF; and that he must be affectively to man what he effectively is *in reality*, ALL IN ALL. But what, in the long aftermath of these surprising conversions, must he learn to say about himself? If God is the only substance, and if ideas are His only a form of creative expression, what can Edwards say about the ontological status of that human form of consciousness which regularly receives those ideas called nature or, by a different law no less regular, the special idea called grace, and which reflects on the conditions and meaning of that reception?

Common sense or pragmatism is, here, no solution. Furthermore, to weaken and grant a quasi-substantial (even if purely "spiritual") existence to man is to sin against sovereignty; it is, very likely, to commit the "unpardonable sin" against the Spirit whose intimations of sovereignty have seemed to complete the guesses of metaphysics. One possibility, of course, is to permit, or even encourage the entire collapse of man back upon, indeed into God—a reckless philosophical gambit, particularly for any authentic son of the Puritans, and counterintuitive in one who, quite unlike Emerson, continued to revel in "the discourse of theism." But while it may be impossible to show that Edwards ever adopted such a position, still it is in that direction that the logic of idealsim seems bound to move; and it is with a position very like pantheism that we will see him struggling when, in the crucial work on *Original Sin*, he is forced to face the outer limits of his most ingenious system.[38]

In order to provide an adequately "conclusive" account of the *Original Sin*, it may be helpful to treat other major works (and other significant dimensions of Edwards' career as a Christian Philosopher) somewhat briefly and indirectly. From one point of view this may seem a dubious strategy indeed, for we are just now arrived at the "period" of Edwards' more full and explicit, public philosophizing. *The Freedom of the Will* completes the analysis of volition begun in the *Religious Affections*, and it can be argued that this effort constitutes Edwards' principal claim both to modernity and to serious consideration as a major figure in the history of philosophy. Moreover, the brief but brilliant *Nature of True Virtue*, which also intervenes, is in fact the single work by this "very eminent Christian" which is purely philosophical in structural essence. At issue, over all, might be the justice (and the relevance) of the claim that Edwards' philosophical terms change "in his later and maturer works."

At the same time, however, to place concluding emphasis on the *Original Sin* is more than an abbreviating convenience or an argumentative strategy. For several reasons. On the one hand, according to the model of the Edwardsian career I am proposing, the *Freedom* and the *Virtue* both amount to species of polemical delay; in both, though especially in the *Freedom*, Edwards argues penultimate points against peripheral persons. Only in the *Original Sin* does he come back, once again and perhaps inevitably, to the very heart of his own problems—which, as we have seen, loom everywhere in the early works, palpably present in their visible absence. And on the other hand, according to the model of Edwardsian criticism I am enacting, it is only in the *Original Sin* that philosophy and theology assume their "exemplary" role and relation. There, most clearly, a whole metaphysic is explicitly brought to bear on a crucial theological issue. Let us look at this second, more formal problem first.

The *Virtue* tries to exclude specifically Calvinist (or even Christian) theology altogether. But it preserves its philosophical purity "artificially," as it were, by maintaining a strict "academic" separation of "disciplines" in which the author himself does not ultimately believe, and which may not reflect the true state of mind or soul of any actual believer, or any doubter either. The case is not without instructional value to Christian academics who might wish to see some particular philosophy established on a secular basis alone; and less tendentiously, it does represent, de facto, one of the models according to which a Christian can "do philosophy"—with his Christianity as glaringly absent and obvious as his metaphysics might be in a work on grace.[39] But it does not, quite evidently, introduce us into the psychological or imaginative mixture at the heart of that Christian Philosopher we call Jonathan Edwards. From this personal center he is deliberately holding us off.

From this point of view—that of persons as against disciplines—the *Freedom* is clearly more instructive. It is, in its aggregate, some explicit sort of Christian-Philosophical hybrid; and, in that regard, its mixed mode is a somewhat fairer model of Edwards' own mixed mind, as he struggles with opponents who are finding some brand of common sense philosophy sufficient to overturn the venerable teachings of the reformed tradition. At the same time, however, we are likely to find its peculiar mix just a trifle odd—as, formally, at least, theology is brought to the aid of philosophy rather than the other way around. The Christian's problem of "Freedom" may take its ultimate beginning in the literary interpretation of St. Paul, but Edwards' own book begins in a very strict and modern (analytic) manner. Edwards defines the area of freedom through a careful analysis of the terms used in moral discourse and then tries to show that other analyses will always prove incoherent. So far so good: it is Arminianism and not (as charged) Calvinism which is introducing unintelligibility into the moral world. But obviously Edwards feels challenged to meet another charge as well: that Calvinism is inconsistent with Christian revelation as well as with man's ordinary sense of the moral life. And so theology enters as Edwards begins to appeal—as if to a "fact"—to that perfect sort of "virtue," perfectly consistent with moral determinism, which Scripture forces its adherents to suppose as the moral habits of God and Christ. It is at this point that the modern reader, fairly addressed at the beginning in terms of his rationality alone, may begin to have difficulty with his own presence in Edwards' audience.

I do not mean to suggest that nothing like this ever happens in the *Original Sin*. Early in that work, indeed, something even more troublesome seems to occur: Edwards begins with that much discussed and much heralded purpose of presenting a fully empirical and fully historical account of the moral state of mankind relative to depravity or its opposite, but he proceeds immediately to treat the Judeo-Christian Scriptures as if they were a neutral account of the problem, and, what is probably worse, he presents an analysis which is thoroughly infected with definitions of depravity and integrity which it is the very purpose of many books of that Scripture all tendentiously to prescribe. The procedure is not even quite circular, and so no one should ever claim that Edwards' *Original Sin* is notable for its academic or disciplinary purity.[40] All I mean to suggest is that by the end of the *Original Sin*, things have got themselves instructively straightened out. Thus, when all the chips at last are down, and that ultimate Christian premise of a universal Fall in Adam is placed rationally on the line, the full weight of Edwards' reason is brought to its defense. For this once, at least, Edwards tries to prove that what his tradition holds most sacred in faith is entirely consistent with the highest reason of things.

Which brings us around to one other, less formal consideration: the degree of "ultimacy" which the varieties of "reason" in Edwards' later works may be supposed to possess. Here the *Freedom* is the more obvious case.

In spite of Edwards' repeated insistence that the *Freedom* was his absolutely crucial work contra the Arminians, and notwithstanding the high valuation placed on parts of it by modern philosophical commentators, it is really impossible to feel that it is a work in which all of Edwards' intellectual cards are out on the table. We may utterly reject the hostile view (of Conrad Wright) that Edwards does no more than throw sand in the eyes of his already dim-sighted opponents by tacitly adapting their confused terminology to his own special use, and then utterly demolishing a position which no one really held; but still we are left with our feelings about what the book's most able and sympathetic critic (Paul Ramsey) calls its "bracketing." Seeking "to catch the agent in the very act of willing or choosing, and to give an accurate report of what goes on in the soul or mind in the state of willing and at the time of willing," Edwards consistently excludes from analysis ("brackets") everything which goes before that very act—including, of course, the process by which the strongest inclination has come to be the strongest.[41] Even if we leave aside the opportunity to question the ultimate usefulness of this procedure in producing any clarification beyond the tautological discovery that yes—by and large, on the whole, and in the end—we always do do pretty much what we will to do; and even if we decline to object that the sense of "will" emerging from such a procedure amounts to something like "motor signal sent by the brain to the limbs in walking" and is, at very least, most unlike the more passive sense proposed in the initial conflation of will with affection, inclination, desire, and preference; even if, in short, we feel Edwards solves the problems he elects to face, we may still be left a little unsatisfied.

Possibly we even feel defrauded, in a way we never do in, say, "A Divine and Supernatural Light." Edwards is now "doing" philosophy: let him really do it. Obviously he *has* a theory of what goes on before the act of willing. Obviously, as I have already suggested, every reader senses that his theory has something to do with his Calvinism.[42] And obviously, as we are now in a position to observe, it has very much to do with the kind of simple ideas with which a person has been furnished. But none of this comes out. What we get instead—"to make a book," as a hostile reader might have said if Melville had been the author—is, negatively, the furious attack on the incoherence of other supposed theories of will and, just a bit more positively, the elaborate demonstration that it is those supposed theories and not Edwards' own which are inconsistent with the ordinary moral life and the extraordinary virtue of God and Christ. We can understand the human and the rhetorical situation perfectly: Edwards is defending as much of his total system as has been challenged by Arminian writers on the will. And we come to the end, I think, less assured that either moral action or Christian virtue requires us to will our willings than we might naïvely have asserted at the ouset. But surely our main response is that Edwards has left out some important pieces of his own intellectual puzzle. Things we easily infer and kindly supply in works of piety we begin to hold out for in works of technical philosophy. It requires an effort of judiciousness to avoid critique.

80

It is easy to see that Edwards' terms have indeed changed. But an adequate understanding of this fact involves our seeing that they change in the same way and for the same impatient reasons they had changed in the opening of the *Religious Affections*: the pressure of somebody else's liberal "anthropology" is distracting Edwards away from his own proper study—the metaphysics of sovereignty. If we sense any of that higher and more imaginative science amid the empirical observations and logical (or Scriptural) argumentations of the *Freedom*, it is only, implicitly, in Edwards' claim that man, however "free" to execute his intentions, is nevertheless not possessed of any originating "power" over them. That "power"—which Locke had suggested might be all we really mean by substance, which Newton had imagined to hold atoms together and apart, and which Edwards had identified as the continuous, regular, and creative "will" of God—belongs to God alone.

Contra Luther, whose *Bondage of the Will* Edwards means his own title to disturb, man may be truly said to possess a certain "freedom," to dispose his limbs as his life shall lead him to see fit. But in no sense does he ever attain that originary "power" which is really the same as substance and which served, in the eighteenth century, as a sort of holding place for the idea of autonomous selfhood.[43] And so, whatever the *Freedom of the Will* may say to historians of philosophy, its literary meaning (provoked by and expressed with reference to misguided and inept "men of God," such as Whitby and Watts, who imagine that something like self-determining power in man is necessary to the cause of religion) is something like this: For God's sake hold your tongue about "the freedom of the power of the faculty of will" and let me love BEING.

Accordingly, the most sympathetic view we can take of the *Freedom* is that it is not the book Edwards' system put him in the most powerful position to write. The subject may have aroused his considerable talent for polemics, but it did not draw out his ontological imagination. Those arrogant Arminians needed to be answered; and if, in the end and *faute de mieux*, the task fell to Edwards, well, so be it. He would answer them, for the most part, only on their own terms; that would, of course, involve changing his own. And while the process of learning to meet worldly adversaries on the empirical grounds of rational psychology might be part of a philosophical maturation, it is probably wrong to think of the *Freedom*, admiringly, as a work in which Edwards begins to work himself out of his childish, imaginative idealism.

The *Virtue*, at first glance, seems an entirely different sort of work: it is much less exasperated in tone and, as I have suggested, much more "pure" in disciplinary mode. Far more coolly, now, Edwards sets about the task of trying to say what kind of "beauty or excellence" both "natural" and "true" virtue may amount to. The search-and-destroy polemics have largely disappeared, even though Edwards clearly has certain ill-considered and/or sentimental users of Francis Hutcheson very much in mind. Nor is there any overt attempt to correlate his proofs from natural ethics with scriptural teachings which everybody is supposed to know and accept, even though it is perfectly plain that Edwards' prime law of "benevolence to Being in General" is intended as a counterpart of the first great "commandment"—to love God with one's whole mind, heart, and soul. In short, Edwards seems totally in control: the argument seems to be, if not quite metaphysical, nevertheless exclusively *his own*. And to the extent that one can agree (with Roland Delattre) that the section on "Excellence" in Edwards' "Notes on the Mind" provides us with his key term, to that extent one would have to posit the fundamental importance of the *Virtue*.

But though it can be argued that "excellence" is the highest name for the expressive activity of God on the practical or moral side, and though "beauty" may be the primary attribute by which He is apprehended by other minds, still it cannot be maintained that this is His highest name or the ultimate aspect under which the metaphysician must regard His essence as such. That of course must always remain the name and the aspect of BEING. And so, however useful we may find the *Virtue* to our own situation in ethics or aesthetics, or however satisfactory we may judge its methodological purity, to

81

which I have alread referred, it seems clear that it is not *quite* the book which takes us back to the ultimate, lurking, and essential Edwards. And we must be very careful, at some level of criticism, not to confuse our academic judgment that Edwards may have done his most effective philosophical thinking when he was provoked, by the fashionable ideas of others, into the subsidiary disciplines of psychology, ethics, or aesthetics, with our literary perception that his own organizing insights and most fundamental intentions lay in the area of idealistic metaphysics.[44]

We may sense, perhaps, that we are on the verge of something crucial in this area when we find Edwards stressing that the "analogy" between "secondary" (or, as it were, material) and "primary" (or, as it were, spiritual) excellencies may be perceived only by those who have already had experience of the latter, more real sort; that "Saints" (to use the language Edwards here strictly excludes) can see the world as God's perfect poetic body, whereas others see only forms and relations. Thomists, we may remind ourselves, would appear to teach otherwise—that the *analogia entis* works "up" as well as "down," before as well as after the operation of grace; that analogy beginning all innocently with the natural constitutes, in fact, the natural man's most available and direct road to God. And elsewhere, we may happen to recall, Edwards is frank and emphatic that his own ("modified Platonic") *analogia generis* is similarly necessary for all philosophical knowledge of God.[45] How, we may find ourselves wondering, are these two different accounts of the order of analogic operations supposed to cohere? Unwilling to press such matters, however, Edwards passes over the question of why the analogy in question here should work one way and not the other. For our present, limited, ethical purposes it is enough to learn that no sense of proportion between the image-and-shadow-beauties of the creation and the spiritual excellencies of the Creator can be perceived by the mere amateur of natural harmonies, and that such a proportionate sense is "the consequence of the existence of [true] benevolence; and not the ground of it."[46]

Edwards knows perfectly well that he is flirting with the edge of his own metaphysical abyss, and he very consciously pulls himself back. He allows himself to imagine that his reader may be worried about that absolutely first question of why the natural and the spiritual worlds should be analogous or "correspondential" *at all*. But he raises the question only to "bracket" it: "Why such analogy in God's works pleases him, 'tis not needful now to inquire."[47] Followed out, such a problem would lead to first-form questions about BEING ITSELF, perhaps to the ultimate theological question of its Trinitarian structure; all such questions are being put off, presumably, for a more direct and comprehensive treatment elsewhere in Edwards' many-mansioned summa. For the present inquiry it is sufficient to observe that it did in fact please God to establish analogy or correspondence of the secondary with the primary beauty as a "law of nature," just as He was pleased to establish, at the secondary level itself, gravity. What we could possibly understand by "gravity" or what a "law of nature" had to signify in the physics of idealism, Edwards will not tell us here. Once again we are put off.

It is just this sort of deferral or bracketing or evasion which does not occur at the defiantly Puritanic conclusion of the *Original Sin*. There, finally, where Edwards' theological difficulties are deepest, he brings forward his most fundamental, original, and authentic metaphysical insight. The "distinguishing mark" of the *Original Sin* is that in it, alone among the published essays and treatises, Edwards is willing to bring the full weight of his idealistic metaphysics—preserved intact from his earliest unpublished works—explicitly to bear on a problem that has taken its rise in the traditional interpretation of a specific Scripture by a historical community of believers. And that, I take it, is a rather perfect model of the faith-and-reason problem as most commonly apprehended: rational speculation brought in to the aid of traditional (if reformed) belief.

In writing about the *Original Sin* one is tempted to suggest (in imitation of Henry Adams, writing about Aquinas) that here Edwards placed the last stone in the bold, aspiring, and majestic arch that was his own Puritanic version of the Christian-Philosophic summa. What holds one back, chiefly, is an ironic sense of an opposite sort of truth—namely, that the place where Edwards' theology and his metaphysics come most tellingly together is the same place where his whole edifice trembles and threatens to collapse, into tautology if not into ruins. Or, to change the metaphor, when he brings his highest philosophic reason to the rescue of his deepest Puritanic faith, we are forced to notice how profoundly problematic both are, and for precisely the same reasons. In any event, it must be with some such sense of final systematic catastrophe or embarrassment, shadowing an ultimate imaginative triumph, that we approach the conclusion of the *Original Sin*.

83

For the purpose of displaying Edwards' daring but also perilous rescue of theology's embattled first premise by an almost wildly imaginative appeal to philosophy's last word on idealism, it is not particularly necessary to judge, or even carefully to trace, the progress of the admittedly "impure" argument that winds its way through *The Great Christian Doctrine of Original Sin Defended*. It is absolutely necessary, however, to see just where we are when—in Part Four, Chapter III—Edwards makes his fervent "appeal to such as are not wont to content themselves with judging by a superfical appearance and view of things, but are habituated to examine things strictly and closely."[48] We need to understand not only the specific intellectual issue which occasions but also the contextual pressures which motivate this remarkable direct (and for Edwards nearly unique) appeal to a strictly philosophical audience. The terms of this address are so unlike those of the *Freedom*, which makes its decisive appeal to the usual meaning of "freedom" in ordinary moral discourse, that we can hardly fail to sense a state of intellectual crisis.

At issue, most specifically, is "that great objection against the imputation of Adam's sin to his posterity [namely] that such imputation is unjust and unreasonable, inasmuch as Adam and his posterity are not one and the same" (389). It is perfectly true, of course, that the legalistic or "forensic" idea of God's "imputing" Adam's sin to anyone else will always present serious rational difficulties. And nowhere, I suppose, will these be greater than within a "Calvinist" emphasis on God's *voluntaristic* sovereignty, where God's will or word or wisdom (as distinguished from some norm of universal rationality) is held to be the sole, the essential, and even the "constitutive" rule of justice. Furthermore, since imputation is one of only two principal explanations of the relation between Adam's original sin and our sinful origination available to Edwards, and especially since it is the one most relied on in his particular tradition, he seems bound to face the problem in a fairly direct way.[49] To "bracket" this question would amount to the most serious sin of intellectual omission. And so when Edwards does face the question of trying "reasonably" to explain God's "sovereign" decision to regard all men as having sinned in Adam, that moment, whenever it occurs, must be fraught with a certain tense excitement: a melodrama worthy of Miller himself.

But in addition to these "traditional" difficulties, Edwards has some specific rhetorical and even logical problems of his own making. One almost imagines they are deliberate—to make the chapter in which he appeals to his first philosophy as dramatically climactic as he senses it is intellectually crucial. And these emplotted difficulties also add to the interest of what turns out to be, for a loyal enough Calvinist, a remarkably rationalistic attempt to prove that what God declares to be the case in "imputing" Adam's sin to each and all of his individual children is also highly consistent with the nature of "things," as that scheme can now be understood according to certain "late improvements in philosophy" (385).

Edwards is not, of course, going to assert that "the great Christian doctrine of original sin" is, in all its reformed ramifications, a self-evident truth, like an axiom in logic or geometry; from his early proposition that "it is necessary some being should Eternally be,"[50] for example, nothing follows relative to Adam and us. Edwards even seems willing to concede that our own situation, as corrupted children of Adam, might have been otherwise, had God decided, declared, or "constituted" things otherwise. As a contingent arrangement, that complex determination is, unlike the necessary economy of the Trinity, incapable of rationalistic proof a priori.[51] But Edwards is going to assert that to understand and rationally accept the justice of God's imputation of Adam's personal guilt requires no *special* invocation of divine voluntarism, and no understanding of the nature of reality, beyond what any decently reformed (i.e., idealistic) metaphysics will furnish. In order to show this, Edwards seems to have arranged his book so that he will have to appeal to his metaphysics, and to his fiction of an audience willing to witness the appeal, only once, and at precisely the right time. So that if our sense of personal engagement and embattled challenge is strong, our sense of strategy is even stronger.

Edwards has been arguing (as the burden of Part One) that all men do fall to sinning, seriously and repeatedly, almost as soon as they are able; and as for the competition between sin and virtue, who will seriously contend (he asks) that there is much true virtue in all the world? As a literary inventory of the human scene, Edwards' gloomy survey matches anything in Ecclesiastes, or Augustine, or Melville; as poetic invention, his myth of the Fall can fairly stand beside that of Plato and Cardinal Newman. And whatever we may think of the moral or sociological "science" involved, it is necessary to "grant" (even if we do not "concede") a universal tendency to sin if we are to follow Edwards' strategy. From such a "steady tendency" he imagines any reasonably empirical person will necessarily infer a "steady cause." An adequate cause, he argues, could only be corrupted principles of perception and inclination, a corrupted "nature," that is, in the common parlance; and, as it seems evident to him, Scripture's "genetic" explanation of this natural given would seem to be Adam's Fall and not any malign creativity on God's part.

That Scripture actually does teach, clearly and throughout, such an interpretation of the human condition becomes the necessary exegetical substance of the argument in Parts Two and Three—as the *Original Sin* begins to reveal quite clearly that its founding mode is scriptural theology and not rational philosophy, and certainly not empirical science. With impressive learning and marvelous hermeneutical clarity, Edwards argues that John Taylor and other "liberal" Christians are making literary nonsense out of both Testaments; that to reject the premise of original sin as Scripture's *donnée* and initial plot-event is not only to reject Paul's masterful exegesis of Genesis and everything since, but also to render the account of redemption literally as irrelevant as the redemptive act itself would be, on liberal premises, spiritually "nugatory."[52] In short, the Christian Scripture makes no decent "literary" sense unless universal depravity is a fact, with Adam figuring as somehow the cause or root explanation.

And so by the time Edwards comes to his last part—"Containing Answers to Objections"—he understandably supposes that very much is already accomplished: liberal anthropology has been denied de facto; and liberal hermeneutics have been vigorously disputed, from the structural integrity of the privileged text itself. Edwards' implied audience, let us recall, is entirely Christian in professed loyalty; whatever the exact state of its "backslidden" relation to the reformed tradition extending itself to the Founders of New

England, it still honors Scripture as God's uniquely revealed word. To show, therefore, that the very coherence of Scripture depends on the perfect parallelism of Adam and Christ as root cause and root cure of the human condition would be, to them, somewhat more than the exemplar in structural criticism it may be to us. And by the end of Part Three, Edwards imagines he has essentially proven the complex original sin case by showing just that. But though his work as reformed sociologist and as exegete is now completed, his work as Puritan Philosopher is just beginning. Far more than mere odds and ends of leftover reflections, his "Answers to Objections" are identically that work.

What Edwards' liberal or "supernatural rationalist" opponents are objecting, most simply, is that Scripture could not *possibly* teach what Reformed Tradition says (Paul says) it teaches, because such a "truth" would be radically inconsistent with all the rest of reality. Adam *cannot* be the cause of our sin because the sinful choice, like any other human choice, is an absolutely free and completely personal thing: God could not make a man sinful in Adam any more than he could make him a carpenter through his father's election of that calling. Bad example might count for very much, sadly, but there must always be some personal choice, or "sin" makes no sense at all. Hence any religious system founded on the premise of sin prior to individual human choice disqualifies itself at the outset. Scripture *cannot* teach that and still be Scripture. Our own minds must judge: God himself cannot reveal what is unreasonable, cannot declare the inherently unintelligible to be anyhow true.[53]

Or, alternately, if we supposed that somehow He could, He would not be God to us. A "god" who could make us guilty in Adam, thousands of years before our birth into actual human personhood, would be in effect a devil-god, a poisonous moral monster worse than any fantastic Dr. Rappaccini. He (and not we) would truly be the "author of depravity." The only proper response to such a god would be an Ahab-like defiance. God must be good as well as reasonable or life is absurd and not worth living.

The question of how such a full-bodied rationalism came to have widespread credibility within a basically voluntarist tradition is a fascinating one, as Perry Miller long ago remarked, but it need not detain us here.[54] Probably it is sufficient to observe that here, as elsewhere, Edwards felt the popular threat of philosophical objections to the religion of his tradition. Or perhaps we may want to observe that a thinker who began his intellectual career with certain "ontological" (perhaps even "Cartesian") reflections on the rational necessity of Absolute Being within a universal system of noncontradiction is probably not the man to ask whether his opponents can draw Leviathan up with a hook and let it go at that. What concerns us, more fundamentally, is the strategic disposition of the answer Edwards gives to the many-headed but really single-minded liberal objection against the rational justice of the Puritan scheme.

How, we might ask ourselves, has the problem of "imputation" come to be the great objection? Clearly it is one such. Arguably it is the one to which many others might be reduced. But such a reduction would have to be *made*. And my own (penultimate) point is that Edwards has, quite specifically, made things just this way: so that, when the last or greatest objection is made—about Calvinism and Reality—he can respond with a single metaphysical proof of their utter consistency.

As a "first" objection, Edwards gives the obvious and humanly very telling liberal protest in its moral form: "men's being born in sin, without their choice…is inconsistent with the nature of sin" (375). Surely this might be the last or climactic objection in somebody's scheme, but Edwards treats it (here at least) in a perfunctory way. To be sure, he has answered it at great length elsewhere, in the *Freedom*, by arguing that the premise of choice before choice is an incoherent theory of human action; that to avoid the trap of positing an infinite regress of choices we must come at last not to an Ur-choice but to some principle of nature (of perception and inclination) from which all choices can be thought to proceed. He has alluded to this performance earlier in the *Original Sin* and he merely mentions it here; he does not mean to repeat himself. This might be simple weariness. Or it might be intellectual economy: explicit reference to careful work done elsewhere is, as all scholars must know, not the same as "bracketing." But still this psychological and moral problem might have been presented as an ultimate one. We can easily imagine how, if "Freedom" really were the intellectually crucial and not just the polemically prominent case, Edwards might come around to this place at the last, and end by showing—once more, with feeling—that "it all" hinges on the observable structure of human motivation. Patently it does not, as Edwards' strategy shows.

Somewhat longer and more energetic is Edwards' answer to a "second" objection—that to suppose a corrupted nature as the fountain of all men's sinful choices is "to make him who is the author of their being, the author of depravity" (380). Edwards presumes that this objection implies some active "corrupting" on God's part, and so he answers with the essentially Thomistic (and surely borrowed) theory of the *dona superaddita*, the reinvention of which some critics have taken as a major accomplishment.[55] Simply put: Adam had certain "gifts" or "principles" which we do not now naturally possess (which are, in the simplified Edwardsian economy of grace, nothing but the fruitful results of a certain simple idea of God); when Adam sinned God withdrew those "principles"—necessarily, since God's own Spirit-as-Idea could not be supposed to maintain residence in a house of sin. All we inherit from Adam, therefore, is a *lack*, and hence the whole course of man's depravity can be explained without for a moment imagining "*God's putting* any evil into the

87

heart, or *implanting* any bad principle, or infusing any corrupt taint, and so becoming the *author* of depravity" (383).

Under this negative hypothesis all we need to explain (according to Edwards) is why God might be thought to have *withheld* from us the principles he *withdrew* from Adam. It is not, emphatically, an Augustinian case of "rotten root and rotten branch"; that inelegant (arguably Manichean, blatantly materialist) paradigm drops away even before Edwards brings forth his idealism. It is much more nearly a case of "imputation," though Edwards lets us know that this formulation is "vulgar" rather than philosophically precise; and if Edwards assumes the burden of the traditional term, he changes its meaning even as he does so. Under his "Thomistic" hypothesis of gifts-withdrawn, "imputation" is less accurately understood as a case of God's "thinking" guilt "onto" or "into" his posterity than of God's regarding Adam and his posterity as sufficiently identical to "justify" the decision to withhold from the latter what was positively forfeited by the former—so that, without gracious protection, men universally become the sinners we observe them historically to be. Quite obviously, questions of rational justice are still deeply at issue here, but the tendency of Edwards' argument is to minimize them by shifting the ground from legal or moral theory to metaphysics. Given Edwards' subtle redefinition of the problem, "imputation" turns from the moralistic question of how, in all justice, God could make or declare all men to be sinners before any human act on their part into the ontological question of how, in all reason, God could possibly treat Adam and all other men as the same moral person.

What happens over the course of Edwards' several "Answers to Objections" is that the various meanings which are subtly merged in the simple but powerful liberal protest that God "cannot make another man sinful in Adam" are subtly taken apart into three very discreet objections, each of which can be met on its own proper philosophic grounds. The protest from freedom is answered in terms of Edwards' own "necessitarian" theory. Then comes the argument concerning what William Ellery Channing would call "God's moral character," and here Edwards easily exonerates God from the charge of active intervention or positive malfeasance. What this analytic scheme leaves for last—strategically, so that the smart and final confrontation will take place on Edwards' own sovereign territory—is the question of identity. To a carefully set up "great" objection, that "Adam and his posterity are not one and the same," Edwards thinks he has had, all along, just the right reply.

The notion of Adam's "federal" headship, his status as humanity's "parliament man," might have satisfied certain "lawyers" who, in their struggle against Tudor and Stuart monarchs, may have thought legal models were perfect paradigms for reality, and who, in the heat of revolution, did not adequately consider that Adam might be holding his place without benefit of universal suffrage.[56] But it would not satisfy Edwards the Cartesian, the Cambridge Platonist, the Newtonian, the Lockean (perhaps, by now, the Berkeleyan and even the Humean); certain "late improvements in philosophy" have persuaded him that legalism is every bit as quaint as the Ramist dichotomy. Above all, it will not satisfy Edwards the great rationalizer of sovereignty, who thinks he knows a perfectly metaphysical reason according to which Adam and his posterity can indeed be "one and the same." To be sure: any perfectly sovereign, voluntarist, "Calvinist" God might simply "think" Adam's guilt "onto" or "into" the rest of the race with as little embarrassed concern for pitiful human standards as any perfectly sovereign, nominalist, "Lutheran" God might declare a man "just" without any reference to the observable state of the ethical case. And though Edwards is perfectly capable of making the nominalist/voluntarist statement that reality is, after all, only and exactly what God declares or wills it to be—and of backing it to the hilt with an idealism suited to the purpose— he does not *merely* say that.

What he says most generally, in his climactic Chapter III of Part Four, is that "no solid reason can be given, why God, who constitutes all other created union or oneness…may not establish a constitution" whereby Adam and his natural posterity "should be treated as one" (405). The privileged modern reader, who has made her survey of Edwards from the 1829 text of Sereno Dwight, or the 1980 version of Wallace Anderson, is likely to hear the Edwardsean pun on *solid* and know where she is at once: back in the world of Edwards' early essays, especially that "Of Atoms and of Perfectly Solid Bodies," where (as Anderson had earlier argued) Edwards' "immaterialism" had begun. It began, plausibly enough, in the perception that "solidity" means nothing but "resistance," which is the same as God's immediate "power," so that—however incredible it seems to the imaginations of the vulgar—perfect "solidity" is nothing but the atomic unity of divine creativity.[57] Anyone who hears that Puritanic pun on "solid" hears Edwards asserting that those who are "habituated to examining things strictly and closely" will know that the problem of unity and multiplicity is, like the problem of solidity which underlies it, a rational problem in divine "constitutionality" and not a sensory problem of touching or counting. And, ultimately, the mystery of the "atomic" unity of the whole race is not much more (or less) subtle than that of the "powerful" constitution of what appears to us as material substance. Like Emerson, Edwards too can make reality "oscillate a little and threaten to dance" whenever he wishes; but most unlike him, Edwards most needs that magical power in reference to the corporate sinfulness of the whole "body" of man.

Critics have often given the impression that Edwards' philosophical solution to the theological problem of original sin was to create, ad hoc, a perilously outre theory of identity, which his successors (understandably) refused to touch with a very long pole. The alternate and more favorable theory

89

would be that Edwards brilliantly—but "metaphysically," somewhat in the manner of John Donne—imagines an original defense of the humanistic unity of the whole "mainland" of mankind.[58] The truth may be somewhat simpler, though it may imply as great a degree of intellectual daring, perhaps even of desperation, as either of the existing suggestions; and this in spite of the highly self-conscious strategy we see at work.

What essentially happens in the answer to the liberals' "great" objection is that Edwards reminds his readers how utterly and literally true it is that all reality depends on the creative idea, will, and power of God. John Taylor and others have appealed to this idea in an attempt to show that Calvinists blaspheme in imagining that God, who creates every soul directly, brings forth every man in sin. Having evaded this criticism with his borrowed theory of the added-gifts-withdrawn, Edwards now turns the idea powerfully against his adversaries, in a philosophical way they could scarcely have expected, but with a problematic force that threatens to leave them, as Christians, speechless, whatever their feelings about "solidity." Nothing created, Edwards argues, can in the last philosophical analysis be validly considered as *anything but* God's will and idea. What we ordinarily refer to as the "law of nature" must appear to the view of those not content with judging things "by a superficial appearance" as *merely "God's Sovereign Constitution"* (404). "Constitution"—which might well be a crucial term in anyone's definition of the idea of "Covenant" as a stipulated or immediately willed and in a sense contingent form of causality— is here being applied to the entire range of reality. If events like faith and justification go together only because God has (intelligibly and fitly) decreed or constituted affairs so that this is so, the same can be said of all other events which men perceive as sequential or lawfully causal. The world proceeds because and just as God immediately constitutes it, without any sort of material or other troublesome, substantial intermediation.

Such an insight, obviously, has powerful implications for the theory of "identity." The appearance we call "the moon" remains identically itself, from moment to discrete moment, not by any causative virtue in its "substance" which, not being an inherent part of God's own being, it utterly lacks; but only by virtue of God's creatively willing its phenomenal continuance at every instant of man's perceptual time. We might say it continues relatively unchanged because its "atoms" continue so; it is, presumably, *still* as proper to say that "God, in the beginning created such a certain number…of such a determinate bulk and figure" as it was in the early essay on "The Mind";[59] but only if we still remember that empirically occult entities are nothing in fact but ideal loci of God's creative will. How much more evidently, then, the case of acorn and oak, and the child that fathers the man: how can we account for the identity of these through time without supposing an "immediate *continued* creation of God…out of nothing at *each moment*"? (401). To suppose otherwise

THE EXAMPLE OF EDWARDS

is to give "substantial," that is, *competing* existence to things other than God and so to deny his inspired and exhaustive self-definition as BEING ITSELF.

To suppose that created existences *in any sense* cause the effect of their own continuance from one instant to the next is not only (stupidly) to fail of complete application of Taylor's own "Newtonian" premise that "God, the original of all being, is the only cause of all natural effects" (401); it is also (blasphemously) to contradict the biblical teaching—well and one might almost say necessarily supported by idealist philosophy—that in God "we live, move and have our being" (404). As soon believe, with Aristotle and the Pagans, in the existence of uncreated matter from all eternity.

Even the stubborn problem of "the personal identity of created intelligent beings" yields to the keen analytic reduction: Ockham's secular razor, sharpened by Edwards' holy idealism, is cutting down unreality left and right. Will anyone suppose that human memory exists apart from continuous divine volition? That the remembrance of things past can "continue to exist, but by an arbitrary constitution of the Creator"? (399) Can *sameness of consciousness* really explain what causes Adam to remain Adam? Or Jonathan, Jonathan? Liberals like Taylor might indeed be guilty of the fondly self-flattering thought that one's his own self-awareness at a human point "n" may somehow cause or predict a similar awareness at "n + 1"; but this psychological sense of self-identity can be maintained, apparently, only at the sacrifice of philosophical self-consistency. A sufficiently reformed ontology—the Edwardsian difference—knows the idea of a "substantial" human identity to be illusory; and no such thought would ever, we must suppose, occur to Phebe Bartlet or Sarah Pierrepont.[60]

And so the conclusion relative to Edwards' "present purpose" is almost too obvious to rehearse: since there is no identity or oneness "but what depends on the *arbitrary* constitution of the creator...no solid reason can be given, why God...may not establish a constitution whereby the natural posterity of Adam...should be treated as one with him" (403–5). And that really is as far as reason can go. In a world where the solidity of the resistance of the power of the atom figures—indeed embodies, except that there are no "bodies"—the all-creativeness of the everywhere-active and immediate will of God, it is not surprising that neither solid material substances nor personal human integers really are exactly what they appear. In such a world, Edwards asks, who can give any "solid reason" why Adam and Jonathan are not just as much "one and the same" being as are the excited boy observing spiders and the philosopher in exile ministering to Indians?

Edwards does not claim, we should note, that any John or Jonathan may have ordinary experience of that particular order of divine "constituency" under which a man is, in the creative thought and by the sovereign will, and for the powerful purposes of God, united to Adam and fairly called by that nighest name. We might infer that intimations of this order of ideal unity come in the same way as does the sense that a person-as-branch may be united to Christ-as-vine; indeed the negative or preliminary part of conversion might be the symbolic moral perception (which the idealist philosopher might then explicate) that, indeed in the sight of God I am no different from, am really *nothing but* the old and fallen biblical Adam. But such speculations—which might lead us to the suspicion that the order of our union with Adam is a literary order only, an order of meaning and not at all of being—are well beyond Edwards' present, valid, and unbracketed purposes. He is not, let us recall, required to do it all on the strength of reason alone. He has observed, as he assumes any person may observe, a universal depravity. He has powerfully argued that his opponents cannot really consider themselves Christians unless they admit, on revelation and in faith, that the true name for this state of affairs is an Adamic original sin. And then, finally, against the objection that this cannot, in all reason, possibly be the case, he has shown that in the highest reason our being united to Adam is no less possible than anything else in this whole unsolid and "oscillating" but lawful world. And there the argument stops, where surely it must.

To be sure, Edwards provides us, in a footnote, with a highly baroque image in which, despite the phenomenal obstacles offered to the vulgar imagination by a show of time, space, and substance, we seem to see "the heart of all the branches" of mankind universally and as one being concur "when the heart of the [Adamic] root, by a full disposition committed the first sin" (392). But we make a mistake, I think, if we take this offering for more than it is: an Image, out of a personal and speculative book of Images, offered in a foonote, by an imagination which apparently does not let imagistic absurdity embarrass or hinder its idealist purposes. The image will not "explicate" in such a way as to tell us more than we already know. If it works at all, it is only as most of Edwards' more famous Images work—to illustrate the already understood truths of a philosophy of sovereignty. The ultimate fact about Edwards as "poet" would seem to be that his imagination can use instances of the "secondary" beauty or harmony to illustrate truths arrived at by his modern philosophical "way of ideas," but it can never simply get to God through nature.

However that may be, Edwards rests his case at the end of the *Original Sin* not in an image but in a metaphysical argument, contra a complicated but pseudo-philosophical objection offered by his humanistic, liberal, and imaginatively "vulgar" opponents: since all reality is a "constitutional" expression of God's lawful power, and since not even human identity is an exception to this principle, philosophy can never be invoked to invalidate the obvious scriptural teaching about Adam's sin and man's depravity. His argument may be, in the end, only a special way of saying that reality is whatever God says it is; and this, philosophically, may be about as perilous as the purely Calvinistic teaching that "the will of God is the highest rule of justice; so that what he wills must be considered just, for this very reason, because he wills it."[61] But it is an argument which, in its philosophical form, Edwards held back for a long time, however consistent it may have been with his earliest idealism.

It came out when he thought it had to, when he faced an objection proportionate to its own Puritanic seriousness: it came out as a sort of dangerous and last-ditch maneuver of Christian Philosophy, precisely when the very intelligibility of Scripture's long-received sense was most deeply embattled. "Reality"—the nature of things and of the human constitution—was being invoked as a crushing counterargument to the founding premise of Orthodox Historical Christianity: in Adam's fall we sinned all, somehow. Rational objections against the legitimacy of God's sovereign dealings with His individual creatures and literary objections against the typic organization of his Adamic plot are both answered with a philosophical definition of God's declarative but also, thereby, constitutive relation to all other reality. A moment of rare intellectual crisis it most certainly was. Well passed, perhaps, for anyone blessed enough to think so. Unless Perry Miller is right—that there are going to be, not images and shadows, but echoes and specters.

Many morals press, but the present essay owes itself a concluding word on the cogency of Edwards' Puritanism as Christian Philosophy. In this dim but colorful light it seems fairest to regard Edwards as one of the last, perhaps *the* last arguably major Christian thinker to work within, or in sight of, the familiar problematic of Reason and Revelation, just prior to the powerful influence of the Higher Criticism. In this aspect he is a sort of "Last Medieval" for, by the end of his century, or certainly by the beginning of the next, Christian thinkers were discovering, to their dismay, that the status of Scripture was itself the primary problem they had to face. Epistemological, now, and not merely hermeneutical, it turned out to be an all-engrossing one, and everywhere Christian intellectual energy fairly consumed itself in the attempt to discover what sense history could make of the very idea of a "supernatural" revelation.

A partisan reading, of the Perry Miller sort, might claim that Edwards actually overleaped this historicist phase of the contest between Reason and Revelation, that his radical Protestantism always supposed that the truth of Scripture appeared to the eye of faith and not to the positivist researches of the textual critic, or—if this is any different—that its authority rested squarely on its congruence, imagistic and operational, with the nature of things.[62] But it is hard to imagine that if he had been born fifty or a hundred years later, he could have resisted taking avid intellectual notice of the curious textual news coming out of Germany. And the normally resistant reader will surely wonder if Edwards would have rested so much on his idealist theory of identity if the no-way-intuitive fall-and-redemption myththeme of Adam and

Christ had not absolutely required it. As always, perhaps, the faith and the philosophy called each other forth and went along together.

Yet this last great figure of the old style of established religious thought is not without continuing human interest, even in his great moment of making humanity disappear. Indeed, the socio-logical flavor of that moment makes it one of his most attractive: for longer than anyone can really remember, we've all been saying we believe this hard saying about Adam; and so we should, it being Paul's own originary way of inflecting the Christ-event itself; now, if we really do believe it, it is incumbent upon us "to get over the difficulty, either by finding out some solution, or by shutting our mouths, and acknowledging the weakness and scantiness of our understandings" (395). Edwards is no human comedian, but we ought to be able to smile at this, as widely and as ruefully as when, much earlier in his career, he compares certain overcivilized objections to the social tone of an Awakening to those of a person who, kneeling in the fields, praying desperately for rain in the midst of a great drought, should become revolted by the fact that a sudden gracious downpour has made him wet and muddy. Oh please, dear God; ooh, yuck. True Religion may actually require us, Edwards everywhere implies, to say what we really mean.

Some things really do change, however, and when the Christian problem moves from the reasonable support of well received doctrine to the epistemic condition of that reception itself, Edwards has only a little more to say than have Locke and Newton, Malebranche and Norris. And what he does have to offer—implicitly in the *Original Sin* and the *True Virtue*, and in so many words in the precocious "Fifth Sign" of "Part Three" of the *Religious Affections*—may well suffer some loss of credibility with all those whom Edwards' theory of identity could only stun.

In one sense Edwards merely raises the crucial but resistant problem of personal identity to another level, with ghostlier demarcations: our inability to understand—or to imagine, except in some baroque figure—our moral oneness with Adam is rationalized by the open discovery of our inability to say very much about the problem at all. Worse yet, the net effect of Edwards' logic is not to answer but merely to cancel certain fond but familiar questions about the ontological status of man, considered as a "created intelligent being." Indeed, creation in the "image" of God comes to have a somewhat narcissistic overtone. To the extent that (embarrassing) questions about the whence and the whither of our *selves* continue to occur to our natural experience—and are not once and for all answered in the virtually mystic experience of the All in All—we may find that Edwards' deconstruction has simply left us behind. And, to say the worst, to the extent that a theory of creation which is total, continuous, active, and in the end ideal makes it hard to think of the human being as ever really very far "off" from God, to that extent the ordinarily gripping religious question of how to get "back" may lose some of its fatal fascination. Calling Edwards' position "panentheist" rather than "pantheist" helps a little, but only temporarily, to conceal the implication that the Edwardsian metaphysic solves the Problem of Man by making it disappear.[63]

Above all else, therefore, the example of Edwards provides the opportunity to observe that Christian Philosophy—even in its Puritanic variety—is interesting only so long as its practitioner can keep the world from collapsing back into the capacious and omnicompetent mind of God. The premise that God so wills (or "so constitutes reality") will always suffice for a last explanation, and it may be in some cases the only remark we can honestly make, but the game of philosophy requires that all other plausible and non-self-contradictory movements toward explanation be tried first. When this obviously last gambit is made, the game is clearly over.

We may wish to credit Edwards with holding off from the public announcement of his final appeal as long as he did—temporally, at the end of his career, but also intellectually, so that his *Freedom* and his *Virtue* could be written at all, and make the important clarifications they do. Yet if the instincts of this essay are right, we sense everywhere that Edwards' apocalyptic master-move is coming—that his own footnote to Plato can hardly wait to be written, that it is foregrounded in the traditions of nominalism and voluntarism that so thoroughly inform the tradition of Protestant intellectuality, and that it is given a powerful and appropriate new motivation by the idealism Edwards adopted so early; in short, that it is *toward* the end of the *Original Sin* that Edwards' imagination and his system both inevitably tend.

95

We should allow, perhaps, that even when it ends there, it provides the only really satisfactory explanation of the nearly universal Christian teaching that the world, created in time and *not* (contra Aristotle) coeternal with God, would in fact disappear if God for a single instant withdrew His noetic and willful support—that being, in Edwards' system, all the reality it ever really enjoyed. We might even suggest that the Protestant emphasis on sovereignty achieves a sort of satisfactory or necessary last phase in Edwards' system—where the Lutheran *sola gratia* and the Calvinist *soli Deo gloria* are both swallowed up in a pietistic and but also metaphysical *Solus Deus*.[64] But irony and a sense of historical completion remain small recompense for the stalemating of philosophy and the disappearance of man. So it may be most "safe" (in Luther's own sense) to sound the cautionary note: Ockham's razor can be a double-edged sword; and also, beware of explanations which prove too much.

If there is any other concluding observation to be made, it may concern, less sententiously, the relation in Edwards of theology, philosophy, and imagination. It may be appropriate to suggest that the problem—and finally the harmony—of theology and philosophy is only part of the story; that what controls that relationship, from deeper down in some intuitive grasp of reality which (like Kierkegaard's leap of faith) occurs somewhere beyond the legitimate boundaries of biblical interpretation, and which (like Poe's guess about God's plot) is quite different from both induction and deduction. I have no wish to end by undervaluing my own old-time project of estimating Edwards' stature as a Christian Philosopher, but I do wish to suggest that a less intellectualized view is just as true. The categories are necessary to maintain a steady view of Edwards' argumentative intentions at every point, but as the insistence on the personal location of those categories was itself meant to suggest, the most fruitful approach to Edwards may not be strictly academic or categorical.

If, for example, we are still asking which *really* came first for Edwards, the theology or the philosophy, the faith or the reason, the religious commitment or the intellectualization, we may find ourselves with an unanswerable question. Sovereignty was clearly a "given" of his Puritanic childhood and Calvinist instruction. He may indeed have had early "objections against the doctrine of God's…choosing whom he would to eternal life, and rejecting whom he pleased," as he confesses in the "Personal Narrative."[65] But unlike many others (including Franklin) he never rebelled. And if he places his conversion relatively late in his young manhood, still we might not want to write off the significance of his early pietistic experiences, in the history of his imagination, as easily as he might, in the progress of his soul. What we seem to see is a young person being authentically religious in a venerable Puritan way, and then, in close combination, discovering the all-creative power and all-encompassing nature of God in philosophical speculations *and also* experiencing a powerful but hardly instantaneous conversion which completed and transformed the early piety even as it gave further validation to the most problematic elements in the speculations. The public life, thereafter, is spent first in promulgating the piety; then in defending it with philosophical idioms which are neither within nor too far removed from the common understanding of things; and finally in rescuing it with his own very first insights, however problematic to the "vulgar." Throughout the whole career, that is, the Edwards "ego" has a very compelling experimental unity.

Deepest down, perhaps, we find not a metaphysics (which "prepared" for a conversion), nor yet a piety (which found its way to the inevitable intellectual idiom), but rather some remarkable capacity of Puritanic imagination, as rare and productive in its calmly idealist way as was the ragged baroque of Edward Taylor. Its quality is best described in the negative, but from Edwards' own early writings; it is most unlike that materialist faculty—"fancy," as they will be calling it—whose "prejudices" seem naturally to grow in every man "by every act of sensation" and which, unless opposed by mental culture or spiritual discipline, cause men to "roar out, upon the mention of some very rational philosophical truths."[66] Overcoming the prejudices of that sort of imagination would, of course, be the first step on the road to any consistent idealism. But possessing an opposite sort of power, imaginative still, but not really sensory in origin, would seem to guarantee Edwards' whole career. A capacity to suspect that reality, including the sources of the self, might be very subtle, and a power to suspend belief long enough to wonder *how* subtle, may tell us more than anything else about the unity and the priorities of a mind which saw spiders and thought "teleology," which learned of atoms and guessed "power," which experienced both nature and grace and leaped to "idea," and which ultimately contrived to hand the whole world, including its own consciousness and that of every other man, over to *God Alone*.[67]

Such an imagination can seem, as it did to Perry Miller, impressively scientific, but it is not, therefore, without a fundamental flaw or besetting vice. As it maintains, in its intuitive phase, an almost mathematical purity, discrediting substance and looking only for the law, so in its expressive phase it tends to be not only "angelic" but even "deific." It can discover, everywhere, images of an ideality already guessed or given, but its "Puritanism" can neither rest in images nor *simply* recommend phenomenal nature as the mind's road to God. As such, it is an imagination which Emerson—so like Edwards in so many ways—would have to outgrow before he could become, in the modern manner, a "fluxional" symbolist; the "slippery Proteus" was not so easily caught.

But whatever the problematic consequences of this Puritanic Imagination for the literature of the *American Renaissance*, the consequences for Edwards' own systematic thought are fairly clear. Edwards may have been, even as Miller claimed, a poet who happened to work in ideas, but he was a poet whose imagination could do some things and not others; equally important, his imagination expressed itself in some ideas and not others. Again and again it availed itself of idioms—both theological and philosophical—more satisfactorily expressive of essential simplicity than of existential complexity. In one critical formulation, Edwards' neoplatonism deals more effectively with Being than with becoming. And perhaps an equally strong case could be made that his philosophical insights into Being-in-General count for more than his theological observations about God Incarnate.[68]

Most of Edwards' idioms are meaningfully related to existing Protestant options or to the developing style of philosophy, in the early "modern" period, as it paralleled or deliberately tried to mock the ideal patterns of early "modern" science. Back beyond that they are Platonic, idealist a fortiori. To quibble about the real influence or supposable reduplication of Berkeley is as quaintly aside from the main point as to argue about whether the revolution in thought effected by Descartes, Locke, Newton, and other "Giants" of the seventeenth century is "modern" in a full or only in a self-styled "period" sense. Our problems of thought remain about the same, whomever we decide to blame.

97

The clear and important point about Edwards is that some strict given of nature or some equally inevtiable Puritan Project of Being everywhere bent him toward one "way" of explanation. Along that way he can give essentially Christian ideas, like grace and creation, a respectable standing within an idealist metaphysic. Or, alternately, he can offer, within that same metaphysic, a Christian understanding of secular ideas like cause, sense, analogy, necessity, and identity. "Philosophically" his position flows from a singular identification of substance as that which enjoys the absolute privilege of simple self-existence; "theologically," such an insight readily supports, or is supported by, Scripture's treasured revelation of the Divine Name. Either way—and however the shifting moods of criticism may valorize the result—the definitive Puritan premise of sovereignty has found its authentic and most durable intellectual champion. Others might challenge that premise, one way or another, with more or less of a philosophical effect. But no one could live to confess more completely or express with more determination the proposition that the God who alone saves is the same as He who alone exists.

CODA (1995)

Idealism Without the Subject

Maybe Miller should have called Edwards "postmodern." True, that momentous term of art was not readily available in 1949. Yet one scarcely forgives Miller's genius for failing to predict that, having survived yet another Great War, Modern Memory would itself require subdivision; that humanistic intelligence would soon declare itself launched (or perhaps merely adrift) on still another historical epoch, even less friendly to its own cherished illusions. For how else could this embattled disciple of Henry Adams have made it clear, to all but the *most* determined misprision, that—prolepsis of Emerson notwithstanding, and "pantheist" or not—Edwards was anything but a humanist progressive like ourselves?

Miller might have helped himself (and us) a little if he had more patiently explained that his own modernity was nothing like the "High Modernism" about to be reified in Departments of English nor anything akin to that secular-humanist "Modernism" that so appalled first the Papacy and then the Evangelicals; that his own agnostic neo-orthodoxy found the "modern" universe intellectually complex, morally grievous, and in no sense very friendly to Man, the "reed which happens to think." Even more useful, perhaps, would have been some correlation of his various formulas for placing Edwards. For example: was the "typologist" who anticipated Emerson more faithfully than had Swedenborg the same as the near-contemporaneous "naturalist" who would require so little time with James and Freud "to catch up completely"?

And if so, in what sense would that make Emerson's naturalism also quite modern? Miller's far-reaching and unexpected claims might still have provoked those studies which studiously show that Edwards' ethical thought did not entirely dispense with faculty psychology and that it was, recognizably, a version of eighteenth-century moral sense theory; that his "scientific" writings are not only nonmathematical but are at times a trifle adolescent, however late he set them down; and that his historiography was of course "Puritan."[1] But it might have been possible to prevent the truly obscene spectacle of a whole host of critics trying to appear more correctly "historical." Possibly the case required the full-scale Derridean insult: deconstruction as a lesson in shame. Apply as needed.

Lacking the appropriately evocative terms, however, Miller did what he could—to indicate that Edwards had boldly parted company with many a Rationalist who felt, there in the Age of Reason (or here in the Academy) that the Problem of the Universe (or of the Human Sciences) was well on the way to solution, structuralist or otherwise. Declining to name names, he nevertheless as good as predicted that many American literary scholars were yet to discover the real Edwards, not well behind them on the road to eventual enlightenment but, like a specter risen from the premature burial of repression, blocking their pathway still. Much of this premonitory sense he expressed elliptically or by hyperbole: literary discourse is like that, and the publications of modern symposia are still trying to figure it out.

Yet two things ought always to have been clear. First, that Miller found Edwards' cosmos more dynamically mysterious—and for *that* reason more modern—than the one customarily evoked in the age that followed Newton's reduction of a universe of motion to three elegant laws. And second, that he judged Edwards' account of the "affective" springs of human behavior (and the "deterministic" definition of "will" it implied) more philosophical, and more likely to be ratified by post-Freudian psychology and cognitive research than one based on the notion that "freedom" implies, anywhere, "indifference"; or on the more radical claim that a consciousness of motives, and of a luxuriant deliberation among them, implies "self-determination" or anything approaching to what we might call full "self-presence." That is to say: Miller thought he recognized in Edwards' reduction of matter-as-substance to energy-as-divine-power some fearful forecast of our own less-than-nuclear universe; and, he came as close as anyone in 1949 could come to recognizing that, in the name of Empiricism and under the aegis of Sovereignty, Edwards had launched his own attack on the "philosopheme of the subject."[2]

We need to notice that, for all his legitimate inheritance of Puritan sensitivity, Edwards is not in truth a very "subjective" writer. To be sure, the early "Diary" makes a brave show of painful self-diagnosis: in recognition of an atypical "preparation" and a convicting inability to "feel the Christian graces sensibly enough," it affects for a time to suffer the terrors of unregenerate self-hood, but before long it buries us under a list of Resolutions extensive enough to break the back of some typological camel.[3] Much more expressive of the native Edwardsian mind and manner are the "Miscellanies" and related entries in the "Images of Divine Things," in which excited perceptions of the way "things" have to be and mean crowd out all sense of the self as philosophical subject, even as a starting point; if "Edwards" appears here, it is only as the irrepressible (dare one repeat the word "hubristic"?) intellectual who can't wait for the maturity of consideration and comprehension of plan to write it all up—in a series of divine advertisements whose dedication ought to read: I wish to thank the Being of Beings for outering himself in such a way as to make all these correspondances inevitably appear. And, significantly, this sense of outrunning wonder at the way the world appears to the renewed sensibility is much more a distinguishing mark of the "Personal Narrative" than any Rousseauvian or "Pre-Romantic" suffering or celebration of the sensibility itself. Every inch a Puritan, Edwards is yet in no danger of providing one more chapter in that account of "Origins" in which the Self gets trapped inside the very Self it needs to hate so much.[4]

Nor does any of the major treatises proceed with a familiar account of what the writer, at the present moment—with or without the dressing gown he does or does not wear, when he writes, dreaming or not, beside the fire in his study—can find his present experience to entail or to exclude. He makes bold to pronounce, in the *Freedom* as elsewhere, about exactly what we all mean when we use certain familiar words, and he goes right on to argue that we never can have the experiences implied by other, more metaphysical accounts of "willing." But he never dramatizes his own (or any) private consciousness as a starting point or model. He never finds his own "self" reduced to "some perception" because, unlike even the most discreet and mannerly Hume, he never once goes off looking for it. What he finds, instead, is that volitions draw men out into the world by permitting them to enact their preferences, and he denies, with arguments furiously invented to refute positions which no one seems to espouse, that anyone can self-consistently hold out anything else in the name of "freedom." But he declines to imagine how it appears, to the inlook of consciousness, when anybody makes a choice; or when, in the *Virtue*, anybody naturally loves wife or child or homeland or graciously expresses that rare consent to Being in General.

This characteristic avoidance of private consciousness could be method, taste, inhibition, or merely an inability to see the direction in which the "modern" world was likely to drift. But the truth of the matter is that—outside the cases reported in the various Narratives of the various Awakenings—the Edwards corpus contains few temptations of the "psychological" sort. The pleasures of his text are emphatically speculative and logical rather than dramatic and literary. Indeed it is almost as if he declined to imagine the Self in order to avoid the spreading temptation to reify it; to invest its vicissitudes, that is, with more "substantial" reality than he imagined them to possess.

There are moments in the *Freedom* when this (negative) point threatens to emerge as such—in anticipation of the metaphysical eruption at the end of the *Original Sin*. They occur whenever Edwards is being most careful to suggest that "the will" is not properly described as a separate "faculty," that men perform acts of willing but that they do not "have a will" (except in the colloquial sense of having made a determination). The obvious point, well made by Edwards' careful and sympathetic commentators, is that he does not wish to split the human personality or reduplicate its structure of authority; phenomenologically (and *morally*) speaking, the buck has to stop somewhere, and Edwards wishes to say that it stops with the man and not with "the will."[5] But lurking in these agitated passages is the further implication that if "the will" were a "faculty" it might have to inhere in a "substance"; or, more likely to the view of the nonphilosopher, it might come to seem a kind of stand-in or code or shorthand or symbolic language for the Substantial Self itself. One hears the problem in the tone of the deadly earnest but often bewildered adversaries: my choice must be, in every supposable sense, my *own* choice, based on motives uniquely and controllably my *own*; even sin, to be sin, must be *mine*. So alerted, one repeatedly senses Edwards' prime fear: that "a free will," in the late-scholastic parlance of the liberal Christians of the mid-eighteenth century, is coming to represent a sort of pseudo-philosophical advertisement for the newly invented and potentially "autonomous" Self. A Self that may be said to be *something*, in any idiom one cares to adopt. And this, of course, is the outcome Edwards has dedicated his intellectual career—sworn on the altar of God, so to speak—to prevent and deny.

None of this latter-day sociological horror is meant to obscure the fact that Edwards' deconstruction of the substantial self is attended (Miller might have said "fraught") with the most serious difficulties. Professionally speaking, the manner and force of its climactic revelation, at the end of the *Original Sin*, went a long way toward limiting the influence that very serious and intelligent work might have had, even among his avowed disciples, in the eighteenth and nineteenth centuries. And from the standpoint of systematic integrity or self-consistency, the problems it leaves (or creates) may be no less difficult than the ones it solves or obviates, even as the most able editor of the "Miscellanies" has recently remarked. Edwards' intentions—to account God the only true substance or fully real being—seem clear and deliberate, but some of the consequences of this position seem inadequately thought through.

Against Locke's "dogmatic" insistence on the material reality of the "primary qualities" of extension and solidity, and in some unknowable substrate that must be thought to underlie these not-quite-prime realities, Edwards early and easily concludes that this supposed "substance of bodies at last becomes either 'nothing' or nothing but the Deity acting in that particular manner in those parts of space where He thinks fit. So that speaking most strictly there is no proper substance but God Himself." Reminding himself that he speaks "at present with respect to bodies only"—but taking quiet pleasure, perhaps, that the Aristotelian rumor of the co-equality of the material universe with God has finally been squelched—he concludes (this famous "Corollary 11" of his essay "Of Being") with the exclamation of "How truly then is He said to be *ens entium*."[6] Too likely to take this last remark as piety merely—as we tend to read the "Being in General" of the *True Virtue* as but a philosophical euphemism for the "God" we all know and distrust—we should remind ourselves that there is a determined literal meaning to Edwards' "wee scrap of Latinity," that he clearly means to name God what he has just, within the stipulated limits, demonstrated Him to be, namely the real being of everything else which is anywhere taken by anyone to exist in any way. And if we hear him indicating that he intends to apply the same logic to souls or spirits as well as to bodies, we may need to catch our breath: you mean to argue that our souls, which Plato and Descartes in one sense and Berkeley in quite another hold to be all that we *really* are, are themselves also nothing but timely manifestations of God's sole but expressive power?

And of course he does mean precisely that: "souls," or created spiritual substances, which (along with the Angels) Berkeley took to be, as minds, the only real entities other than God in the Universe—wherever that was, in or out of Augustinian Time and Newtonian Space—are not themselves self-existent in any sense cogent enough to qualify as what philosophers had fallen into the habit of calling substances. The text is entry number 267 in the "Miscellanies." There, in amplification of an argument that goes "I think, therefore God exists," Edwards wonders where to find the cause of any new thought:

> It is not in antecedent thoughts, for they are vanished and gone...But if we say 'tis the substance of the soul, if we mean that there is some substance besides that thought that brings that thought forth, if it be God, I acknowledge it; but if there be meant something else that has no properties, it seems to me absurd.[7]

Just like matter, that "occult substrate" which could be nothing more "substantial" than God's own continuous exercise of power, the human spirit or soul reduces to the very same ongoing—needful and continuously forthcoming—creative energy. And by this astonishing account, God not only furnishes "nature," to the entirely spiritual mind of man, in the form of continuous and regularly communicated ideas, He also furnishes, at the very same time, and in just about the same creative way, the receiving mind itself. Clearly we are very near the end of something or other.

Platonists though they have often been, Christian Philosophers have never taught the eternal existence of the Soul from the beginning. Once called by God into existence, however, this "incorruptible" spiritual substance is usually said to have its own capacity to go on forever. God could, of course, destroy this subtle substance He has made, whatever some brash young first-time whaleman might rhetorically declare;[8] but in the most widespread account He is not expected to do so. The quality of matter is always somewhat strained, but the soul is really real. Confiding thus, an Anglican Bishop (of Irish origin), wishing one day to refute (or at least to embarrass) the materialists, gave his sentiment divine against the real being of matter: phenomenal it was, and no substance at all; but not to worry, as the spiritual being of God and the similar (though vastly lesser) being of the human soul made knowledge altogether proof against illusion. An inspired thought it most certainly was: instead of relying on revelation to counter Aristotle's Pagan (and potentially Manichean) view of the existence from eternity of the material universe, the sufficiently epistemological Christian could see, in the strict empiricism of his own analysis, that matter is something which merely appears and, as God exists, appears just exactly as His steady law decrees.

Inspired, Edwards may (or may not) have thought—the evidence is less clear than with Emerson.[9] Counterintuitive, perhaps, but who would need a philosophy that merely registered the common sense? Absolutely elegant and altogether nondisconfirmable in any event. To say, in the next place, that all our affairs go on just as before is merely to notice that the evidence for the claim of Berkeley (or Edwards or Emerson) and for the claim of common sense is exactly the same: things appear, but it really *could* be, all of it, nothing more (or less) than God's will and Idea, and we could never know the difference. What if, as I tease my students, with wit borrowed from the later Emerson, Life is a just some really "mammoth" cave which (contra Plato) you never do get out of; or perhaps "We all live in a yellow submarine." Or, to vary the figure again, in a direction they find more familiar, maybe reality is, all of it, "virtual"; maybe "we're still on the holodeck."

Inspired or not, however, Berkeley's ready and easy way with matter is by no means as far as our thought can proceed in this phenomenological—but also, happily, theist—direction. Fine as far as it goes, Berkeley's magical ontology is everything but Puritan. It delivers God from his age-old competition with the ugly countersubstance of matter, and it rescues knowledge from the splendid but labyrinthine subjectivity no pre-post-modernist knows any way to praise. But it leaves man, religious man, well assured of the stability of his knowledge in God, and with the further conviction that, though he is not truly a thing of matter, he is something quite real nevertheless. Not more real,

103

perhaps, there now being no apt standard of comparison, but much better—a spiritual substance, created by God and hence not self-existent, but endowed with all the enduring privilege of real being. I think, therefore God and I are both spiritual substances. Who could ask for any thing more?

It is fictional, of course, to imagine Edwards actively intervening in the Berkeleyan plot at just this point—exactly as he and Berkeley had both interrupted the Lockean account of the extra-mental existence of material substance. But the two analyses look suspiciously the same: the occult—nonconscious or subphenomenal—soul is a real substance no more than is the power underlying the qualities we perceive as outlying material reality. Nature is God's ideal effect and so, a priori, almost, is the human soul: can we really imagine that the flimsy tissue of our thinking is more real-in-itself than the things we see or taste or build? God, the *ens entium*, is the real being of the thinker no less than of the thought.

Shocked by the extremity of this insult to the substance of Western Thought—and indeed to the dignity of Man—my earlier account of Edwards buried the crucial text in a footnote and turned to a final critique of the *Original Sin* and to a prosy estimate of Edwards' stature as a Christian Philosopher. No absolutely *false* conclusions here, perhaps, but the assumed calm of those passages may serve as a reminder that the intimations of real being (not to say of immortality) can vary with age, or with what an original Emersonian philosophy would call "mood." At very best, I supposed, the ending of the *Original Sin* raises the mystery of "identity" to another level but leaves human beings wondering whether it is reasonable to worry about their life and death or not; it forces us to recognize Edwards' one-real-being metaphysics as the astonishing yet almost predictable equivalent in philosophy to Calvin's insistence on the sovereignty of God's electing decrees, but that the reduction of the spiritual soul as well as the material world to the power of God may amount to a sort of end-game in the Western philosophy of "substance." What else could one say?

Frightened I may have been, but kindly I was in comparison to Edwards' recent editor who, coming to the same recognition, observes that the climax of the *Original Sin* was the inevitable outcome of a metaphysics invented long ago and that this metaphysics makes the Universe so totally an affair of *Solus Deus* that, "instead of guaranteeing the value and immortality of intelligent creatures, [it] leaves God finally alone, talking to a reflection of himself in a mirror." The wonder, this editor remarks, with understatement truly bathetic, is that Edwards "never seems to have been aware of this potential objection."[10] Perhaps, now that the manuscripts in question have received their definitive modern edition, some other poor philosopher will try to reconcile Edwards' wish to say, sometimes, with conventional Platonism, that spiritual substances are more real than the material sort, with the outrageously more commanding claim that God, the presently active reality-principle of everything anyhow "else," is the only Being to deserve the name of substance. But that study will involve us in the more painful discovery that, ever since we stopped treating substance as an Aristotelian "category," a form of predication rather than a department of real being—a thing sayable, what Melvillean satire called a "dicible"[11]—we have never more than half known what we were talking about.

But even here Edwards might be most useful. Even if we begin by assuming his puritanic analyses do no more than spoil or cancel the games of identity and substance afoot in the seventeenth and eighteenth centuries, his philosophical example, brave or bizarre, deserves to be stirred into the mix of the account we give of western metaphysics, as it barely rises up from the preliminary self-critique of its own epistemology, in that crucial "early modern" epoch. In one modest (Americanist) example, James Hoopes devotes a chapter on the career of "Consciousness in New England" to Edwards' skillful and, in context, entirely plausible avoidance of the most "substantial" problems in which Descartes, Locke, Berkeley, and Hume seemed (otherwise inevitably) to have entangled themselves. In the dogmatic outcome, the painful "conundrum of personal identity" actually "delighted" Edwards, making it easier for him "to believe that, in regeneration, God might arbitrarily create a new man or a new woman." And the differential process is just as revealing: "Like Berkeley, Edwards rejected as occult, as unperceivable, any substantial constitution of the universe. Unlike Berkeley, he made no exception for the soul."[12] Like Hume, furthermore, Edwards denied that the self was anything but its ideas, unless—as he was *not* embarrassed to allow—that "thing" were the self-sustaining power of God. Some endgames may still be games and, though Hoopes stops short of saying so, this comparative account makes Edwards a "player."

The same moral might be drawn from a second, less modest but also more "negative" example. A recent account of the course of modern philosophy "From Descartes to Hume" does an admirable job of showing that there is less difference between the "traditions" of British Empiricism and Continental Rationalism than most histories of philosophy ask us to credit: all the thinkers in question are epistemologists at the outset; all are thus idealists in some sense, and none can really sustain the distinction between "experience" on the one hand and "consciousness" or reason on the other. More to the present point, however, all the philosophers in question have similar embarrassments with the idea of substance—material, or spiritual, or both—as something which depends on nothing else, *except perhaps God*, for its own real existence. It is, pretty clearly, all one extended, early modern family.[13]

To make the demonstration most complete, the cosmopolitan author self-consciously includes the curious but to him legitimate example of Berkeley and even of Malebranche, along with the more widely appreciated ones of

Locke, Hume, Descartes, Leibniz and Spinoza. Which leads one to wonder: if Malebranche, whose "Cartesian" opposition between material and spiritual substances was so radical as to require the invention of an "occasionalist" theory of knowledge, in which God has directly to provide the appropriate spiritual idea just when (and every time) any man has the relevant material sensation; and if Berkeley, whose inspired dismissal of material substances left God no less important (or less busy) in the accomplishment of any human knowledge whatsoever; then why not Edwards, whose system is no less counterintuitive and altogether more elegant? Especially as it shows all the others, at a stroke, how not to have the problem—of man, as a sort-of substance—they clearly are having; or else, at the very least degree of intellectual sympathy, as it realizes the deconstructive dead end everyone else is trying so hard, so awkwardly to avoid.

With or without Edwards in the mix, it should also be possible to show that the problem of (substantial) human identity goes hand in hand with that of (self-determining) human freedom. The Early Modern Philosopher may or may not be carrying, in silence, a brief for the immortality of the human soul, but he is everywhere heavily invested in the (perhaps related) idea that we are, all of us, responsible moral agents.[14] We must be, therefore and at all events, sufficiently the same from moment to moment—from evil intention, to guilty deed, to civilized trial and sentence, to solemn repentance (if any), to lawful execution or painful durance of just retribution—to make the entire legal and social process make sense. All of which seems to require that the human person be something *like* a substance, whether the emergent profession of philosophy can detect its *self* beneath its operations or not. Equally required, if not self-identically entailed, appears the sort of will which, faculty or operation, habit or quality, can make its *own* determination. How else could any bar judge any way but—as our language is forced to pun on itself—arbitrarily? And so, one way or another, those noble anticipators of our present distress all make a mess of "substance" in the name of "freedom." Inevitably, or so it seems, until one notices that Edwards has none of these problems. Others as difficult, perhaps, but not these.

Introspection can locate no "thing" that goes between (or lies under) the flow of our thoughts; if it could, that thing would be then one of those thoughts. Nor can we detect the thing that goes between the motives, not "the will itself," nor yet—without committing ourselves to one of those explanatory appeals that never ends its hapless retreat—the motive that led our motive to become our motive. Nor is any of this required by a conscientious account of moral sense: judgment may well go to the motive, but freedom means simply that a motive is enacted without obstruction, not that it came to be *the* motive all by itself or all by our self. The finest, most civilized morality asks if we did what we intended, that is, if we knew what we were doing and meant to do just that: much less than speculative philosophy which, on one account, enjoys the prospect of going on forever, even if in a regress, can the practical reason afford to ask what motivated the motives. It really is, for Edwards, all part of a single schema: Calvin's needful construct, no doubt; Scripture's subtlest sense, perhaps; but neither of these in a way Locke's *Sophia Laici* or Hume's Background for Backgammon could find reason to discredit as such. His example ought to be included.

Included, that is, in our histories of Western, and not just American Philosophy—a signal instance, at the very least, of what it would look like for philosophy in the eighteenth century to *admit* it had a social agenda and then, so motivated, to have the courage of its analytical convictions.[15] The will is "free" only if one is careful about what is really sayable on this subject. And the reed which happens to think does not for that reason appear to be a substance: better get a new way of affirming the unique importance (or generic self-interest) of human beings.[16] Included, also, in our surveys of American literature in ways that pay more than lip service to the notion that he is (of course) a major figure in the history of something or other: theology, philosophy, philosophical theology, whatever.

He did indeed indite a "Narrative" or two, but to call the one "Faithful" was to claim much more than that he meant to tell the truth, and it may be time to notice that his very brief essay in the genre of self-writing is neither very "Personal" nor at all friendly to the emergent cause of self-invention. Citizen Franklin, just literary enough to be ironical about that project, and Quaker Woolman, who thought he could blame his nightmares on the Spirit, do far better to satisfy our insatiable appetite for personality and to hold the fort of fiction until Foster and Rowson, Brackenridge and Brown begin to earn the chief glory of every people. Edwards is for something else. One forgives oneself the rigors of trying to teach (sophomores) the one "short book," the *True Virtue*, as a sort of philosophical and cultural critique of all novels, present and future, that seek to register the senitmental basis of natural morality; but anybody who has come to college (or to class) "freely," on their own account, can see what's up in Edwards' preliminary excursus on *The Will*; and anybody who has (in some earlier class on Cotton and Hutchinson) sat through one's embarrassed explanation of the fall in Adam or of redemption in Christ can see it all come real in Chapter III of Part Four of the *Original Sin*. Are we being interdisciplinary yet? Any more so, do we think, than when we search for texts to convict Edwards' straitened appreciation of the native culture of Stockbridge?

Or perhaps the pedagogic spirit does ebb, in some relation to a literacy which, without being mathematical or scientific at all, becomes more computerish with every passing term. Better than nothing, then, surely, are the old standbys, with some sense that they are *our* only ways of getting at something,

107

some not-quite-thing, that is hard to say but which (as Derrida himself admits)[17] refuses to be left entirely out of account. Edwards, that is to say, has his own "idealistic" sense of substance or reality, which he insists on applying, full force, to the touchy question of the human "self." And he does it just about everywhere—even, one is finally forced to recognize, in that worst of all the old chestnuts, the "Sinners in the Hands of an Angry God."

Did it frighten or merely bore the high school students, who used to remember it and nothing else about Edwards, whom they frequently confused with an Edwards Taylor, who was himself insufficiently distinct from John Cotton Mather? Did anybody ever learn to love the efflorescence of its "imagery," of spiders and fires, and bent bows with piercing arrows about to be let fly, and sweeping floods but barely held back? Or to take seriously the altogether pre-demythological theodicy of which that imagery is one distinguishing mark? Or to appreciate the text as a fearful exercise in the post-Lockean linguistic enterprise of preaching the simple ideas *themselves*? Well, no matter. Edwards is always Edwards, and we ourselves, so alerted, can hardly miss the lurking point—about those sinners who think they are "something":

> you find you are kept out of hell, but don't see the
> hand of God in it, but look at other things, as the good
> state of your bodily constitution,…and the means you
> use for your own preservation. But indeed these things
> are nothing; if God should withdraw his hand, they would
> avail no more to keep you from falling, than the thin air
> to hold up a person that is suspended in it.[18]

You think, apparently, that your bodily, or indeed your spiritual substance guarantees your continued existence from now to now-plus-one, but the Being of your being is nothing but God's power; and who knows, it might even convert you to know it. At very least, like chicken soup or preparation, it couldn't hurt.

Only out here in California, perhaps, are we regularly reminded that our "foot shall slide in due time." It is the price we pay, no doubt, for living in a place where the sun seems to "ever shine," as a certain Puritan poet had wished it might. Fair is fair. But even those who stand by their teaching that "Every man is sufficient to his condition" should remember that the man who taught us that teaching had also taught that "God is the substrate of the human soul"; that he was taught so by Edwards who, modern or not, had also wanted to teach that even thinking reeds need something real to lean on.

"THE CORN AND THE WINE"

Emerson, Theism, And The Piety Of Herbert

ALTHOUGH EMERSON'S appreciation of the "metaphysical" poetry of George Herbert has scarcely gone unnoticed, no one has quite thought to cast Herbert in the authorizing/inhibitive role of "precursor." The reasons would seem obvious enough. First of all, in general, Emerson's immense authority over *subsequent* (American) poetry and prophetic writing has often made it hard to think of his own literary projects as profoundly influenced. Secondly, in the particular case, the determined traditionalism of Herbert's piety and the elaborate sacramentalism of his symbolic practice appear simply alien to Emerson's increasingly secular habits of thought. And though there is only slightly more historical distance between Emerson and Herbert than between, say, Wordsworth and Milton, no "high argument" in Herbert has seemed to forecast Emerson's revolutionizing doctrine of the "original relation."[1]

We know enough not to take that famous formula too literally, particularly in the literary sense, and especially if we have read Emerson's late essay called "Quotation and Originality." Even apart from its recent emphatic, indeed climactic treatment, the essay stands to remind all readers, philosophically, that "All minds quote" and also, anxiously, that there is something "mortifying" in the discovery of everyone's inability to escape that "perpetual circle" of quotation, which argues the "very small capital of invention." The essay has its expected "turn," of course, and the echo of *Nature* (itself an echo of Jefferson) forbids us to conclude that "the existing generation is invalided and degenerate." And yet the very universality of the problem tends to throw our attention away from the tense question of one writer and one other. So does the doubleness of the conclusion: on the one hand, platonically, "the nobler the truth or sentiment, the less imports the question of authorship"; and on the other hand, therapeutically, "there remains the indefeasible persistency of the individual to be himself."[2]

Thus it is not entirely surprising to find that Bloomian accounts of Emerson's career as a most *readerly* writer will have much to say about the rhetorical laws of Emerson's iterated recoveries from paralysis to power and very little about the dynamics of his encounters with a (lengthening) list of likely influences. Indeed, the shape of the problem may survive from Bloom's own invention: Milton, before he rose up to threaten the Major Romantics, had his own "strong" Renaissance and Classical poets to work through and face down; but the case of Emersonian "priority" is made to look much simpler. Milton and Emerson both inspire chapters called "In the Shadow of," but only Milton merits one on himself "And His Precursors." One wonders if the system, otherwise quite elegant, is not in this instance missing at least one term.[3]

Belatedness is admitted, of course, particularly in the work of Julie Ellison, who senses that the problem was, in Emerson, so acute as to require the leveling devices of the "higher criticism." First the institution of the "Lord's Supper" and then, in six pages, the literary giants of Romantic "England" must feel the force of a criticism powerful enough to clear a space for the Spirit amidst any imaginable terrain of interpretation or speech.[4] Where Moses and Jesus must fall at a stroke, who in fact can stand? So that the problem of belatedness—that is, of literary authority and freedom—tends to become a tropological metatheme: powerful but empty, a drama without characters. Except perhaps Emerson, too aggressively, himself. Or language.

From one point of view, the missing term may be Jesus himself, that strongest of all the prophets who, though he wrote no text, was nevertheless, according to Emerson's early reading of his own tradition, always being given credit for absolutely everything truly thought and said. But that thorny problem would require an essay in its own right, possibly one in which the paradigm of literary anxiety threatens to collapse into a more purely psychic (or religious) archetype.[5] And always there are, we somehow sense, painful persons closer home. There is Edwards, of course, whose strength has shown itself to even Bloom. Channing is "weak," we sadly fear, but there appear to be moments when Emerson himself was not so sure; from which moments we may yet learn that strong and weak is a sliding scale, and that the difference may be largely situational.[6] Then too there might be the "text" of America itself—barren as a landscape of epic and lyric, but teeming with a host of Jeremiahs who appear to speak with one authoritative voice on the unavoidable issue of apocalyptic repetition and difference. Again, though, another essay.

More recognizably "literary" are the (separate) problems of Wordsworth, Coleridge, and Carlyle, all of whom are revealed by the recapitulating gestures of *English Traits* to have been anxious-making in the extreme, whatever might be supposed in the basis of their political separation and generic dissimilarity.[7] And Swedenborg: a rank self-parody in most textbooks of intellectual history, but a conscious stone in the building of Emerson's emergent theory of symbols. And Montaigne, whose *Essays* Emerson explicitly challenged himself to "mend." And Fox. And Luther. And possibly even Plato (or Plotinus), when all the footnotes had got themselves suitably arranged.

Yet not quite "Everybody." And probably not simply prior-writing-in-general. For as "Quotation and Originality" goes far to suggest, the writer may always leave the *parole* which suffers and take sides with the *Langue* which secures universal meaning by his pain. In fact Emerson (whose little poem on "Forerunners" might appear to authorize the entire psycho-literary project we are still assembling) appears to have picked at least his *literary* quarrels with uncommon specificity and canniness. Shakespeare and Goethe easily transcend the "representations" to which they are reduced. Both are "criticized," as sharply as the triumphant Plato himself, yet both are meant to survive; neither comes close enough to touch Emerson's own project, career, selfhood. Milton—absent from the *Representative Men*, but well represented in the *Early Lectures* and Journals—appears to hurt Emerson chiefly as contestant in the agon of Virtue: "He did not love it more than I."[8]

Finally, as it seems, Emerson is altogether modest (or fearful) enough to let the Really Great be really great. And probably we should sense that his strategies of aggression are largely just that: strategies. The Ellison plot—of ritualized literary defeats and critical recoveries—is, she (sometimes) reminds us, more plot than psychograph. For what real glands could possibly pump Emerson through the rollercoaster ride she describes? What actual human memory could keep forgetting that one really is permitted to write? More likely, Emerson learned, early, to do certain (sublime) things very well and was willing to repeat them, often but consciously, till he felt his point was truly taken. A philosophic point, in fact: the human mind may or may not retain or express "the Idea according to which the Universe is made," but human being is always adequate to its own situation; as soon stop writing as believe the world's store of original energy is ever spent.[9] Thus Whitman heard the master. And thanked him for the favor.

Yet there do seem to be instances when—consciously or not, but surely enough either way—Emerson finds himself truly troubled by the example of a writer he much admires, truly uncertain he can go on with his own project, even his own life, unless he can dispose of another man's literary facts. Good writing was, to Emerson, always a sign of truth, so that he scarcely knew what to make of a case of eloquent or trenchant error. The universe seemed, suddenly, incoherent. Confident that he could "translate" the spiritual doctrines of all manner of Platonists and Christians into his own naturalized supernaturalism, he nevertheless discovered, occasionally, some node of real difference, some fact of authentic religious experience he could no way assimilate. Somebody had to be *wrong*. All minds might share, with perfect equanimity, the glory of discovering and publishing some Truth which all minds do really share; and we have yet to appreciate either the catholicity of Emerson's spiritual taste or the precision of his literary appreciations. But evidently there were limits.

George Herbert, I mean to suggest, is one such limit. He is surely not the only one such, and he may not even be the greatest (or "strongest") of the Standard Authors Emerson found the need to resist, deny, defeat, disprove. But the very limitation of the instance may provide an element of welcome specificity in the recent context of rhetorical largesse. Further, the precise nature of Emerson's growing resistance to the exemplary poet-priest may serve to remind us of the class of propositions which generate Emerson's career as a writer; propositions which we structuralize at some expense of local meaning. And finally, and with some historical caution, we may begin to sense, in the force of that resistance, some remnant of a puritanic absolutism which, in the later phases of its refusal to settle for less than the really real, found itself resisting the dearest figures of the familiar religion, including the trope of theism itself.

The last chapter of *Nature* presents us with the largest and most famous but also perhaps the simplest case of Emerson's "critical" response to Herbert: fairly or unfairly, Emerson "uses" a large, central portion of Herbert's "Man" to help ease his own transition from analysis to prophecy, from the epistemology of "Idealism" and the uncertain metaphysics of "Spirit" to the proclamation, in "Prospects," of Nature's apocalyptic disappearance. Yet as the full nature of even that internal transaction is by no means self-evident, a word of repetition may well be in order. Nor will it do to forget how radically Emerson's evident truncations alter the full sense of the Herbert poem. Clearly Emerson does not want the whole doctrinal package.

Coming just before the more fictive and "fabulous" voice of the "Orphic poet," the Herbert claim exists to be transcended, even if in a manner not yet entirely certain. Evidently Emerson regards it as a sort of historical marker or philosophical holding place. And yet, for a moment at least, Emerson appears to take the argument ("from design") quite seriously, even as he had throughout the "lower argument" of Chapters II through V. In teaching that "Man is all symmetry,/ Full of proportions, one limb to another,/ And all to all the world besides," Herbert's perception has hit on that "class of truths…which draws men to science."[10] And further, though Emerson does not say so explicitly, he may be letting Herbert's list of what Nature does "for us" express the otherwise submerged philosophical pun that unites his naturalist appreciation with his idealist epistemology. Since the world is so thoroughly *for us* as an end, perhaps that is its only mode of real being. So that in terms of what is actually quoted, there scarcely seems to be a quarrel at all.

Similarly with the very brief citation earlier: in the (logically) originary chapter on "Commodity," a single near-couplet from Herbert's eighth stanza serves to conclude, with finality, and to epitomize, with entire authority, a paragraph largely and grandly instancing "the prodigal provision that has been made for [Man's] support and delight on this green ball which floats him through the heavens." There is no "eyeball" excess here, to be sure, yet Emerson may well sense the risk of romantic indulgence in his own dilating rhetoric. Accordingly, he appears to let Herbert make the point with simple sense, in words which any man might use:

> More servants wait on man
> Than he'll take notice of.

That, we are all supposed to know, is the name of that tune. And though Herbert himself might still be puzzling over the oddly Biblical implications of "prodigal," Emerson simply goes on to his next point. So long as Order rules, who cares who wins the game of teleological stylistics?

But our sense of literary (and intellectual) contest sharpens dramatically as soon as we permit ourselves to reread the three stanzas of "Man" which Emerson has declined to reproduce. They are, of course, explicitly "theistic," devotional, and pious, in the most ordinary Christian sense. And Emerson— who wrote repeatedly on the philosophy of "composition," who clearly understood and arguably accepted the theory of "organic unity"—knows quite as well as Brooks and Warren the inevitable effect of settling for passages we have underlined and quoted out of context. So that the aggression appears not only deliberate but even philosophical: evidently we are invited to accept

Herbert's central Man and corresponding Nature, but discouraged from considering his intentional God.[11]

The speaker of the Herbert poem has, at the unquoted outset, "heard this day" (where, exactly, we are left to wonder) "That none doth build a stately habitation/ But that he means to dwell therein."[12] Now what "house," he begins to meditate, could ever be more "stately" than is "Man" himself?—even as the poem's central stanzas go on to instance and explain, in words and music which Emerson, patient ephebe, can lovingly transcribe in full. And then, finally, a "conclusion" to this first hypothetic, then prayerful little pseudo-syllogism; but one no more quotable by Emerson than was its (dramatic) major premise:

> Since then, my God, Thou hast
> So brave a Palace built; O dwell in it,
> That it may dwell with Thee at last![13]

Nature may be a house most "fit" for Man, but Man is a house by God made fitting. Evidently Emerson likes Herbert's proleptic science better than his preparationist theology.

Or than his poetry, someone might think to say, as the conceit of a house dwelling with God seems worthier of the typological temper of Edward Taylor than of his most accomplished master. Yet if this reason of taste were any part of the logic of Emerson's exclusion, it could only be in some relation to the argument which had generated a metric perfection but an imagistic absurdity. Taking "argument" first in its ordinary, dialectical sense, we see at once that Herbert's reasoning is more pious than reasonable: syllogisms conclude with formal certainties, not existential imprecations; and further, entirely as to fact, if man already predicts or recapitulates the perfect harmony of an unfallen creation, what gift need be superadded? Leave off this begging; confess the case. And then, taking "argument" in its "high," Miltonic (or is it only its Wordsworthian?) sense, we understand the lopping off at once: none of Emerson's fablings of the Universal Plot can find any part for a personal God; nor can his mature, self-trusting soul find much sympathy for those which can.[14] We do, Emerson appeared to feel, grow out of that.

In the end, therefore, Herbert's poetic proto-science may have glimpsed the point of Universal Law, but plainly it failed to grasp its true sovereignty. The august "doctrine of analogy" this Christian poet took as handmaiden to religion, not as Religion Itself. And then the poetic Parson took his spirit back to church. House of God, indeed.

Thus *Nature*'s rejection of what Herbert surely took to be his main or "strong" point is largely a matter of silent, strategic, perhaps (Emerson thought) even polite omission. Yet not entirely. For although the logic of

Herbert's theism disappears utterly, his conceit of the "house" comes back to haunt Emerson's very last paragraph. And with its appearance comes the uncanny sense that Emerson may have caught himself in or near the unlovely act of winning too easily, over a "forerunner" who once had been an entirely "happy guide." This second thought (if that is what indeed it is) speaks well for Emerson's intellectual honesty, and possibly of his sense of the hidden strength of the Herbert poem.

Having decently averted his gaze from Herbert's too Christian sense of personal dependence, Emerson immediately announces that he will "conclude" his work with some (larger) "traditions of man and nature, which a certain poet sang to me."[15] Yet this prediction is not entirely accurate: the "Orphic" utterances (of things once known now hid from the human mind) are obviously more suggestive of Emerson's own present "conclusions," but they do not at all end the essay. Instead, after interpolating four paragraphs of some more or less fabulous neoplatonism, Emerson follows up his *Also Sprach* with several pages of prophetic commentary on this more or less self-generated version of the perennial philosophy: a "fall" from power, hints of "miraculous" recovery, a call to the redemptive "marriage" of mind and nature, as Romanticism platonizes Christianity without missing a note. And then— within some final and more "properly" Emersonian evocation of that day when Idea shall be All in All—this stunningly cosmic re-write of Herbert 's homely plot:

115

> Every spirit builds itself a house; and beyond its house, a world; and beyond its world, a heaven. Know then, that the world exists for you...Build, therefore, your own world.[16]

Overfull in itself, the passage is, in relation to Herbert, almost too simply pointed to need commentary. Herbert's house-builder, the familiar "God" of Christian theism, has turned into Emerson's "spirit," clearly no member of the Christian nucleus. But then so too has Herbert's house—Man. Pantheistic or not, the conflation effectively rules out prayer: I may not "loaf" that much, but I surely do "invite myself."[17] And then it also liberates a new style of teaching and command, grammatically sound, but lapsing at last to a sort of (literally) self-fulfilling prophecy. In the old mode, descriptively, the winds do blow "for us," in genus or in sum. Prophetically, however, "the world exists for you"— which no human "subject" has ever apprehended in the plural. As souls are not saved, so texts are not read, "in bundles." And just so: the mind which understands the radical dependence on the mind of that "perfect phenomenon" we call the world will scruple not to make and remake itself a(t) home.

In some rare sense, therefore, the determination of meaning in Emerson's *real* conclusion really does depend on the virtual presence of the absent

Herbert lines. And the effect, I have suggested, deserves to be called "uncanny." Yet not, I think, in the most fashionable sense; for what is "returning" here has been excised without ever really being "repressed." In this case, at least, the ego knows its fear—as clearly as the philosophic man recalls the Christian child. And, haunted by absences as it is, the gay science of the Emerson text may yet support the claim that the differential writing we call literature is explicit and therapeutic, not secretive or anxious.

What is truly uncanny about Emerson's use of Herbert, accordingly, is the very open directness of its oppositional strategy: nobody likes a quibble, and Herbert is a wonderful poet; but theism is initiatory, as Taylor seemed to sense; and Edwards did well to speak of Being in General. Not quite the "measles, mumps, and whooping-cough of the soul," precisely, it is, for Emerson, a prime instance of the fallacy of "personating" which his own Unitarian sermons had tried (tactfully) to expose. "The Father" is a capital trope of the Christian tradition; but as Jesus himself had known it (Emerson thought) entirely as such, was it not about time "to drop all personification" at once? Herbert is an observer of exquisite perception, but "The soul knows no persons."[18] And nobody can follow the perfectly explicit allusive signals of *Nature* without noticing the criticism.

Biographers do not know when, precisely, Emerson stopped "believing" in a personal God. Presumably he did once so believe; and the death of his wife Ellen—though unmarked by the sort of theistic apostasy so shrilly proclaimed by Henry Adams—may well have taken its toll.[19] But as the problem here is "Herbert" and not "God," perhaps we can turn to one more (still preliminary) example of Emerson's open quarrel with Christian poesy, and with concepts which appear to survive the death of the traditional deity.

The text (and the issue) is "Grace," familiar to us as it heads the selection of "Poems" in the virtually standard anthology of Stephen Whicher. Accepting the traditional dating of 1833, and declining to gloss the title from any of Emerson's later valorizations of this "Barbarous and Sacred" term, Whicher notes only the contrast of this (early) poem with Emerson's later "self-reliance doctrines" and includes it as a sample of the "Calvinist-bred mood of self-distrust which he was already endeavoring to throw off." One instantly sees why:

> How much, preventing God, how much I owe
> To the defences thou hast round me set;
> Example, custom, fear, occasion slow,—
> These scorned bondmen were my parapet.
> I dare not peep over this parapet
> To gauge with glance the roaring gulf below,
> The depths of sin to which I had descended,
> Had not these me against myself defended.[20]

The "depths of sin" sounds as if it were the explicit fear of Aunt Mary Moody, the "valued adviser" who, in "Self-Reliance," is remembered as warning that one's "impulses may be from below, not from above." And if it took some years for Emerson to learn to say out loud that he might be willing to "live then from the Devil," he had already vowed (as Whicher notes) "I will not live out of me."[21]

In itself (as critics used to lisp their creed) the poem scarcely calls for further notice. The close-reading pedant will observe that the one odd word, "preventing," both translates and puns on St. Augustine's notion of "prevenient" grace, which prevents sin by coming along in advance of the appropriate "occasion." And the long-seeing ironist will smile to think how faithful logic here prevenes the moral challenge of Yvor Winters: example, custom, fear, and lack of occasion all evince the efficacious work of generations of organized Puritan repression; of course Emerson could afford, in such circumstances, to trust himself.[22] Even to advise many other post-Puritans, similarly repressed, to do so as well.

But all of this changes as soon as we realize that the eight lines of Emerson's "Grace" appears to rewrite and reduce—explicitly, but this time silently—Herbert's perfect sonnet, "Sinne." As the point is taken in at sight, the poem is worth quoting in its entirety:

> Lord, with what care has Thou begirt us round!
> Parents first season us; then schoolmasters
> Deliver us to laws; they send us, bound
> To rules of reason, holy messengers,
>
> Pulpits and Sundayes, sorrow dogging sinne,
> Afflictions sorted, anguish of all sizes,
> Fine nets and stratagems to catch us in,
> Bibles laid open, millions of surprises;
>
> Blessings beforehand, tyes of gratefulnesse,
> The sound of glorie ringing in our eares,
> Without, our shame; within, our consciences;
> Angels and grace, eternall hopes and fears.
>
> Yet all these fences and their whole aray
> One cunning bosome-sinne blows quite away.[23]

The first effect of this comparison is to assure us how well Emerson knows the social text of Christian grace. All of Herbert's wonderful specifications—

parents, teachers, pulpits, Sundays, all of them both telling and embodying, fairly or not, the reasons reason gives for patient service—are all abstracted up into Emerson's one line: "Example, custom, fear, occasion slow." Then too, of course, Emerson entirely lets on that these graces are rarely met with graciousness: "scorned bondsmen" as "parapet," and parapet, as Castle Dismal. But the surprise, the Emersonian difference, lies in the Herbertian conclusion. Like a mortar shell, perhaps, one cunning "Christian" bosome-sinne blows the whole damn thing. For Herbert. But not for Emerson: Grace works. And even if we resist the Devil's reading—according to which Emerson is actually meditating some "plunge" into the Self, whatever it should turn out to be, and that he actually blames some social construct named "God" for "preventing" this dangerous but necessary experiment so long—even so, we cannot overlook the point of radical dissent: the speaker may still be thanking "God," but he is not praying for anything. Secure, furthermore, he seems unlikely ever to be repenting. And his mood, just now, seems a little dangerous, as if he might indeed "throw off."

The problem of that mood will come back, with an interesting reversal, in our next (climactic) example. But here it is the formal problem which should take our attention: what are we to make of a rewriting that appears as silent as it is entire? Is there in fact any reason to retain our model of adequate literary consciousness, as against that of anxious repression?

Oddly, the bibliographic history of "Grace" may provide a clue. The poem is, undoubtedly, "early"; nor are we surprised to learn it was never printed in any of the poetic collections Emerson himself arranged. Yet it did not, as we might also have suspected, go unpublished in the author's lifetime. Rather, he included it, anonymously, along with other poems he regarded primarily as records of personal development, in the pages of *The Dial* (January 1842). After which, one ill-starred but finally successful attempt was made to reprint it; not by Emerson, but by William Henry Channing, who thought to set it as an epigraph to a chapter he was editing for the *Memoirs* of the recently drowned Margaret Fuller Ossoli.[24] So placed, it had a curious poignancy, which Emerson himself might have approved: there, but for the grace of something or other, might he himself have gone, into sexual irregularity, perhaps, or even into Revolutionary Politics.

Yet the poem was almost displaced from this setting, and the story of its disappearance is as revealing as it is humorous. After looking over Channing's chapter of their joint project, Emerson wrote to his collaborator as follows:

> For your mottoes to your chapter, I saw that the first had the infinite honor done it of being quoted to Herbert! The verses are mine,—'Preventing God,' etc.,—so I strike them out.[25]

Other editorial considerations reversed this decision, apparently, for the verses do appear—unattributed and even untitled—as one of several epigraphs to chapter seven of the *Memoirs*. Evidently the moment of embarrassment passed. Possibly Emerson merely reminded himself that "it never troubles the simple seeker from whom he [has] derived such or such a sentiment."[26]

The point, of course, is not that Channing should have recognized the verses as Emerson's, or even that Emerson should find it (in whatever tone) an "infinite honor" to be mistaken for Herbert, but merely that some more or less literate reader made the inevitable, the well-nigh "correct" mistake. Of course it isn't Herbert. How could it be? Herbert's purchase on Grace is anything but secure, and his sound is never (finally) sullen or threatening. Yet the connection is otherwise too obvious to miss: someone is very precisely rewriting and unwriting Herbert in a single gesture of imitative cancellation. The rest is criticism.[27] Including, perhaps, the observation that Emerson declined, for the moment, to tear off an "Ode" to the earnest and usually half-right collaborator.

And then, finally, the fair doubt whether what was obscurely clear to Channing in 1842 could ever have been well hid from Emerson himself. Most likely not. Most likely, a poem not written for publication was written, instead, for the private purpose of working out the difference between the terrific clarity of the seventeenth-century sight of sin and troublesome obscurity of the newer age's dim half-sight of Self. Of the changing figure of "God." And of the philosophic revisions all his pomps and works might have to undergo if the Idealist, no longer a minister, were yet to remain, in any supposable sense, a Christian. Herbert was perhaps the greatest of the "minor" poets in English. But he was also, and perhaps in some relation to his evident minority, quite wrong about "sinne."[28]

Which brings us round to our titular—and hardest—case and question. The case: the possibility of a significant, perhaps strategic echo of Herbert's masterful "The Collar," in Emerson's masterly "Address" to Harvard Divinity School in 1838. We can afford to overstate the question just a little: could the Emerson who had to keep distancing himself from the structures of Christianity and from the received interpretations of canonic Christian texts ever be quite free from the need to keep confronting the apposite example of George Herbert? And also, more particularly, could Emerson ever finally expel himself from the Christian community without somehow answering the opposing logic of the one poem which most famously declares that move to be childish?

Much has already been teased out of the remarkably rich and compressed first three paragraphs of Emerson's still stunning "Address." Particularly noteworthy is Jonathan Bishop's demonstration of the economy with which they

119

recapitulate the entire doctrine of *Nature*; equally impressive is his suggestion that they insist their "text" is organic nature as much as a previous essay. And Joel Porte is entirely convincing in his reading of the literary (Biblical) overtones of Emerson's apparently innocent (naturalistic) reference to "the balm-of-Gilead."[29] And more may yet be lurking. Particularly if we are willing to suppose that Emerson is not only going on from Nature but also, and perhaps more dangerously, that he is also going back to the moment (and the issues) of his 1832 resignation from the Christian ministry. And overwhelmingly, I think, if we are prepared to consider the complex figure of "resignation" in Herbert.

In at least two, ironically competing senses. First of all, obviously, Herbert is always resigning himself to the will of his personal God—to the general justice of His ways, and to the recognition that childlike submission alone is the path to mental health. Rebellious self-assertion has its appeal, of course; and one can scarcely grasp the gentle force of Herbert's "grace" without a prior sense of his unruly "nature." Yet one hardly needs to be a Puritan to know that the Self is always a delusion and a snare. The point is simply "Christian," and Melville's Father Mapple will never make it better than Herbert himself. Repeatedly. Yet nowhere more energetically than in "The Collar," where the bridled Christian cries "No more. / I will abroad"; then raves his fulsome fantasy of "throwing off," not only his repressive ethic but even his ministerial role and garb. And just here we find our ironic second sense: unless he can be reconciled to the way of his "Lord," the Herbert speaker will have to resign from His service.[30]

In the end, of course, he does not "throw off." Arrested by a voice calling "Childe"—and calling attention, thereby, to the childishness of his "choler"— he resigns himself to that "yoke" the Christian must feel as sweeter than any marriage-tie but also to that clerical "collar" that only Puritans reject as papist symbol of fallacious priesthood. That is to say: as Herbert's most vividly dramatic speaker resigns himself to the will of his personal God, he simultaneously, and in the same mental act, abjures some rebellious plan to abandon the ministerial calling and career. So understood, "The Collar" stands forth as the most powerful poem in English about the (rejected) temptation to apostasize; and also, at the same time, as the strongest claim and evidence that one need not separate the poetic role from the priestly. Small wonder, then, if it had indeed caught Emerson's anxious notice—if not in 1832, when he did in fact resign his post at Boston's Second Church, then certainly in 1838, when he repeats and publicizes that resignation in the single most famous apostasy in American literary history. Elsewhere one merely "peeps" over the parapet; here one fairly plunges.[31]

This much analysis is prejudicial, obviously, in advance of any verbal sign; yet it may be necessary to suspect this much in order to hear one when it comes. It comes, as I sense, embedded in the dense and richly argumentative center of Emerson very ornate first paragraph. At issue, evidently, is some sort of "communion." Not quite the sort they have practiced in the churches, to be sure, and therefore not the one Emerson had tried to nullify in 1832, but a real communion, nevertheless. Mysterious, wonderful, and grateful to the soul, its prime quality is yet its universality. Indeed it is more "open" than anything dreamed of in the ancestral philosophy of Solomon Stoddard, which formed a significant part of the logic behind the earlier "Resignation Sermon."[32] For in the unspeakable but intelligible and practicable lesson of the world, "the corn and the wine have been freely dealt to all creatures." From which it follows, as the "transparent" night the "refulgent" summer day, that while no man is fairly collared by the rites of sectarian tradition, all men are rightly "constrained to respect the perfection of this world, in which our senses converse." Denial here would be not a chargeable apostasy but a self-evident blasphemy, of the most wicked, Manichee sort. And faith here begins, at the level of the senses, the salvation of the Soul. "This is the meal pleasantly set": put down your Herbert; take up your Whitman.[33]

Yet if the "Song of Myself" helps measure the vast distance between Emerson's utterly philosophical "constraint" and Herbert's more personal "resignation," a simpler point requires no later vindication. For surely "the corn and the wine" of Emerson's originary natural communion are meant to echo and supplant the logic of Herbert's most sensuous temptation:

121

> Sure there was wine
> Before my sighs did drie it; there was corn
> Before my tears did drown it;
> Is the yeare onely lost to me?

Herbert's "yeare" has been contracted to Emerson's "summer," then exploded to a single, perfect Now; but a subtler point survives in wicked metaphysic wit. Here is substance which "needs no transmuting."[34] We scarcely need to change a name. And yet by some rare miracle of transignification, Herbert's nature has turned from "sinne" to "grace."

There is, of course, one small metonym. Herbert's corn and wine turn communal only at the end, and then entirely by implication: submitting to his Lord, a would-be Priest to the Temple will resign nature's pagan plenty and settle for the elements of his Lord's own Supper. No "metaphysical" violence here, for Herbert's "corn" means "bread" already: his corn is simply "grain," most often "wheat"; and anyone may take part for whole, cause for effect. But American English—like Bloom's "American Religion"—obeys other laws of reference, so that when Emerson says "corn" he means either "maize" or "Herbert's pagan temptation turned natural sacrament."[35] Language is indeterminate. And Emerson's communion saves even the Indians excluded by Stoddard. But we know where we are: Emerson's repressed Unitarian audience is being told to look for the original means—and also the final seal—of salvation precisely where Herbert had found only the reason of rebellion. The nature and the grace which God has joined together, the logic of some (otherwise) gentle "psalmist" has "rav'd" to set apart. Perhaps the Puritan party is larger than we had supposed.

Much of Emerson's compressed, allusive point must appear evident on the surface of his own conscious rhetoric. Clearly the Transcendentalist must reject the conservative Christian dichotomy of nature "versus" grace: one more well-made opposition that can no way survive the deconstructive logic of Natural Supernaturalism. And this particular prophet had long ago rejected the claim that any part of real religion can be at all instituted: Truth is true whether Jesus said it or not; and no form of communion can expand or contract a single degree beyond its natural guarantee. Clearly all do partake of the same wondrous food and drink. We may even labor the obvious to remark that Emerson once again rejects the implication that there is anything at all "personal" about the expansive submission religion appears to require: as soon "worship a whig" as kneel before a "Lord."

Yet there is, lurking in that largely "oedipal" issue of the nature of the authority to which we do (at last) submit, the narrower and riskier one of the psychology of religious sentiment in the adult worshiper. Why does one—finally, and contra both Herbert and one's Aunt Mary Moody—decide to abandon the holy office? And why might one yet resign from the whole system of moral resignation? Not to have a better time of it, surely. For the way of self-reliance would require, Emerson already saw, its own quite severe laws of self-surrender.

Doubtlessly Emerson could notice, with full sympathy, the clear implication that there had been something "childe"-ish in all of Herbert's crying and striking of "the board" which feeds us. Well to come out of that furious little petulance. But what, then, of the child-like-ness of the ending?—wherein, reminded of his dependence as well as his penchant for petty resentment, the chastened Herbert speaker takes up his yoke again, as meekly as Hester Prynne picks up her scarlet letter. Is that all there is? The lapse from wilfull and sensual self-seeking back into the inevitable or enforced recognition of enduring childhood, or servitude, or both? May no one ever, in poem or in life, find reason to rebel and conscience to press on into some other kingdom? The kingdom of Manhood, for example? Sure there was protest before these gentle psalms did quench its manly force. And confirm, thereby, the poet's own minority.

At issue, therefore, is more than "just" the spontaneous, naturalistic redefinition of Herbert's entire sacramental system. Equally contended for, as some

legitimate part of the same theological issue, is the psychology of adult apostasy and mature conviction which, by Emerson's logic, Herbert has simplified
out of existence. And that, ironically, in a poem so virile that one may almost
fail to notice either the triviality of the psychological case or the puerility of
its solution.

The evident doubleness of Emerson's response—to the manly vigor of
Herbert's rhetoric and to the childish weakness of his virtue—is perfectly confirmed in another, much more full and clear, even "imitative" response to "The
Collar." Written in 1834, "early," at the very outset (apparently) of Emerson's
fullest period of Herbertian inspiration,[36] the initially quiet "Each and All"
ends with a carefully staged scene of dramatic reversal which both flatters and
annuls its obvious source of poetic inspiration. After meditating on the subtle
and largely unrecognized communion of each with each, a sober speaker sage-
ly concludes that "All are needed by each one"; that in very fact "Nothing is
fair or good alone." He next reports three separate instances of the utter illu-
soriness of beauty shorn of full relation. Precipitately, then, and with some
noticeable agitation, this would-be connoisseur repents too much:

> "I covet truth;
> Beauty is unripe childhood's cheat;
> I leave it behind with the games of youth."[37]

Already "abroad" in the fields, the rebellious speaker finds no altar "board" to
strike, yet we recognize the Herbert haste at once. Some unripe disciple has
worked himself up for a change of gods.

Prematurely, of course, and wilfully too, as the thought of the "All" is not
yet counted in. But how exclude the cosmos? So that it comes as not very
great surprise when its messengers one by one surround and overcome this
false adulthood. A little "ground-pine" curling, a "violet's breath" inhaled, and
(at the top of the scale, perhaps) a soaring of "eternal sky," and lo, an instant
reversion, to the way of Nature once again:

> Beauty through my senses stole;
> I yielded myself to the perfect whole.

Keats is here, no doubt, reducing and identifying the categorical grasp of "all
ye know on earth." But Herbert wrote the magic change of phase. Except
that, crucially, in the milder Emerson drama the speaker is de-converted, to a
sacramentalized version of the pagan lure. And also, obviously, no gracious
voice need call the hectic tyro's childish bluff. Constraining the would-be
ascetic to "respect the world in which our senses converse," Nature itself has
won its perfect lover back.

From the verge, it appears, of the usual mistake of setting beauty against virtue.[38] The opposition seems adult and strong, like the tough-minded, "Puritan" relation of nature to grace. The weakness shows, however, in the intrusion of God as a personal voice; in the implication that the Herbert speaker, called off a truly infantile desire, will yet remain more a Child of God than a philosophical adult; and finally, in the exclusion of the gracious All which comprehends the ragged each. "They reckon ill" who leave that out.

As when they reckon on "Vanitie"—in poems which not only gloss "The Collar" but cover the entire field of Herbert's Christian partialism. Herbert's "fleet astronomer" can solve the "spheres" with principles he "knoweth long before" as laws of his own nature; and his "subtil chymick" can work the same way to "devest/ And strip the creature naked." But his religious "man" enjoys no such a priori advantage, never finding Deity by natural prediction. And paradoxically not, as the moral law appears innate along with the rest:

> What hath not man sought out and found,
> But his deare God? who yet his glorious law
> Embosomes in us, mellowing the ground
> With showres and frosts, with love and aw,
> So that we need not say, Where's this command?[39]

As the first part of the poem perfectly expresses Nature's full doctine of the attraction of Emersonian science, so the conclusion goes far to prepare the way for the moral strategy of that first, remarkable, liberating/constraining paragraph of the "Address"; for there we do begin, unarguably, in a world already mellow with love and awe.

Yet the check is as complete as the invitation: some unique incapacity of nature determines man to seek and not to find his own "deare" God. And so the final lines—when they too are included in the *Memoirs* of Margaret Fuller—must be answered with a maxim out of Fichte: as "thorough integrity of purpose is itself the Divine Idea in its most common form," so "no really honest mind is without communion with God."[40] Purity of heart annuls all dualism. To seek is everywhere to find. Even as the first chapter of *Nature* had originally supposed, with Herbertian echo and corrective: "Embosomed for a season in nature," man searches for no answers not already prefigured in his own being. The law is not so much embosomed in us as we are in it. And its first clue, furthermore, is always organic delight. So that Herbert's other timely warning about "Vanitie" entirely lacks adult advice:

> Then silly soul, take heed; for earthly joy
> Is but a bubble, and makes thee a boy.[41]

And so it appears, from Emerson's complex but no longer very orthodox point of view, that the pagan temptations of "The Collar" are "Cavalier" indeed. Either they are nature's graces in transparent disguise or, sad to say, they mark a stage of reflection too nakedly primitive to be dignified by the name of major poetry. What boyish joy could the poet-priest have possibly been meditating? Had he thought we meant to ravish virgins?

Accordingly, Herbert's entire elaboration of naturalistic impulse and vitalist resentment can be sustained only in the mode of a melodrama beyond anything imaginable in the context of "Each and All," and quite unlike the scenes of Emerson's own "antinomian" temptation.[42] And then, finally, predictably, Herbert's resignation is more than a little too pat. Too lucky, in one sense, since in really reckless moods God's "preventing" voice is rarely heard in time. But also, when we do decide to drop this personification, it is simply false and injurious to moral sense. Can we not think, somewhere, of a going on to the beauty of virtue which is not, at the same time, a going back into childhood? "The Father" is a trope of man's divine original, not his lasting dependency. Virtue is, accordingly, the mark of the soul's divine majority. As it is the burden of the entire "Address" to propound and exemplify, if not quite to "argue." Its final call, in fact, is for a new Teacher who will "show that the Ought...is one thing with Science, with Beauty, and with Joy."[43]

Thus it is that, as we let the Herbert logic begin to work—to read "The Collar" through Emerson's eyes—we find ourselves objecting to the entire poem. It is all just as if we were fully expected to learn that neither its initial violence nor yet its terminal mildness is entirely "one with the blowing clover and falling rain," nor even quite compatible with the psalmist's own "showers and frosts" of "love and awe." Another dualist plot which did not quite inscribe itself. A miracle of rhetoric, merely; in the service of the soul, "monster."[44]

Or else, if this is too harsh a conclusion, how better might we account for— situate and comparatively apprehend—the studied yet apparently inevitable calm of the massive heterodoxy laid out in the first three, allusive paragraphs of the "Address"? No outbursts and no dramatic oppositions; only the steady tendency (or "myth") of regular philosophic derivation. Passion, perhaps, as the senses are indeed "constrained"; but no eruptions of will and no interposition of persons. Grace works because Nature is Supernature, always already. So the heart of man is well prepared, always, for the process of redemption to begin. So the instruction of man in "what is above him" may proceed, not by opposition to the world found so ready to hand and tongue, eye and mind, and not through a series of moral spasms, but calmly, steadily, and with uniform trust. For virtue (we are told) can be nothing but the soul's highest communion with the unitary and invariable system of Being. Completing, in apotheosis, a process which begins with "corn," it leaves us, quite literally, no place else to seek for life and health. We could not go "abroad," even if we would.

Except that Emerson had taken, just after his resignation from the Unitarian ministry, his own little tour of Europe. We might allay our anxiety by calling this timely trip a pilgrimage rather than a moral holiday (or a "moratorium"). But we would have no Emersonian authority for doing so: to run off seeking vice, or even entertainment, is simply unserious; and to go abroad for virtue (or selfhood) is philosophically incoherent. Probably we must admit the irony and call it "just personal."[45] But even that admission must serve to remind us that Emerson's victories over Herbert may not all be as clean as we have made them seem. That is to say, in part at least, that orthodoxy may be a stronger (mis)reading of the world than Emerson ever quite lets on; and also, perhaps, that Emerson never did fully explain the nature of his own submission to the severe and impersonal terms of Virtue, or Law, or the Beautiful Necessity. No doubt some readers had flat out "rather be 'a pagan'"; or a "childe."

But rather than hectoring Emerson to produce—out of Fichte, perhaps—some further, less imperfect moral tuition, it may be more profitable to conclude, however briefly, with a consideration of the problem Emerson named "The Problem," in a poem which seems to reason on the claims of poetry and priesthood without benefit of Herbert's clerical influence. Does it appear that Emerson can solve his problem any better without Herbert than with him? Or is Herbert's displacement Emerson's very solution?

The first thing to notice about Emerson's "Problem"—why, loving the things of religion, am I not content to be a "churchman"?—is that it is solved before it is even fairly posed. Technically, that is; but perhaps psychologically as well, as if some agon now were really past. The initial formulation of what "I like" takes four lines; the "yet not for all" that, another two; and, then, the specific "why" requires a couplet of its own. Yet the accomplished, intertextual reader of the "Address" knows he has heard Emerson's definitive remark in the second line, only formally parallel to the first:

> I like a church; I like a cowl;
> I love a prophet of the soul [.][46]

Churches, cowls, and (in the next line) "monastic aisles" are one thing, the soul quite another. And though it might seem possible for "cowled churchmen" to prophesy on behalf of that encompassing and transpersonal reality, it has not been Emerson's Christian experience that they often do. Nor could he himself "endure" to wear "the vest" which signifies a disciple of the historical Jesus more clearly than a "newborn bard of the Holy Ghost." Attracted by even the trappings of divine service, Emerson—no Puritan in the ordinary sense—will yet wear the livery of no "Lord."

What follows, of course, is both too famous and too remarkably expressed to be paraphrased here, as Emerson proceeds to evoke that truly "secular" spirit which produced—indifferently, so to speak—the Pagan, the Christian, and the Natural wonders of the world. All purposive, to be sure, but all without a trace of the purpose one senses in the enlisted arguments of one's own most un-catholic tradition. An "organic theory of art" we readily notice; and also, obviously, an "'ecstatic' theory of nature," though quite without the "frolic" element of "The Snow-Storm."[47] But more important, perhaps, an impersonal theory of religion; one which leaves almost anyone named "the good bishop" with a "faith" as sightless as that which church-outed John Milton.

It requires only a little psychobiographic acumen to suspect that Emerson may be thinking of a "bishop" nearer home than "The Shakespeare of Divines"; that the image of William Ellery Channing is as clearly visible as the "cowled portrait" of Jeremy Taylor.[48] And it is only slightly more "impudent" to wonder what has become of Taylor's Anglican contemporary, George Herbert, in a poem which mentions "cowl" and "vest" but never, oddly, "collar"; in a poem whose title imitates Herbert's most familiar form of poetic naming—"The Agonie," "The Banquet," "The Call," "The Discharge," "The Foil," "The Glance," "The Holdfast," and dozens more besides. If the question is at all fair, then the answer can be only a little cruel: problems we have already declared solved, or which perhaps we cannot solve, we may begin to leave unstated. Sooner or later: exit Herbert, enter the Soul. We do have to get on.

Thus it may be only a little fanciful to rename Emerson's "The Problem" as "The Answer"; or even as "The Good-Bye," to the long provocative but finally inadequate example of the single most accomplished poet-priest in Christian lore. And to see, herein, a de-christening more significant than the encoded baptism cum ordination of the Divinity School "Address" itself. For Emerson—embracing prophecy but translating and subsuming Jesus—was evidently bent less on service than on ecstasy, if only in its literary form.

Where Herbert went, after his resignation to "The Collar," was on (as he surely thought) to a book of prose which Emerson can scarcely not have known: *The Country Parson*, whose virtue is its caritas more than its inspired expression.[49] But the Emerson who had positively hated the round of parish visitations that so crowned the career of fellow pastor Henry Ware, and who had more recently characterized the entire "Unitarian Association" as "the prose of prose," had long since said goodbye to all that. Preaching was wanted, clearly: a Sabbath for the Soul, in the "Address"; and, later, as one possible "whip for the top."[50] But not the corporal works of mercy.

And not, less prejucicially, the "vested" interest of some local sect or "Cultus." As "the soul knows no persons," so the prophet knows no "Lord"

but Law. The rest, even at the level of preaching, is all benighted consolation—
"a Night-chair at sickbeds and rheumatic souls."[51] As the corn and the wine
have indeed been dealt to all creatures, so the poet must be priest of a religion
more universal than Universalism and yet more unitary than Unitarianism
itself. Dualism means drama, of Herbert's self-conflicted sort. Psychologically
intense, no doubt, but faithless in the end. Herbert's poems are, to Emerson,
complicated, fascinating, and accomplished. Vigorous, even; but not "strong"
because not philosophical. Churchmen enforce the anxious death of Self. But
the poet of the future will proclaim the common life of Being. And, as
Edwards himself might be got to admit, all the rest really is just personal.

PLEASING GOD

The Lucid Strife of Emerson's "Address"

IT SEEMS a long time since Transcendentalism could mean, blithely, "a little beyond," and since Emerson himself could appear, with benignant vagueness, as "friend and aider of those who would live in the Spirit." And yet, despite a well established and deepening tradition of intellectually precise, even philosophical criticism, a version of the old temptation remains strong: to take the compressed and highly dramatic utterance of an Emerson lecture-turned-essay as aiming for something less (or more) than intellectual completion. For Emerson's larger prose effects, "architectonics" has often seemed a safer word than "structure," and local assertions have sounded more like stylized or encoded maxims of personal insight than like "propositions." Moreover, all of Emerson's venerable authorities seem quoted only to have their power nullified by the speaker of the moment. Oral in inspiration and conversational in mode, the (new) Emerson text transcribes a Babel of voices which only imperfectly translate the "One Mind." Possibly Transcendentalism is coming to mean "a little different."[1]

Solid intellectual commodities may still be had, perhaps, but only at some noticeable discount: Unitarian self-culture, if not imperial Selfhood; Kant's critique of metaphysics, if not Jacobi's Saturnalia of Faith; idealism's nostalgia and grief, if not the Soul's fatal power. Heat lost equals coolness gained. Except, as the career moves, for the friction of the transition itself. But then— once again, clearly—process is the most important product.

As it will be impossible to deny that Emerson himself abets, even encourages this highly mobile, almost kinetic response, so it will be fully appropriate for a certain brand of Theory to tell the tale of Emerson's "indeterminacy."[2] As the monolithic typology of *Nature* slides toward the "fluxions" of "The Poet," Swedenborg is not the only ideologue to be warned that "the slippery Proteus is not so easily caught" (IV, 68): possibly Emersonian meaning is altogether a matter of difference. "Self-Reliance" solemnly promises the moral revolutionary that "all the sallies of his will are rounded in by the law of his being" (II, 34), but as it utterly fails to recoup an "aboriginal Self on which a universal reliance may be grounded" (II, 37), it leaves us with a particularly nervous choice: either fly at once to Edwards' sovereign recognition that God is indeed the "occult substance" of human being, or live with the indefinite postponement of self-identity, a law always to be written. So that the unsettling confession of "Circles" may be philosophic as well as generic (to the *essai*) or whimsical (to the individual): "I simply experiment, an endless seeker with no Past at my back" (II, 188). Thus the provoking question of "Experience"— "Where do we find ourselves?" (III, 27)—may actually be inquiring how anybody at all can go about locating the self; and then the essay's final daring, not to presume to give the order of its own life-stages, may express a modesty positively poststructural.[3] Confess it: One cannot step in the *same* river once.

Until that plot is fully written, however, and until its radical skepticism is reconciled with Emerson's never-failing faith that "the moral sentiment...never forfeits its supremacy," and amounts, in fact, to "the final solution in which all skepticism is lost" (IV, 103), many local embarrassments remain. That is to say, not all of Emerson's refusals of finitude assume so fashionable a form of deferral. Some sound distressingly like evasions.

Nature's climactic chapter assures us that many wonderful truths "arise to us out of the recesses of consciousness" (I, 38); but while we are puzzling over the pun on "recess," it merely offers us the table of contents of a neoplatonic treatise on "Spirit" that never does get written, a "groundplan" for a structure never nobly erected. "The American Scholar" premises its program of literary independence on the fable of the "One Man," but when prophetic push comes to propositional shove, it can only warn that the "reason" of our creative self-trust is "deeper than can be fathomed,—darker than can be enlightened" (I, 53, 65). Nor do the lectures on "The Philosophy of History" (nor their concentration into the single essay "History") effectively solve the antique arithmetic of the one and the many. And the "Address" itself—the very text we are preparing to rationalize—comes round to the expectation, less than the confident prediction, of "the new Teacher" (93) who would regularize its intuition and realize its prolepsis. Often enough, it seems, Emerson makes appeal to some body of intellectual work not yet accomplished. No wonder Andrews Norton was upset. Increasingly, as in the aftermath of the "Address," Emerson steadfastly refused to explain or defend his compressed and unsettling pronouncements.

Not that Emerson would have improved his reputation by responding to the "pure rage" which led Norton to "appeal from a commencement ceremony at the Harvard Divinity School to *The Boston Daily Advertiser*"; but somewhere, perhaps, he might have indicated how it is not an inconsistency to wish for a Teacher of a doctrine that "cannot be received at second hand" (80). Probably Emerson owed no reasoned reply to Henry Ware Jr.'s glancing sermon on "The Personality of the Deity," or even to Norton's very pointed discourse on "The Latest Form of Infidelity": neither of these responses picks up the essential line of his argument, any more than George Ripley's tantalizing position papers had exactly anticipated it. Yet more than one modern scholar would have been aided by some more exact location of the "Address" in relation to the "Miracles Controversy."[4] And then there is the matter of Ware's personal letter about the ambiguities and (to his mind) dangerous tendencies of that "Address." Here, privately at least, Emerson *might* have offered a word in season.

Instead, of course, he merely mocks his own (supposed) incapacity to reason or argue, even as he affects to wonder at the storm of counterprotest his remarks have created. Always regarding himself as the "chartered libertine free to worship & free to rail," and always counting himself "lucky when [he] was understood," how has he now come, all suddenly, "near enough to the institutions & mind of society to deserve the notice of the masters of literature & religion"? Then, while the (privileged) modern reader is trying to imagine what real or imagined slight Emerson is avenging here, the satire presses the advantage of its altogether passive aggression. Continuing mindful that there is "no scholar less willing or less able to be a polemic," Emerson protests that he "could not possibly give...one of the 'arguments' on which as you cruelly hint any position of mine stands."[5] Cruelty, indeed. Quite the equal of anything in Hawthorne's "Custom-House." And less plausibly motivated, so far as the baffled outsider can tell: "What? Me think?"

Hence it is that an alert but essentially conservative brand of modern criticism, scarcely less tolerant of polemics than was Emerson himself, reluctantly concludes that Emerson does not always play the game of thought quite fairly (or not at least quite sociably); and that he gives his reader every right to ask what personal strife lies just behind the scene of his rational engagement. What *has* Ware done to deserve this? Surely it was not quite a fault in this mild man to have succeeded so famously in the profession Emerson resigned when he could not reform. Is his doctrinaire earnestness, here, any more punishable than the homiletic bathos of Barzillai Frost, the pulpit-usurping formalist the "Address" had made to represent—not quite fairly, as it seems—the spiritual depletion of the entire Unitarian movement? Perhaps the ultimate "reason" of certain Emersonian utterances lies not in the public arena of philosophy and theology but in the more obscure (yet not altogether inexpressive) region of personal competition or literary anxiety. Perhaps Emersonian culture ends not in "headache" but in analysis.[6]

An apologist might propose that Emerson's letter to Ware actually expresses an entirely serious intellectual point: cruelly or not, it means to suggest that his problem of explanation is not *sui generis* at all; that in fact we *never* know "what arguments mean in reference to any expression of a thought." If so, then the metaproblem may be more complicated than we have so far supposed; and Emerson may owe clarification not to doctrinal conservatives like Conrad Wright and David Robinson but to a philosophical reactionary like Yvor Winters—perhaps to the institution of philosophy itself. That is to say: when explanations become even more oracular than the original formulations themselves, some question of fitness remains: as if, piously asked for the outline of his sketch of the Deity, Emerson had replied that "line in nature is not found" (W, IX, 14).[7]

The problem, then—significant enough to warrant a longer-than-usual discussion—is simply to propose a "psycho-social" reading of Emerson's "Address" that yet gives adequate attention to its domain and decorum of argument. Granted its personal urgency, does it nevertheless pay a "decent respect to the opinions" and the capacities of its presumed audience? What, accordingly, can we say about its "form"? Is there anything in either its generic implication or its particular composition which would entitle its author to feel he had made his matter clear enough, as clear as that matter admits, so that further commentary would be gratuitous and painfully beside the point? And what *is* that matter? Beyond its general but also traditional premise that religious truths are "spiritual" rather than "notional," subjective rather than historical, and short of its tendentious but not unsupported conclusion that New England Unitarianism had dwindled to a cult of personality, does it frame any historically intelligible proposition of natural or scriptural theology? Does it say what it means by the "moral sentiment" (77)? Does it at least hint how that "solution" dissolves skepticism itself?

Is there, in short, an Emersonian *doctrine* worthy of its prosy name? Or is all just tonal objection and pious postponement, which we have fallen into the habit of regarding as different enough, somehow, to be thought of as "literary"? We should beware, of course, of asking too much, all at once, particularly from a statement which (Emerson knew) was definitively ending one career and sense of identity and which (accordingly) we expect to be doing a fair amount of work that is not precisely philosophical. But unless it does at least some of the implied intellectual work, we may have to conclude, with Norton and Ware, or with Yvor Winters, that Emerson is best understood as a confused thinker and a failed Christian. And await his redemption as discourse or as *differance*.

If historical imagination is any guide in such matters, it probably took the original audience of Emerson's "Address"—the assembled faculty and student body of Harvard's (graduate and increasingly professional) Divinity School— a moment or two to get over a certain electric thrill at the lavishly sensual, even "voluptuary" mood of its opening sentences. Possibly it took several moments more to realize that the "aureate" language of the first paragraph was designed to give way, by a law already approximated in *Nature*, to the idiom of philosophical idealism. It may even be fair to suppose that most of these "liberal" (yet really somewhat cautious) Christians never did get over Emerson's uncanny ability to derive the active moral faculty from a process beginning most naturally in the reactive passion of the "organic faculty": what, after all, did one mean by calling the moral sense a *sense*?[8] But surely no one left Divinity Hall without realizing he had heard an utterly religious discourse; essentially a sermon.

133

Though the context was school and not church, the sober commencement of several divinity students rather than the solemn ordination of a single minister, the evidence suggests that Emerson meant to raise the spiritual tone of an event that threatened to be merely "academic." Indeed that complex intention defines the formal irony of the famous first paragraph, which Emerson made not only arresting but also as religious as he knew. Argumentations might develop along the way; and with them, certain unhappy charges and specifications so local as to be almost personal. But apparently he felt that none of those things could fairly follow unless one began with an experience of "the holy," one which no audience, "in its senses," could possibly resist. Others might discover the religious impulse, long ago, in ignorance or in fear; but for Emerson the entire enterprise was presently null and predictably doomed unless it might arise from a lively response to the (mysterious) excellence of the world "in which our senses converse" (76). In that regard, at least, religion could not be other than "natural." And, as the alternative was some *contemptus* that never could entirely evade the charge of Manicheanism, even "schools" needed to recognize the point: being is good, even at its furthest remove from the blissful One; nor is our lowest reception of it anything but "perfect in its kind" (I, 11). So if the initial dose is strong, it seems nevertheless essential, originary.

On the one hand, of course, no one familiar with Emerson's earlier, more ordinary performances as a preacher could be surprised to hear him begin with the irresistible grace of "Summer."[9] Nor, alarmed as that institution might become about the implications of "Natural Supernaturalism," was the Unitarian pulpit altogether hostile to the matter of Romanticism. On the other hand, however, it might well have been disconcerting to hear Emerson thus poetically launch the career of the Soul from a "desk" whose decorum was less affective than intellectual. A Sunday morning sermon on the spiritual use of Nature was one thing, uplifting in its way, unless one somehow got too far too fast. But a Sunday evening lecture-turned-sermon on the primacy of natural experience—delivered as a sort of summa of religious schooling— was something else altogether. As if an ordinary commencement speaker should take for his text: "One impulse from a vernal wood."

Nor will it do to suppose that the academic challenge was particularly innocent, however we construe the reply to Ware. A letter to Carlyle, written at about the same time, records Emerson's clear (if retrospective) sense that he had "written & read a kind of Sermon to the senior class of our Cambridge Theological School."[10] And the substance of that sermon reveals a "kind" that is entirely familiar: by the time Emerson is transmuting the "moral" (77) into the "religious sentiment" (79), he is evidently expounding the "doctrines" he has meant to derive from his Ur-text of Nature; and when he begins to enumerate and then prejudicially illustrate the defects of historical Christianity, the traditional reader clearly sees he has passed on to the needful "application" or "use." Indeed it is hard to resist the conclusion that the "Address" is, in formal terms, one of the most traditional sermons Emerson ever gave.[11] Deliberately. As part of the insult.

Yet it is this very sense—of a studied determination, from the outset, to "read them a sermon," to teach them (at last) some absolutely fundamental religious truth—which raises the question of strife or local competition in its most distressing form. Possibly Emerson was discovering more about the anxieties of his peculiar psyche than he was managing to reveal about the steady calm of the impersonal Soul. Especially as the Journals record, before the public fact, a number of uneasy anticipations of the complex psycho-social act he was about to perform.

Clearly Emerson wanted to believe not only in the inevitability (and therefore the pious reception) of the proposition he was preparing to deliver, but also, and perhaps more so, in the unalloyed purity of his own motive. Indeed those two austere conditions went hand-in-hand in his well developed theory of "prophecy," a form of authoritative yet disinterested proclamation, not at all an argumentation. Bolder than he had dared to be in 1832, and well aware that he was indeed preparing to deliver some doctrine "which shocks the religious ear of the people," he needed also to feel that he was merely redirecting the general impulse of worship—from Jesus, the principal avatar and example, to the "moral sentiment," the divine principle itself. How could that be bad? Above all else, however, he needed to trust his own sense of lucid authenticity:

> When I have as clear a sense as now that I am speaking simple truth without any bias, any foreign interest in the matter,—all railing, all unwillingness to hear, all danger of injury to the conscience, dwindles & disappears. I refer to the discourse now growing under my eye to the Divinity School. (JMN, VII, 41–42)[12]

This remarkable passage may help explain the surprise Emerson felt at the fury he evoked. But, like all whistling in the dark, it invites us to ask what fear is being repressed.

Elsewhere, as it seems, Emerson's self-estimate was a little more self-searching. He warns himself to "beware of Antinomianism" (JMN, V, 496), but also, and more fundamentally, he notices that those rare moments in which the impersonal beauty of truth was sufficient to raise him "out of fear & out of time" were altogether transitory: "Strange the succession of humors that pass through this human spirit. Sometimes I am the organ of the Holy Ghost & sometimes of a vixen petulance" (JMN, VII, 9). Timely warning, as "petulance" would be no bad name for the feelings aroused by the tireless visits and tiresome preaching of Henry Ware and Barzillai Frost; and by the dismal spectacle (as he saw it) of an entire generation of Unitarians who had exchanged their literary birthright for the "intense grumbling enunciation of the Cambridge sort, & for scripture phraseology" (JMN, V, 471).

Harsher names might be applied to Emerson's increasing impatience with "old man" Ripley, the step-grandfather whose "foolishest preaching" on the punitive local consequence of the Second Coming "bayed at the moon," and whose bespectacled but still perplexed eyes not only typified "Moabitish darkness" but actually "reminded one of the squash bugs who stupid stare at you when you lift the rotten leaf of the vines" (JMN, VII, 22). And possibly only clinical language applies when all such "grandfathers" are required not only to "hush" but to "die," so to "let the new generation speak the truth" (JMN, VII, 39). Clearly it had been a danger, if also somehow, painfully, a necessity, for the Emerson who wanted to abandon much of the tradition in which he first thrived, to keep attending regular Unitarian services, whenever he was not himself engaged as "preacher of supply." And evidently his "bias" or "interest" in the matter of the "Address" was not so much "foreign" as familiar, even if one takes no proximate account of the provoking influence of his (absent) father's inhibiting strictures on the "transcendental" tradition of Ann Hutchinson and Jonathan Edwards.[13]

Still, the Journals are not without anticipations of a somewhat more intellectual sort. Conversations with the "friendly Youths" of the Divinity School repeatedly turned Emerson's attention to the question of "Theism" and reminded him that many persons not *yet* overcommitted to Unitarianism's evolving creed found his views of the "impersonality of God desolating & ghastly." To them he would simply confess, as never to Ware:

> I cannot find when I explore my own consciousness any truth in saying that God is a Person, but the reverse. I feel there is some profanation in saying He is personal. To represent him as an individual is to shut him out of my consciousness. (JMN, V, 457)

A hostile analysis might suppose that Emerson, fearful of the Edwardsian sovereignty, dimly suspected that a personal God would so exhaust the condition of personhood as to leave the humanist without resource. A more forgiving (and equally philosophical) reading would merely observe that, as Emerson's idealism never could theorize a union of persons, so God, to be "in" man, had to exist as a principle prior to all individuation. It might, in the end, even blame Fichte. Or Descartes.

But instead of spelling out this implication, already hinted at in *Nature*—that the "Self of Self" cannot be imaged as an infinitized human personality—a second conversation rather easily diverts attention from the logical implications of theological tropes to the rhetorical conditions of the local clergy.

> The Divinity School youths wished to talk with me concerning theism. I went rather heavy-hearted for I always find that my views chill or shock people at the first opening. But the conversation went well & I came away cheered. I told them that the preacher should be a poet smit with love of the harmonies of moral nature:—and yet look at the Unitarian Association & see if its aspect is poetic. They all smiled No. A minister nowadays is plainest prose, the prose of prose. (JMN, V, 471)

Unwittingly, perhaps, but notably in any case, the movement of this evaded confrontation appears to imitate in advance the structure of the "Address" itself which, after its opening invocation, moves through a highly suggestive but elliptical discussion of the problem of personality versus divinity to a frontal and absolutely confident assault on the spiritual condition of the local "Cultus" (81). Perhaps it would not be unfair to conclude, simply, that an anxious Emerson always felt surer of himself in the mode of satire than on the ground of theory.

And yet, as Emersonian "prophecy"—the absolute and impersonal duty to proclaim what ought to be evident to all—involves neither satire nor theory, it would be a mistake to stop at just this point, even in the shadowy domain of private pre-text. Evidently Emerson, despite his protest, needed to use his "Address" personally, to "resign" once more: not from a parish this time, and not necessarily from preaching; not even from all one might ever mean by a large and expanding tradition of "liberal Christianity"; but from the by now too-established sect of Unitarianism. Thus his withering attack on its clergy, together with his most cordial invitation to those "friendly youths" not yet so established, is far more than an afterthought. Neither is it, primarily, a way of shifting the ground from an argument he could not win, against the old guard, to a quarrel he could not lose, with the new (including, by literary implication, us). He needed to justify himself. Yet the verdict upon "the famine of our churches" (85) had to be a necessary conclusion as well as an inevitable outcome.

Along with so much else, the Journals frankly propose that "there is no better subject for effective writing than the Clergy":

> I ought to sit & think & then write a discourse to the American Clergy showing them the ugliness & unprofitableness of theology & churches at this day & the glory & sweetness of the Moral Nature out of whose pale they are almost wholly shut. (JMN, V, 464)

137

We might worry, of course, just what "artistic" goal Emerson means to propose by "effective writing"—suspecting, as always, that his concept of religion was too literary by half, just as we can observe that the actual implementation of his plan is neither disinterested nor even, in all supposable senses, fairly representative. But we do him less than intellectual justice if we entirely shift the ground of our criticism from the prophetically general, which he steadfastly sought to occupy, to the anxiously personal, which he tried his best to abandon.

We do well, in this regard, to remember that Emerson did not, in the end, write simply a discourse *on* the American Clergy. Formally, at least, his satiric remarks occupy no such independent status. They offer themselves, rather, as the inevitable Application of some doctrine about which all theologically literate persons had inescapably to decide. Acceptance of that doctrine is highly prejudiced, of course, by the "conversionist" epistemology in whose rhetoric it is embedded: those who cannot accept the saving insight as propounded to the intuition first mark themselves as spiritually (or hermeneutically) blind; then they fall perforce into the sad condition of belatedness which, except for some apparently indestructable habit of solemn speech and pious reception, were impossible to distinguish from usurpation or fraud. But such is always the urgent rhetoric (and the circular logic) of those who seem to see "The Danger of an Unconverted Ministry."[14] And as Emerson quite deliberately activates that lapsed but latent and dangerous tradition, it will not do to deny him the power and peril of his choice. Emerson knows his precedents. And Spiritism is like that.

So, for that matter, may be poetry: after some more or less self-parodic placement of and commentary on its peculiar code, we either do or do not understand and believe in (i.e., love) a poem. And in these terms we may yet come to take seriously Emerson's meta-critical claim that "Jesus [was] a poet & his labor a poem" (JMN, V, 482). One consequence of this poetic re-vision would be a renewed estimate of Emerson's charge that the Unitarian clergy was simply "unpoetic." He might intend less that preacher A or B was boring or inept than that an entire readerly community had committed itself to a naïve, if ever so "historical" reading of its founding text. Possibly the post-Enlightenment imperative was not at all to ignore or suppress supernatural claims that could not be rationalized.[15] Certainly it was not to insist that certain tropes were privileged beyond all question, merely because "We love to address the Father" and find the tendency benign.

This same "poetic" context may eventually help us to a sympathetic understanding of Emerson's relation to Jesus—surely the "agon" of most crucial importance to the enduring significance to the "Address." As Jonathan Bishop shrewdly observes, Emerson ventures to translate Jesus' commanding words into his own more softly suasive idiom. Noticeably that translation involves an equation of the moral with the esthetic. Arguably this "erosion" spells a rhetorical defeat for Emerson exactly where he had planned a philosophical victory, or at least a prophetic standoff. Expecting some strong redefinition of "the new Christ," we are offered only "the reception of beautiful sentiments." And as that result *can* seem more sentimental than sublime, we may end up preferring the Jesus original to the Emerson translation. An ironic literary outcome, surely, and not without implications for the competing philosophical senses of history, persons, and "the body."[16]

In any event, however, a simpler point is perfectly clear: the moment of confrontation with Jesus is—like Edwards' bout with Identity—as deliberately staged as it is anxiously motivated. More than his quarrel with Ware or Frost, Emerson's contest with Jesus (and with Unitarian Christology) is essential and long-standing. Largely repressed in earlier utterances, it is here publically announced and practically adumbrated. A prophet of the highest order, Jesus is scarcely to be placed beyond the range or the need of interpretation; his *words* require "translation" no less than those of Luther, Fox, or the Swedenborgians, all of whom had rightly produced their own lively translations.[17] Further, as the opening of the "Address" means to propose that the esthetic experience leads on to the moral, so Emerson can hardly be criticized, just here, for translating the eventual back into the originary. Indeed he might well argue, in his own defence, that his "reduction" was really a necessary re-authentication, a returning of a more complex and socialized idiom to its simpler, more organic form. Jesus had spoken as a reformer of the Jewish legalism, beautifully internalizing "the Law," but addressing the matter of justification still. Law remained the premise of Paul. But surely Joy was the condition of Life.

Or, if that were available mysticism rather than valid interpretation, one had at least to say what Jesus had "meant," by glowing word and more radiant example. The poem was wonderful but it did not explain itself. Not even the words announced their full intent. Even if they were, at all events, the very words once spoken—which "criticism" was less and less prepared to affirm with certainty. Yet whosoever words they were, they either did or did not recapitulate the structure of reality, summarize the limit possibility of the human case. If they did, they were God's own words, whatever scholarship might conclude about the fidelity of the literary executors of Jesus. If not, they were merely words. To suppose otherwise was to maintain, in awkward liberal form, the orthodox fallacy of linguistic presence. Worse than a failure of Enlightenment, this ghostly reverence was in fact idolatry.

And that—negatively considered, at least—is the true propositional setting of Emerson's Divinity School "Sermon." Only momentarily does it reinvoke the issue of "Miracles." Only indirectly does it question "The Personality of the Deity." Only by implication does it threaten to undermine a social order based on sacerdotal hegemony. Only by exemplum does it satirize local ineptitude. Most directly it charges that the Unitarians had, in the name of religious liberalism, selectively idolized the tropes of the historical Jesus; and then, by the familiar literary transference, they had fallen to excessive regard of his literal person. And this while strenuously denying, as condition of their sectarian integrity, that Jesus had ever really claimed divine entitlement.

The Unitarians had, of course, their reasons, as any moderately patient account of their own conservative but evolving logic(s) could sufficiently show. With controlled *impatience*, however, Emerson seeks to derive their spiritual attenuation from their intellectual confusion. Assumed, no doubt, is some new and evolving hermeneutic, to which Schleiermacher, Herder, and even Strauss may yet provide the clue. Expressed, however—and even announced, in the form of a cardinal New Testament "text"—is an utterly coherent, if "poetic" Christology. Not precisely a theology of "Christ Crucified," though even that might be (imperfectly) implied in Emerson's poetic restoration.[18] But quite self-consciously a theory of God-manifest. And with that, a justification of nonpersonal spiritual authority, all of it depending on some necessary, if "allegorical," distinction between the historical "Jesus" and the sover-

139

eign "Christ." All of it designed, thereby, to transfer worshipful imitatio from the historical fact to the divine principle.

Accordingly, the insult could hardly be more studied, the "sermon" more pointed: the "Address" means to force, once again, some absolutely crucial distinction of theology, one actually better observed by the Orthodox (and the Quakers) than by the Liberals. Personal anxiety there clearly is, as Emerson seeks both to define and to occupy a space for his own deed of prophecy. Even more relevant, however, may be a meta-rhetorical condition we could name "the anxiety of audience," as Emerson proposes to address the Unitarian intelligensia on the issue of their own deepest insecurity. Granted: the historical Jesus could not "also" be—identically, or by mystic participation—the principle of effective creation (and/or efficacious holiness). And yet he had, in despite of Unitarian uneasiness, indeed claimed to embody as well as to express Divinity. To the death he had claimed it, when the merest verbal refinement or ambiguity about his divine claim could have got him off the cross. Not to be repressed or elided, however, this scandal evidently required translation. And, discoverably, such translation is the positive work of Emerson's "Address."

To claim that the "Address" is in fact a sermon, that it offers itself (accordingly) as a gloss on a text of the New Testament, and that its domain is (formally, at least) as much scriptural interpretation as rational speculation, is not at all to undermine the structural significance—or the literary power—of Emerson's "philosophical" beginning. The first three paragraphs do indeed recapitulate and refine his earlier derivation of all the contiguous and hierarchical faculties of "the Soul." To that extent Emerson's "text" is indeed "Nature," as previously written by himself, or as eternally preinscribed in the world's own proto-linguistic structure.[19] But this textual outsetting is by no means complete until Emerson has specifically identified the outcome of his own, impressively homegrown "phenomenology of Spirit" with the biblical "Christ." As soon as Emerson's nameless and utterly nonspecific representative of "the mind" has "opened" so far as to realize, absolutely, and as good as declare, categorically, that "He ought," so soon is "the end of the creation answered." But in that same moment we recognize—identically, despite the shift in idiom—the beloved Son with whom God is "well pleased" (77).

The familiar text is merely "echoed," we might nervously observe; yet familiar as it is, it is also plainly announced. And with it Emerson clearly discovers the utterly lucid purpose of his most provocative opening. What he has been pressing toward, all the while, with an urgency that sinews the lavish expansiveness of his prose poem to the "refulgent summer," is the New Testament text which first establishes, or publishes, Jesus as in fact "the Christ"—forcing the faithful interpreter to pause once again on the distinction between historical person and divine office or function.[20] Those who have ears had better learn to hear.

The exact "source" of Emerson's specific "text" is almost certainly Matthew 3.13–17, but it is important to remember that Mark and Luke produce almost exactly the same formula of Christic recognition and endorsement: "This in my beloved Son, with whom I am well pleased." And even John delivers a version of the scene to which Emerson means to direct our attention.[21] It is, of course, the baptism. About to begin his public ministry, Jesus (after a "long foreground somewhere") has come up to the Jordan, to encounter John "the Baptist," the self-conscious precursor, to be baptized by him, even though anyone familiar with the plot in advance might suppose, with John, that their roles were about to get painfully reversed: Me? Baptize You?! Yet the ritual washing is accomplished, with the minimum of social awkwardness; and it—along with the dove descending and the miraculous voice of endorsement from heaven— is duly, indeed redundantly recorded. When God talks, the reader had better listen.

The scene comes early in the text of all four of the received gospels, earlier in some than in others. In no account, however, is it anything like a literary "beginning." In no account, that is, does "the Christ" simply burst on the scene, full-formed by the will of the Father. Extraordinary revelation there well may be. But no magical advent. Clearly the moment is an event as well as an origin. The "Christ" is divine, no doubt, but evidently "Jesus" was not always already that, an avatar looking for a place to occur. Unlike the mysterious "claimant" of romance, the gospel-hero must undergo somewhat more than the discovery of his own true last name. And evidently something comes before that.

For John, what precedes is, famously, the massive a priori of his own *logos*-theology: the eternity of "the Word" and the urgency of its manifestation in the "flesh." Then, in but an instant of real time, the epoch-making recognition or "witness" by the Baptist. Equally abrupt, yet fundamentally historical, Mark begins with a summary account of the preparatory mission of the Baptist, including his most humble sense of being the precursor merely. Luke, at some opposite extreme of personal interest in "the historical Jesus," tells the entire tale of family preparation, elaborates the "Christmas" event complete with shepherds, and provides as much as most readers have thought relevant or recoverable from the natural life of Jesus within (and, once, in the temple, without) his "holy family"; then, finally, the baptism. Falling somewhere between, Matthew provides a rapid-fire account of the authentic genealogy, the marvelous "annunciation" to Mary, the miraculous virgin birth, and the providential evasion of Herod; but then, again climactically, the same remarkable change of phase. Jesus of Nazareth was born of woman, and no doubt; but

141

the Christ has still to be manifest. Divinity lurks, but the heavenly opening occurs just "now."

The "Spirit of God" descends, dove-like, and the voice from heaven endorses, just when the conscience of Jesus as good as demands baptism from the scrupulous, protesting John—reminding his reluctant kinsman that, whatever else may be true, it is surely "fitting for us to fulfill all righteousness." Miracles attend the baptism of Jesus, but they are not his own. His own may follow, variously motivated by the plea or the challenge of the moment; and their effect on unbelief will be at least as various. But in the moment his way is simply to refuse to be put off from his own sense of duty: to submit, not to John, but to the transpersonal authority that is over them both, and to the universal typology of water, which may forecast Emerson's own preferred figure of Spirit. And the heavens open in response to just that. Poetically considered, it is the same as if some precocious solution were already given; as if some mere acolyte had guessed the riddle of the universe.[22]

Thus is the first realization of the divine Christ identically "the end of the Creation" (77). Not the end of the world, to be sure, but an apocalypse in good conscience. Well might the heavens open: someone without "any foreign interest in the matter" has dedicated himself to perfect righteousness. As the dedication seems somewhat legal or ritualistic, in the Jewish manner, it will scarcely count as the final word in the history of absolute commitment, but it represents a completion so perfect that nothing to follow can be imagined to please God differently or better. A crucifixion might confirm the intent, but it could never improve the meaning.

So are we forced by sermonic context to reconstruct Emerson's latent but active interpretation of text. And, while we are about it, we swiftly infer a crucial principle of his reading of the New Testament: "Jesus" is everywhere taken to name an authentic, partially recoverable and largely admirable exemplar in the history of mankind's literally episodic but morally continuous attempt to express the holy; "Christ," however, belongs to an entirely different order of reality. Not simply another, truer name for the same singular personage, a patronymic hidden until revealed, it designates, instead, an ideal or at least an "allegorical" possibility, one which the "inspired" gospel authors have sufficiently evoked in a single literary moment—proving, in that moment, the quality of their own inspiration. Coming up from some obscure "historical" beginning in Galilee, Jesus goes on to generate, famously, a public record of teachings, miracles, sufferings, and death over which the pious seem destined to struggle with the sceptics forever. But Christ expresses that condition of dedication which the pure of heart experience as the inevitable foundation of their identity, which Kant named a structure, and which Hume could assuage only by an occasional, friendly game of backgammon.

If the Scriptures were to be trusted as in any manner historical, Jesus was in fact a most remarkable man. In one sense, a singular exception: in claiming divinity, he revealed himself "the only soul in history who has appreciated the worth of a man," the only fair expositor, so far, of the grand premise that "God incarnates himself in man." Yet the divinity he calmly claimed was not in the least personal, was not in any sense his *own*: "Having seen that the law in us is commanding, he would not suffer it to be commanded. Boldly, with hand, and heart, and life, he declared *it* was God" (81, emph. added). To be venerated, therefore—worshiped even—was not *him* but *it*. And thus the heavenly voice commending the dramatic revelation of this saving insight must itself be heard poetically.

As doves descend only as a literary sign of some authentic manifestation of spiritual intelligence, so God "himself" can never truly say his sense in articulate human speech. A rare trope, and rarely to be used. But when more appropriately than when somebody has grasped "the thought that is parent of the universe" (IV, 103)? Whenever lowly man shall attain to say "I love the Right; Truth is beautiful within and without, forevermore" (77), then, surely, may the speechless but symbol-generating God be thought to utter his perfect pleasure. Then only can we recognize the capital figure of the "beloved son."

Problems abound, of course, only some of which are specifically addressed in the course of Emerson's primal sermon. When and how has Emerson learned to read Scripture just as he does? Whose principle suggests that we may trust the naturalistic detail literally and look for allegory only when we encounter the marvellous? And what, finally, is the stable, philosophical source of the allegory? Such things nowhere authenticate themselves. It is one thing to suppose that there are, in "all those religious writings which were in their origin poetic" certain "ecstatic expressions which the first user did not know what he said" (JMN, VIII, 74), but quite another to know the order of reality in which such inspired utterances happily participate. Whose lucid categories guarantee Matthew's prescient half-knowledge that Virtue is indeed the End of the Universe?

What should be clear beyond cavil, however, is that Emerson's Divinity School Sermon deliberately conflates the outcome of his one most stable religious phenomenology with Scripture's account of the moment when Jesus of Nazareth stood revealed as the "beloved" (that is, "chosen") expression of divine purpose.[23] That he felt no particular uneasiness about translating providential direction as universal teleology. And that he was absolutely assured in his determined philosophizing of the baptism scene, relocating the emphasis on "miracle" from the trope of magical discovery to the reality of spiritual dedication.

Most of Emerson's Journal entries in the wake of this condensed exegesis seem either tense and tight-lipped or else vaguely hurt and defensive. Yet as

143

the shock eases and the repression lifts, one remarkable passage reveals, at a stroke, the hermeneutics that ought to have been clear to an audience no less well prepared than it was anxious:

> You prefer to see a dove descending visibly on Jesus; I too acknowledge his baptism by the spirit of God. And which is greater & more affecting, to see some wonderful bird descending out of the sky, or, to see the rays of a heavenly majesty of the mind & heart emitted from the countenance & port of a man? (JMN, VII, 236)

How, Emerson must have been wondering—how, without admixture of superstition—could anyone construe his text otherwise? Had they not read their Paine, let alone their Hume? Admitted on all sides, apparently, was the (Channingesque) principle that "it is the distinction of Christianity, that it is moral" (JMN, IV, 383).[24] How, therefore, to contend for some *other* superiority as well, some ghostlier variant of the old claim of mystic derivation and magical advent? Were not that miracle, taken at face value, as monstrous as any other?

Granted the Spirit: was not the Christ perfectly recognizable as such? Had not Channing's admirable view of the Christian "Evidences" long since conceded, if not gloried in, just this point? Had not Ripley already elaborated this "better mode of evidence," out of the Soul no less than out of Germany? And had not the claim in fact been Jesus' own? As he had asked the agents of ill-tempered unbelief "Which is easier?"—to cure the soul or the body?—so Emerson asks, "Which is greater?"—to take the point of the sovereignty of the Spirit in its own terms or to refer it to signs of a more positive order? Say the secret word and divide the Godhead. Or perhaps the Spirit was *not* in fact being granted, any more than the difference between the career of Jesus and the Life of Christ. Perhaps the Unitarian reduction had been as devastating as it was complete. And perhaps Emerson's sermon was, in its revolutionary way, as Trinitarian as it was Christological.

After all, the same text which forced distinction between Jesus and Christ also provided one of orthodoxy's few scriptural reasons for insisting on the tripartite division the Unitarians found confusing, or distracting, or simply inelegant. Yet possibly the old instinct had been sound, in its own poetic-predictive way. Occult entities were not to be multiplied, but cases had to be covered. And there, in any event, they all were: prophet, bird, and heavenly voice. The problem involved more than counting, of course, and surely there could be no return to the vexed question of "persons": "the Soul" knew them not. Certain it is, however, that Emerson's *final* application concerns not any longer the identity of Christ but the universality of the Spirit. That too, we ought to recognize, was part of the insult: the old way, poetically considered, was the truer.

Yet that is also ahead of the argument. For the body of Emerson's sermon—extraordinarily patient by the standards we have been discovering—takes great pains to get its audience past the the complex question of the "limited personality" (JMN, VII, 167) of the composite "Jesus Christ." And some of these pains are doubtless Emerson's own. Lurking, that is to say, and not very well concealed, are signs of a long-standing problem: the psycho-literary meaning of Emerson's natural supernaturalism; his need, that is, to deny that the powerful prophecy of Jesus left room, in latter days, for interpretation only. Nor, given the clear determination of Emerson's textual strategy, will it reduce the impact of his theological daring to reconsider its relation to his keenest sense of writerly strife.

We need to set figures such as Frost and Ware aside from the most significant plot of the "Address": local effects rather than root causes, they seem epiphenomenal to Emerson's private quarrel with Unitarian Christology; response to them would take the form of prophetic anger, not literary anxiety. Neither will the looming presence of "Pope" Andrews Norton quite unlock the secret of Emerson's rebellion against belatedness and repression: learned as he was, and utterly committed to the conservative implications of his burden of the past, he embodied a position first too predictable and then too self-assured and acrimonious to activate Emerson's nicest uncertainties; somebody had to be retrogressively, defensively wrong, and Norton easily filled up that "infidel" identity.[25] Yet short of the ultimate example of Jesus—itself reconceived as not quite ultimate—there intrudes the instructive lesson of William Ellery Channing, oddly predictive of the finally inescapable problem. Indeed we get the impression that for a time the two are mixed up together in Emerson's religious allegiance.

In the end, of course, no guide could be truly "happy" if his path led at last to an acceptance of the one-time significance of the historical Jesus, however perfectly imitable his own exemplary "Likeness to God" might prove: what the soul craved was not perfect recapitulation but "original relation" (I, 7). Yet clearly this admirable religious personage, this "bishop" to the emerging Transcendentalists, had pointed a way once joyously followed. And as Emerson's originality comes to seem a series of significant departures or differences, so his decision to abandon Channing's high road of liberal intermediation may stand out as a literary event of the first magnitude. For it overstates the anxiety of this influence only slightly to suggest that Emerson had begun his career as a "professional" Unitarian more as a convinced emulator of Channing than as a convicted disciple of Christ.

145

Most noticed in Emerson's famous (1824) dedication of his time, talents, and hopes to "the church" is its actively literary character: "passionate love for the strains of eloquence" appears to count for at least as much as the sublime veneration of "the laws of Morals." Equally noticeable, however, and no less problematic, surely, is the clear implication that Emerson's desire "to put on eloquence as a robe" (JMN, II, 242) involved as well the wish to don the mantle of Channing. Recognizing an "immoderate fondness for writing," and needing to justify or redeem a "reasoning faculty" regarded as "proportionately weak," Emerson offered "Dr. Channing's Dudleian Lecture" as the very "model" of the religious work his own self-puzzling mix of faculties might hope to produce.

Assuring himself that "the highest species of reasoning on divine subjects is rather the fruit of a sort of moral imagination, than of the 'Reasoning Machines,' such as Locke Clarke and David Hume," Emerson specifically invokes the sanction of Channing's "Evidences of Revealed Religion." Its sweeping, ascending, and not quite argumentative method provides the enabling condition of his own career, especially as the faculty which produced that discourse seemed "akin to the higher flights of fancy" (JMN, II, 238).

Arguably the terms of Emerson's uncertain but very earnest dedication would be clarified by the application of some still inchoate distinction between the fancy and the imagination; so that it may indeed be impossible to overstate the transcendental stimulus Emerson would yet receive from Coleridge. Or perhaps it may yet come to appear that James Marsh's 1829 edition of the *Biographia* was second in importance, that year, to Sereno Dwight's publication of the *Works* of President Edwards. Unarguable, however, is the observation that the aspiring divinity student—reminding himself in 1824 that "in a month I shall be legally a man" (JMN, II, 237)—adopted the mentor who was preparing him for graduate study at the Divinity School as his model of ministerial efficacy. He wanted to be like Channing when he grew up.

Nor is it difficult for the reader of Channing's 1821 Dudleian Address to imagine what form the imitation would take: Emerson wanted to re-do (perhaps out-do) the higher logic of Channing's rather special treatment of the Christian "evidences"—to find a way to preclude Hume without ever quite answering him in his own terms. Well begun by Wesley T. Mott, the *whole* story of Emerson's relation to the themes and emphases of Channing's preaching may have to await a widespread assessment of the entire corpus of Emerson's Unitarian sermons, as they now appear in a full-dress modern edition; yet the influence of Channing's strong suggestion seems strikingly clear from the pulpit productions of "Young Emerson" long in print. In marked contrast with the historical, even "positivist" import of the authoritative teaching (and then the magisterial tome) of Andrews Norton, Channing exhibits an extreme friendliness toward, even a rhetorical emphasis upon certain "internal" evidences of Christianity's saving truth. Indeed the text in question works (as I have suggested elsewhere) toward a brief but climactic expression of the position which Ripley would famously propose and defend in the much-discussed "Miracles Controversy"; namely, that the adequate evidence of Christianity's unique status as divine revelation is not positive but "moral," that its acceptance depends less on the authority of its witnesses or the credibility of its miracles than on the vital appeal it makes to the religious sensibility of the individual believer.[26]

Traditionally, of course, "internal evidences" referred to the question of the authorial integrity of the Scriptural texts themselves, their manifestation of an organic wholeness which resists the suspicion of clever, collaborative imposture and convinces the reader that some whole story is being faithfully presented. Nor is Channing's alertness to modernist literary fallacy quite keen enough to prevent his own manipulation of this perilous argument. More significant, however, is the fact that his treatment of more extrinsic matters is itself highly internalized: putative miracles are declared meaningless apart from the moral character of the agent supposed to have performed these feats of magical power and from the end of the teaching they are purported to validate. Moreover, Channing's real miracle is, first and last, the altogether unpredictable yet utterly imposing character of Jesus himself: standing in the place where many had come to expect "a triumphant leader" of the subjugated Jewish nation, this astonishing Messiah confidently pronounced "the abolition of the peculiarity of Moses" and calmly proclaimed the universal application of love. Well might history blink. Even the literary "invention" of such a character, at such a time, Channing would regard as miraculous. So that his inspiring address closes not with arguments but with the mere observation of the perfectly efficacious "adaptation" of the Christic teaching to the "noblest faculties" of man. Surprised at first, honest souls then (and later) recognize their salvation when they hear it announced. Thus the "conviction of the divine original of our religion" rests at last on evidences utterly unlike those propounded by "the learned books of Christian apologists."[27] Wisely, certainly, the Soul embraces it own.

All this, of course, is *very* old news by 1838, as the pretext of the "Address" includes not only the logic of Channing and its amplification by Ripley, but Emerson's own revisions of that logic in the sermons following his "approbation." A version of the sermon we have known as "The Authority of Jesus" (LXXVI, May, 1830) defines every one of Jesus' prophetic strokes as "a naked appeal to every man's consciousness whether the fact be so or not," and suggests that it is his entirely internalized understanding of "command and obedience" that "more than miracles...moves the whole frame of human nature" (CS, 2: 361, 364). The crucial pronouncement on "Miracles" (CIII, Jan., 1831) brands those outward wonders "a lower species of evidence," addressed to

147

"ignorance" and far outweighed by "internal evidence"; so that "the truth taught in the New Testament will stand by itself" (CS, 3:82). And a sermon given at the moment of resignation from the Second Church, and pointing toward the meta-Christianity of many of his later teachings (CLXIV, former- ly "The Genuine Man," Oct., 1832), emphasizes the "absolute sovereignty" not of Jesus but of the receptive sense to which he had spoken, a supreme univer- sal Reason in your mind which is not yours or mine or any man's, but the Spirit of God in us all."[28]

As this frank naturalization of "the Spirit" may suggest, Emerson's position is already diverging from that of Channing; yet it is *from* that position that the Emersonian difference must be estimated. In one sense, Emerson comes to sound more like those most radical of the Puritans, the Quakers, than like any more famously liberal group.[29] But that is only to observe, once again, the cru- cial fact about his relation to available religious tradition: namely, that Emerson's mature version of Christianity was more a poetic reinterpretation than a rationalistic reduction of the complexus of orthodoxy. And we can sus- pect it gave him pause, even pain, to discover that not even Channing was pre- pared to move in that nonliteral direction. "Proto-transcendentalist" Channing may have been, but nothing more; for in the last analysis he refused to displace the historical Jesus from the cardinal premise of his syllogism of salvation.

Such a consideration adds "psychological" interest to the justly famous Journal passage of 1 Oct., 1832—in which Emerson willfully determines to consult his "own heart at first" (JMN, 4:45); and in which, it can be argued, he reveals more of the reasoning that led him out of the Unitarian ministry than in the Resignation Sermon itself. No local names are mentioned this time, only the supposedly universal one of Jesus, at the mention of which, Emerson noticed, minds as well as knees were being bent in awkward ways. Yet, given the logic of the position set down for refutation (or "transcen- dence"), it is impossible to avoid the inference that, formally at least, it is *Channing's* Jesus being rejected as ultimate religious warrant. Repressed, accordingly, is this painful irony: having suggested to Emerson that Jesus is rec- ognized as the Redeemer "because he declared...those truths on which the welfare of the human soul depends," Channing was yet unwilling to deny that there was *also* some "peculiar designation to the office of Messiah that gives authority to his words"; unwilling to say quite simply, that is, that it is "his words that mark him out as the Messiah."[30]

It comes to appear, accordingly, that the private rationale of Emerson's abandonment of the ministry is as nearly allied to the rejection of Channing as his dedication had been to the adoption. Emerson stopped being like Channing when he declared himself in *fact* grown up. Or when he found him- self able to formulate his own religious first premise: more internal still, and

148

separable in principle—if not quite separate in fact—from any historic example.

Announcing a full and final internalization of the problem of evidences, the passage in question also predicts (or actually announces, though long in advance) the pseudo-Dudleian job of work the Divinity School "Address" would have to perform. If no one else came forward to perform it sooner. Or if it would take that long for Emerson's mighty repression to permit an open response to his own private challenge: to say *all* that seemed implied in the new epistemology, whether the prophet of that position realized its last implication or not. For public as well as private reasons, then, the familiar passage is worth quoting at length:

> Has the doctrine ever been fairly preached of man's moral nature? The whole world holds on to formal Christianity, & nobody teaches the essential truth, the heart of Christianity for fear of shocking, &c. Every teacher when once he finds himself insisting with all his might upon a great truth turns up the ends of it at last with a cautious showing *how* it is agreeable to the life & teaching of Jesus—as if that was any recommendation. As if the blessedness of Jesus' life & teaching were not because they were agreeable to the truth. Well this cripples his teaching. It bereaves the truth he inculcates of more that half its force by representing it as something secondary that can't stand alone. The truth of truth consists in this, that it is self-evident, self-subsistent. It is light. You don't get a candle to see the sun rise. Instead of making Christianity a vehicle of truth you make the truth only a horse for Christianity. It is a very operose way of making people good. You must be humble because Christ says, 'Be humble.' 'But why must I obey Christ?' 'Because God sent him.' But how do I know God sent him? 'Because your own heart teaches the same thing he taught.' Why then shall I not go to my own heart at first? (JMN, IV, 45)

It really is all in that remarkable meditation: the invention of Transcendentalism considered as a perfect deconstruction of the very Liberal Christianity in which Emerson had long been preparing. And anybody who yet believes Emerson is not a prime religious thinker, nor an utterly lucid commentator on the state of his own professional art, should try explicating that whole passage some time, including its echo of what Thomas Shepard and John Cotton said to one another, long since, about a candle and the sun.

The opening question, about the "fair" preaching of "the doctrine...of man's moral nature" is a little less rhetorical than it appears. The answer is *no*, of course: "Nobody teaches the essential truth." But this discovery of universal dereliction proves a personal blessing as well as a public scandal: a prime

149

confusion of thought—and perhaps a failure of courage as well—has crippled the teaching of religion everywhere; but it has also left open the space in which someone might yet (re)publish the saving news. Liberal Christianity had done much, it appears, but not everything; not even the one essential thing, for which earnest intelligence seemed to be crying out. It required only that some inspired (or merely honest and clear-sighted) person step forward and set the matter straight. You don't need a Higher Critic to work out the Yankee logic of cart and horse.

Yet unless the person so tempted were impossibly unselfconscious or intolerably arrogant, this perceived failure of "the whole world" might give pause as well as occasion: perhaps there are good and sufficient reasons for not saying what is never said.[31] The private self could simply be wrong, God knows, however convinced; and so, "beware of Antinomianism" (JMN, 5: 496). Or else, even if stunningly correct, it might be largely misunderstood or misapplied, producing deleterious effects on a religious community not so bad it could not be made worse: too much criticism might easily bring on a "cold denying irreligious state of mind" (JMN, VII, 255). And deep down, of course, there was always a personal element, one's *own* "fear of shocking"—including, quite plausibly, one's reluctance to appear to outstrip, or show in a bad light, the guides who had brought one to the brink and then pulled back.

Not Frost or Ware, quite clearly; those lesser ephebes were not even, as Emerson finally convinced himself, the good and faithful students. Not Norton, presumably, so like other "Popes" in his failure to grasp the principle of human subjectivity. And not even, in a different sphere of influence, Coleridge, who—not yet having condescended to Channing or, worse, carried on about his own baptismal anniversary—seemed safe in the pantheon of International Romanticism.[32] But quite predictably Channing, who had in fact shown the way and whom, indirectly at least, the opening of the passage identifies as one who had stopped short of the evident spiritual terminus. Not even he, Emerson manages to imply, had "fairly preached" the importance of "*man's* moral nature" (Emphasis added).

Of *God's* moral nature, perhaps, so long as one retained the machinery of theism. Certainly Channing's epoch-making "Unitarian Christianity" (1819) had openly announced a "greater stress" on "the *moral perfection of God*" than on its two supposed "great points," namely, the strict unity of God and the consequent subordination of Jesus. Even here Emerson may have discovered problems eventually, as Channing's emphasis on God's "proper" (univocal) "benevolence" made his (capitalized) theory of God's "Parental character" seem scarcely a metaphor at all. But it would have been ungenerous to deny that Channing had been both vigorous and timely in his attack on the personalized version of Edwardsian "sovereignty" and on the New Divinity's conception of depravity as a sort of divine "constitution." Or that Channing's highly rhetorical outburst against a divine slander which had "arrogate[d]...the name of orthodoxy"—itself elaborated into the tendentious but highly effective polemic of "The Moral Argument Against Calvinism" (1820)—had almost single-handedly created a world in which some fair consideration of man's moral nature had begun to be possible.[33] For the fiction of imputation had been an impossible foundation on which to erect a liberal anthropology. And of course it precluded, a priori, a phenomenology of spirit in any way distinct from the narrative of some surprising conversion.

Still, another truth had to be recognized as well: when Channing's "Unitarian Christianity" came round to the question of "the moral nature of man," as the fifth and last of its practical deductions from a Scripture "rationally" interpreted, not much energy remained. What might have been a powerful climax—or else, at very least, an explicit invitation for more and bolder work to be done—became instead a sort of cautious self-defense. As the rhetoric is noticeably less vigorous, the prose less assured than on some earlier points, so the logic is extremely circumspect. And the main purpose is highly conservative: to assure the custodians of orthodoxy, ever on the alert for incursions of mere natural religion, that the so-called Unitarians "do not mean to deny the importance of God's aid" in the formation of "true holiness"; and to make it clear to all sober students of the history of enthusiasm that, as conscious opponents of radical awakening or instantaneous conversion, they would not bury the reason of virtue in the sensation of grace. As if Ellery Channing had turned himself back into Charles Chauncy, the cautious hero of Emerson's most conventional father.[34]

Thus the definitive manifesto of the newer, more "liberal" religion had ended with a judicious statement of the anti-Calvinist emphasis on the innate "sense of duty" as the "foundation" of all virtue. But it stopped well short of a "fair"—that is, full and general, open and unbiasaed—exploration of the religious consequences of what was, in New England at least, a radical moral doctrine. It thus demanded further thought, even if it seemed not at all to invite it. Nor, as Emerson's universal negative implies, had anyone (including Channing himself) yet answered the demand.

But the implication of Channing in Emerson's private announcement of transcendental departure is more than a rhetorical inference or even a psycho-structural inevitability. The peculiar shape of Emerson's final, self-thwarting argument identifies itself as distinctively (if parodically) Channing's own. After Emerson has moved, at the center of his meditation, through a querulous version of his already familiar argument about the authority of Jesus—not designation of person but inherency of principle—he proceeds to imagine the current state of Christian apologetics in this light. Most obvious about his final bare-bones dialectic is the fact that he is presenting the case of "historical Christianity" in a way that calls attention to its own near circularity. Just less

151

obvious (yet perfectly so, to the reader of Channing's "Evidences") is the fact
that, ironically, it is Channing's gesture of internalization which produces the
inelegant, indeed embarrassing overdetermination. If, on premise, we can, and
if in all good faith we *must* ask our "faculties" about the truth of the words of
Jesus, can we not suitably inquire of those same faculties in some more direct
and original manner?

Of course it is those very faculties that have introduced the unstable, even
disruptive element into an otherwise tidy (if tedious) form of historical argumentation. Ironically, therefore, the Channingesque premise serves chiefly to
ruin a formula that not even a latter-day revival of Arianism had been able to
unsettle. Believe (or obey, or imitate) Jesus. Why? Because God sent him. So
far so good, even though Jesus is admittedly God's "inferior." Now, *how do I
know* God sent him? How indeed? Not only Andrews Norton but the assembling sect of American Unitarians, in perfect agreement with William Paley
and with conservative Christians everywhere, wished to declare for "miracles":
his wonders prove his words. In New England, at least, and in prediction of
Emerson, Channing had been boldly forward in emphasizing the internal rat-
ification.[35] And rightly so, Emerson clearly felt. So that one *now* one replies
that Jesus is believed—indeed "is Christ"—"Because your own heart teaches
the same thing he taught." Why then not, Quaker-fashion, witness a Christ
nearer home than Jerusalem?

Evidently it takes God to know God, even as Cotton had tried with
increasing exasperation to explain to certain "Elders" who thought the Spirit
might be inferred by a logic of works. And though the question had moved
far off from the quaint calculus of sanctification and justification, the attempt
to discover something already necessarily there continued to seem "operose"
in the high Protestant sense of "worksy." And also, in another sense, just silly:
like taking a candle (or indeed a well trimmed lamp) to assist the sun's own
morning self-discovery.[36]

Thus the logic of American Unitarianism had, in Channing at least, come
round to a very curious position. A holding place, in Emerson's view, and—
unless a whole culture should suffer excessively from "fear of shocking"—not
likely to hold for long. Jesus had not been (nor had he actually claimed to be)
"of the same substance" with the Father. Yet he had been, avowedly and cred-
ibly, a uniquely designated bearer of the message of divine benevolence, and
of the need for the benevolent redirection of human impulse. His appearance
had been, therefore, an altogether necessary intrusion into the history of spiritual endeavor which were, otherwise, not salvation-history at all. The soul
needed to recognize the authority—and to heed the word—of this signally
anointed teacher, who was also, somehow, the only perfect practitioner of a
saving virtue otherwise not quite knowable as such. And yet, in this most liberal construction of the historical plot, it could recognize that publication of

virtue in its own terms. Authentic recognition was thus not extrinsic, by miracles, but properly internal, by confirmation of inherent capacity and a priori
expectation. Thus the Christic message could not be *entirely* unknown. And if
not, the venue of religious argument needed to be changed.

So long as "miracles" remained in place—the plausible answer of the common sense to the question of "How do I know God sent Jesus?"—the liberal
apologetic survived intact. What ruined it was not the frank and entire human-
ization of Jesus so much as the ambiguous and partial internalization of the
burden of revelation. Its obscure naturalization, so to speak. So long as the substance of the divine communication seemed sufficiently paradoxical or
strange, miracles provided the shock or "affront" needed to propel human
capacity beyond its customary expectation of encountering "the same." And
under that regime, no one could object to the habit of centering religious
attention on the person who worked wonders to confirm his unique teaching credential, his right to propound a strange new creed: not God, yet a sine
qua non of divine pedagogy, such an agent surely commanded all solemn
attention. But when Jesus, no longer a Jewish blood-sacrifice or an Anselmian
atoning substitute, was thought to declare, with clarity and emphasis, something the soul was supposed to know, dimly, but always-already, the sense of
his centrality was profoundly altered. And relentless attention to the historical
Jesus now easily identified itself as the latest form of idolatry.

Any such outcome was, of course, intensely ironic within the framework of
Unitarian rhetoric. One of its strongest practical or "moral" arguments against
the trinitarian separation of powers had been, all along, that the extreme reverence paid to the character and activities of the historical Jesus distracted the
mind of the believer from its ultimate, transhistorical (yet still Fatherly) object.
Denial of incarnate divinity would work, Channing insisted, to prevent this
embarrassing deflection of "worship."[37] And Emerson's own Resignation
Sermon confessed "Unitarianism" in just these terms, namely, "that every
effort to pay religious homage to more than one being goes to take away all
right ideas" (W, XI, 18). Yet the continued, urgent, and (by Emerson's account)
widespread reliance on the literal content of Jesus' own ministry—including,
as it seemed, the endless requotation of his very words as the Q.E.D. of every
moral argument—seemed even more likely to confuse or dilute the religious
sentiment. And not less so, surely, after the "Arian" reduction of his status.

Elsewhere, a little later, Emerson would protest the self-dramatized claim
that "Jesus was the perfect man," denying he possessed the attributes of "cheer-
fulness," "the love of Natural Science," or any "notable kindness for Art." Such
arguments will seem absurd, of course, wherever Jesus' prime annointment is
to the oxymoronically combined office of priest and victim, but Emerson's
doctrinal world makes them seem almost relevant. Did he wish to "resemble
Jesus [rather] than any other man," he would suspect himself of "superstition"

(JMN,V, 71–72). And this form of personal resistance—as strong, surely, as the hatred of "grumbling enunciation of the Cambridge sort" (JMN, 5:471)— would last at least as long as the composition of the *Representative Men*, in which Jesus does not appear as even one of several, having given up the "Mystic's" place to Swedenborg.[38] The implication, quite obviously, is that in the area of character or behavior (of "manners," even) the demanding but possible and in a sense necessary *imitatio Christi* had degenerated into a slavish attempt to reproduce the sentiments, in the very language, of a singular historical figure, the *imitatio Jesu* merely.

In 1832, however, as of the moment of Unitarian resignation, which was also, identically, the transcendence of Channing, the Emersonian response assumes its properly literary character. Jesus—who was not God, and whose inspiring words mattered only in so far as the soul offered its own inspired testimony—was being accorded an authority which, formally, he could not possibly possess. And also, materially, this "benign" (JMN, 5:71) but limited man, who wrote nothing of his own, was being given credit for the precocious enunciation of everything that was or could be, in a moral sense, true. What else, in the literary sphere, could one understand by "worship" but a "cautious showing" how everything good "is agreeable to the life and teaching of Jesus"?

Of course it will not do accept Emerson's perceptions and protests as a disinterested account of contemporary practice; so that neo-Unitarian scholarship may wish to assess the figure actually cut by Jesus of Nazareth in the public preaching and private piety of the whole range of Emerson's quondam teachers and peers. The point here, however, is severely logical. And, in an equally severe sense, psychological. The subtler reasons of Channing's "Evidences" had led Emerson, more surely than they had led Channing himself, well past the point of direct reliance on the words of Jesus. The faculties which recognized his message were the same faculties which might explore, independently, its foundation in the nature of things. And (though there may be other considerations as well) the inhibitory power of Channing's influence, both public and personal, looms large among the reasons why Emerson held back from *full* publicity, for almost six years, the thought that empowered his resignation; and that also—by repression and sublimation, perhaps—gave an oddly plausible meaning to his first attempts to establish himself in a secular career.

The striking thing about the "shape" of that career is the way in which the brazen challenge of 1838 appears to proceed so perfectly from, indeed to follow so inevitably upon the modest resignation of 1832. The logic was all there, developed out of the sermons Emerson had been giving for several years.[39] And yet it would take almost six more years before Emerson would say what he really meant to any wider audience. The famous sermon on "The Lord's

Supper" openly questions, in the strenuous German manner, whether Jesus had ever "*meant* to impose a memorial feast upon the whole world" (Emphasis added). Then, almost as an afterthought, it manages to imply the irrelevance of any such intention, even if it *could* be proved: no merely historical figure enjoyed that much power over what Emerson invokes Jefferson to call the "living generation" (W, XI, 7). And then, very quietly, Emerson went to Europe.

He came back, in one sense, well assured: no one over there knew more than he was telling; if anything, less somewhat than once they had told. Thus a growing confidence marks the philosophic ambition of his unfolding sequence of "Early Lectures," from the unwonted experiment of "Science" (1833–34) to the utter command of "Human Culture" (1837–38). And yet Emerson appears significantly to have changed the subject. It would be a mistake, of course, to think of the import of these early lectures as altogether "nonreligious," or flatly to contest the antique and now venerable observation that Emerson never really stopped being a preacher.[40] Yet as he scrupulously regards the secular nature of his new, non-Sabbath occasions, he everywhere preserves a non-biblical sense of issue and idiom. The early lectures are *not* sermons. Nor do they threaten anyone's dogmatic slumbers. Not even his own, one is tempted to suggest.

To be sure, he continues to deliver many of his older sermons, as "preacher of supply"; and these are, despite their noticeably mixed content, formally religious. Yet they do not say, outright, the thing he had come to the verge of saying to his congregation but then confided, modestly, to the Journal. They only prepare to say, and then do not quite say, the thing that needed saying. Earnestly. Religiously. In the manner of a prophet. In the most august and traditional, the most sacred language a modern man might dare, without superstition, to employ. Against this standard, indeed, *any* repetition must seem inauthentic. Like stalling. Or filling in the time, against the moment when something new would have to be written, if he were to have his whole say on the issue that had generated his first great crisis. Something not to be given as adult education or as Sunday substitute.

Nor—once we begin to induce in ourselves this curious sense of suspended teleology—does either *Nature* or "The American Scholar" supply the link of missing intermediation between the time "t" of the resignation and the "t₁" of the "Address." The *Phi Beta Kappa* gesture can be *made* to seem perfectly parallel to that of the Divinity School: a declaration first of literary and then of theologic independence. And one certainly can, if one wishes, unify almost everything Emerson wrote up to and including *Essays, First Series* under the rubric or topos of the One Man: thus "The American Scholar" frankly proposes that ideal type to the humanist, while the "Address" overtly assures the religionist that the historic Jesus neither fulfills nor abrogates that typic iden-

155

tity. Yet one must be seriously insensitive to the implications of occasion and audience to sense more similarity than difference: the first opportunity was a lucky break for a scholar of Emerson's middling academic record, and it provided a rare opportunity to alleviate, for intellectual Americans, the burden of the long literary past. But the second was like some bizarre 1960s miracle: the dropout had been asked to edify the graduates. And (though not even the earnest youths could know this) he had been invited to invent the occasion of his own emancipation: to enact for himself, even as he declared it for others, the right to preach the moral sense without anxiously deferring to the one really sovereign influence. And one must be stone deaf to the tonalities of the sacred not to hear the difference between "I greet you on the re-commencement" (I, 52) and "In this refulgent summer" (76). "The American Scholar" refers to its occasion, very personably, as "our holiday"; but every word of the "Address" insists on a holiness that is not *ours*. The one is determined to be timely and trenchant. The other confesses itself to be inspired.

The problem of *Nature*'s failure to fill in the psychic and rhetorical gap is too complicated to consider in detail, related as it is to the vexed question of whether that work is quite a "characteristic" Emerson performance. (Many readers appear to think not, and yet insist on it as the invariable starting point of the career we teach and write about as "literature"; a very queer procedure, as the editors of first the *Early Lectures* and now the *Sermons* have exasperated themselves to argue.)[41] But the present point can be put quite simply: the Resignation Sermon clearly implies that the stature of Jesus is the standing problem of the age, and the Journal passage of the same moment proposes to measure that stature against the standard of "man's moral nature." It even implies that such measurement is to be Emerson's proper task, that performing it (however imperfectly) will mark the completion of his own intellectual majority. And *Nature* does not even attempt that work.

In the course of its mixed philosophical argumentations, Jesus merely figures the "devout" aspect of Nature—a "she" which "stands with bended head, and hands folded upon the breast" (I, 37); a sentimental picture, surely, even if the beloved Charles had helped Emerson draw it.[42] Or he appears on a short list of prophets who recognized Nature as "ever the ally of Religion" (I, 26). Or else he marches in a very long parade of miracle workers, from "earliest antiquity" to "Swedenborg, Hohenloe, and the Shakers" (I, 43). More important, perhaps, the complex structure of that many-stranded treatise actually manages to blur the transcendent importance of the principle which was supposed to measure, encompass, and eventually supplant the overly favored personage. Treated as "Discipline," the moral sense comes *after* the discussion of "Beauty" and "Language," to be sure, so that Emerson can be taken as neither an esthete nor semiologist. And it does of course precipitate the famous leap into "Idealism": if Man's moral discipline is indeed "the Final Cause of the

Universe"—and if that function depends altogether on perception and relation and not at all on the oldtime premise of material substance—well may
one doubt "whether nature [here *un*capitalized] outwardly exists" (I, 29). Yet
as the logic moves on, urgently, from this critical negative to the pure (if merely formal) positive of "Spirit," the moral interest clearly gives way to some
mystic (or Fichtean) ontology. And the final predictions of "Prospects" concern power rather than obligatory instruction or needful submission: no doubt
Emerson believes the "I Ought" (79) conceals and then reveals a powerful
prophecy of the "I Can," but the argument goes by too fast.

The opening "summa" of the "Address" is, of course, nothing if not rapid-
fire, but now the "moral" order is both clear and emphatic: idealism lurks in
science's inevitable insistence on "law," and law was itself the coded message of
nature's correspondant appeal to "every faculty." Then—crucially, as the opening mind realizes that "the laws which traverse the universe" actually "make
things what they are" (76)—the attention necessarily shifts to the mind itself;
for where else, properly speaking, can *law* be thought to exist? Revealed in the
very next moment, however, and more by sublime reversal than by "analogy,"
is the new, moral sense of law: not the cosmic or universe-creating conclusion
that such things always occur or cannot appear otherwise, but a self-differen-
tiating sense that the mind's expressive "I" must act in accordance with the
splendid but unforgiving Appearance called the world. This "mere illustration
and fable of [the] mind" (76) becomes at once a *moral* fable. But in that same
moment the mind irresistably introjects the self-creating sense of "duty": the
world is "the mind's" promulgation of law, but this law is one "I" must obey.
Precisely as, for the first time, "I."[43]

Here, surely, and not before, is Emerson's most coherent masterplot, the
firmest "Groundplan" of his "Metaphysics of Morals."[44] Clearly it is one
which critics worried about the anarchic tendencies of Emerson's thought
would do well to keep in mind: the fearsome Emersonian "I" can scarcely be
said to exist prior to or apart from an original sense of submission to law; to
be human is to be obligated. Or, more forcefully still, the conscious acceptance
of duty is the single austere condition of credible selfhood. The point may also
bear importantly on the interpretation of "later Emerson," particularly on
"Experience," which consciously tries and knowingly fails to locate a noumenal self by introspection or by "pure" rational derivation. The Emersonian
"self" is inherently "practical," in Kant's peculiar sense: constituted morally and
no other way, it remains a moral entity or it vanishes. Obviously no speculative truth can count as "mine"; and—at the opposite extreme of epistemological inquiry—even pain proves less "incorrigible" than merely "evanescent."
But duty remains, as long as "I" live. And its thought is both debased and incoherent except as my own.[45]

157

Yet a simpler point deserves emphasis as well: just here does Emerson attempt his own fair preaching of "man's moral nature"; here, for the first time, do we sense that he has set out *directly* to answer the challenge he set himself in 1832. The works that fall between "The Lord's Supper" and the "Address" are all quite wonderful in their way. Taken together, they constitute a brave sort of philosophical downpayment on a career in prophecy; and, given his notorious resentment of the philosopher's need to "mince his words & fatigue us with explanation" (JMN, V, 31), the combined result speaks enormously well for Emerson's intellectual good faith. He really was being about as careful (and as patient) as a prophet can afford to be. Still, it is impossible to avoid the suspicion, retrospectively, that Emerson was nervously omitting to say the one thing he supposed it was "given" him to say. Or to keep from imagining that, were Emerson somehow permitted to confess the substance of these "early" works to a modern analyst, that shrewd psychic observer might say something like "Waldo, you appear to be intellectualizing."

Probably he realized the fact himself. Though generally quite satisfied with the integrity of his success as a lecturer, he nonetheless criticized himself, in March, 1838, for the failure of his most recent lecture series ("Human Culture") to "state with directness & conspicuously" his definitive claim: namely, that "you can never come to any peace or power until you put your whole reliance in the moral constitution of man & not at all in historical Christianity." The point had been implied, of course, as it had been latent in most of what he had written since 1832, but that fact only made more conspicuous the refusal to be explicit. And as Emerson proceeds, once again, to elaborate his lesson to himself, the tendentious reader can both sense the urgency and guess the logic of the "Address" itself:

> The Belief in Christianity that now prevails is the Unbelief of men. They will have Christ for a lord and not for a brother. Christ preaches the greatness of Man but we hear only the greatness of Christ. (JMN, V, 459)

Evidently it was about time—not only to set the cart and the horse in proper philosophic alignment, but to rearrange as well certain other, more "familiar," relationships. If God himself were a "Father" only by a trope of origins, then surely it made no sense to reintroduce a sovereign moral (or literary) authority in the person of a human prophet. Evidently the prospect made him angry.

And yet, given the intensity and the longevity of this repressed concern—the philosophical but also clearly personal need to bring Jesus down to proper size and into human perspective—the remarkable fact about the "Address" is the relative mildness of its rhetoric of reduction, the actual friendliness of its strategy of revision. It seeks not at all to triumph over or to supplant but merely to equalize the authority of Jesus. Remarkably, it purports to claim not the least but rather the most which could still, within the limits of the available logic, possibly be claimed for the truly revolutionary significance of that Jesus whom they called the Christ. Not (on premise) God, and not (therefore) to be as good as worshiped, he remains—or, rather, he stands forth revealed for the first time as—the "only soul in history" (82) who has seen and announced some altogether necessary point. Shorn clean of all superstitious foreknowledge or prearranged divine programming, he nevertheless utters a thing hidden from the foundation of the world. Not magically, so far as the limits of human knowing could ever know, and not on his own authority. But "in the Spirit": on the basis, that is, of some profound yet utterly natural intuition of a truth that is, potentially, within the common domain and which must be received not as "his" but as true to the common sense of how things really are. He utters his truth de facto, that is to say. Poetically, it also appears, so that the "fact" is yet in need of suitable interpretation or idiomatic translation, but truly and well. Thus a figure of singular supernatural function is transformed, at a stroke, into a signal religious genius. Quite an unusual put-down, we ought to notice.

We also notice, of course, that the natural generosity of this estimate permits Emerson to appear, like Jesus himself, as a radical reformer rather than as an apostate: no more an opposer or a rejecter of Jesus than Jesus himself had been of Moses or Abraham, Emerson wishes only to restate, with appropriate clarification—and with vernacular eloquence idiomatically renewed—the essence of the Christic message as he had come to understand it. And it may be only a little cynical to observe that Emerson's logic (or strategy) actually enables him to enlist the sanction of the great teacher for his own doctrine of the moral sentiment. In his wake, though not at all "on his authority," and against the traditional yet idolatrous "exaggeration of the personal" (82) importance of Jesus, Emerson will point not to the man (or his miracles) but to the truth he insisted upon: the duty and the self-identical power of the soul to "love the Right" (77). It may be fair to quarrel, just here, with the textual basis of Emerson's "reading" of Jesus; but not, I think, with the purity of the position that reading produces.

We may even wish to observe that this position makes it reasonable for Emerson to blame, not Jesus, but a variety of followers ("in the same, in the next, and the following ages") for the idolatry of person which, far from dismantling, the piety of the Unitarians had awkwardly reinscribed. Jesus taught the truth. Yet he taught it perforce poetically—the failure to regard which fact could produce only "distortion." And so it lamentably occurred. In a "jubilee of sublime emotion" Jesus had indeed claimed to be divine; but when ordinary language "caught this high chant from the poet's lips," it utterly literalized (and personalized) the meaning; thus

159

> The idioms of his language, and the figures of his rhetoric, have usurped the place of his truth; and churches are not built on his principles, but on his tropes. Christianity became a Mythus, as the poetic teaching of Greece and of Egypt, before. (81)

No one in Emerson's liberal audience would any longer descend to declare that "This was Jehovah come down out of heaven," and "I will kill you, if you say he was a man" (81). But a divine claim had indeed been made. And it required translation still. Emerson's prime literary duty is to make that translation. We may remain unconvinced that it is entirely adequate. And, on the authority of "style" alone, we may altogether prefer Jesus' outrageous "I and the Father are one" and "Before Abraham came to be, I am" to Emerson's better socialized "Through me, God acts; through me, speaks" and "Would you see God, see me; or see thee, when thou also thinkest as I now think."[46] We may even suspect some metaphysical relapse when Emerson declares, elsewhere, that "If Jesus came now into the world," he would say not "I" but "You, YOU!" (JMN, V, 362). But it is impossible to deny that Emerson has deliberately, systematically put himself into the position of *having* to paraphrase the poetic utterance. Like Edwards seeking out some "great objection," which only his own arcane metaphysics can explode, Emerson is arranging to meet his prime hermeneutic challenge head-on.

And it may be that the literary implications of this position are as interesting as any other. What it had come to mean to worship Jesus, apparently, was to be bound to repeat his own words; or else, at very least, to refer all further words to his. The result might be linguistic or phenomenological impoverishment and, hence, a resentment of the authority that enforced this utter belatedness. But it could hardly be literary competition in any ordinary sense. The Unitarian Jesus was not God but he was (in Emerson's view, at least) the precursor who could, by definition, not possibly be surpassed. To demystify him altogether was, on the other hand, identically to install him as the sort of religious genius or "poet" with whom one was invited, indeed required to compete. He had said the truth, in his own language, the idiom historically available to him. The religious world somehow conspired to misunderstand. Someone had to try again, in other words, to the same purpose. Readers are free to conclude that Emerson fails, that he in fact loses in the literary contest so artfully arranged. But criticism is bound to conclude that he loses in a game of his own inspired devising.

Surely Emerson realized he was entitled to the sanction of Jesus only so far as he could earn it—by a convincing translation of the truth he understood him to have taught. And here, at least, he is not that anxious about the question. He has derived, as he imagines, the essence of religion. Jesus, he supposes, had intuited something of that same essence. He might be wrong, of course, like anyone at any time. But the confidence of the "Address" is that he is, like anyone at any time, more apt to be wrong about Jesus than about the moral sentiment. If Jesus had *not* taught the divinity of that, preeminently, then Emerson's position was significantly more lonely; but not, he thought, any less self-evidently true. For otherwise the cart were still before the horse. And it is this rare "philosophic" poise—built up, it may be, from the "intellectualizations" of his "Early Lectures" and from *Nature*—which ultimately controls the revolutionary logic of Emerson's Divinity Sermon.

The "Address" opens, as we have seen, philosophically. "Poetically," if one insists, but this means only that Emerson is certain he can derive his categorical (and self-creating) imperative from a phenomenology which begins in that organic "joy" his (Romantic) generation identified as the experimental source and rhetorical effect of lyric poetry as such.[47] The crucial consideration is that, sermon though it is, it begins with a reading of Nature (including the faculties or capacities of human nature) rather than of Scripture: the "text," that is to say, is announced only *after* the originary derivation is complete. Indeed, by Emerson's logic, the text becomes satisfactorily intelligible only insofar as it has received some effective philosophical prediction. No one ignorant of the inevitability or givenness of "the moral sense," he means to suggest, could entertain any but the most literal and personal notions of a divine "sonship" or of what it might mean, a-theistically—and without filial resentment—to "please God."

And no doubt Emerson believes his present instance may stand for the general homiletic case as such. Traditionally, of course, sermons declared their "theological" loyalty by presenting the text *first*, according it thereby an absolute pride of place and implying that the operations of philosophical reason all come later, to "open" it merely, or to suggest that what was authoritatively received was also consistent with humane learning; or else, in the most rationalistic version of the tradition, to show that divine revelation must be exactly as it is.[48] The liberals, however, had been steadily undoing this pious but not inevitable assumption for quite some time: from Locke's epoch-making essay on "The Reasonableness of Christianity" to Channing's sect-securing account of "Unitarian Christianity," a new consensus was forming around the suspicion that no one can read a "scripture" in philosophical innocence. Evidently some altogether human thinking has operated to privilege one piece of writing over others, to install it as "revelation" in the first place: unlike manna, it never quite falls from the sky. And just less obviously, an act of interpretation (of de- or re-troping) always constitutes the "meaning" of any passage we might announce for commentary and enforcement: God reveals himself to readers, not geese. Channing may have outraged the orthodox by emphasizing the highly "metaphorical" nature of the "literal" in Christian

Scripture, and he may irritate our own more pervasive skepticism when he proudly declares that "we must limit all these [tropological] passages by the known attributes of God."[49] But at some level he would seem to have a point: something always comes before "the text."

To this extent, at least, Emerson's natural supernaturalism is in perfect agreement with the supernatural rationalism of his Unitarian tradition: as no one can read without language, so no one can interpret a text apart from prior knowledge.[50] Of course Emerson's ultimate position lies well beyond this prime interpretative consensus. His "poetic" opening plainly suggests—what he elsewhere makes explicit—that philosophy is itself, after all, only a kind of writing. From this it may well follow that what precedes the text is always some *other text*; and thus the "hermeneutic circle" is (un)resolved into a sort of "grammatological spiral." Sufficiently drastic for the present occasion, however, is his evident implication that the "disciplines" of natural and scriptural theology are by no means so distinct as they have been made by tradition to appear; that their separation is less epistemological and absolute than operational and generic. It remains true to say, dramatically, that for Emerson the one "subsumes" the other, as revelation reveals by emphatic instance rather than by privileged invention.[51] But this is only to repeat a more famous point: there is only one scene of efffective mentality in Emerson: "Man Thinking" (CW, 1:53).

And indeed a more modest (or less self-aware) version of the same insight already lurks in Edwards' utterly rationalistic attempt to recoup Calvinist theology as metaphysical Idealism. From that bracing example we have seemed to learn that natural theology is when we think about God *without*, scriptural theology when we think such thoughts *with*, an already priveleged text open before us. Thus the "content of revelation" will mean the thoughts a particular community can think about God, at any time, without abusing either their text or their minds.

Once again, however, the local point may be as interesting as any other: assuming the new, naturalized relation between faith and reason, Emerson sets out to reform the sermon as methodically as he does to reformulate the relation between Jesus and the moral nature of man. Inevitably. As the task of pious thought was to make some apt translation of the tropes of one's tradition, so the duty of faithful preaching was to make clear the inevitability of that very act of interpretation. Such, it appears, is the solemn obligation the sermon ends by inviting a generation of new-fledged ministers to share—on their acceptance of which, it more than implies, the fate of the ministry entirely depends. Nor is the gesture merely polite or (at the end, finally) self-effacing: as no (post-primitive) religion could exist apart from a subjective or "original" experience of the moral sentiment, so no continuation of the present Christian dispensation could pretend to more authority than is generated when readers agree their book tells a truth they must, "in the Spirit" (as sharers of the "One Mind"), embrace. A "regulative idea," perhaps, but not less noble (or necessary) for that reason. The minister of the future might wish to testify in terms of the quality or condition of his own first *recognition* of the truth in the Scripture's account of Jesus, but only as an instance or an invitation. Once the standard of truth had moved outside the text, the minister had to behave himself like any other teacher of literature.

Yet the revolutionary nature of Emerson's position may be felt most powerfully by marking its dissent from the tradition of separation (and of hierarchy) that strictly regulates New England's most "institutional" form of pedagogical preaching. His sermon is *not*, of course, a "Dudleian Address," as was Channing's "Evidences," the significantly so-identified precursor text. Benign as his literary fortunes had been, early and late, Emerson never had been and never would be asked to contribute to the maintenance of that endowed ritual of public faith; his early signing-off from the establishment—if not the upsetting implications of his unific logic—had seen to that. Possibly he noticed the vacant professional space; arguably he relished the present occasion as the lucky chance to fill it in. But plainly, and at some level strategically, his long-delayed and remarkably-authorized "Sermon to…our Cambridge Theological School" meant to place itself within the still habitable territory of the Dudleian sequence, to reform its constant doctrine and to unify its artificial multiplicity.

From its post-awakening outset in 1755, the sequence of lectures endowed by Joseph Dudley had to cover four (apparently) discrete but (as it seemed) equally essential issues: the certainty of God's existence from the light of nature, the demonstrable authenticity of the Christian revelation, the errors of the papacy, and the validity of non-Roman "orders." By the turn of the nineteenth century, however, the latter two topics had lost much of their urgency: satisfactory usage insures—is all we can mean by—"legitimacy." But the vitality of the first pair of topics actually increased, in proportion to the rising credibility of their denial. And just as the internationally respected William Paley had had to produce *two* books of evidences, natural and scriptural (confusable only in hasty footnotes),[52] so the official preachers of New England's establishment had vigorously to maintain two separate but equal arguments as the twin foundations of an appropriately enlightened or sufficiently intellectual religion. The undeniable evidence of God's intelligent existence was plainly writ in the beauty, order, and design of the natural world; and (or *but*; the emphasis could vary with the rationalistic confidence of the preacher) a distinct supernatural revelation had been superadded to define and insure the relation between virtue and ultimate human destiny. The certainty of this latter, verbal communication was of a different order—historical rather than esthetico-scientific—but it was *not less* for that reason. Only a Pauline "fool" could deny the one; only the invincibly ignorant would challenge the other.

In a provocative essay called "The Insecurity of Nature," Perry Miller has suggested that by the 1830s the equilibrist emphasis of the latter-day Dudleian structure was showing signs of stress, and that in 1851 Fredrick Henry Hedge as good as declared its premise "obsolete." Hedge's argument (and also Miller's) is that those Christians who pretend, on some "forensic occasion," to speak from nature *alone* are like "'children playing blindfold, and pretending to walk with their eyes covered, while at every turn, they peep beneath the bandage.'" The epistemological point is well taken, Cartesian example to the contrary notwithstanding: what we believe, we believe; what we doubt, we doubt. More relevant, however, is Hedge's contention that the distinction between natural and supernatural religion is outdated and false; that (in Miller's summary) "all religions, like thoughts themselves, are simultaneously natural and supernatural, and who can tell which is which?"[53] Relevant, but also (by now) somewhat belated, since the same point had been the evident implication of Emerson's "Address": all religious thought is *thought*, and New England's well regulated little Dudleian two-step was more quaint than any minuet.

Nor could Emerson's singular intention be more pointed than it is. As his sermon's "application" is an updated version of an Awakening monition against an "unregenerate ministry," so his "doctrine"—equivalent to but not derived from his "text"—is a timely conflation of the two Dudleian (or Paleyesque) cases of evidence. Never officially invited to deliver a single, proper Dudleian Address, Emerson evidently fashioned his Divinity Sermon as two such addresses in one. *As* one. Deliberately. The universe evinces divinity, as the initial, speeded-up version of *Nature* clearly means to remind its well accustomed audience. And (or *but*, but only by generic insult) the process of noticing this fact is not different from recognizing the authority of "Christ," non-personally considered.

The order of the world prepares for and reflects, indeed *comprises*, the moral order: necessarily, and in full despite of Calvin; for no such order could possibly be imposed from without. By *anybody*. Constituted as ideal invitation and (identically) as norm, the universe offers intimations of "laws [which] execute themselves" (77), in consciousness and in society no less than in so-called "natural" phenomena. Other forms of creation are thinkable, no doubt; some may even be possible. But no other is so agreeable with the premise of obligation as Emerson's (post-Kantian) generation could best conceive it: categorically: in the practical order, that is, unconditionally. No other, surely, was compatible with religion in any but a primitive sense of fear or personal placation. The highest law—indeed the highest supposable case of consciousness in the universe Emerson conceived—is expressed in the "necessitated freedom" of the "I ought." Not in the pseudo-imaginative "I AM" of Coleridge who, if he had read his Fichte, had not read him close enough; for that thrilling claim really did amount to an Edwardsian blasphemy.[54] And surely not in the "Thou shalt" of Moses, reliance on which left one a child, and in the (tribalist) Old Law still. But in "original" recognition of and entire reliance on the inherence, the self-evidence, and the (eventual) triumph of duty conceived as essence and embraced as destiny. An honest proposition and a clear one, I think we may safely conclude.

Such a condition—of the sort of "selfhood" conferred by the ecstatic acceptance of the inescapable morality of human being—Emerson plainly posited as "the end of the universe," begun from eternity (no one knows how) and that way tending, constantly. No wonder it scandalized him to hear that "they have said in the Churches…'Mere Morality'" (JMN, IV, 382): one's very self depended on it.[55] And particularly as the category of moral selfhood corresponded to or translated, satisfactorily for the first time, their own cherished notion of "faith," on which, he agreed, any respectable salvation of any credible soul had always depended. And most especially as it had become his settled hermeneutical belief that such had been the translatable substance of Jesus' own (entirely tropological) message.

We smile, perhaps, the first time we hear Emerson evoke Kant in describing Jesus as a "minister of the pure Reason" (JMN, V, 273). Jesus has, of course, nothing whatever to say about the sorts of considerations Kant would regard as "pure": he utterly lacks, as Emerson himself truly noticed, the "scientific" interest. And no one has ever confused the crabbed technicalities of even Kant's "practical" idiom with the commanding accents of a Jewish prophet. Yet Emerson makes his suggestion strenuously (and often) enough for us to consider taking it seriously. Sympathetically considered, the claim would mean, first of all, that the certainties of Kant's second critique are truths of "reason" rather than of "experience," and that, as such, they are as "pure" as practical (i.e., moral) matters ever become. Nor would Emerson be the first (or last) philosopher to hold that opinion. But it would also mean, evidently, that there is some deep structural similarity between Kant's "categorical imperative" and the sort of immediate and unreasoned but absolute commitment Jesus seems everywhere to require, sometimes actually even to provoke. The notion of the religious "leap" is post-Kantian, of course, but Kierkegaard was not the first to notice that Kant's destruction of rationalist "metaphysics" had the motive of clearing a space for Protestant "faith." Perhaps Jesus had been, in the utter subjectivity of his implied standard, one of "the moderns" after all.[56]

Yet however we decide this large historical question, the smaller, generic point survives: Emerson's deliberate mixing together of the two (still viable) Dudleian matters is based on a clear refusal to honor the venerable separation between natural and revealed theology; and it aims to redefine, for all (non-fundamentalist) religion of the future, the epistemology of "the sermon."

165

Revelations are recognized as such—indeed are such—so far as they draw the veil from something inevitable, though oddly unrecognized, about the structure of the world. Morality is part of that structure: everywhere appearing, it sooner or later discovers itself not as morose resignation to the inherited terms of social repression, but as the gladness of a durable selfhood. Would it be so bad if sermons reported just *that* good news?

This would be the appropriate place—if ever—to wonder whether Emerson has not somehow "mystified the moral." Perhaps he has. But only if that charge is taken to mean that, inspired by Kant, Emerson came to regard morality as a structure rather than an arrangement, and that, in perfect parallel with (if not in literal imitation of) Fichte and Jacobi, he identified its appearance as the world's highest and, in a teleologic sense, "last" expression of the divine. And it might also be fair to admit, in another idiom, that he does not adequately differentiate his moral sentiment *as faith*, and also *as selfhood*, from the ordinary operations of "conscience," or from the daily, hourly pursuit of what his tradition once called "sanctification": like John Cotton, perhaps (and unlike the "doubly" protected Edward Taylor) he let his miracle of justification overwhelm all other attendant and allied considerations.[57] It would be quite false, however, to imagine that Emerson was merely "sentimental" about the sentiment of virtue. The early Journals may fondly confess that the ideal of "moral perfection" of which Milton was "enamored" had affected himself as well—had "separated me from men,...watered my pillow,...driven sleep from my bed"—but they also make it clear that the principle involved here is one "which I cannot yet declare" (JMN, IV, 87). And we should notice that when, by 1838, Emerson was indeed able to declare his principle, all the weepiness has disappeared. The words of the "Address" are defiant words: he stands here, he *cannot* other. So that analyses which associate him with the eighteenth as against the nineteenth (or the sixteenth) century are likely to be subtly, learnedly misleading.[58]

By calling virtue a "sentiment"—or the moral sense a "sense"—Emerson means primarily to deny that it is, formally, a conclusion to an argument or that, psychologically, it is ever truly experienced as such. To say that it is "an intuition," which "cannot be received at second hand," is only partly to say that the quality of its subjectivity (or "privacy") is such that it cannot be taught by or learned from another; that, socially considered, it follows upon "not instruction, but provocation" (80). It is also to say that it is neither the result of a conditional proposition founded on sense observation nor yet a practical application of or transfer from the realm of speculative reason. It is, rather, the inevitable term of a certain sort of experience as such; one which individual consciousness discovers precisely as its own but also, equally precisely, as necessary and binding; one which is, therefore, precisely and perfectly subjective without being in the slightest degree whimsical. One's duty is quite one's own;

but it is no less *duty* for that reason. To say more were to "spend the day in explanation" (II, 30), not to say in "critique."

Yet Emerson also wishes to suggest that the "sentiment of virtue"—unlike the thought of consequences or the idea of punishment—is constituted as a matter of "reverence and delight" (77). "Delight" points backwards, of course, to the natural joy in which the career of the soul was thought to begin, and thus it means to warn that what Freud will call the "Discontents" of "Civilization" will not cover the entire case of man's conscious separation from nature. Civilization, which Emerson comes to call "society," indeed appears as a "conspiracy," against the authentic subjectivity of every human subject; but only to the extent that someone or some group with power false-ly objectifies the contractual (or otherwise co-operational) nature of his or its authority. Further, civilization itself, though it might on merely Hobbesean premises be tried, would surely fail were it not formed in some image of the moral sentiment itself; were its well socialized "Thou shalt" not some primi-tive reminder, or typic prediction, of the truly originary "I must" of human consciousness as such. As it is later indictated that "the indwelling Supreme Spirit cannot wholly be got rid of" (80), so it is here implied that we can never entirely give away—sordid boon—our own lively heart.

But if "delight" suggests the preservation (indeed the redemption) of the organic at the level of the moral—so there cease to be, now, "levels" at all, but only a single self-affirming but suitably opposed and lawfully limited con-sciousness—it is the element of "reverence" which prepares for or even begins the transition from what might be called the "merely" moral to what (Emerson felt) anyone might recognize as the specifically religious. It is, per-haps, the single "move" Emerson makes in the doctrine/reasons section of his sermon that we could wish either firmer or better elaborated. Yet he does mean, clearly enough, to establish some important distinction between the "moral" and the "religious" sentiment; between, that is, the philosophical fact of obligation and the sense of "holiness" that may well attach to it.

Rejected of course, and necessarily so, is any traditional notion that, beyond mere morality, religion properly begins as soon as the moral agent refers his being, including his behaviors, to some onlooking, paternally-concerned cre-ator-person.[59] Substituted instead, again necessarily, given the system so far, is the idea that religion arises from a little further reflection on the self and its correlative world as forming a complex and wonderful moral spectacle or sys-tem. The moral sense awakens, naturally, inevitably, because it is indeed a *sense*: as the eye cannot choose but see, so the human being cannot avoid choosing (or refusing); and that, always, under the aspect of the right or the good. But something is added, apparently, as soon as somebody notices that this structural necessity, absolutely subjective in its unique manifestation as first-person-sin-gular, is yet not entirely private or self-limiting in its implications; that "the good" is not only that which "I" must do, but that it really is, undeniably, *good*. The system cannot manifest itself except to a subject; but it does not cease to be a system therefore. And—praise God!—it works.

Naïveté lurks nearby, of course. And some form of it may be inadequately prevented by Emerson's notion of "Compensation" which—long held and well developed but not yet written out as an "essay"—appears to intervene at just this point.[60] Emerson may live (and write) to repent his "early" view of the way some "rapid intrinsic energy worketh everywhere, righting wrongs, correcting appearances, and bringing up facts to a harmony with thoughts" (78). And we may learn to call the rare melancholy of this literary repentence "later Emerson":"the world I converse with is not the world I *think*" (III, 48); "the laws of the world do not always befriend" (IV, 100); "all is riddle, and the key to a riddle is another riddle" (W, VI, 313). We may also notice, as words like "worketh" drop away, that an increasingly secular Emerson repeatedly reminds himself that "Nature is no sentimentalist," and so it will not do to dress up the "terrific benefactor" called "Providence" in the "white neckcloth of a student in divinity" (W,VI, 6,8). But we are also to notice that a more fundamental conviction, set forth in the very first sermon, is *never once* put into question:"He who does a good deed, is instantly ennobled himself[;] he who does a mean deed, is by the action itself contracted" (78). And this *further* moral fact is, for Emerson, the ultimate reason of religion.

In its first manifestation simply a given, the moral sense provides in turn the basis of what Emerson names "the principle of veneration," what we might call the sentiment of "the holy": the feeling that we do, once in a while, tread on sacred ground and might do well to take off our shoes. This principle, which "successively creates all forms of worship" (79), appears to be immortal, whatever the human appetite for idolatry. It operates purely, however, as soon (and for so long) as "compensation" can be experienced as a self-executing and perfect law of spiritual formation and growth, not as a calculation and not as a rough or approximate medium of worldly exchange. True religion occurs when somebody manages to notice that virtue is not a temporal hedge against an eternal future, not what the socialized have learned to settle for (instead of pleasure), not even the rare if mixed pleasure of pleasing the parent; but that it is in fact the end for which—and by which—the "soul" is created. The sense of obligation simply *is*; but men worship whenever they are astonished to discover that by accepting this inevitability they come to be themselves.

With a fair poetic prophecy of this lucid sense of human calling Emerson entirely credits the historical Jesus. For its perversion he altogether blames the history of "Christianity": what appears only as "intuition," and is fully verifiable in practice, is superstitiously ascribed to the unique supernatural authority of an (oxymoronic) divine person; and then, more "rationally" as was thought, to the privileged tropes of a magically annointed teacher. Risking (but not really fearing) the charge (and indeed the logical possibility) of reformulation-as-apostasy, Emerson overcomes anxiety—hesitation, delay, "fear of shocking, etc."—well enough to declare that in this "refulgent" universe the pure of heart are blessed as such. Or if not, then one had "rather be 'A pagan'" (82). The rest would seem to be history. Or criticism. And a little satire.

Yet these worldly matters cannot be said to exhaust Emerson's capacity for sermonic application: his last words are as "spiritual" as they are forward-looking and hopeful. As no American Jeremiad would dare conclude without a final, upturning "use" of comfort or encouragement,[61] so Emerson himself cannot end without offering some favorable prediction for the future of religion; at least for its most durable (and literary) fixture, the "institution of preaching" (92). Emerson's "comfort" is that, in this line at least, there is indeed much to be done; and that, if done "in the Spirit," the doing cannot fail.

Surely it is incautious to imagine that this "anticipatory" Emerson—who ends his discourse still in expectation of some new Teacher, some rare Koenigsburg Wordsworth or Lake Country Kant, who "shall show that the Ought, that Duty, is one thing with Science, with Beauty, and with Joy" (93)—might be regarding *himself* as a much-awaited, long-delayed New Comforter or Paraclete. Visionary predictions he may utter, but no delusional fantasy.[62] Here as elsewhere in Emerson's Holy History, there is only one Age or Kingdom: one which we can call the Age of Man so long as we remember that it is also one, eternal Age of the Spirit, and that "Man" here signifies Emerson's perfect (and always potential) "One Man," that mythic First-Born of Creation who should embody the Spirit entire. Then too, the preacher who thought only to naturalize and so to equalize the authority of Jesus has no wish, at the end, to reabsorb it all into himself; but rather, and explicitly, like some latter-day Jesus saying "You," to disperse it as wide and democratically as the gracious mystery of inspired speech can permit. To require all possible disciples "to refuse the good models" (90) is surely to define the present text as occasion and "provocation" merely, to decline the available opportunity to become (at the very least) the "Dr. Channing" of the next dispensation. Indeed Emerson's literary history recapitulates his theology: all actual speech (or "writing," if one insists) is always-already belated; "in the Spirit," however, no one is further off from the beginning or closer on to the end. As every origin is also a climax, and every "moment" a potential apocalypse, so Emerson would be embarrassed to regard himself as more than a single harbinger, among many.

Yet there is something utterly "Pentecostal" about the close of Emerson's "Address," some urgency of vision which begs a new typology of the Spirit. Beginning here. The prediction is general and not personal. And it is, of

169

course, *only* prediction: nothing final is here fulfilled. Yet it is impossible not to sense that Emerson feels himself in touch with some transcendent moral energy. Or else, at very least, that he finds himself speaking within the frame of some powerful mythic structure, and that he expects his audience to feel it too, and to respond accordingly. Assured by the very resonances he would invoke, he really does foretell something new in the sensibility, and hence in the success, of religion.

Nothing sectarian, of course. And nothing in the way of ritual, about which Emerson appeared to feel there was very little to be said on *both* sides. On the one hand, flatly, "faith makes its own forms"; thus it were ridiculous to imagine some Americanist version of the Oxford Movement, some (finally) post-Puritan enrichment of public ceremony. On the other hand, however—as the opportunity to address yet another Dudleian matter opens up before him—Emerson explicitly resists the once-powerful temptation of Rome-bashing: "A whole popedom of forms, one pulsation of virtue can uplift and vivify" (92). Evidently the pure of heart find all outward things pure. Or else, by the powerful light of Emerson's unique Puritanism of the Moral, everything *else* becomes a thing indifferent.

Idolatry is possible, to be sure, and nothing less can be charged against any doctrine or usage, however reverent, which diminishes the sovereignty of the intuitive knowledge of moral obligation or distracts from the allied, specifically religious sense that the system of the universe is such that the lover of virtue puts on "the safety of God" (78). Thus there will be no new sacraments, those specially empowered rituals once thought so essential to the life of grace. Radical Protestantism everywhere reduces the number of those signal occasions to just two, a unique Baptism and the movable feast of the Lord's Supper; and Emerson—consciously reliving the moment when he declared that the repetitious rite blunted spiritual desire with historical memory and made an idol of the literal Jesus—is far from wishing to multiply, once again, the popular store of occult transactions. Guilty (enough) of mystifying the moral, and chargeable (certainly) with allowing all the old supernatural *valeur* to shine forth from the poetry of his naturalized religion, Emerson nevertheless leaves no doubt that he has moved, once and for all, beyond the reach and the lure of religious magic.

Still there is something uncanny about the "sacramental" composure of Emerson's final remarks: not especially agitated or hortatory, his Pentecostal predictions evidently proceed from a trust in powers not altogether rhetorical and not properly his own. He even predicts the success of agencies or energies beyond his present power to anticipate or project. Promising an outpouring of ecstatic speech which shall renew all the tropes of religious discourse, all he can actually recommend—all indeed he can soberly imagine—is…more preaching. Yet he appears to be expecting some sort of miracle.

To be strict, we should remember that he is recommending a *reformed* preaching, not the pure word or perfect example of the historical Jesus, but the saving power of man's moral self-revelation as the telic last incarnation of the Soul; fairly begun here, but to be spread and developed everywhere, to perfection, perhaps just that will be potent to cure the religious malaise of the nineteenth century. A less friendly view would suggest that Emerson's mystification was merely to presume and trade upon some diffuse and unspoken sense that the sermon had itself already become invested with magical properties; that in New England, at least, that one species of formal address had long since absorbed all the potential energy of the latent or lurking presence of the Spirit of God.[63] But that cynicism would have to survive Emerson's own remarkably undeceived, virtually deconstructive analysis of the elements or features which survive from the former religious regime. The entire heritage of puritanic, indeed Christian culture is reduced to a linked pair of "hereditary advantages": "the Sabbath," as an established and durable symbol of sacred time and space, and the "institution of preaching" (92), that well accepted but actually quite remarkable agreement that the regular "speech of man to men" may at some times be granted exemption from the ordinary designs of rhetoric; from the logic, that is to say, of power or control merely. Astonishingly!—and despite redundant provocation to the contrary—people keep coming to church on Sunday; they sit there and let you fumble at their soul. At one level, evidently, the "miracle" would seem to be nothing more marvellous than a perdurable obstinacy of religious audience.

Minimally, therefore, Emerson wishes merely to establish or assure the more hesitant members of his proto-ministerial hearers: many things will pass away from the childlike Christianity in which they (like Emerson earlier) had been nurtured; but heaven and earth seem scarcely more obdurate than the human need for some serviceable adult faith. This thing cannot be "conferred," of course; it cannot even, properly speaking, be taught. But it can, wondrously, be provoked. And it can, at the same moment, and in the same (mysterious) manner, be *confirmed*. The precise laws of the moral sentiment "refuse to be adequately stated," yet we do "read them hourly in each other's faces"; and though refusing to be quite "spoken by the tongue" (77), they yet require some testimony more open and more "philosophical" than the sympathetic or the furtive glance. Hence the role of the preacher, who confirms and is himself confirmed in the act of pronouncing, in and around the sacred precinct of the ineffable, that the "'open secret' of the universe" (JMN, 4: 87) is in fact true. And as there remain some reasons to believe that to confirm intuition is not always the same as to sacralize rhetoric, I think we can afford to trust Emerson on this point: the Church survives because the confirmation of faith is a public and a social event; and whenever people actually do feel confirmed by

171

preaching—when thcy do not grow "petulant," or fall asleep, or look out at the snowstorm—the occasion is as sacred as anything we can imagine.

Further, as Emerson's most direct and legitimate audience is a group of would-be ministers, his exemplary "confirmation" may also serve as something of a reformed "ordination"—a directive to cherish and foster, though not at all an authoritative conferral of power to perform, the holiest "orders" there are. The graduates still require, as Emerson realizes, the call of some particular church; nor, as his logic well indicates, would he at all wish to challenge the by-now august body of "Congregational" theory on this point. And yet, as the fourth and final Dudleian subject comes into view (and even into latter-day relevance), Emerson clearly means to evoke and to celebrate some element of mystery that continues to associate itself with the "calling" in question.

On the one hand, clearly, neither he nor anyone else in the world has the gift to make a "priest"—forever, in essence, for all and some. Virtue puts a "mark upon the soul," but nothing else does: as soon consecrate a "poet" to the (Wordsworthian) office of "man speaking to men."[64] On the other hand, however, some specific transaction seems absolutely required: the power of expression is free and (potentially) universal, but the right to preach is always by consent of those preached at. And that contract may not be as simple as first appears. Arranged by covenant, no doubt, the "institution of preaching" seems yet to have foundation, if not precisely "in nature," then at least in the all-but-ineluctable sense of the holy; and in this rudimentary way, at least, it seems more ordained than invented. Ordination to the ministry would seem to involve, therefore, the conscious offer and the solemn acceptance of a privilege more vulnerable to spiritual abuse than to deconstruction. What the "ordained" minister must recall, always, is that his audience will feel the sacredness of the preacher's "right" because it is one they also share:

> for they with you are open to the influx of the all-knowing Spirit, which annihilates before its broad noon the little shades and gradations of intelligence in the compositions we call wiser and wisest. (91)

There really is but One Mind: to forget which were sacrilege.

Yet the sacrament whose power Emerson would draw on and energize most fundamentally is that of baptism, even as his choice of "text" would indicate. Not the initiatory or proto-typical baptism of water, to be sure; such "Christenings" never had made Christians, even if Christian were the only or inevitable thing to be. But the confirming and ordaining baptism of the Spirit which, gathering up much of the potency of other pseudosacraments, unites all virtuous men in that rare, yet "common" priesthood of believers. Not that Emerson himself is to be thought of as "baptizing" his audience—any more than he is, in the magical sense, ordaining them; any more than Peter, for example, baptized, or confirmed, or ordained those fearful but also prayerful men (and women) once gathered in a certain famous "upper room." He merely supposes an undiminished survival of energy, from that occasion to this.

What was predicted at Jordan—awkwardly, when John and Jesus agreed to let the Spirit cancel the need to compete for typological priority—and what was gloriously yet *not entirely* fulfilled at the first "Christian" Pentecost—when a group of "post-Christian" apostles were so "filled with the Holy Spirit" that they "began to speak in other tongues, as the Spirit gave them utterance" (Acts 2:4)—receives here not its completion but merely its relevant contemporaneous translation.[65] Enabled here is precisely the possibility of yet-original and always-various religious speech. Baptism of the Spirit, it appears, is whenever several human individuals become convinced of the unarguable validity of their individual yet identical commitment to the saving power of the moral sentiment; and when, thus fortified, they decide to go public with the good news. Bereft of the assuring presence of a once available prophet, but absolved at the same time of the utterly hypnotic authority of his "style," disciples go forth to preach. Disciples not of the historical Jesus but of the Spirit's own Truth. Freed at last, evidently, is the transpersonal power to proclaim the safety of Virtue, the last expression of the Soul. And who knows what might follow from that?

If Emerson were praying for the tongue of flame to descend, on the graduates if not on Andrews Norton, the wish does not quite find expression as image. And if he seriously imagined that his sermon would by itself create and send forth, "replenished," an entire cadre of post-sectarian poet-priests, he may well have been disappointed. Theodore Parker would issue his own version of the natural-supernaturalist call in 1841, and Hedge (as we have seen) tried to halt the Dudleian charade a decade later, but Ripley merely exchanged his liberal pastorate for the more literal pastures of Brook Farm, and Brownson's moral agitation moved him first to Democratic politics and then to Roman Catholicism. Among the "literary" disciples, Henry Thoreau and Ellery Channing both failed to find either a position or a stance from which to preach the moral sentiment; and, closer to the church, Unitarian preaching went on pretty much as before, except as its official notice fell off from the "Miracles" to the "Confessional Question."[66] Yet none of these ironies—and not even those deliberately enforced by Hawthorne and Melville—can cancel the ardor with which Emerson "look[s] for the hour when that supreme Beauty, which ravished the souls of those Eastern men…shall speak in the West also" (92). What Emerson anticipates, apparently, is not just another Revival, to prove the tropes of inherited Scripture could still be given lively and efficacious application. What he predicts, instead, is a renewal of prophetic activity powerful enough to prove that Age of Revelation remains altogether open.

Accordingly, Emerson would not be flattered to learn that, in the space where he had expected the Spirit, Ignorant of "persons," to "rekindle the smoldering, nigh quenched fire on the altar" (92) of the Religious Sentiment, his own bold writing ushered in only an American Renaissance. That it did *just* that has become the prime fact of our literary history. But Emerson himself had foretold something a little different, more recognizably "religious."

Imagining, most immediately, a renewed subject and style of preaching, and prepared to accept, at worst, a somewhat rectified or regular Jones Very, Emerson may well have "rubbed his eyes" when, after a time, the newest "bard of the Holy Ghost" (90) appeared in the unlikely guise and unlikelier garb of Walt Whitman. Yet the shock had to be one, in part at least, of recognition, for what the "newborn" song "assumed," primarily, was the demystification of The Word and the liberation of The Spirit, in all its infinite variety of worldly manifestation. Whitman meant to "preach," clearly enough, yet no one would be misled by usage into listening to his revolutionary verses, any more than they would come by custom to hear an Emerson "lecture." The accents of the streets of Brooklyn were as different from those of the fields of Concord as the literary historian can well imagine; but then the Emerson who had complained so bitterly about the tyranny of the "grumbling enunciation" of Cambridge and the "phraseology" of Palestine (JMN, 5: 471) was in no position to anathematize this latter-day experiment in language. And if organic delight had come sexual, finally to overwhelm the moral sentiment it was supposed to provoke and enliven, still Emerson may well have known he had only himself to blame. Who knew? Who indeed could *ever* know what form, cut loose from some authoritative Word, the Spirit might yet assume?

174

Seeking but to liberate and to sacralize the preaching of the moral sentiment, and yet praying for some truly impressive display of the Spirit beyond even that, Emerson's "Address" succeeded most signally in baptizing the doctrine of the difference of American literature. Miracle or Monster: the jury is still out.

Not even Jonathan Bishop—our ablest reader of Emerson as theology *and* as literature—knows quite what to make of the power of Emerson's still emergent example, un-Christian (and often unruly) as he takes its impact largely to be. Yet he is right to insist that to evaluate Emerson we must hold him in the closest comparison, even in dialogue, with the doctrinal expression and the moral consequences of historical Christianity. To that powerful premise I would add only that we need to do this in order even to *understand* him: dependent as are most of his "doctrines" on his power to transubstantiate (or at least to transignify) the terms of a tradition elsewhere thinning out to water, they need to be read, first of all, as natural translations of all the old supernatural wonders. Bishop is also correct to notice that, verbally at least, many of

Emerson's most "literal" translations of the recorded sayings of Jesus are colored by an idiom of virtue-as-beauty which may strike the ear tuned to sterner accents as somehow weak.[67] But he is wrong, I think, in one quite specific way, about the scriptural provenance of Emerson's "Address," and the misprision may have important consequences.

To claim that the "only analogue" in Scripture of Emerson's "Address" is the scene of "Jesus teaching in the temple" is to run the risk of misidentifying the primary audience; to think of Emerson as addressing chiefly the professors rather than the students—who issued him his unlikely invitation, and on whose renewed preaching he clearly staked any viable, or credible, church.[68] And this emphasis may well lead us "back" (as it seems) to some more than ample insistance on the centrality of Emerson's contest with Jesus. Emerson wishes to embarrass the position of "the Elders," of course, and his success in this rear-guard action will be greatly strengthened, he knows, if he can in fact co-opt the authority of their unique prophet, capture even his *words*. But as he ultimately relies on some logic of the Spirit, he is plainly willing to do without the historical Jesus if he must; and what he wishes most fervently is that, thus armed, he can win the minds and hearts of the new generation.

It is thus possible to overemphasize the fact that Emerson wants to be understood not as an "apostate," who would renounce or deny it all, but rather as the "heretic" who, like Jesus in the temple, desires only to "announce the real truth of a message which the apparently orthodox have somehow missed."[69] The fine line of that distinction is always difficult to draw in practice, and it is plainly the intent of Emerson's natural supernaturalism to blur it beyond recognition. That he did not do so with *universal* effect is well established by the orthodox charge of "Infidelity," implying that he was, after all, only a sort of platonistic Tom Paine. Perhaps such distinctions point more usefully to event or outcome than to intention. And it certainly does not appear that Emerson is everywhere taken as but the new Luther.

It is inappropriate, perhaps, to look for a single Biblical analogue to the occasion of Emerson's Divinity School Sermon. Clearly Emerson means to evoke the baptism at the Jordan, but he does so without for a moment considering himself the present-day incarnation of any of the principals: not Jesus and not John; certainly not the bird. And not the Voice either, whose words he takes for his text. As soon would he imagine his own rhetoric to be the efficacious cause of the revival of that original Pentecost where nobody baptized anybody else. What happens in myth may always be true in the spirit, but it never will bear literal repetition. And surely the Emerson who read the entire typological sequence as an effective cancellation of prophetic anxiety would be chagrined to learn that he was, after all, only competing.

So much for in-house debate. Sufficiently clear and significant to conclude the present "provocation" is a simple, altogether literary point: what resonances do we hear when, opening our text, we hear Emerson read again his little sermon to the Theological School? Echoes from *Nature*, most assuredly; and also, as we begin to recover Emerson's explicitly religious beginnings, echoes of his Unitarian sermons as well; as importantly. Yet part of the impact the "Address" *still* makes depends on our chronogically arranged sense that Emerson is also saying somewhat more than he dared say before, something he knew he had *finally* to say. Instructed in this context of "daring," we begin to hear, behind the accusations of and arguments with real but unnamed adversaries, the finished form of the conscientious—but also anxious—conversations once conducted only with his journal, wherein he had indeed learned to do all the voices: Frost, Ware, Channing, even Jesus. We may even learn to hear, more distinctly, all the "philosophical" references, however smoothed out by the not-quite-spiritual unction of Emersonian rhetoric.[70] And in the midst of this intertextual medley, we should also learn to hear Emerson's graceful yet insistent announcement of Biblical text, and to listen for all the changes rung, deliberately as it seems, on the Scriptural song of the Spirit, whose baptism into Virtue Emerson took to be the one religious mystery ever worth celebrating.

We do not know whether our learning to do this, however lucidly, will manage to please God or answer any supposable end of creation. We suspect that it will not, in all probability, save us from having to face the differential or "negative" theology that everywhere haunts the failure of the doctrine of theism. But it should allow us a fuller appreciation of an American writer who worked conscientiously and with marvellous *elan* to anticipate that peculiar condition of the postmodern world. And—with "criticism in the wilderness" still—we could do much worse.

176

FOOTSTEPS OF ANN HUTCHINSON

A Puritan Context for *The Scarlet Letter*

IN THE first brief chapter of *The Scarlet Letter*, the narrator pays almost as much attention to a rose bush as he does to the appearance and moral significance of Puritan America's first prison. That "wild rose-bush, covered, in this month of June, with its delicate gems," contrasts with the "burdock, pig-weed, apple-peru" and other "unsightly vegetation," yet all flourish together in the same "congenial" soil which has so early brought forth "the black flower of civilized society, a prison" (48).[1] Thus early are we introduced to the book's extremely complicated (yet not quite postmodern) view of the natural and the social. Moreover, as the rose bush appears to offer Nature's sympathy to society's criminal, it becomes essentially associated with Hester Prynne, almost as her symbol. Accordingly, criticism has been lavish in its own attention to that rose bush: it has, out of perfect soundness of instinct, been made the starting point of more than one excellent reading of *The Scarlet Letter*; indeed the explication of this image and symbol ranks as one of the triumphs of the (now) older Hawthorne criticism.[2]

But if the internal and, as it were, natural associations of this rose bush have been successfully elaborated, its external and "historic" implications went largely ignored. Yet not for any fault of the narrator. This rose bush "has been kept alive in history," he assures us; and it may even be, as "there is fair authority for believing," that "it had sprung up under the footsteps of the sainted Ann Hutchinson, as she entered the prison-door." We are, I suppose, free to ignore this critical invitation if we choose. Obviously we are being offered a saint's legend in which Hawthorne expects no reader literally to believe. Perhaps it is there only for the irony of "sainted"—a trap for D.H. Lawrence or other romantic readers; for Hawthorne's strict and largely unforgiving narrator will have nearly as many reservations about Hester's sainthood as John Winthrop had about that of Ann Hutchinson. Certainly the language of flowers is a more available aid to interpretation the overdetermined system of historical curiosities we have learned to call "The Antinomian Controversy." And Hawthorne himself may be partly responsible for the idea that he was not all *that* serious about all those old books he used to borrow from the Salem Athenaeum.

Still, a conscious decision *not* to look for and press a Hester Prynne/Ann Hutchinson association might be risky, the result of an old-fashioned bias about what can and cannot count as "internal" to the text. Most simply put, we should not regard Hawthorne as a casual name dropper unless he *prove* himself one. Surely we should prefer a more rather than a less precise use of literary allusion, not only in this opening reference but also in a later one which suggests that, except for the unlooked-for existence of Pearl, Hester "might have come down to us in history, hand in hand with Ann Hutchinson, as the foundress of a religious sect" (165). The references are pretty precise: Hester walks in the footsteps but—unlike the Quaker Mary Dyer, perhaps— not quite hand-in-hand with Ann Hutchinson. And before we invest too heavily in any of his professions of scholarly innocence, we might remind ourselves that Hawthorne did write, near the outset of his career, in clear and close dependence on "a good many books,"[3] a pretty well informed sketch called "Mrs. Hutchinson." He mentions her again, prominently, in those reviews of New England history entitled *Grandfather's Chair* and "Mainstreet." And here he seems to be insisting on a connection between Hester Prynne and New England's most famous female heretic. The man who created the one and memorialized the other ought to be in a position to know.

Clearly, however, the relationship is not one of "identity": tempting as the view might be made to appear, *The Scarlet Letter* is probably not to be read as an allegory of New England's Antinomian Crisis. Hawthorne's historical tales seldom work quite that simply: "The Gentle Boy," "Young Goodman Brown," and "The Minister's Black Veil" all have something precise and fundamental to say about the Puritan mind but, in spite of the precision with which they are set or "dated," they are not primarily "about" the Quaker problem, the witch-craft delusion, or the Great Awakening. Their history is not quite that literalistic. And here, of course, the setting is "literally" Boston, 1642 to 1649, not 1636 to 1638.[4] More importantly, but equally obviously, the career of Hawthorne's fictional Hester Prynne is far from identical with that of the historical Mrs. Hutchinson. However "antinomian" Hester's views may become, it would be unforgivable to forget that her speculative career is inseparable from adultery and illegitimate childbirth, events which have no literal counterpart in the life of the prophet Hawthorne calls her prototype. And—as a newer sort of historical criticism has suitably emphasized—Hester is never ostracized from the scene of her crime and prosecution; she stays in Boston of her own will, leaves when her lover's death severs the most obvious connection, then executes a very curious "return,"[5] long after the dust of Dimmesdale's dying confession has settled.

Important as are these simple differences, and as dangerous as it must always seem to turn away from the rich particularity of Hester's own love story, Hawthorne himself seems to have invited us temporarily to do so. And if we follow his suggestion, a number of similarities come teasingly to mind. Like Ann Hutchinson, Hester Prynne is an extraordinary woman who falls afoul of a theocratic and male-dominated society; and the problems which cause them to be singled out for exemplary punishment both begin in a special sort of relationship with a pastor who is one of the acknowledged intellectual and spiritual leaders of that society. No sexual irregularity seems to have been associated with Mrs. Hutchinson's denial that converted saints were under the moral law, but (as we shall see later) no one could read what seventeenth-century Puritan observes said about the "seductiveness" of her doctrines without fearing sexual implications everywhere. Evidently such implications were not lost on Hawthorne. Further, though with increasing complications, both of these remarkable and troublesome women have careers as nurses and counsellors to other women: Ann Hutchinson begins her prophetic career this way, whereas Hester Prynne moves in this direction as a result of her punishment. And most significantly—if also most problematically—both make pronouncements about the inapplicability of what the majority of their contemporaries take to be inviolable moral law.[6]

To be sure, it takes Hester Prynne some time to catch up with Ann Hutchinson; but when Hawthorne says of Hester, in the full tide of her later speculative freedom, that "the world's law was *no law* for her mind" (164, Emphasis added), we may well suspect that he intends some conscious pun on the root meaning of "antinomianism." If Hester's problems begin with sex more literally than do Ann Hutchinson's, her thinking eventually ranges well outward from that domestic subject. In some way, and for complicated reasons

179

that need to be examined, Hester Prynne and sex are associated in Hawthorne's mind with Ann Hutchinson and spiritual freedom.

So teasing do Hawthorne's connections and analogies come to seem, that we are eventually led to wonder whether *The Scarlet Letter* shows only this one set of historical footprints. If Hester Prynne bears relation to Ann Hutchinson, would it be too outrageous to look for similarities between Arthur Dimmesdale and John Cotton, that high Calvinist who was variously asserted and denied to be the partner in heresy? And—granting that what is involved is neither allegory nor roman à clef—might there not be some fundamental relation between the philosophical and theological "issues" raised by the Antinomian Controversy and the "themes" of Hawthorne's romance?

To the first of these questions, a certain kind of answer comes readily enough. Although the portrait of Dimmesdale is physically unlike the one Hawthorne gives of (the older) Cotton in his early sketch of "Mrs. Hutchinson," their positions are disturbingly similar: both are singled out from among distinguished colleagues as models of learning, piety, and affective preaching; and both relate very ambiguously to a wayward woman on trial. It is impossible not to feel that John Cotton's drastic change of relation to Ann Hutchinson—a phenomenon as fascinating to scholars now as it was momentous to Puritans then—lies somewhere behind Dimmesdale's movement from partner in to judge of Hester's adultery. Both men sit in public judgment of an offense against public order in which there is reason to believe they may bear equal responsibility with the criminal.

Although his sketch of "Mrs. Hutchinson" suggests in one place that her enthusiasm had earlier been restrained from public manifestation by the influence of her favorite pastor, Hawthorne actually takes a rather harsh view of Cotton's role in her trial: "Mr. Cotton began to have that light in regard to his errors, which will sometimes break in upon the wisest and most pious men, when their opinions are unhappily discordant with those of the Powers that be" (XII, 222).[7] That is to say: Cotton and his female parishioner have been what their society calls "antinomians" together, both "deceived by the strange fire" (221), but the respected minister saves himself. Not all modern commentators would agree that Cotton's behavior is to be judged this harshly, but that is not the issue here. At some point Cotton did clearly reverse his relationship to Ann Hutchinson, reproving doctrines she thought were faithful to his own emphasis; and clearly Hawthorne's view of Cotton has influenced his treatment of Dimmesdale.[8] Except for the rather too delicate question of who first lit the strange fires, both Mrs. Hutchinson's treatment by Cotton and Hester's by Dimmesdale might almost be subtitled "Seduced and Abandoned in Old Boston."

Although the significance is completely ironic in *The Scarlet Letter*, both pastors are reminded by their colleagues that "the responsibility of [the] woman's soul" is largely within their sphere; Wilson's urging Dimmesdale to press repentance and confession upon Hester sounds a good deal like an ironic version of the ministerial pleas which Cotton, because of his doctrinal affinities with Ann Hutchinson, so long refused to heed. And to the end, both men are spared from denunciation by their partners. Although Puritan defenders of Cotton's doctrinal reputation (like Cotton Mather) insisted he had been slandered by even being named in the same breath with the seductive Mrs. Hutchinson, there is no evidence to suggest that the "abandoned" one ever pointed a finger of public accusation at Cotton, or reproached him for infidelity to what she continued to believe were their shared experiences and beliefs. Cotton alone, Hawthorne reports, is excepted from her final denunciations. And in spite of Dimmesdale's false and unfaithful position on the balcony overlooking her scaffold, of his own part in her troubles, Hester "will not speak."

The Cotton/Dimmesdale analogy may seem treacherous on these internal grounds alone. After all, Cotton is not named by Hawthorne and Mrs. Hutchinson is. But there are also arguments which "implicate" Cotton in Dimmesdale—external reasons for believing that John Cotton could not be far from Hawthorne's mind when he wrote of the Reverend Mr. Dimmesdale. And in the light of these, the very omission of the name of Cotton seems glaringly to call attention to itself. The historically alert reader of *The Scarlet Letter* comes to sense the presence of Cotton's absence on almost every page.

First of all, in the public judgment of Hester, Dimmesdale stands as the partner of John Wilson, at the head of the Boston church of which Hester is a member: Wilson is the fervent, Dimmesdale the reluctant enforcer of discipline. Now it seems to me inconceivable that the man who wrote about the Hutchinson situation explicitly three separate times, using highly detailed contemporary sources as well as later histories (and who built into *The Scarlet Letter* certain details so minutely accurate as to convince one careful critic that he wrote the romance with a number of books open before him) would not know that the famous partnership at Boston throughout the 1630s and 1640s was Wilson and Cotton.[9] It might be too much to suggest that Dimmesdale is conceived and dramatized as a younger version of Cotton, one whose pastoral involvement with Hester Prynne amounted to a less metaphorical seduction than Cotton's relationship with Ann Hutchinson; but it is hard to believe Hawthorne could pair Wilson with *Dimmesdale* without thinking *Cotton*.

Several other, more curious "displacements" also implicate Cotton. Hawthorne had certainly read in Mather's *Magnalia* of a case in which John Wilson and John Cotton joined together publicly to urge public repentance upon a woman who had killed an illegitimate child; Mather's account surely lies somewhere behind Hawthorne's first scaffold scene. Also, Hawthorne could scarcely have not known that it was with Cotton's death in 1652 that

181

the fiery signs in the sky were associated—not with Winthrop's in 1649. One could argue, of course, that this points away from Cotton, but just as cogently one can say that Hawthorne cannot make the transference without having Cotton in mind, and that the reader who knows the facts will make the application, especially when, standing on his midnight scaffold, Dimmesdale applies "Cotton's" sign to himself. And finally, it was not exactly a secret (despite Mather's silence) that Cotton's son, John Cotton, Junior, was deprived of his pastorship and excommunicated from church membership in the Plymouth Congregation for the sin of adultery. Perhaps Dimmesdale is to be thought of—metaphorically, and with a certain rueful irony—as a sort of embodiment or offspring of Cotton's principles.[10]

All of this may not add up to a completely rational calculus of "influence," but it does suggest that, at some level, *The Scarlet Letter* reflects a complicated response to more in the historic Puritan world than Ann Hutchinson alone. To this point, however, we still know very little about the importance of historical context to the realized intentions of Hawthorne's first long romance— as opposed, that is, to some complex, Road-to-Xanadu association that lies somewhere behind it, perhaps even close to its source. The rest of this essay is conceived as a cautious and tentative answer to the less positivistic question of what *The Scarlet Letter* might come to suggest, in a religious-historical way, if we indeed permit it to call up a fairly extensive set of associations from Puritanism's most crucial controversy.[11]

182

The place to begin an exploration of the inner similarities between Hester Prynne and Ann Hutchinson is with a closer look at Hawthorne's early sketch. In many ways a puzzling piece of historical fiction, the sketch does clear up one fundamental point immediately: Hester's difficulties, with sex and with social relation more generally, can be compared to those of Mrs. Hutchinson because those very "historical" problems can themselves be made to seem flagrantly gender-specific. The sketch introduces itself, too heavily, as a lesson in that forlorn subject which hapless males used to call the nature and role of women. First presented as "the female," Mrs. Hutchinson is offered as a forerunner of certain nameless public, writerly ladies of 1830, and the line from Hawthorne's catty remark here about "how much of the texture and body of cis-atlantic literature is the work of those slender fingers" (XII, 217) to the more famous but equally sexist one later about "the damned mob of scribbling women" seems to run direct. The revelation is damaging enough, but fairly simple: Hawthorne enjoyed competing with women for the readership of magazines and gift books at the outset of his career as little as he did for the "gentle reader" of romances later.[12]

But if Hawthorne's own sexual politics seem too painfully easy (and largely irrelevant to the present question), certain subtler forms of the feminist problem treated in "Mrs. Hutchinson" throw an important light on Hester Prynne (as well as on a significant woman-problem in Hawthorne's larger career). Once we read on and apprehend Hawthorne's dominant image of Ann Hutchinson—formerly a spiritual counsellor to Puritan women, interpreting to them the best of the patriarchal mind, now a prophet in her own right, giving voice to a new spirit of freedom and embodying within herself a new awareness of female intelligence and social power—we immediately grasp the significant context of Hawthorne's views of the later Hester Prynne.

In the now-famous epilogue which Hawthorne calls a "Conclusion," Hester has returned to Boston to wear her scarlet letter "of her own free will," with something approaching an internalized acceptance of its appropriateness. She now appears to accept as reasonable what in the forest she tried to deny and many years earlier she could, in very much the same words, only rationalize: "Here had been her sin; here, her sorrow; and here was yet to be her penitence" (263).[13] But this is not the whole story. Whether to affirm a yet undestroyed inner direction and unreconstructed self-reliance, or else to assert once again the mortal irreparability of ruined walls, the narrator informs us that Hester is still a visionary and has become a counsellor to women. Earlier, even in her most antinomian moments, she had stopped short of that critical move from undisciplined private speculation to unsanctioned public prophecy; providentially she had been prevented from joining hands (metaphorically) with her sister Hutchinson, because "in the education of her child, the mother's enthusiasm of thought had something to wreak itself upon" (165). Now, although Hester has apparently picked up and pieced together again "the fragments of [the] broken chain" formerly cast away; although "the world's law" is now apparently some law to her mind; and although she would might not now claim for her adultery a totally sufficient "consecration" in feeling, she has now found a way to make public her ideas about sexual justice.

Earlier she had pondered the "dark question" of the "whole race of womanhood": could its lot ever be a happy one without a tearing down of "the whole system of society" and an essential modification of "the very nature of the opposite sex" (165)? Now—with important modifications of tone and in separation from all traces of antinomian self-justification—her ideas are expressed to other women, especially those whose lives have been made miserable through excess or absence of passion:

> Hester comforted and counselled them, as best she might. She assured them, too, of her firm belief, that, at some brighter period, when the world should have grown ripe for it, in Heaven's own time, a new truth would be revealed, in order to establish the whole relation between man and woman on a surer ground of mutual happiness. (263)

What Hester's experience comes to finally—in an epilogue, and after a painful and complicated development forced upon her by others—is some insight about the double standard, or perhaps about we have learned to call the "new morality."

Thus, if we can bear the temporary reduction of difference to doctrine, it is easy to see that Hester passes through a phase of antinomianism comparable to (though not identical with) that of the historical Ann Hutchinson, only to emerge as a version of the sexual reformer already "typed out" in Hawthorne's "figure" of Mrs. Hutchinson as independent and reforming "female." And though the equation might need to be clarified by an examination of the precise quality of Hester's antilegal phase, we can already calculate that her final position is, in Hawthorne's mental universe, just about halfway between the baffled protest of Ann Hutchinson and the boldly prosecuted "lawsuit" of Margaret Fuller; and we can sense that when Hawthorne describes her later career as counsellor to troubled and searching women, he has certain seventeenth-century, Sunday evening doctrinal meetings and certain nineteenth-century "Conversations" just about equally in mind. One thing this clearly suggests, in consequence, is that interpreters of the problem of women in Hawthorne can make a less autonomous use of Margaret Fuller than they have sometimes supposed.[14]

To this point, as I have indicated, Hawthorne seems open to the charge of a fairly radical sort of reductivism: he seems to have presented an historical woman whose heretical ideas once caused a profound religious and social crisis as a simple case of uneasy or misplaced (female) sexuality; and the opportunity to reduce Hester Prynne to a woman whose sexuality got quite literally out of control and never did entirely recover itself is therefore ready to hand. Such a reduction is, presumably, as distasteful to old male literary critics as it is to avowed feminists.

The way to stop being offensive about Hawthorne's use of the "female" Mrs. Hutchinson as a type of Hester Prynne is *not*, therefore, to appeal to the psycho-historical interpretation of Mrs. Hutchinson's career. It is probably of some value to notice that its author, Emery Battis, devotes almost as many pages to the complicated female problems of her relation to her strong father, her weak husband, and her beloved pastor as he does to her ideas; that he unashamedly argues for a relation between menstrual cycle, pregnancy, menopause and the more public aspects of her career; and that he introduces his treatment of the character of this unusual woman with the astonishingly Hawthornean speculation that "had she been born into a later age, Mrs. Hutchinson might have crusaded for women's rights."[15] It is perhaps more than a nice polemical point to observe that Hawthorne is not alone in reading sexual implications in Mrs. Hutchinson's theologic and prophetic career, but the observation leaves out all the subtle considerations. They concern not only the ways in which Ann Hutchinson and Hester Prynne are related in a very serious approach to the "theological" meaning of sexuality, but also the historical reasons Hawthorne may have had for linking enthusiasm, individualism, and femaleness.

If we glance again at the early sketch, we can notice that, embattled and argumentative as it is, it is yet about sex in some more elemental way than our loose discussion of "feminism" has so far indicated. With structural intention—and not, pretty clearly, by obsession—the sketch tries hard to focus on several scenes in which Mrs. Hutchinson is the center of all male attention, prophesying doctrines that astound the male intellect. Most of the "historical" facts are there, but only a fairly well informed reader can feel assured of this; and except for an initial, one-paragraph reminder, the facts seem to fall out incidentally, so as not to distract from the dramatic confrontation. The implications, in turn, are not in the ordinary sense "theological": there is no mention of the famous eighty-two errors Mrs. Hutchinson's original protest is said to have spawned, as there is, self-consciously, in *Grandfather's Chair*; we are, historically and psychologically, beyond that sort of consideration. The issue is not sanctification as an a posteriori evidence of justification, but the woman's own prophetic abilities. Having formerly cast aspersions on legalist doctrines of salvation, the enthusiast now claims the spiritual "power of distinguishing between the chosen of man and the sealed of Heaven" (XII, 224). What further need of witnesses? Clearly the progress of the strange fire of her enthusiasm is far advanced.

Nor is there much ambiguity about the source and significance of that fire: Mrs. Hutchinson's spiritual openings and leadings are closely linked to her female sexuality. Although her "dark enthusiasm" has deceived the impetuous Vane and the learned but mildly illuministic Cotton, it is clearly her own "strange fire now laid upon the altar" (XII, 221). The men, variously affected, must make of it whatever they can. Hawthorne does not quite identify enthusiasm with "the female," but we do not distort his intentions if—supplying our own italics—we take as the very heart of the sketch the following sentence: "In the midst, and in the center of all eyes, we see *the Woman*" (XII, 224). This is still sexist, no doubt, but it is no longer petty or carping in the familiar, competitive way. Mrs. Hutchinson's influence is profound. Even the male chauvinist is compelled to admit it. The impulse to challenge the Puritan theocracy's dominant (and socially conservative) assumptions about "visible sanctity" evidently comes from a fairly deep and powerful source. It seems to be coming from some "female" principle.

Evidently, in Hawthorne's view, awakened women accept the inevitability of a given legal order far less easily than their male counterparts. And clearly this is the central issue. What caused a state of near civil war in Boston and what creates the crackling tension in Hawthorne's sketch is Mrs. Hutchinson's proclamation—variously worded at various times, but always as far beyond the reach of the "trained and sharpened intellects" of the most scholastic Puritan controversialists as are Hester Prynne's sexual feelings—that "the chosen of man" are not necessarily "the sealed of heaven." Here, in her last, most devastating, and for Hawthorne most problematic formulation, Mrs. Hutchinson is claiming that sort of direct inspiration and divine guidance necessary to distinguish between true and false, spiritual and legal teachers. But she has been forced to this last claim by the pressure of investigation and over-response; this, presumably, is what you are made bold to say when facing the legalistic scruples of John Winthrop—not to mention the holy wrath of Hugh Peters, the satiric antifeminism of Nathaniel Ward, and the sheer adamant intolerance of John Endicott. And behind her last, sadly self-conflicting claim (as Hawthorne well knows) lies a series of far less drastic attempts to affirm that the Spirit does not always obey the laws of ordinary moral appearance. And even though she has moved from the socially upsetting to the politically dangerous, the weight of Hawthorne's subtlest moral judgment falls no more heavily on her head than on those of her disturbed and anxious judges.

In simple ironic fact, she appears as their natural opposite—private experience exacerbated into individualistic heresy by their organized, legalistic intolerance in much the same way as Hester's later denials are induced by the violence of the community's over-response. Beginning, apparently, with only a purer sort of Calvinism than was customarily preached in New England, Mrs. Hutchinson's ultimate claim to a self-sufficient illumination seems a predictable response to an emerging Puritan orthodoxy which, in its undeniable tendency to conflate the visible with the invisible church, was really claiming that, for nearly all valid human purposes, the "chosen of man" were indeed and indentically the "Sealed of Heaven."[16] If the community chooses to overextend, indeed to mystify its corporate authority, the individual will call upon the deepest interests of the passional self to nullify it all. Or at least, as it appears, the woman will.

What Hawthorne's figure of Mrs. Hutchinson suggests is that "the woman" is not by essence the safe and conserving social force the seventeenth and the nineteenth century (and much Hawthorne criticism) decreed her to be.[17] Exactly to the contrary, female sexuality seems, in its concentration and power, both a source for and a type of individualistic nullification of social restraint. Obviously Hawthorne's feelings about this are not without ambivalence. Personally, of course, he might always prefer some less powerful, more submissive "Phoebe," and in one way or another he would continue his Miltonic protest that "Woman's intellect should never give the tone to that of man," that her "morality is not exactly the material for masculine virtue" (XII, 217–18). But his clear recognition of the antisocial meaning of self-conscious female sexuality, first formulated in the theological context of Puritan heresy, goes a long way toward explaining the power and the pathos of Hester Prynne.

Hawthorne reformulates his insight in "The Gentle Boy." Despite the complexities introduced by a "calm" male enthusiast and by the presence of the "rational piety" of that unreconstructed lover of home and children named Dorothy Pearson, we can hardly miss the elemental clash between "the female," Quaker Catharine, and the entire legalistic, repressive Puritan establishment. Against that male system of enforced rationlistic uniformity, she extravagantly testifies to the reality of an inspired and pluralistic freedom. Her response is, of course, extreme; Hawthorne is no more than faithful to history in judging it so, though he does not have her go naked, for a sign, in the streets of the Puritan capital. But, in a terrifying and elemental way, her response is effective. Tobias Pearson can only puzzle over and feel guilty about his drift toward the sect whose doctrines he thinks quite irresponsible, but this "muffled female" must stand up in the midst of a Puritan congregation—authoritatively and symbolically divided, by a wide aisle, into male and female—and denounce the minister's cruel and sterile formulations of the Puritan way.

The relevance of Quaker Catharine for Hester Prynne is simple and evident: here is the woman who has *not* been prevented from joining hands with Ann Hutchinson; her enthusiasm (and her sufferings) are such that not even little Ilbrahim can hold her back from a career of public testimony to the autonomous authority of conscience itself. Quaker Catharine does, if only in fiction, "come down to us in history, hand in hand with Ann Hutchinson." No doubt several historical women lie behind Hawthorne's figural portrait of Quaker Catharine, but surely none more powerfully than Mary Dyer, Ann Hutchinson's strongest female ally—who literally took her hand and accompanied her out of Cotton's church after her excommunication, went with her into exile, and (years after Mrs. Hutchinson had been providentially slaughtered by the Indians) went on to become notorious in the Quaker invasion of Massachusetts.[18]

Accordingly, another level of history is also involved. Virtually all commentators have recognized that in New England, in dialectic with the Puritan Way, Ann Hutchinson and the Quakers go together; that the latter represent, chiefly a more organized and self-consciously sectarian espousal of the values of individual (or "spiritual") freedom which lies close to the center of Ann Hutchinson's protest. If one is committed and hostile, the cry against both is simply devilish and seductive enthusiasm, unregenerate impulse breaking all bonds of restraint and decorum. If one is committed and sympathetic, the cry is just as simple: the martyrdom of human dignity and divine freedom by aggressive repression. If one is a terribly cautious modern commentator, one is likely to pity the victims and worry that both the Hutchinsonian and the (seventeenth-century) Quaker doctrines do rather tend to elevate the "individual conscience above all authority"; that both promote a "monistic egotism" which tends to dissolve "all those psychological distinctions man [sic] had invented to 'check, circumscribe, and surpass himself.'"[19]

None of these formulations would have been unfamiliar to Hawthorne. And neither would his knowledge or speculation be significantly advanced by the modern historian who, after discussing the Ann Hutchinson question as a "Pre-Quaker Movement," begins his chapters on Quakerism proper with the observation that as in London and at the great Universities of England, "so too, the first Quakers to reach the American hemisphere were women."[20] In every way it comes to seem the reverse of surprising that radical freedom and awakened female sexuality are inextricably linked in Hawthorne's most obviously historical romance. History itself had forged the link.

What is perhaps surprising is that Hawthorne is as sympathetic to a sex-related understanding of freedom as he is. The female protagonist of his "Mrs. Hutchinson" is a troubled and dangerous woman; his Quaker Catharine becomes, in her "unbridled fanaticism," guilty of violating her most sacred duties (even if Ilbrahim is not a Christ figure); even his Hester Prynne is not quite the "Saint" she has occasionally been made out to be. But here—as in his later, largely private encounter with the aroused female novelists of the 1850s—Hawthorne sympathizes with the problems as deeply as he fears the dangers; his compulsion to record warnings is no stronger than his desire to discover the laws by which powerful half truths generate their opposites or to feel the pain of those being destroyed by that implacable dialectic. The context of the sex-freedom link in *The Scarlet Letter* is not adequately sensed, therefore, until we are in a position to measure Hawthorne's emotional distance from his seventeenth-century sources who first raised the issue of sex in connection with Ann Hutchinson's law-denying theology.

The measurement is swiftly made. It begins with Cotton Mather and runs backward directly to John Winthrop and Edward Johnson.[21] All three are, through the typology of Ann Hutchinson, important sources for *The Scarlet Letter*. And except that they are all highly scornful in tone, it might almost be said that these Puritan historians themselves began the transformation of Ann Hutchinson into Hester Prynne. Certainly they reduced Ann Hutchinson to a sexual phenomenon far more egregiously than did Hawthorne. It might even be argued that his own reduction is nothing so much as a fictional way of identifying theirs.

The emphasis of Cotton Mather's treatment of the Hutchinson controversy is double—but not very complex or subtle. On the one hand he utterly rejects the charge that his grandfather John Cotton was hypocritical in declining to espouse Ann Hutchinson as his partner in heresy: it is not, he pedantically insists, a case of a Montanus refusing to stand by the side of his Maxilla;

rather, and obviously, of a notorious woman whom an infamous calumny connected with the name of an Athanasius. (One thinks, perhaps, of certain obdurate refusals to believe Dimmesdale's final confession.) On the other hand, more expansively and with more literary flair, he is perfectly determined to treat the sectaries themselves in a frankly sexual way.

The following reflection—from a special sub-section titled "Dux Faemina Facta"—may stand for Mather's strict theological antifeminism:

It is the *mark of seducers* that *they lead captive silly women*; but what will you say, when you hear of *subtil women* becoming the most *remarkable* of the *seducers*?...Arius promoted his blasphemies by first proselyting seven hundred *virgins* thereunto. Indeed, a *poyson* does never insinuate so quickly, nor operate so strongly, as when *women's milk* is the *vehicle* wherein 'tis given. Whereas the prime seducer of the whole faction which now began to threaten the country with something like a Munster tragedy, was a woman, a gentlewoman, of "an haughty carriage, busie spirit, competent wit, and a voluble tongue."[22]

The quotation marks around the final descriptive phrase point back, of course, to a contemporary phase of antifeminist response to Ann Hutchinson. As usual, Mather, the indefatigable historian, is only elaborating, with a sort of goofy elan, the facts and the emphases that have come down to him.

But equally important in the "Wonderbook" which so pervasively influenced Hawthorne is the primary sexual language which informs Mather's account. Far more memorable than any formulation concerning the self-evidence of justification is a bastardy metaphor which helped to inspire and to shape *The Scarlet Letter*: the doctrines of the Antinomians are "brats" whose "true parents" are to be discovered by the guardians of orthodoxy. And related to this basic concept is the whole grotesque business of the "very surprising prodigies" which were looked upon as testimonies from heaven against the ways of the arch-heretic: "The *erroneous gentlewoman* her self, convicted of holding about *thirty* monstrous opinions, growing big with child...was delivered of about *thirty* monstrous births at once." Or—behold the Puritan wit—perhaps "these were no more monstrous births, than what it is frequent for women, laboring with *false conceptions*, to produce." Again, none of this is strictly original with Cotton Mather: the heretical-idea-as-illegitimate-child conceit is in the windy and wonder-full pages of Edward Johnson; and Winthrop himself labors the ugly details of *monstrous births*—which are at least the providential consequence of her criminal heresies. But the full "literary" elaboration of this sort of talk is Mather's, and his account seems most to have influenced Hawthorne.[23]

189

The influence is very curious. On the one hand, Hawthorne specifically declines to repeat the story of monstrous births in his "Mrs. Hutchinson"; such details are fitter for the "old and homely narrative than for modern repetition" (XII, 225). And the sketch makes no use of any bastardy metaphor. On the other hand, however, in a rather startling display of creative process, it all comes back in the story of Ann Hutchinson's typic sister, Hester Prynne. Not only does Hester conceive a very real, natural child to accompany (and in some measure embody) her quasi-Hutchinsonian conception of spiritual freedom, but she finds it almost impossible to convince herself that Pearl is not in some sense a monstrous birth. Along with many other characters in *The Scarlet Letter* (and not a few incautious critics), Hester daily stares at the child, waiting "to detect some dark and wild peculiarity" (90), unable to believe that a sinful conception can come to any valid issue. This might be no more than the too-simply-Puritan inability ever to separate the moral order from the physical (like looking for one's own "A" in the midnight sky), but with Mather's elaboration of Johnson and Winthrop behind it, it is evidently a bit more. As almost everywhere, Hawthorne seems to be making Hester Prynne literally what orthodox Puritan metaphor said Ann Hutchinson was "really" or spiritually.

One more telling detail from Mather, to which we can only imagine Hawthorne's convoluted reaction: not quite faithful to the wording of Winthrop, Mather has John Cotton express the opinion that Mrs. Hutchinson ought "to be cast out with them that 'love and make a lie.'"[24] Except for this peculiar formulation—which is not really related to Mather's basic set of sexual equivalences, but which just happens to read like an epitome of Dimmesdale's career—nearly all of Mather's basic vocabulary is second-hand. Mather's own debts are tedious to detail, and clearly Hawthorne could have got all he needed from the *Magnalia* (though it is clear he read most of Mather's sources independently). The basic antifeminist construction seems to originate with Winthrop, not only with his famous characterization of Mrs. Hutchinson as "a woman of a haughty and fierce carriage, of a nimble wit and active spirit, and a very voluble tongue" but also with the clear implication in his whole account that one very deep issue is Mrs. Hutchinson's female invasion of male "literary" prerogative. Mrs. Hutchinson insists, out of Titus, that "elder women should instruct the younger"; Winthrop might admit, under exegetical duress, that "elder women must instruct the younger about their business, and to love their husbands and not to make them to clash," but his deeper feeling is rationalized in Timothy: "I permit not a woman to teach."[25]

This last makes the sexual politics of Hawthorne's remark about women's intellect not giving the tone to men's seem liberal. It also enables us to imagine, by simple contraries, what new and surer "relation between man and woman" Hester is teaching at the end of *The Scarlet Letter*. But this is still too easy.

If there is one formulation behind those of Cotton Mather worth savoring on its own, it is something from Edward Johnson. His impassioned account of the seductive appeal of Mrs. Hutchinson's doctrines gives us the clearest sense that Puritans themselves feared sexual implications more profound than those involving ordinary decorum. Upon Johnson's return to New England, he was alarmed to discover that a "Masterpiece of Woman's wit" had been set up by her own sex as a "Priest"; and Johnson was invited to join the cult:

> There was a little nimble tongued Woman among them, who said she
> could bring me acquainted with one of her own Sex that would shew
> me a way, if I could attaine it, even Revelations, full of such ravishing joy
> that I should never have cause to be sorry for sinne, so long as I live.

Here, as clearly as we need, is the simply hostile version of Hawthorne's suggestion that "woman's morality it not quite the standard for masculine virtue," as well as the perception, registered in anger and in fear, that antinomian doctrine is not separable from the tone and from the unsettling consequences of awakened female sexuality.[26]

To write *The Scarlet Letter* out of Hutchinsonian materials Hawthorne would have to feel that tone, but he would have to feel other, different ones as well. Fear "the woman" as he might, he would yet sense the justice of setting her—in reality, and as a symbol of radical and self-contained moral freedom—against the omnivorous legalism of the Puritan establishment. If he would reduce the prophetic Ann Hutchinson to a female "case," his reduction would be less drastic, and more considered, than that of his ancestors. And he would preserve, amplify, and revalue certain deeper hints. *The Scarlet Letter* might not be "about" the doctrines of Ann Hutchinson, but it would be, consciously and emphatically, about antinomianism and "the woman."

191

We are now, finally, in a position to "begin"—to look directly at Hester walking in the footsteps of Ann Hutchinson, and to approach *The Scarlet Letter* itself in an historical context Hawthorne seems urgently to suggest. Legitimately, that task would require twice as many pages and distinctions as we have already set down. But perhaps the sympathetic reader will waive his right to charge doctrinaire reductionism against a somewhat schematic reading of Hawthorne's love story in the Antinomian context.

The Scarlet Letter is, as I have suggested, not roman à clef: we are not to search for secret informations about literal, existent singulars in the seventeenth-century world. Neither is it quite an "allegory" of the deep significance of a theological controversy: the Antinomian Crisis has historical ramifications which defy critical ingenuity to discover in *The Scarlet Letter*. And yet, to repeat, it is about antinomianism and "the woman."

It is, as in one considered formulation, about "passion and authority," but it is not about those human realities considered timelessly and as such. The experiences of Hester and Dimmesdale are subject to an exquisite (and painful) historical conditioning. Their Puritan world may be, as in another formulation, some version of the "modern" world, but that is far too imprecise to account for the historical specificity of Hawthorne's realized intention and stable achievement. To be sure, *The Scarlet Letter* details the items of Hester's beliefs even less than the early sketch specifies those of Mrs. Hutchinson, and yet the romance undoubtedly and unashamedly is, as one excellent reading describes it, a "literary exercise in moral theology."[27]

That theology is, so far as the characters are concerned, "Puritan." So profoundly Puritan are the historically conditioned experiences of Hester and Dimmesdale, in fact, that *The Scarlet Letter* must be seen as Hawthorne's way of testing the limits of Puritan theology as a way of making sense out of some deep and passionate forms of human experience. The limits of that theology are understood by Hawthorne to be—what I take it in fact they are—antinomian; and those antinomian limits of Puritan theology are associated by Hawthorne, as they were by his orthodox predecessors, with "the woman." When the limits are reached, as historically they were and as philosophically they must be, the theology fails what a twentieth-century critic of Puritanism has called "the pragmatic test." And as the theology fails, *The Scarlet Letter* becomes (in the context of the Hutchinson problem, at least) a powerful contribution to what one nineteenth-century critic called "the moral argument against Calvinism."[28]

The Scarlet Letter is about the reasons why "the woman" Hester Prynne reaches certain antinomian conclusions not unlike those of Ann Hutchinson, and why, though her progress seems somehow necessary, and though personally she enlists our deepest sympathies, the teller of her tale—and perhaps the tale itself—enforces her step backwards from those conclusions. More elliptically, it is also about Dimmesdale's lesser portion of the "strange fire"; about the failure of his Cottonesque, all-but-antinomian theology; and, in the end, it is about Dimmesdale's—and the Narrator's—"neonomian" emphasis on "the law" and "the sin." If we understand Hawthorne's relation to Mather, Johnson, and Winthrop properly, we can profitably view *The Scarlet Letter* as Hawthorne's differential version of the *Short Story of the Rise, Reign and Ruine of the Antinomians, Familists, and Libertines*.

In these terms, Hester's career is fairly easy to plot. At the outset she is hardly to be seen as an antinomian in full cry. But she is conceived, like Hawthorne's Ann Hutchinson, as a woman who bears "trouble in her own bosom" (XII, 219), and her "desperate recklessness" on the scaffold, symbolized by the flagrancy of her embroidered "A," and issuing in "a haughty smile, and a glance that would not be abashed" (52), seems deliberately to recall Mrs. Hutchinson's courtroom defiance:

> She stands loftily before her judges with a determined brow, and, unknown to herself, there is a flash of carnal pride half hidden in her eye, as she surveys the many learned and famous men whom her doctrines have put in fear. (XII, 224)

That might describe the original Hester easily enough. She begins, let us say, in a not very repentant spirit. The limits of her defiance are yet to be explored, but strong hints of her later denials and unorthodox affirmations are already there.

To be sure, Hester feels a deep sense of shame, and we scarcely need the still, small quasi-authorial voice of a young woman spectator to tell us so; the reduction of Ann Hutchinson's doctrinal bastard to a living illegitimate child must, in a Puritan community, at least, count for something. And yet even here Hester feels little enough of what our moral pedantry would insist on calling "guilt." Just after the trauma of public exposure, she does confess the real wrong she knows she has done to Chillingworth; but defiance—of hopelessly unqualified and painfully uncomprehending male judges—seems clearly the dominant element in her early characterization. It is probably true to say that, short of the "epilogue," Hester is nearer to "repentance" at the very opening of *The Scarlet Letter* than she ever is again. But she is not very near it. And by the time she finds herself in the forest with Dimmesdale, she has evidently found her own way never again to "have cause to be sorry for sinne."

In preparation for that antinomian moment, the narrator severely instructs us, Hester's "whole seven years of outlaw and ignominy had been little other than a preparation" (200). The moment includes not only the decision to cast by all outward pretence of living by the Puritan "world's law" and run away with Dimmesdale but also, and even more radically, her attempt to convince that unreconstructed Puritan theologian that what they earlier did "had a consecration of its own"—they having felt it so and said so to each other. The painfulness of Hester's development toward this moment in no way lessens our sense of its inevitability. From the first she has seemed perilously close to defying her judges with the affirmation that her spirit posits and obeys its own law.

The Narrator, a curious, sternly moralistic character in his own right, seems convinced that Hester has indeed sinned—deeply, and "in the most sacred quality of human life" (56); at one level of our response, the seventh commandment remains real enough. But what he urges far more strongly is the outrage to both human privacy and human conscience perpetrated by the "unpardonable" Puritan practice of exposure and enforced confession.[29] And

193

he also feels, with Hester, that her adultery was, in quality, not simply or entirely evil: the sacred is present along with the sinful; or, less paradoxically, that Hester has fulfilled her passionate self—felt love, perhaps—for the first time in her not very independent life.

But of course there are no "Puritan" categories for this ambiguity. There is no way for Hester to say to herself that her action (an "experiment," as Emerson's "Experience" might have branded it) had been naturally perfect and yet had introduced an element of profound social disharmony. And there is no way for the Puritan mind to treat her evident unwillingness fully to disown and un-will the affections and natural motions which caused the disorder as anything but a wayward motion of unregenerated natural depravity. She evidently loves her sin, and theocrats in the business of inferring the ultimate moral quality of the self from the prevailing outward signs can reach only one conclusion. And, thus, when the Puritan establishment moves from the fact that Hester has sinned to the conclusion that she in essence is sinful, her rich and ambiguous personality finds no life-saving resource except to begin a career of antinomian speculation, of internal resistance to all those puritanic guilt categories as such.

If Society must treat the negative consequences of one mixed act as the symbol of the depravity of the Self, that Self is likely to respond with a simple affirmation of all its own more profound impulses. If the Puritans begin by turning Hester into a sermon, a type, and an allegory of "Sin," she will end by nullifying their entire world of external law and interference with her own passional freedom. Some Ideal Reader might wish for Hester to stop feeling shame and to confront the real though limited extent of her guilt. But this, in the Puritan mental and social world, seems impossible. Extremes of public legalism seem to breed their antinomian opposite by a law that comes to seem natural.[30] In any event, Hester finds no way to affirm the legitimacy of her sexual nature without also having to affirm some totalized, anarchic spiritual freedom.

Of course she begins in outward conformity, playing the game of "sanctification"—the single rule of which is that the true Self is the sum of all its outward works; indeed, by the time we see her in the chapter called "Another View of Hester," she has learned the game so well as to have covered her undestroyed inner pride with an external appearance "so like humility, that it produced all the softening influence of the latter quality on the public mind" (162). But all the while she is "preparing," moving toward the moment when she announces a doctrine of personal freedom which every orthodox Puritan sensed would lead directly to passionate license and judged a more serious threat to public order than adultery itself. Her own version of the antinomian heresy does not, obviously, express itself in theological jargon; for the most part Hawthorne eschewed it even in treating Mrs. Hutchinson. No dogmatist,

194

Hawthorne is looking for doctrines that make a difference, and the antinomian difference is identically expressed in Mrs. Hutchinson and Hester
Prynne, in association with but not quite reduced to a discovery and affirmation of the legitimacy of their female sexuality. Call it Spirit with the seventeenth, or Passional Self with a later, less guarded but also less subtle century,
one's affirmation is not very different: the significance of a life is not the sum
of its legally regulated outward works; or, more radically, what one does has a
consecration of its own provided the quality of inner feeling is, in a word,
authentic.

Probably this is all too partial a truth for Hawthorne; we may not be wrong
in hearing his own advice when Dimmesdale twice bids the voice of Hester's
moral revolution to "Hush." And yet he seems to understand how it comes
about. He even presents it as necessary for Hester to reach this stage of self-
affirmation and release from shame before she can settle into anything
approaching final peace.

While she cannot affirm her "adultery"—hardly that, given the casuistical-
ly complicated facts of her original case—she cannot truly accept Pearl as a
valid human person. It is probably too much to ask her to accept a good-out-
of-evil doctrine all at once. Certainly it is better to affirm the natural order
than to treat Pearl chiefly as a living sermon; clearly nothing good can happen
as long as the mother is allegorizing the child even as the community has allegorized the mother; and surely a parent who is watching for a child to become
a moral monster will not be disappointed.

195

And then there is the simple matter of Hester's own integrity. Speculating
so boldly and conforming so relentlessly, she has become—no less than
Dimmesdale himself—two people. At one primal level, the whole antinomian
controversy is about the inner and the outer, the private and the public person: what do our outward works, positive and negative, really reveal about our
salvation status, or, in naturalized form, about our enduring selves? The conservative rhetoric of Hawthorne's romance is, of course, busy denying total
autonomous validity to the private or "spiritual" self, and the explicit "moral"
about freely "showing forth" some inferential "token" clearly embodies the
authorial realization that inner and outer can never be completely congruent.
Hawthorne has not written "Young Goodman Brown" and "The Minister's
Black Veil" for nothing. And yet Hester must stop living a life so completely
double. Quite like Dimmesdale, she must heal the wide and deep, "hypocritical" split between her outer and inner self. She may never realize in the way
Dimmesdale finally does the extent to which (or the profound reasons why)
the Self must accept the demystified implications of the visible, and dwell—
though not as the great body of Puritans do—among moral surfaces.[31] But in
the terms of her own developing and self-held theory of spiritual self-reliance,
she must enact, as fully as possible, whatever she most truly comes to believe.

And we sense her self-acceptance and self-affirmation coming. She may seem to wander in confusion, thinking the sun of universal benevolence shines only to illuminate her scarlet letter, and deceiving herself about the real (passionate, confused) reason she remains in New England; but from time to time, when a human eye (presumably Dimmesdale's) falls upon her "ignominious brand," she wills her old passion anew. She may worry about the condition and quality of Pearl's right to existence, but when the watchful theocratic government considers removing her natural child to some more socialized context of Christian nurture, Hester is simply defiant: "I will not lose the child!" (113). She may argue from Pearl's moral use, but she is also affirming the validity of her own sexual nature.

We can say—if we wish to maintain a modern-only reading of *The Scarlet Letter*—that this is all Hester is affirming when she argues, finally, that her adultery had "a consecration of its own"; that Hawthorne has engaged Hester entirely in an overt struggle with the unruly and unsatisfied sexual emotions which the Puritans obscurely felt to lie unsublimated behind Mrs. Hutchinson's public career, and which they clearly felt would be unleashed upon their community by a public acceptance of her doctrine. (Male self-control being difficult enough when all women are passive or frigid.) But if our conclusions concern only Hester's movement from sexual shame to sexual affirmation, then Hawthorne has wasted a good deal of historic understanding and surmise as mere costume and color. It seems far more adequate to say, as we have already said, that Hawthorne regards awakened but not conventionally invested female sexual power as the type—but also as a real historical source—of the individualistic nullification of organized social restraint.

Waiving the problem of vehicle and tenor, we may validly conclude that in *The Scarlet Letter* "the woman's" discovery of an authentic, valid, urgent, powerful, and not shameful sexual nature is not unlike the Self's discovery of its own interior, "spiritual" sanction. The *donnée* of Hawthorne's romance is such that Hester discovers both together, and each reinforces the other.

And further, by way of completing our contextual approach to *The Scarlet Letter*, it seems appropriate to suggest that Hawthorne's treatment of Dimmesdale, the less clearly antinomian partner, provides further, cogent reasons for not divorcing the theology from, or reducing it too simply to, the sexuality. For Dimmesdale's predicament is not to be understood without some fairly explicit reference to the most theological of the antinomian questions, certainly not without a sense of the peculiar moral shapes one can be molded into only by a fairly high Calvinism. Indeed there is, as I have already suggested, strong evidence that Hawthorne thought of Dimmesdale as some intellectual and literary relative of John Cotton. And—feminist favoritism to the contrary notwithstanding—it is Dimmesdale's story too.

• • •

In a number of complex and related senses, Dimmesdale's problem is "hypocrisy." Most simply, he is not what he outwardly appears; he may or may not be "vile," but he is certainly not the apotheosis of saintly purity the Puritan community takes him for. More technically, he is an enforcing agent of public discipline who has himself sinned against a clear and serious public law whose absolute validity he (quite unlike Hester) never questions for a moment, and who refuses to confess and submit to the discipline he has sworn by covenant to uphold and enforce. In so refusing, he may very well be avoiding the question of whether he is really sorry for his sin, or whether in fact he loves his own satisfactions more than he loves God; if so, if Dimmesdale's adultery is really an "idolatry," as in the common religious equivalence, then of course he is a "hypocrite" in the very most technical Puritan sense of all: he is an unconverted man who has found his way not only into but up to the very apex of the purest Church the world has ever known.[32] This is clearly what he fears: that the minister, whose election is sure if anyone is, whose conversion is the norm for the members' admission, and who—at this level, incidentally—is universally revered as a miracle of preternatural holiness and supernatural humility, is really an unregenerate sinner simply.

He fears, but he is not certain. He also hopes. In such tension Dimmesdale is a classic Puritan case of conscience—an advanced and exacerbated form of the too-common problem of lingering sinfulness and naturally attendant doubt which seems to have followed many honest Puritans into full communion with New England's congregations of "visible saints." What, after all, could the unreconstructed Arminianism of natural conscience make of the fact that, after one professed to have received saving grace by the direct operation of the spirit (and had that profession accepted by other spiritual men and women), one continued to be roughly the same sort of moral person one was before?[33]

The simplest answer is antinomianism: "works" argue nothing. The sons of God being under no law, it is as fatal a confusion to argue from the presence of sin to the absence of grace as it to infer justification of the person from sanctification of the life. Grace is a spiritual indwelling, and whatever the Spirit is, is right. Just ask Hester.

Dimmesdale, of course, can accept this limit-interpretation of Pauline and then powerful Protestant theology as little as Cotton could. And yet Dimmesdale seems caught in a trap set for him by certain of the spiritual principles Cotton laid down carefully to distinguish himself from both the covenant legalists on the one side and the "antinomians, familists, and libertines" on the other. Everyone wanted to admit that the forensic transaction of justification did not imply or create immediate and perfect operational sanctity, but Cotton's critics wanted him to narrow the gap as much as Protestant loyalty could possibly admit. They put it to him: when you say "a

Christian may have Assurance of his good Estate, maintained to him, when the frame of his Spirit and course is grown much degenerate: we want much satisfaction."Your doctrine is very dangerous, they instructed him; there ought to be more "Symmetry and proportion" in this matter of "faith and holiness" or you "open a wide door of temptation, as into Sin with less fear, so into a bold continuance and slight healing of sin, and breaches thereby."[34]

As always, the legalists have conceived the problem rather too crudely: Dimmesdale's "continuance," for example, is far from "bold," and his physical and moral self-flagellations amount at some level to more than a "slight healing of sin." And yet there is sense in their position. A man who fears he may be a hypocrite and yet has good theological reasons to hope that even gross sins do not necessarily prove the case either way is likely to clutch at every available theological straw. And indeed Cotton's answer to the legalists offers far more than a straw. It may be worth quoting at some length, for it marvellously illuminates Dimmesdale's predicament. If a man

> know the riches of God's grace in Christ, he ordinarily both may, and (by ordinary rule) ought to beleeve that his justified estate doth still remain unshaken, notwithstanding his grievous sin. For as Justification and the faith of it doth not stand upon his good works, so neither doth it fall or fail upon his evil works.[35]

Cotton's difference from the antinomians is, evidently, a fairly subtle one (and not of primary interest to us here). Of significance is the fact that the strictest Calvinist of New England's first generation appears to provide Dimmesdale with a perfectly plausible way to avoid the obvious, most "natural" conclusion about his technical hypocrisy. And Cotton's analysis comes even closer to our present fictional case:

> Because men of great measure of holiness be apt to live besides their faith, in the strength of their own gifts and not in the strength of Christ, it pleaseth the Lord sometimes to leave them to greater falls, than other weaker Christians, who being of weaker gifts do find more need to live by faith in Christ than upon the strength of their gifts.

It seems to me entirely likely that some conception such as this—a deeply religious man being tested by a great fall—lies very close to Hawthorne's idea of Dimmesdale, that "subtle, but remorseful hypocrite" (144).[36] And that Hawthorne is testing this Cottonesque way of conceptualizing the problem of sin and sainthood as he watches Dimmesdale fail to work out his assurance of salvation in just these terms. For the terms do fail him, even more plainly than, in the epilogue, Hester's appear to have failed her. The psychological dynamic of their failure is delicately wrought, but it is "there," perceptible enough, in the romance itself. To see it requires only to look at Dimmesdale's few key speeches very closely.

We do not begin to get inside Dimmesdale until Chapter X, where "The Leech" is working on "His Patient." With the worst imaginable motives, Chillingworth is trying to get Dimmesdale to do what the structure and the basic terms of the romance clearly indicate he must if he is to save his soul, in any imaginable sense—clearly and openly admit his guilt, whatever the consequences. Dimmesdale offers several "good" reasons why some men find it impossible to confess before the Last Day, or to any hearer except the Searcher of Hearts. His reasons are all, we easily sense, speculative or notional, unreal; the two men are talking "objectively," about "some men." And yet before Dimmesdale waives the whole subject as if "irrelevant or unreasonable," he is betrayed into a modestly revealing hint. The best of his rationalizations is that "some men" do not confess because, in spite of their sin, they yet retain "a zeal for God's glory and man's welfare"; they realize that once exposed "no good can be achieved by them; no evil of the past be redeemed by better service" (132). Hypocrisy, Dimmesdale seems to argue, is not without an important social, even spiritual use.

Chillingworth, however, that perfect devil's advocate, recognizes the desperate character of this logic at once. Hypocrisy for the sake of the kingdom is the worst hypocrisy of all. Would Dimmesdale have us believe "that a false show can be better—can be more for God's glory, or man's welfare—than God's own truth" (133)? The irony here is very keen. It seems impossible to escape the sense that Hawthorne is deliberately playing with one of the most famous arguments in an important Puritan literature of propagandistic self-defense—the idea of "the usefulness of hypocrites." Attacked by English Presbyterians for a wildly utopian collapse of the invisible church into the visible, defenders of the New England Way loudly protested that they fully expected to receive hypocrites into their churches, despite the revolutionary tests for saving grace; that they indeed could rest easy in this practical knowledge, despite their purist theoretic aims, because in outward practice the hypocrite was very often more zealous, set a more striking public example than the true saint. And the most authoritative spokesman for this Puritan "foreign policy" was—of course—John Cotton.[37]

The irony is only slightly less telling when we remember that neither Dimmesdale nor Hawthorne really sees the case in these terms. Hawthorne could very easily accept hypocrites into his church since, so far as we can tell, it is universal and consists *only* of hypocrites who never can fully "show forth" what they ultimately are. Trapped in his historic world, however, Dimmesdale is obviously far from this insight. Indeed he is even further away from it than his use-of-hypocrites rationalization would indicate.

Where he is, morally and theologically speaking, becomes perfectly clear only in the forest with Hester—though anyone versed in the literary cure of Puritan souls may sense it long before. The meaning of his entire predicament is encapsulated into two sentences, and logically enough he speaks them in direct reply to Hester's antinomian plan for adulterous escape:

> "If, in all these past seven years," thought he, "I could recall one instant of peace or hope, I would yet endure, for the sake of that earnest of Heaven's mercy. But now,—since I am irrevocably doomed,—wherefore should I not snatch the solace allowed to the condemned culprit before his execution?" (201)

Again the irony is fairly complex. First of all, we recognize in Dimmesdale's decision to "seize the day" the crassest sort of antinomian response possible for a Calvinist to make: since I am predestined to hell anyway, I might as well... But this is still the least of it.

More crucially, Dimmesdale reveals that he has to this point been looking at his life in a way that is very "properly" Calvinist: he has been regarding all his acts, good and evil, and all his spiritual states and experiences, hopeful and discouraging, not as sequential parts of a moral life that he himself is building, bit by bit, but rather as evidences of his status relative to divine decree. The difference may often seem subtle in practice, but it is profound, and the meaning is to be read in any Puritan diary. One does not repent sin in order to undo it and atone for it and get *back* into the divine favor one had lost; only Catholics and other Arminians think this. Rather, one examines sins, along with every other significant fact about the moral life, in order to detect, if one possibly can, whether or not an eternal decree of salvation has made itself temporally manifest in some conversion, the realization of psychological counterpart of justification, usually issuing more or less "proportionally and symmetrically" in sanctification.

For *most* Puritans sins are, therefore, an essential sign; for all, repentance is an absolutely necessary one. Even for Cotton. The great man may have great sins and not lose heart and hope, but even the great man must find he truly can repent. Gross outward lapses may be at best a crude indicator of the spiritual estate, but enduring love of sin is not.

"Of penance," Dimmesdale admits, of that melodramatic outward punishment and gothic inward torture, there has been a surfeit; "of penitence," however, of that true spiritual rejection of the soul's rejection of God, "there has been none!" (192). And now, he accordingly concludes, things look very bad indeed. He may as well admit he has been, all along, the hypocrite he feared he might be and yet hoped (in spite of his rationalization to Chillingworth) he might not be. In the forest then, finally, after seven years of self-torturing

hope against hope—"forcing hope's faculty," as Taylor's Soul might say—
Dimmesdale gives over the attempt to see himself as the man whose justification does not, in Cotton's words, "fall or fail upon his evil works." Quasi-anti-
nomian to this point, he now concludes that his hope has all been in vain, that
he has not repented his sin, that he has been granted no further spiritual assurances, and that his crime of adultery is precisely what all vulgar Puritanism
would take it to be, "visible" (if only to himself) evidence of a manifest unre-
generacy.

Spiritually, then, Dimmesdale is further from Hester Prynne during their
physical, quite possibly sexual reunion in the forest than he has ever been
before—as far away, in fact, as it is possible to be within a Puritan world. Their
decision to escape, though they may "say it to each other," means two dramatically opposed things. To Hester it is that triumphant escape into the antinomian freedom of spiritual self-reliance; to Dimmesdale it is a pitiful retreat
from the hope-against-hope to that miserable alternative of sinful freedom left
to the despairing reprobate. One hopes their original meeting had involved
more real mutuality.

Thus Hawthorne's subtlest view of Dimmesdale is as a man who is so ineffectual an antinomian as not to be able to overcome the conscientious suspicion that his serious sin proves him in fact a hypocrite; not even with the subtle categories of John Cotton. Hawthorne's men, as we know, are weaker than
his women. Or perhaps it *is* simply that "woman's morality is not quite the
standard for masculine virtue." Or perhaps Dimmesdale is simply honest. In
any event, neither his sexuality nor his doctrine can justify the life he has been
leading or, now, sanctify the new freedom he has been seduced into accepting. He will run away, in a sense, to settle his doubts, once and for all, into a
certainty of reprobation.

If we are sufficiently aware of the positivistic pitfalls, it becomes useful to
speculate about Dimmesdale's fictional relation to John Cotton. Should we say
he is some curious version of Cotton's son, who did commit adultery and suffer ignominious excommunication? Or might we see him as a provisional
John Cotton who by Providential mischance happened to seduce (or be
seduced by) Ann Hutchinson? What if, Hawthorne might have brooded, what
if Ann Hutchinson had literally been what Puritan metaphor implied she was?
And what if Cotton were implicated, literally, to the very extent his English
detractors said he metaphorically was? What, in short, would a "high" but not
antinomian Calvinist do if he had played the part of a sexual Montanus to
some sexual Maxilla? What would a real sin, all sexual, passionate, and ambiguous, do to the delicate balances of personality required to maintain that
exquisite "Doctrine of the Saints' Infirmities"? What sense might a younger,
less robust, less settled version (or disciple) of Cotton be able to make out of

a passionate but unsanctioned love affair, an adultery in doctrine if not in self-conscious fact?

In this light, it is just possible that Dimmesdale owes something to the writings (thought not to the life) of John Preston, Cotton's most famous orthodox convert and disciple. Mather's *Magnalia* calls Cotton the "spiritual father" of Preston, and Preston's most famous work, *The Doctrine of the Saints' Infirmities* (1638), owes a profound debt to Cotton's ideas about assurance in spite of sin. Like Cotton, Preston is at great pains to prove that the Puritan saint "may have many infirmities, and the covenant remain unbroken." But there is one peculiar and illuminating hesitation in Preston that is entirely lacking in Cotton's answers to the American legalists of the 1630s. Unlike Cotton, Preston is extremely anxious about an exception, or at least a possible misunderstanding. Not all sins are to be written off as mere "infirmities"; "some sins" are so radically "idolatrous" that they must be taken to mean that a person has not been in the covenant—that he has been a hypocrite all along. Preston does not specify; but his one hint is telling indeed: the exceptions are sins which "untye the marriage knot" as, in human marriage, "Adultery."[38] That revelation would seem to explain Dimmesdale's career pretty well: the reason he cannot repent is that he is not a saint; probably Preston's emphasis is sounder than Cotton's. And so he gives over the desperate seven-year effort to believe himself not a hypocrite in the worst sense. His peculiar "infirmity" is too real, too true a sign of unregenerate infidelity. Justification and sanctification are not to be conflated, but "some sins" are unsupportable. And thus—until Dimmesdale's very last moment, at least—Puritan doctrines with sexual implications and overtones seem to be damning him as surely as they seem to be saving Hester.

The problem of "Dimmesdale's Confession" may well be, unhappily, every bit as complicated as that of "Hester's Return." There is, first of all, the question of exactly when, and in what mood, he decides to reveal his hidden sin and its curious outward evidence, and *not* to follow through with the plan of escape Hester had formulated for him, for them both, in the forest. Evidently he is still planning to run away when he tears up his old election and excitedly composes a new one: "no public duty unperformed," he had promised himself, with sad self-deception, nor any one "ill performed" (215). And, arguably, the same natural high—begun in the forest with his first taste of "joy" (201) in many years—carries over into the confident but curiously abstracted way he conducts himself in "The Procession" that leads to the site of his final preaching. But where, then, does he change his mind? In the very delivery of that final sermon, as some have held? But how could a poor sinner be converted to the true sight of his very own misdeed by the eloquent proclamation of some "high and glorious destiny" yet to be manifest to this "newly gathered people of the Lord"? Has Hawthorne lost his mind as well as his sense of irony?

In any event, a major reversal does indeed occur, at some unspecified time we have to call the last moment. Ceasing to "live in the strength of [his] own gifts"—even though he has just exercised them magnificently in a sermon almost certainly delivered in self-deception or in bad faith—Dimmesdale asks for Hester's strength and God's grace to help him up the scaffold. Once there, his words indicate that *somehow* he has freed himself from his old Calvinist entrapment. If he has not entirely de-theologized himself, at least he has got his doctrine down to certain saving essentials. Hester calls on his far-seeing vision to predict their final destiny. But Dimmesdale, who has been reading evidences of spiritual *faits accomplis* for too long, rightly refuses to predict: "Hush, Hester, hush!" What has often been called his final "gloom" may be no more than some elemental moral and theological honesty: "The law we broke!—the sin here so awfully revealed!" Stern instructions to an Antinomian. And a curious lesson from seven years of trying to detect Salvation in spite of Sin. Yet these alone must be in their thoughts, their only proper concern. For the rest, "God knows; and He is merciful!" (256).

Law, Sin, Mercy: these, the Narrator is sure, are now the only terms in Dimmesdale's moral scheme. We know there are laws to restrict our Selves in the name of our communities which, well or ill, sustain our common life; we know we break these laws; the rest is up to God. This may or may not conceal Arminian heresy, but its moral conservatism is clearly designed and understood. And though a fair amount of critical literature very effectively warns us not to believe everything we are merely "told," it may be safe to grant the writer of "Young Goodman Brown" and "The Minister's Black Veil," and the creator of Dimmesdale's own problems of ever "outering" what he truly is inside, the right to affirm the operational primacy of "the public." "True-be-true-be-true," one student of mine has parodied the Teller's final moral, waggishly conflating one blue-eyed American bard with another: thematic doggerel is like that. But who knows? Something somehow like it might somehow, like, be true.

It takes Hester longer, and it requires a years-later epilogue, but she too relents from her doctrine of the autonomous private; she too repents, the Narrator is quite sure, turning her worksy game of "penance" into authentic "penitence." There is "compromise" here, if one insists; and politics is, like theology, exactly where one finds it. But the Narrator's sense of moral retribution—and indeed formal closure—is now perfectly satisfied. Hester looks forward to the appearance of some Feminist Reformer, whom one learned critic has soberly interpreted to be Christ appearing in the Female.[39] But evidently she can now separate the valid personal and sexual expectations of her

203

sisterhood from the supposed spiritual freedom of the Self from the world's law.

The final ironies of Hawthorne's use of Hutchinsonian motifs and antinomian ideas are thus striking indeed. If his early sketch seems to reduce a dangerous female heretic to a sexual case, his effort can be regarded as a commentary on a Puritan response as validly as it can be taken for his own, and he puts all the subtlety back into *The Scarlet Letter*. He maintains, even literalizes, all the sexual suggestions in his creation of Hester Prynne, but he leaves them in tension with some very profound (if, for him, dangerous) religious ideas. With Dimmesdale he allows the full theological complexity to operate, though we never forget that Dimmesdale is related to Hester in the sexual problems which form the context of their spiritual struggles. An ideal context, we may feel, given Puritan problems with "privacy" of all sorts. And in the end, after he has fully explored the antinomian and Cottonesque ramifications of his imaginative vision of a Puritan heresy, in doctrine and in metaphoric implication, Hawthorne brings both his principal characters back to some worldly but demystified "neonomian" norm. The ending is by no means "happy," any more than Hawthorne's "Antinomians" and "Libertines" are, in any sense that would satisfy Winthrop or Mather, "Ruined." But their "Short Story" does end in an important transformation.

The Self—if indeed we still believe in such a thing—is not to be inferred from its Works; it is and always has been quite naïve to think so. But sorrow for sin is not to be transcended or "spiritually" suspended in this life. Human beings are more free than any human establishment, theocratic or otherwise, can "tolerate" or even perhaps recognize. But the world's law exists to restrain our disruptive social excesses, however powerful and authentic we "say" their private consecration to be. That, or something like it, equally simple, was the ethical truth to be discovered by following up the footsteps of Ann Hutchinson. Or the shadow of the figure of John Cotton. To press for more would be to invite a more critical, less humanistic analysis of the morally and socially productive power of sexual language in the world of Puritanism. For what lies beyond the doctrine of "the world's law" is, in Hawthorne at least, not some perfect freedom but that calculus of difference we call deconstruction.

204

"THE WOMAN'S OWN CHOICE"

Sex, Metaphor, and the Puritan "Sources" of *The Scarlet Letter*

THE PROBLEM with "source criticism" is that it raises more questions than it answers. Or else, as often as not, it discovers questions where none before existed. We always wish to read the works our author has read, presumably, yet we quickly discover that a text is easier to read "in itself" (as we used to say) than as a function of its "pretexts." Further, the readerly discovery that some apparently unified and powerfully original work of literary imagination actually reveals significant traces of other works can leave us feeling a little let down: evidently the myth of uninfluenced identity, defeated in life, had wished to live on in literary criticism. And finally, the presence of those traces instantly generates a whole new set of difficulties, at a level quite different from the one on which they were first discovered. Why this particular pretext and not others? (Don't all roads lead to Xanadu?) Is the trace in question an unconscious echo or a deliberate allusion? If unconscious, is it therefore accidental and, as it were, meaningless? If deliberate, is it yet the sort of necessary "borrowing" an author has tried but failed to conceal? Or is it in fact part of a pattern or purpose, a constitutive element in some design of strategic repetition and significant difference?

In this last case most of all—but in the others too, in some fair degree—we always want to know what *else* the positive identification of a source can possibly teach us. And this added fact is not always easy to learn. Hawthorne's texts rewrite those of the Puritans. Yet what critical significance are we supposed to attach to that information? Was Hawthorne himself therefore a Puritan? Or just a little short on plots? Or else somehow anxious to disguise present psychic interest as past religious theme?

But to remain with the general case just a moment longer: evidently our discomfort is most acute when a source or pretext turns out to be "historical" rather than "literary," in the ordinary (but now embattled) sense of that word. Books which allude to Shakespeare or Milton may betray, thereby, their want of absolute originality, but clearly they have nothing to fear by way of generic reduction: the texts speak to one another, we tend to assume, and at a level of privilege so rare that no real violation can occur; and thus we spread out an order of literature that retains its purity, even if no individual literary text is ever completely "originary." But what if the pretext is not Milton but Cotton Mather, not Shakespeare but John Winthrop? Suddenly the noble kingdom (or Department) comes under attack. Wordsworth's response to Milton founds the modernist project. But what supposable canon can ever be constituted by folding Winthrop's *Journal of New England* into *The Scarlet Letter*? Only that of "American Studies," presumably, where literary appreciation usually takes a back seat to intellectual or social history.

And yet the evidence accumulates: if the geography and physical setting of *The Scarlet Letter* reveal an author who wrote with Caleb Snow's *History of Boston* "on the desk,"[1] the moral setting and even in some deep sense the plot evidently required of Hawthorne—and may yet demand of us—a pretty fair recall of the matters John Winthrop set out as the essential religious and political story of the first two decades of his holy experiment and Model City. The matter of Ann Hutchinson we may now take for granted: though elaborated by Winthrop in a separate book on the very subject, and then significantly reviewed in Cotton Mather's comprehensive *Magnalia*, the Hutchinson story exists most essentially in the *Journal*, where it figures as something like the definitive (if negative) test case of Winthrop's own special theory of covenant as a fusion of law and love; and it is from that source, primarily, that Hawthorne was moved to create, in Hester Prynne, a female protaginist whose primary distinction is to walk "in the footsteps" of Ann Hutchinson.[2]

A complicated story, to be sure, but even simpler evidences have pointed in the same direction. The classic source study of *The Scarlet Letter* had wanted to emphasize externals, out of Snow's *History*, but it was unable to suppress the implication that both the career and *Journal* of John Winthrop moved everywhere, just beneath the surface. A well nigh definitive essay on the problem of "Public Confession" and *The Scarlet Letter* returns again and again to that crucial document for its most suggestive hints and analogues. And a most able treatment of Hawthorne's connections with the conventions of "Historical Romance" has strenuously to insist that Winthrop ("the founding father *par excellence*") well survives his intriguing displacement by the altogether un-literary figure of Richard Bellingham.[3] So that it may be worth the risk to test, however tentatively, a very suggestive proposition about the intertextual status of Hawthorne's most powerful evocation of the Puritan world—namely, that Winthrop's famous *Journal* is not only a prime and obvious source for Hawthorne's knowledge of "historical backgrounds," but that it furnishes the novel's own most essential themes; that Winthrop's record may itself be a vital part of Hawthorne's own (intensely historical) subject.[4]

A full exposition of that complex proposition would require a lengthy monograph indeed. It would involve, among other things, a full (and fully "literary") reading of the structure and theme of Winthrop's *Journal* itself—and that in relation to many other Puritan writers who struggle to harmonize the differential matters of law and love. It would require an elaboration of the entire seriousness of historical fiction, in a literary climate where such a thing has often seemed either "popular" or Marxist. And it would demand some account of why Hawthorne might have felt intellectually compelled (rather than personally obsessed) by Winthrop's own peculiar mix of moral and political matter. But one has to begin somewhere. And, as Hawthorne himself everywhere implies, there's no time like the past.

Clearly the narrator of *The Scarlet Letter*—however criticism shall come to identify that cautious, even fearful, yet ever polite personage—knows a great deal more about the Puritan world of the 1630s and 40s than he will forceably obtrude on the notice of the less knowledgeable readers he alternately assures and provokes. And much of his learning appears to come, ultimately at least, from Winthrop's *Journal*, which *no* historian of the Massachusetts "Utopia" (47)[5] can escape rewriting, in one way or another. As Bradford's "Plymouth" is someplace else, only Winthrop was present at *this* creation, of which his own prefatory "Model of Christian Charity" served as moral groundplan and exemplar. Yet our narrator also knows enough to trust neither our native sense of plausibility nor our knowledge of actual events. And so before his own narrative has had the time it usually takes an extended fiction to develop a life of its own, he challenges us with an anxious-making reminder that his story really does presuppose a pre-fictive, "historical" world. About which it will help us to know.

207

The clearest example is unmistakeable indeed. No sooner, fictionally speaking, has Hester settled down to "Her Needle" (Chapter V), and to the "morbid purpose" (90) of outfitting "Pearl" (Chapter VI) as her own scarlet letter in human form, than she finds herself called upon to justify the quality and effect of her Christian nurture.[6] Of course the logic of her inquisitors is perfectly pernicious and circular, a theological catch-22 hardly designed to increase our regard for "the New England mind": if Pearl were "of demon origin," then "a Christian interest in the mother's soul required" the guardians of the Covenant to "remove such a stumblingblock from her path." Or—dichotomy as undistributed middle—if the child were indeed human, "then, surely, it would enjoy all the fairer prospect [of salvation] by being transferred to wiser and better guardianship" (100). The modern reader may wonder how any of this "logic" comports with the Decree of Predestination; perhaps Hawthorne's Puritans are no more simply "Calvinist" than those of Perry Miller. But the narrator has other, simpler worries: won't the reader think his psychological romance is taking absurd plot liberties with the political realities of history, slandering the past thereby? And so, in a rather remarkable moment of direct address, he elaborately cautions that reader to remember exactly what sort of a world he or she has entered.

His sober yet knowing little disclaimer is worth quoting in its entirety:

> It may appear singular, and, indeed not a little ludicrous, that an affair of
> this kind, which, in later days, would have been referred to no higher
> jurisdiction than that of the select men of the town, should then have
> been a question publicly discussed, and on which statesmen of eminence
> took sides. At that epoch of pristine simplicity, however, matters of even
> slighter public interest, and of far less intrinsic weight, than the welfare of
> Hester and her child, were strangely mixed up with the deliberations of
> legislators and acts of state. The period was hardly, if at all, earlier than that
> of our story, when a dispute concerning the right of property in a pig not
> only caused a fierce and bitter contest in the legislative body of the
> colony, but resulted in an important modification of the framework itself
> of the legislature (101).

There are, clearly, enough ironies here to keep us busy for a long time. And again our first response may involve simple dismay: trying to justify what, from a later perspective can only seem an unwarrantable intrusion of "federal" power into an entirely local (or "congregational") matter—if not a positive invasion of privacy—our narrator actually succeeds in trivializing the entire process and product of constitutional development in Massachusetts. Surely modern readers merely smile when, elsewhere, a cautious and worldly man like John Winthrop suggests that somewhat of the mind of God may be discovered by studying which parts of a religious book will and will not be consumed by mice. Perhaps we can yet believe it a "majestic idea, that the destiny of nations should be revealed, in [the] awful hieroglyphics, on the cope of heaven" (155). But what order of History or Providence can we possibly invoke when our own vaunted system of "separation of powers" turns out to have been provoked by a pig?[7] Especially when the same "imagery" tells so unhappily against the status of Hester's precious child.

Perhaps the narrator has intended his insidious reductionism: Hester on the scaffold has already seemed herself a Pearl cast before swine; and evidently he thinks that figure may obtain wherever the mysteries of the human soul are forcefully opened to the view of a disciplinary, punishing public. But somewhere the irony is supposed to go deeper. As it surely will for any reader willing to be guided back to the necessary pretext of this nowise innocent little history lesson.

Practitioners of American Studies will know the story of the Pig that Divided the Legislature from the pages of Samuel Eliot Morison's masterful (if filiopietistic) *Builders of the Bay Colony*: the typically American form of "bicameral" legislature came into view just when, in the case of the disputed ownership of a pig, the Magistrates successfully reversed the judgment of the Deputies, thus making good at last their long-standing claim to enjoy the power of veto (or "negative voice"), and pointing the way, thereby, to some future sense of Upper and Lower Houses, without benefit of any Federalist fantasy of an American peerage. In itself a ridiculous instance, of course, but the Lord moves in strange ways; and when was typology ever a respecter of persons? And much the same lesson may be drawn, fairly enough, from the version Hawthorne himself had (unquestionably) read in Snow's *History of Boston*, which "source-critics" may always insist is the real inspiration for Hawthorne's curious aside.[8] But the serious reader of historical fiction may feel himself invited to pursue the tale back to its ultimate source, from which Snow's nineteenth-century account is itself obviously derivative: the first-hand, eyewitness participant's account in Winthrop's *Journal*, without which the story had not survived at all.

The specific reference would be to an entry for 22 June 1642—a date which, on other grounds, we might wish to fix as the absolute beginning of *The Scarlet Letter*'s own scaffold scene action.[9] But the episode is crucial to a story and a logic which extend both backwards and forwards from this specific moment; and which, along with the story and logic of the "rise, reign, and ruin" of those libertine familists we know as the "antinomians," make Winthrop's *Journal* an organized and vital history rather than a series of needful annals. Taking close account of the sexual crimes eventually prepetrated by all those who espoused the higher liberty of the Spirit, Winthrop is equally watchful of all arguments for civil privileges greater than those granted by the

209

Massachusetts "Charter" or logically inconsistent with his own sense of the
nature of human government. Indeed the theme of the *Journal* is precisely
those excesses committed in the name of some "liberty," of nature or of charter, other than that implied in his initial definition of "charity," according to
which civil order is altogether impossible without a number of severe (and
recognizable) forms of subordination. And though Winthrop is glad of the
political triumph of his Upper House of fully chartered Magistrates, his more
somber concern, here as elsewhere, is for the whole tenor of political wrangling about "rights" which give it context. The mordant realism of his earlier
comment remains in force: "how strictly the people would seem to stick to
their patent, where they think it makes for their advantage."[10]

What emerges from the restrained and largely unrhetorical pages of
Winthrop's *Journal*, from the beginning, and down to the mid-1640s at least,
is the sad and often exasperated feeling that a whole variety of misunder-
standings about "liberty" are abroad in his land. On the one hand, obviously,
but not quite originally, a few "antinomians" ("bold sensualists" as Emerson
might have called their parody of Self-Reliance) were invoking spiritual liberty to cover their own sexual license; and on the other, a rising and all too
politicized populace was demanding ever greater legal clarification and political voice. Apparently almost everyone wanted a full and written set of "positive laws," to specify Moses and to limit the discretionary authority of the
Godly Magistrates. Worse yet, a party of Freemen were quibbling and quar-
reling in ways which forced a single, precarious, territorial guarantee to bear
the undue strain of full constitutional development. Lust, Winthrop must have
felt, he would always have with him. But an outbreak of hermeneutics he had
hoped to avoid.

What is signaled by the narrator's curious aside, then, in Winthrop's
American Ur-world and in his own most orderly imitation, is the presence of
an extreme political anxiety at the heart of the Puritan system, uncertainty and
strife where there should have been holy consensus. Pious wish had fathered
no very stable political fact. A world where a pig can alter a legislature is a
world of flux, where any novel decision might yet produce the most unlooked
for and far-reaching consequences. And the reader who had expected a monolith was just plain wrong.

Suddenly the dis-agreements hinted at in the chapters of Hester's exposure
and judgment come into sharp thematic prominence. The narrator's explicit
sense of violent moral "outrage" (55) is set against his subtler evocation of
political confusion and even experimentation. Sensing legal ambguity as well
as moral complexity, perhaps, the "magistacy...have not been bold to put in
force the extremity of our righteous law against her" (63) which is, as a particularly ugly member of the female populace has already reminded us, death,
"both in the Scripture and the statute-book" (51–52). Suddenly Hester seems

caught up in the midst of a constitutional crisis, at a moment of historical unfolding that is arguably more "crucial" than of the "Antinomian Controversy" of the 1630s.[11] An entire "Way" is at issue. And, unless Hawthorne himself is being both prurient and reductive, the whole crisis seems to take Hester's "adultery" as its fitting symbol. Superficially, at least, Winthrop had tried to keep his sexual cases separate from his political ones. But here they stand wholly conflated. Leaving readers to wonder what strange principle of fictional displacement can substitute Hester herself (rather than Pearl) for Winthrop's problematic pig.

The answer is a little complicated, as we may fairly expect. And it requires that we stay *with* the Winthrop source—literally, still, and well before we should think to tease out its own sexual politics. But the invitation (possibly it is a demand) is clearly present in Hawthorne's text. And this time it points to its own most outrageous manipulation of history: the problem of "Governor" Bellingham.

The same chapter which seeks to defend Hester's summons to "The Governor's Hall" (Chapter VII) actually begins with a political reminder of a lower order, but one which turns out to involve us in *The Scarlet Letter*'s famous historical "mistake." Remember, it says, that by "now" (1645) the man we're politely referring to as "Governor Bellingham" is no longer the actual governor of Massachusetts. Yet the course of fact or probability is scarcely violated, "for, though the chances of a popular election had caused this former ruler to descend a step or two from the highest rank, he still held an honorable and influential place among the colonial magistracy" (100). Once again, but with results even more devastating, the narrative evokes ironies which survive and all but swamp the factual disclaimer. Specifically, we are being reminded that, even as a *mere* Magistrate, Bellingham commands considerable judicial authority, though obviously much less than he had that day in June 1642, when he stood on the Balcony of Judgment above Hester's Scaffold of Shame. And yet it is this very reminder—of the political ouster of Bellingham—which forces us to advert to the originary lie we have already been led to believe: the real-life governor of Massachusetts Bay in June of 1642 had been John Winthrop; Bellingham's political defeat had occured the month before. For reasons we need to think seriously about, the narrative is now fussing about niceties where before it had flatly said the thing which was not.

In one sense the news is not so new. Source critics have long known about the "displacement" of Winthrop by Bellingham; nor has responsible speculation failed to produce plausible explanations of why, within the conventions of Hawthorne's peculiar subgenre, the sly little metonym seems justifiable and even necessary.[12] Yet looked at in the light of the information furnished by

211

Winthrop's *Journal*, the matter seems the very reverse of innocent. Much more is at issue, evidently, than either the freedom or the mimetic exigencies of "romance." And, judged in that same light, the narrator's remark about "the chances of a popular election" turns out to involve an irony more vicious than anything Hawthorne ever penned in his own political defense.

Bellingham's political story, leading up to his defeat in the Great and General Election of May, 1642, is, for one thing, about as unlike Hawthorne's own recent, more debatable dismissal from the Salem Custom House as we could imagine.[13] Bellingham was, after all, himself the candidate rather than some mere pork-barrel appointee, and his own recent behavior formed the well known substance of the political argument against him. Furthermore, that behavior had been explicitly sexual. Indeed it seems essentially accurate to say that Bellingham had been voted out of office, in May of 1642, for conduct not so different from Hester's own. For which he was punished—somewhat unequally, as it may appear—with the sort of political reprimand which forced him "to descend a step or two from the highest rank." Evidently the *real* politics behind *The Scarlet Letter* are, quite apart from the ultimate implications of Winthrop's rhetoric, themselves intensely sexual.

Bellingham's story is not nice, but it is fairly simple. Widowed, at age fifty, and wishing to remarry, during the term of his own governorship, a young woman of twenty, he simply declared the wish a fact, on the strength of his own considerable authority. No problem, as he may have thought: Puritan marriage being civil affair, no benefit of clergy need apply; and was he not, at the time, the highest civil officer in the land? Yet Winthrop and many others were deeply distressed. Anxious to get on to other matters (including the case of the eighty-year-old Reverend Mr. Batchellor who, "having a lusty comely woman to his wife, did [nevertheless] solicit the chastity of his neighbor's wife"), Winthrop turns aside to point out that "the young gentlewoman was ready to be contracted to a friend of his, who lodged in his house." Then, conceding this point of honor, which Bellingham "excused...by the strength of his affection," he presses two more official charges: that Bellingham "would not have his contract published...contrary to an order of court," and that "he married himself contrary to the constant practice of the country."[14] Strange covenant, this, with no banns, and no civil witness. Perhaps Bellingham felt that what he did "had a consecration of its own." Perhaps he and his stolen bride had "said so to each other" (195).

The attempts at prosecution which followed proved ineffectual, as Bellingham refused to "go off the bench" for his own trial. But as Winthrop's later editor remarks, "After such an experience of Bellingham, it is not strange that the colony should restore its chief dignity to Winthrop once more in May, 1642."[15] And the reader of *The Scarlet Letter* is now in a position to grasp the wicked logic of its major historical fabrication. Bellingham and not Winthrop sentences Hester, for the keen historical irony involved: but for the grace of his Magistracy (or his maleness?), there go he. Or, to put the matter less allusively, the demoted "Governor" Bellingham stood, in June of 1642, not as the accuser but as the accused, in a rather tensely central case of sex and constitutionality in the unfolding experiment of Utopian Massachusetts. A largely forgotten case, perhaps, except as *The Scarlet Letter* goes well out of its own fictional way to remind us.

At one level the joke is fairly nasty—rather like the local Justice of the Peace who, accustomed to rail against the morals of the young, is himself, one Saturday night, taken in adultery. (Let him who is without sin...) Yet here too the irony may go deeper. Possibly we are to wonder about the fate of the distinctive covenant of marriage in the midst of a society which is, on one side, redundantly over-covenanted already and, on the other, likely to produce prophetical critiques of all merely contractual arrangements. Winthrop believes in love, though he might begin by calling it "charity." And he resolutely believes in the law, if only in the form of "an order of court." Yet how are these conflicting loyalties to be harmonized? How "like," in the end, are law and love?

At very least the "matter of Bellingham" reminds us just how literally sexual are the historical matters that lie at the "source" of *The Scarlet Letter*. Perhaps Hawthorne's romance is indeed more about sex than that "guilt" we used to notice, in dutiful recognition that the drama of the book itself is all painfully (if not quite penitentially) after the fact of Hester's unique sexual transgression. And if so, perhaps it is about that curious, slandered, but intensely historical subject of sex in the world of the Puritans. Not in the world of the "bourgeoisie," where texts enough already inspire the researches of Peter Gay or (at a more "powerful" level of discourse) Michel Foucault, but in the American seventeenth century.[16] The subject might be only, as we might say, fidgeting, metaphorical, since Hester does seem designed to "figure" something or other, and since, in the end, language (and its silences) *will* always come in the way. But perhaps even that possibility deserves further attention. Granting, for the moment, that all sex is the same elemental fact of nature; or even, more tendentiously, that the matter or theme of the "triangle" really is "eternal"; we may yet wish to ask if there was not perhaps something different—distinctive and revealing—in the way Winthrop and his Utopian Puritans thought and spoke about such matters. Certainly this is the implication of Bellingham's *other* sex scandal of 1641–42, which may also have left its traces in Hawthorne's text.

This second, really ugly case implicated Bellingham not as a principal but as a judge, and also, it oddly appears, as something of what we would now call a "sexologist." And it involved all of Puritanic New England in a question we might associate with one of the more explicitly sexual utopias of the nine-

213

teenth century more readily than with Winthrop's (or Bellingham's) Boston—
with Finney's Oberlin, for example, or with the Oneida Community of John
Humphrey Noyes. Yet it truly appears that the anxiously developing legal
establishment of Massachusetts (and Plymouth, Connecticut and New Haven
as well) needed to determine, just then and just there, the true import of
human sexuality: time out, so to speak, while the facts of life are driven into a
corner, assessed, and published to all those validly concerned. Specifically, the
matter involved the question of "natural" and "unnatural" sexuality, including
the prescribed Scriptural penalties for sins of both sorts. But the *essential* question, of the "meaning" of sex itself, clearly lurked. And the reader of *The Scarlet
Letter* needs to know that Hawthorne has ascribed the opening of his most
explicitly sexual romance to the one moment when much of colonial New
England seemed to have sex on it official and conscious mind.[17]

Though the (expurgated) twentieth-century version of Winthrop's *Journal*
decently averts its gaze, the 1825–1826 edition we know Hawthorne read
gives all the lurid (or pathetic) details. The two prepubescent daughters of a
certain John Humfry were repeatedly "abused"—"especially on the Lord's
days and lecture days"—by a series of "rude servants," and also by others of
the better sort who happened to be, temporarily at least, men without women.
These "very foul sin[s]" went for a long time unreported, yet they did eventually reach the light of Puritan mind.[18] As the matter became public, it fell to
the court of the woman-snatching Bellingham to decide the appropriate
penalty for what our own sociological wisdom calls "child sexual abuse." And
as the question arose at the very moment when the nexus of all crime and
punishment was publically at issue, it drew for the full subtlety of the Puritans'
"scholastic" intellect, even as it paralyzed their legal machinery for the better
part of two gubernatorial terms.

On the one hand (Jesus and the Pharisees to one side), the "judicials" of
Moses clearly made "adultery" a capital crime, precisely as Hawthorne's liti-
gious matrons had been quick to observe, so that the *married* abusers could
always be executed on that score. Yet something else seemed involved as well.
Did not the *age* of the abused females essentially matter, even if one or the
other seemed from time to time to consent and "[take] pleasure in it"? An earlier case had already aroused Winthrop's keenest legal faculty. A boy convicted
of raping "a child of 7 or 8 years old" escaped with a severe whipping (the
punishment for "single fornication") because the penalty for rape "was not
death by the law of God." And yet Winthrop suspected that

> by the equity of the law against sodomy, it should be death for a man to
> have carnal copulation with a girl so young, as there can be no possibili-
> ty of generation, for it is against nature as well as sodomy and buggery.[19]

And so in the present instance as well: as the females in question were well below the age of child bearing, had not their *penetratio* (the records here lapse into Latin) been significantly unnatural? Evidently the breach of sexual covenant was not the only source of capital matter.

Rational men may disagree, of course, and yet they needed to know the answer to the "great question" of "what kind of sin this was, whether sodomy, or rape, or etc." And so it fell to Bellingham, himself not *much* better than he should have been, to compose a sort of sexual questionnaire, seeking "to know the mind of God by the help of all the Elders of the country, both our own, and Plymouth, and Connecticut, New Haven, etc."[20] What he had to ask, of every duly constituted congregational officer, was what exactly rational men might understand the Pentatuch to mean by "sodomy"; and, more specifically, what precise acts of sexuality a Bible State was bound to regard as capital offenses.

The answers Bellingham received (a sample of which the modern reader may consult in the definitive edition of Bradford's *Plymouth*) are revealing in the extreme.[21] And more than a little depressing, perhaps, to anyone seriously anticipating "some brighter period" when a "new truth" should "establish the whole relation between man and woman on a surer ground of mutual happiness" (263). An *old* morality still, and with a vengeance.

Yet the point is not so much the number of sexual practises declared to be capitally sinful: nothing significant is added by the observation that the world has since discovered it can tolerate a good deal more dysfunction, experiment, and preference than the Mosaic law supposed. Somewhat closer to the mark would be the observation of how little attention—namely, none—is given to the plight of the young females in question. Unmentioned except as the legal premise or sinful occasion, they are effectively reduced to animal status: lying with them has been, evidently, a lot like lying with a ewe or a mare. And worst of all, perhaps, is the old-time ease with which the obscure teachings of Deuteronomy and Leviticus are referred back to some lucid and cleanly standard called "nature," leaving the reader to wonder how to name the urge whose expression had caused the case to arise in the first place. For surely we are reminded that, like so much else, the puritanic understanding of sexuality tended too readily to presume its competence to settle any contested point.

Everywhere the discussion centers on the question of *penetratio* versus *contactus et frictatio*, and everywhere the distinction between the natural and the unnatural is referred to some terribly material concept of "cleanness," until one almost wonders if the two young women in question may be thought to have "chewed the cud and divided the hoof."[22] So that whatever sociopolitical logic operated to forgive the sexual misdemeanor of Bellingham himself, the more primary categories that emerge from his questionnaire must be judged primitive indeed. Without at all privileging his own (AIDS-terrorized)

215

understanding of human sexuality, the modern reader of *The Scarlet Letter* is forced to conclude that the men who judge Hester Prynne do not appear to know what-the-fuck they are talking about; and that the famous displacement of Winthrop by Bellingham means to call attention to just this unhappy fact.

Surely some such charge is implied by the arresting and otherwise highly gratuitous accusation made by the narrator as he seeks to characterize those judges. Granting that their somewhat spurious "dignity of mien" owes much "to a period when the forms of authority were felt to possess the sacredness of divine institutions"; and conceding (with some irony, given what we know of Bellingham) that "they were, doubtless, good men, just, and sage"; he means nevertheless to impugn their present competence absolutely:

> Out of the whole human family, it would not have been easy to select the same number of wise and virtuous persons, who should be less capable of sitting in judgment on an erring woman's heart, and disentangling its mesh of good and evil, than the sages of rigid aspect towards whom Hester Prynne now turned her face (64).

A remarkable passage indeed, the reader is bound to feel, especially from a narrator who ends by praising Hester's return to serve the standards of the community so viciously attacked. Yet the present thought insists on itself: the men on the balcony above Hester are utterly unfit to "meddle with a question of human guilt, passion, and anguish" (65). Whatever the Biblical premises of their utopian state, their sexual categories are wildly inappropriate to the present instance.

And the relevance of the second Bellingham episode is only heightened when we learn the other questions in his timely little survey. A second seems to have asked for help in deciding—as in the legal inquisition surrounding the shame of Hester's sexual reduction—"how far a magistrate might exact a confession from a delinquent in capital cases." And then, filling out the syllabus of the historical mind in question, what is to be done "for the maintenance of the trade of beaver?"[23] So much for the "strangely mixed...deliberations" of that "epoch of pristine simplicity." And small wonder if the narrator should wish, however illogically, for a "Papist among the crowd of Puritans": not that his Canon Law would seem, by comparison, a triumph of humane sensibility, prosing as it does about "the natural female vessel"; but possibly some remembered image of the "Divine Maternity" (56) might fairly redress the uneven contextual balance. And surely that image would redeem Hester no more unfairly than she is degraded by the one more nearly provided—of an "iron-visaged" old dame replacing Hester's curiously stitched letter with "a rag of mine own rheumatic [i.e., menstruous] flannel" (54). Evidently it is very hard, the early scenes of *The Scarlet Letter* suggest, to take the right tone about sex. And no easier then, certainly, than now.

Yet those same scenes appear to suggest that this unsolvable problem is also a vital one, that Hester's sexual transgression stands at the center of and indeed epitomizes a highly public and utterly crucial moment in the development of the Puritans' Model City. To be sure, the narrative will presently turn inward, to an exploration of Hester's own mixture of shame, hysteria, and even antinomian rebellion; and then, even more so, in the case of Dimmesdale, so that "The Interior of a Heart" (Chapter XI) can all too easily come to stand for the true domain of Hawthorne's version of "psychological romance." But at the outset, insistently, and throughout the rest of the tale, by intermittent reminders, we are forced to notice that Hester's deepest difficulty is that she has created a problem her peculiar world does not know how to address, let alone solve. And yet one that world feels it *must* solve if it is to maintain its covenanted identity and get on with the task of elaborating its own peculiar institutions. Failure here is failure *simply*, we are plainly led to feel. No ambiguities, please: "cemetery" and "prison" in all realism provided (47), let's get this awkward affair of the flesh rationalized before the law and press on into the Kingdom. What further need of witnesses, really? Mark her with *something* and then get this City moving again.

Nor should most of this pressing, oppressive background have ever been anything but obvious: Hester challenges a whole community in an absolutely fundamental way, and the range of inappropriate attitudes taken by Ministers, Magistrates, and Populace alike reveal the anxiety appropriate to the discovery that some splendid intellectual edifice has been reared on a foundation of murk. Bellingham's questionnaire may betray no qualm appropriate to his own personal situation; possibly he thought of his own sin as altogether "natural." Yet Winthrop's *Journal* eventually reveals the same sort of hesitations that undid the splendid confidence of Bradford's *Plymouth*—as antinomians, servants, even Christian Magistrates all fall back into the common, if multifarious, condition of natural desire.[24] And so, ironically, it requires the meretricious rhetoric of the explicitly hypocritical Dimmesdale to lend the situation of Hester its needful complexity; for evidently some "quality of awful sacredness" (114) will always escape the utopian rationalism of the judges she has to face. Even as they try to name all things to the use of their own holy politics.

Yet the subtler implications of Hawthorne's studied historicism evade us still. Granting that Bellingham's (fictional) judgments of Hester are themselves significantly hypocritical; and that (historically) his sexual questionnaire epitomizes a very old morality; yet no accomplished reader of Puritan literature can tolerate the slanderous implication that the Builders of the Bay Colony were, to a man, nothing but bourgeois legalists flourishing some quaint utopian metahistory. Winthrop, for example, was a fairly accomplished writer of love letters, and no one need accuse him of being an "old man" who had "lived so long and forgotten so much that [he could not] remember anything [he] ever knew or even heard about love."[25] And other evidence indicates that the American Puritans did indeed possess their own highly developed idiom of the sexual sacred.

Of the first generation only Cotton fully explicated the sacred love poetry of Canticles, and not so well, it has come to appear, as Edward Taylor later. Clearly Cotton's rhetoric nowhere courts the transport of mystic sexuality. And the critic may even conclude that his American performances *plainly* eschew not only the Pentecostal "Tongue of Flame" (142) but even the more modest, Dimmesdalean "eloquence and religious fervor" (66). Still, his meditations on the "kisses of his mouth," which are "better than wine" are part of the relevant historical context; and evidently they matter in a tale which implicates Cotton almost as directly as Hutchinson.[26] And everywhere else, the reader of *The Scarlet Letter* needs to learn, the expounders of official Puritanism appropriated the facts of sexuality to the new life of Grace and the Church. "Weaned affections" was a lively cliche of Puritan poetry and preaching, not at all a dead metaphor: if one could give up sucking at the teat of the world, he would yet find sufficient nourishment "out of the Breasts of both Testaments."[27] So that the ironic career of "Governor" Richard Bellingham tells us only part of what we need to know about the sources of *The Scarlet Letter*'s sexual setting and theme.

The now familiar story of Hester Prynne as a sort of "literalized" Ann Hutchinson tells us just a bit more: Hester's sexual threat to her holy community seems but Hawthorne's ironic embodiment of what Puritan rhetoric implied was really or deeply true of her historical counterpart. When Hutchinson taught spiritual liberty, including a liberation from the Pauline anxiety of mind and members, the Puritans could hear only a distinctively "womanly" licensing of the passional self; so that a subtle Protestant heretic was reduced to a sort of libertine, and to a wily (female) seducer, assaulting (male) continence as a sort of first principle of redeemed society. Here, as elsewhere, the Puritans could never come to the end of their own sexual *entendre*. And Hawthorne merely brought their urgent language game to full sexual life.[28]

Yet the discovery of an exuberant life of Puritan sexual metaphor—now mystifying their own doctrine, now discrediting another's—may only serve to deepen our sense of how utterly unsolvable, "puritanically," the case of Hester Prynne will prove. Any symbol system that turns out to be all "tenor" and no "vehicle" will not only produce awkward "allegories," but may result, more seriously, in an impoverished vocabulary of practical life. And so it may well have been with the Puritans, decent men and women, doubtless, but inveterate symbolizers of sex.

Though too complex to argue here, the historical formula may be simple enough: taking natural life (too readily) for granted, Puritans valorize salvation and the life of grace; "coarse" enough (as Hawthorne suggests) about the ordinary details of coupling, fecundation, pregnancy, and nurture, these eminent pre-Victorians turn all their subtlety to the "higher" task of discovering and organizing the typology by which such things mean, beyond themselves, in a decently spiritual way. Better to marry than to burn, clearly, for how could one on fire with fleshly lust successfully meditate the logic by which sex and marriage have been made types of the soul's closing with the Heavenly Bridegroom or of Christ's espousal of a truly Virgin Church? Yet where everything is always already symbolic, the real world may have trouble finding its own language. Perhaps it will yet appear that the profound Puritan interest in the theological, ecclesiastic, and even political analogies of sex and marriage all but displaced their more literal curiosity and judgment. Possibly their metaphors obscured rather than redeemed their own sexual life.[29]

Here Dimmesdale—though without precedent in Winthrop—would seem to be the most obvious case. Though the casual reader may infer that his seven-year regimen of fleshly self-crucifixion is designed to pay back in pain what he once enjoyed of pleasure, the subtler evidence all suggests that his real problem goes deeper and involves a theology less obvious than that of holy masochism. As I have argued earlier, the unspoken premise of his "hypothetical" debate with Chillingworth, about confession, and the last revelation of his somewhat franker discussion with Hester, about repentance, both indicate that he is not so much haunted by the specter of remorse for a single (natural) sexual deviation as he is consumed by fear that his "adultery" is really a classic case of "idolatry"; that is, that he did once and does still love Hester more than God, preferring the creature to the Creator in the one just definition of the unregenerate will. He tortures his flesh truly enough, but what torments him is an (Augustinian) allegory of Saving Faith.[30]

Indeed what else *can* Dimmesdale be thinking, when he tells Hester he has tried to persevere as a chosen saint but now accepts his doom and would even seal it by "snatch[ing] the solace allowed to the condemned culprit"? (201). Social conscience he has seemed entirely to lack, weakly permitting Hester to bear the entire responsibility and burden of Pearl. And, as he has been ignorant all along of the sexual identity of Chillingworth, how could he attach so *much* significance to what his world all but dismissed—with a wave of the whip—as "single fornication"? Only by rejecting Hester utterly, in the end, can this thoroughgoing Puritan ideologue recover his lost, allegorical identity.

Here Hester's case seems simpler, more naturalistic and more truly sexual. When we determine to consider her *as herself*, rather than as some Hutchinson

219

surrogate, we quickly notice that she feels shame, admits that she has wronged Chillingworth, loves Pearl (in spite of certain "monstrous" fears),[31] and wants to live with Dimmesdale; eventually she will propose they simply escape from the Utopia which has allegorized the sexual and mystified the police force. Yet in the end even this most natural of Hawthorne's protagonists is presented as a function of Puritan metaphor. A victim, if not an exponent. Which may be one powerful reason why naturalistic readers continue to identify with her, even after they are shown that the fiercely logical structure of *The Scarlet Letter* points to Dimmesdale as the indubitable center of literary organization.[32] Dimmesdale ably abets the (male) myth he suffers. Hester merely endures it, for seven years; and then she simply nullifies it—though she may also, much later, return to sponsor a new one of her own.

The clearest revelation of Hester's metaphoric enclosure and irruption (and also, not incidentally, of Hawthorne's full debt to Winthrop's *Journal*) comes in her own emotional overflow in the famous forest scene. The force of the moment derives partly from the fact that, unlike almost everything else in that thoroughly prepared-for episode, the outburst comes as a surprise to both Hester and the reader. But also, partly, from the fact that Hester's silent thought seems to be echoing New England's single most powerful figure of social organization. We should proceed with caution.

For Hester's theory of para-nuptual "consecration" (195) and for her later, more energetic proposal of "trial and success" (198) in a world elsewhere, the "antinomian" suggestions of "Another View of Hester" (Chapter XIII) have fully prepared us. Her views horrify the narrator, of course. An accomplished and sympathetic reader of Winthrop, he no doubt considers her plan comparable to that of many other failed Puritans who had "crept out at a broken wall": one more rash assertion of some singular (or, more oddly, dual) "liberty" set against the terms of an earlier covenant of perfect mutuality founded on a holy love transcending both Justice and Mercy. Indeed his evocation of the "untamed forest" as an apt figure of Hester's "moral wilderness" (199) well recalls Winthrop's impassioned protest against the supposed logic of certain backsliders from his utopian society:

> For such as come together into a wilderness, where are nothing but wild beasts and beastlike men, and there confederate together in civil and church estate, whereby they do, implicitly at least, bind themselves to support each other, and all of them that society, whether civil or sacred, whereof they are members, how they can break from this without free consent, is hard to find, so as may satisfy a tender or good conscience in time of trial.[33]

Clearly Dimmesdale himself has felt the force of this sentiment, daring not to "quit [his] post, though an unfaithful sentinel" (197) on the walls separating (but metaphorically) the Enclosed Garden of New England from the Wilderness of the World. But Hester, we know, is not going to be impressed.

Winthrop's "Model of Christian Charity" (which the narrator has, with Foucauldian grasp, blandly assimilated into "the world's law") is now "no law for her mind" (164). Nor, given the ragged terms of her own migration to New England, can the reader entirely disagree. Unless it were when she decided to remain there, to be close to Dimmesdale, morbidly, hoping for some "joint futurity of endless retribution" (80), how had she, any more than Henry Thoreau, ever made a contract with the State of Massachusetts? Yet the surprise—and the full revelation of Winthrop—comes just earlier, in the aftermath of her disclosure of her long-concealed ("second") secret, the identity of Chillingworth. Hardly more ashamed than outraged, Dimmesdale splutters over "the indelicacy!—the horrible ugliness of this exposure" and, forgetting all he otherwise owes the "wondrous strength and generosity of [this] woman's heart" (68), fiercely avows that he "cannot forgive" (194) this one deception so crucial to their mutual conspiracy.[34] Yet he *does* forgive, as we feel he must. And the reason may have as much to do with the suppressed terms as with the "sudden and desperate tenderness" of Hester's impassioned plea.

She merely holds him fast, "lest he should look her sternly in the face." But the narrator appears to know the inevitable language of her silent thought:

221

> All the world had frowned on her,—for seven long years had it frowned upon this lonely woman,—and still she bore it all, nor ever once turned away her firm, sad eyes. Heaven, likewise, had frowned upon her, and she had not died. But the frown of this pale, weak, sinful and sorrow-stricken man was what Hester could not bear, and live! (194–95)

Why the repeated stress on *frown*?—we might be led to wonder. Can mere repetition possibly compensate the effect of a word that seems too weak to capture the force of Dimmesdale's violent energy of resentment? Or the allegorical outrage by which a covenanted community has implemented its unpardonable judgment of a pardonable sin? Or the theological injury of a God who marks the infinite iniquity of any human sin? Yet it is just a *frown* which Hester's life cannot sustain. And the single word is sufficient to evoke the crucial context in Winthrop.

A figure of speech, of course, it nevertheless climaxes the tedious argument whose intent it was, insidious or not, to bind the souls of all his saintly citizens to the social compact they had entered. Therein was "liberty," but only such as "is maintained and exercised in a way of subjection to authority"; it was indeed the same "liberty wherewith Christ has made us free." Then, as if not content with this ultimate mystification (as Roger Williams would see it) of the mere exigencies of discipline in wilderness states and wilderness churches, Winthrop proceeds to suggest how it can all be perfectly naturalized in the typology of Pauline marriage: "The woman's own choice makes such a man her husband," even as the soul must voluntarily enter the covenant of grace, or instituted church, or separated civil polity; "yet being so chosen, he is her lord, and she is subject to him, yet in a way of liberty, not of bondage," even as those who have espoused New England are now "subject" so freely. Indeed the "yoke" of this quasi-marital covenant is as "easy and sweet...as a bride's ornaments";

> and if through frowardness or wantonness, etc., she shake it off, at any time, she is at no rest in her spirit, until she take it up again; and whether her lord smiles upon her, and embraceth her in his arms, or whether he *frowns* or rebukes, or smites her, she apprehends the sweetness of his love in all, and is refreshed, supported, and instructed by every such dispensation of his authority over her.[35] (Emphasis added.)

Just here, along with so much else, is the source of the frown which Hester cannot bear. Yet subversively redefined: the word is the word of Winthrop's Sovereign Lord, but the frown is the frown of Hester's fleshly lover.

The *literal* must pass without much notice: with or without the fortunate example of Milton's Eve, the liberated will scarcely admire the sociology of Puritan wedlock. Nor need we stress the obvious political tenor of Winthrop's "holy pretense": contractual absolutism is absolutism still; and "how like an iron cage..."[36] Closer to Hawthorne's ironic point would be Winthrop's prediction of the way Hester "shakes off" and then "takes up again" the letter (and the cap) which mark her subjection to some diffused but scarcely attenuated male authority—as if Pearl's own "Come thou and take it up" (210) were but one more (absurd) displacement of an ever-present Winthrop. Yet the emphasis rightly falls on the *frown*, the vital clue to the real terms of Hester's metaphorical bondage and effectual rebellion, and of Hawthorne's relentless deconstruction. State, Church, and God himself may frown on Hester, but not Dimmesdale. Political gentlemen may have their pious little allegories; but "the woman's own choice," it finally appears, has made this man her *only* viable lord and husband. The rest is somebody else's quaint little language experiment—magical, as long as it works, but void, and irritating, whenever it does not. And just here, clearly, not, where even Dimmesdale may feel the silent force of Hester's idolatrous substitution of himself in the place of Covenantal Authority.

Ultimately the problem is not Chillingworth, nor any other casuistic instance in "The Doctrine and Discipline of Divorce." The problem is in the

language, reduced to materialistic absurdity on the one side, only to be ele-
vated to mystic overdetermination on the other. Dimmesdale's (Cottonesque)
affair is with the Bridegroom of the (always female) Puritan soul; and the first
love of the Puritan Magistrates is always their own unadulterated system of
symbols.[37] All men and—to be puritanically fair, at last—all women too will
always be sinners in the flesh: Winthrop's Boston is decidedly *not* "perfection-
istic" in the manner of Humphrey Noyes' silver-smooth Oneida. But how *can*
Hester prefer Dimmesdale to God? Or, to be fairer still, to the terms which
empower the Puritan Utopia? Marriages are made by fools like Bellingham;
but only God can make a Type. Which Hester here breaks.

At issue, all along, has been something beyond the more-than-Evelike
"frowardness" of Hester's unruly female sexuality, flaunted however literally in
the "embroidery" of human art. Deeper down, all along, has lurked the problem of her imperfect subjection to the "easy and sweet authority" of those
who teach that, under the terms of New England's most especial covenant, all
valid human willing is but a "true wife," who "accounts her subjection her
honor and freedom, and would not think her condition safe and free but in
her subjection to. . . the authority of Christ, her king and husband." No wonder the narrator finds Hester's outward "humility" (162) so dangerously
deceptive; no wonder he portentously concludes that her "scarlet letter had
not done its office" (166). Its failure is clearly a failure of metaphor. For, given
her "own choice," this woman *will* always choose her own literal lover before
any version of Winthrop's figurative husband, even in hell. Emily Dickinson
herself could scarcely make the blasphemy more blatant.[38]

Hester may or may not continue to believe in the God whose "merciful"
will Dimmesdale closes his earthly career by explicating with such meticulous
orthodoxy. She certainly seems to believe, much later, in the coming of some
new sexual morality, though not by her to be revealed. But what makes her
guilty, in the view of a most unliberated narrator, of a "deadlier crime than [the
adultery] stigmatized by *The Scarlet Letter*" (164) is her flat rejection of the
metaphorical identity between the Pauline marriage and Winthrop's puritanic Utopia—considered as, itself, "the redeemed form of man." Never is her
effective choice between Roger Chillingworth and Arthur Dimmesdale;
always it is between a human lover and the Figure of Salvation in Covenant.
Tempted all along to conform to the Community's constituted disbelief in the
validity of her sexual love for Dimmesdale, she seems nevertheless just waiting
for the moment of her "own choice." And when it comes, she passionately
chooses the literal. To which she *almost* converts even Dimmesdale. Apparently
nature lurks, just waiting for our figures to fail.

The occasion of Winthrop's justly famous "little speech" on the quasi-marital
nature of "liberty" and "authority" had been one more dispute—this time in

223

1645—over the discretionary power of magistrates to intervene for order, wherever the laws or precedents of a newly formed community seemed insufficiently precise to cover the singular human case. And thus it is probably worth noting that "Governor" Bellingham's own intervention into Hester's domestic situation also occurs in 1645, as historical critics have plotted the novel's fictional action against the background of actual time.[39] One more strategically ineffectual displacement of the definitive pretext: Hester's too-casual stewardship is attacked and defended just when Winthrop's own was most authoritatively impugned and philosophically defended; a whole "Way" really *is* up for grabs.

But the "sources" of *The Scarlet Letter* run deeper than the discovery of political confusion beneath the theocratic monolith. For Hester's ultimate rebellion is against a myth far older than that of puritanic consensus. One there from the outset, and written, as it must have seemed, in stone.

Even in his utopian "Model," Winthrop had implied that law was just like love, that civil combinations were but reflections of that more ideal union of man and woman. And nowhere more so than in the "City" his migrant Puritans were about to posit. That everywhere the Citizen had to obey the Magistrate might almost pass without saying, unless some proleptic disciple of D.H. Lawrence should suppose the moral of Amercia was "Henceforth be masterless." What needed stressing, apparently, was the theological guarantee and, even more so, the precise quality of that obedience in a Bible State. As "members of Christ" the citizen his rhetoric hoped to create would discern "his owne Image and resemblance in another, and therefore cannot but love him as he loves himself"; self-love, if one insists, but redeemed by the recognition that ultimately the True Self is always Christ.[40] And thus redeemed, what possibly frustrates an overflowing abundance of love among the members?

Probably the reader of *The Scarlet Letter* should read the full text of the loving outburst which follows, for Hawthorne seems to have recognized it as Winthrop's own theme song for New England:

> It is like Adam when Eve was brought to him; shee must have it one with herselfe: this is fleshe of my fleshe (saith shee) and bone of my bone; shee conceives a great delighte in it, therefore shee desires nearenes and familiarity with it. Shee hath a great propensity to doe it good and receives such content in it; as feareing the miscarriage of her beloved, shee bestowes it in the inmost closett of her heart; shee will not endure that it shall want any good which shee can give it. If by occasion shee be withdrawne from the Company of it, shee is still lookeing towardes the place where shee left her beloved, if shee heare it groane shee is with it presently; if shee finde it sadd and disconsolate shee sighes and mournes with it,

shee hath noe such joy, as to see her beloved merry and thriving; if shee see it wronged, shee cannot beare it without passion. Shee setts noe boundes of her affeccions, nor hath any thought of reward, shee findes recompence enoughe in the exercise of her love towardes it.[41] (Punctuation added.)

Winthrop may go on to point the moral in the Biblical example of Jonathan and David, considered as eminent (if typic) "Christians." But we notice rather that the spiritual point of view is indeed female; that the fervent rhetoric (here) stops just short of predicting Eve's response to an Adamic "frown"; and that in fact it characterizes nothing so well as what Dimmesdale rightly calls the "wondrous strength and generousity of a woman's heart" (68). As if Winthrop were bidding to become a "theological feminist."

Yet the passage is altogether metaphorical: the love is the love of the citizen, under the law; or, in the extreme case, made *painfully* explicit after fifteen years of "libertine" experiment and "constitutional" wrangling, of the saintly citizen *for* the law. Just here is the enthusiastic premise of Winthrop's more than lawyerly vision of holy order in New England—our excuse for treating him as more than a mere "Magistrate," Hawthorne's justification for calling his Boston a "Utopia of human virtue" (47), and Hester's ultimate reason of rebellion. The distinguishing mark of Winthrop's New World Citizen-Saint was precisely his (or, should the case ever arise, *her*) renewed spiritual ability to love the law as the unfallen Eve had once so fully loved the mated partner of her own Edenic soul; or, as that figure takes its final winged flight, as the liberated soul will always love its saving Christ, that one promiscuous bridegroom-lover of all truly gracious souls.

A cynicism suggests itself at once, of course: Winthrop's vaunted "liberty" of law-like-love will actually entitle the saintly citizens of New England to do no other than "those things that qualified magistrates...and learned clergymen" would say they might.[42] But as long as rhetoric matters at all, it is surely worth noticing that Winthrop begins the Massachusetts experiment sounding as much like an arch-enthusiast as like a perfect Tory. And no American Puritan ever gave either a more lyrical or yet a more technical expression of Boston's oddly un-Puritanic variety of sexual politics; neither poets like Bradstreet and Taylor nor theologians like Cotton and Shepard. Always female, the soul of "man" is the subject of one adequate passion, whose sole object is that Divine Other which is Christ; and which, if it does *not* feel, all the rest is legalism surely. Or repression. Or force.[43]

Yet it is not quite cynicism, but merely adequacy to the various dystopian texts of history, to notice that it did not quite work out. Winthrop's *Journal* itself records—ruefully, if not bitterly—the more obvious human failures to meet his holy terms: the antinomian divorce of grace from law on the one side

225

and the altogether loveless quarrel about civil rights on the other. All of which forced him to repeat, for the record, the less lovely side of his complex original thought: "if you will be satisfied to enjoy" such liberties "as Christ allows you, then you will quietly submit unto that authority which is set over you, in all the administrations of it, for your good."[44] Even as Hester Prynne's seven-year submission manages to persuade everyone (except the narrator of her tale) she is only too willing to do. Until her final rebellion, when her "sudden and desperate" seizing of Dimmesdale convinces us that her own text implies a rejection of Winthrop's terms altogether. The law, say the lawyers, is the law; but love involves "a consecration of its own."

It would be too much, doubtless, to suggest that *The Scarlet Letter* fully endorses *this* particular form of antinomian rebellion, which shocks the narrator almost as much as it does Dimmesdale. His "Hush, Hester!" (195) speaks well enough for the civil reader's sense that local customs of courtship, marriage, and divorce are at least as complex and subject to social regulation as Winthrop had implied (whatever Bellingham may have thought). So that "the novel of adultery"—not to mention the more ambitious project of "deceit, desire, and the novel"—will surely survive the worst that Hester's rebellion (or Hawthorne's deconstruction) can possibly accomplish. But it is only fair, and indeed it is somehow necessary, to recognize that Hester's case is not entirely sociological, nor even altogether ethical. Her choice, throughout *The Scarlet Letter*, is never effectively between one and another human lover. Always it is between certain terms of complex socialization which have been mystically equated with the One Love no soul is free to reject and the passional motions of her own female temperament. An unforced option, surely.[45]

Even if it is, theologically speaking, quite like the one Dimmesdale in the end accepts—fleeing from the arms of Hester Prynne to those of the Heavenly Bridegroom his own (rather too "feminine") nature finally manages to prefer. Obviously, though ironically, his decision turns out to be quite easy: all he has to accomplish is the identification of his true self (or soul) as the part of him that really does love his own (Calvinistic) idea of God's "name" and "His will" (257) more than anything else, including Hester, whose fleshly existence his own flesh has found such an idolatrous temptation. Not quite so easy, perhaps, as it would be were he simply a Platonist, fleeing "to the Fatherland" from the wiles of the Aphrodite of generation; for then his soul could remain a masculist after all. But easy enough, as it turns out, for even the *Christian* allegory was made by men; and arguably for the same (Platonic) purpose of escaping "the woman," by becoming her themselves. Not physiologically, of course, but allegorically: by "submission."

Evidently it is not so much "right" as it is inevitable that Hester will regret her own version of this sexually mysterious option. Or at least that she will frankly question, at the end, whether Dimmesdale's authentically (and apocalyptically) Puritan Solution is indeed "better" (254). For to whom, after all, ought she just now submit? Hardly Dimmesdale, for he never has been her "husband"; and it would be only a little cruel to suggest that he is dying to evade that very role. Surely not Chillingworth, whom not even Winthrop would dare regard as a type of Christ. And where is the critic who will propose submission to the Puritan Community?—which never has known exactly what it was talking about. Besides, she has Pearl to consider: better, perhaps, if "we may both die, and little Pearl with us" (254); otherwise it's all too terribly confusing. Evidently the allegory works better for men than for women, whatever John Milton may have thought.[46] And evidently it is easier to be a woman allegorically than really.

Dimmesdale's "bright dying eyes" may indeed look "far into eternity" to see God, but Hester foresees only further years of single parenthood. Nor is her past of any present theological use. Her choice of Chillingworth—if choice it could be called—had not concealed, and could not be made to stand for, her prevenient willingness to accept only such liberty "as Christ allows." Nor could her "adultery"—as it after the fact turned out to be—possibly be construed as a whoring after strange gods. Dimmesdale dies believing he must choose "Hester or God," like some timid version of Melville's Pierre. Hester can only live on, finding time to return to some less utopian New England, free to consider again the proper "terms" of the human sexual relation. Hester "endures" (in Faulkner's sense) to rethink the problem of Hawthorne's "sources," in a world where even the best made metaphors eventually reveal themselves as such. Even if this means only that new ones must be made, in the space that always separates the soul from any supposable object of its own desire.[47]

227

PURITANS IN SPITE

A MOMENT or two before the most recent, well advertised paradigm shift in the study of American literature, an argument about "Puritan Influences" flared up, just briefly, in the pages of a journal soberly devoted to the study of earlier American literature as such. Not the old-time question of whether Perry Miller ever had found a way to get from the seventeenth to the nineteenth century, or whether his speculations about the transition "From the Covenant to the Revival" or, again, "From Edwards to Emerson" were merely thin and putative imitations of his account of the intellectual evolution of New England "From Colony to Province." Not even the livelier question of whether the emergent, more properly political system of Sacvan Bercovitch seemed more likely to capture the later course of American ideology for explanation in terms of a rhetoric that began with the invention of the New England Jeremiad. But much more radically: were there, in fact, any Puritan influences of significance? or was the premise of some puritanic continuity in American literature merely the fabrication of a naïve desire to totalize American literary history in its own nativist terms?[1]

Were "Colonialists"—exploiting their ignorance of British Romantic and Victorian literature—trying to have the whole thing, or at least the American Renaissance, their own provincial way? Or was it just as likely that the cosmopolitan critics were slighting the question of local literary tradition because they were not themselves sufficiently learned in the texts and issues of "Puritan Origins"? Or both? Was everyone just doing what their training had made possible and calling the result "method"? A nice question, which a timely review essay might have tried to answer, before the morale of politics came along to replace the history of ideas.

Even now, in these latter days, when critical interest has turned away from the ambiguous legacy of Perry Miller, one might revive the issue of Puritan influences by trying to pick a quarrel with the implication of Lawrence Buell's large, learned, and withal very correct study of "Literary Culture"—that the emergence of the literary interest in New England corresponds to the rise of Unitarianism.[2] Without challenging the general argument that the liberalism of the later eighteenth century helped to provide a friendly climate for the pursuit of belles lettres, or even the more determined claim of an homology between Unitarian preaching and the themes and forms of fiction, one might yet propose that the enduring power of many antebellum American texts comes in fact from Puritanism: from the dis-ease of its embattled survival, in some instances; or from the violence of its repression; or even from the energy required to meet its "moral" argument head-on. It took a long time, after all, for the liberal movement to insist on itself as such. And it remains hard to dismiss Emerson's claim that American Unitarianism is unintelligible except as a running critique of the older, Calvinistic creed—less "enlightened," to be sure, but also, for that very reason, less embarrassed by the spirit of criticism, and more powerfully positive, therefore, in the force of its mythic formulations.[3]

The spirit and the forms of liberalism come thus to figure as a necessary but by no means a sufficient explanation for the fact and the quality of the remarkable flowering of what used to be called literature in New England. An abstruse point, perhaps, especially where the ruling interest has shifted away from religious discourse altogether. Still, for a spot check of the available intuitions, the reader might try the experiment of comparing Buell's account of *Moby-Dick* with that of T. Walter Herbert, as the two appear, close together, in a recent collection of "New Essays" on Melville's polymorphous and self-deconstructing masterpiece. What Buell explains, very professionally, is the way the gradual erosion of biblical authority had made it possible for *Moby-Dick* to insist on itself as a "sacred text" in its own right. But when asking, in conclusion, "what brand of revelation" this rare formal premise had enabled, he can do little better than endorse and elaborate on Herbert's more doctrinal claim that the book "sets forth a Calvinistic analysis of Ahab's moral strife."[4] The net effect of liberalism, it appears, is to enable a fuller and more critical—more literary—enactment of the prime Puritan agon. Which is not so much different from what we always used to say about the cultural setting of Melville's "Quarrel with God."[5]

But it is not the intention of this essay to pursue the exact conditions of the liberal/orthodox engagement, decade by decade, or writer by writer. I allude to these difficult problems, at the outset, only to suggest how seriously the issue of American religious continuity might still be taken. (And to indicate that my old-fashioned, pro-Puritan bias is willing to take correction). I want in the end to raise only a very simple question: can we really imagine Hawthorne's instructed but edgy evocations of earlier New England, or Melville's preposterous but irrepressible quarrels with God, or Dickinson's finely turned little blasphemies could have been produced anywhere but in the latter days of a Puritanic culture? And even on the less "gloomy" side: does not Emerson's passionate departure from credal Unitarianism indicate a reversion to a familiar if recessive Puritan type as clearly as it does a perfection of the liberal progress?

The process by which all this neo- (or pseudo-) orthodoxy manages to survive or be reinstaurated is a difficult question indeed. So is the problem of the differing modes and degrees of influence or reception. And no doubt a full form of the present argument would have to account for those not insignificant cases—Old Canon and New—in which the old-time religion does not seem to reappear at all. The point here, however, is merely to suggest that "Puritanism" is a category not very easily discarded. Or, more modestly still, to raise the question: can we read the texts we do in fact continue to read without throwing in something somehow like Puritanism to strike the uneven balance? "Culture study" can never quite afford to ignore the religious aspect of culture. And to miss, in New England, the signs of a world once energized and still haunted by the wish to observe the fact of depravity and theorize the rumor of election might count as the latest form of "obtuse secularism."[6]

Emerson is always a hard case, perhaps, but particularly so in the light of our determination to read his "Transcendental" creed as a sort of upper-case liberalism. On this account he takes his place, with perfect linear clarity, right after William Ellery Channing: a prophet of self-culture, in the familiar and agreeable way, yet self-consistent and self-possessed enough to leave off the violent, oppositional rhetoric of "Unitarian Christianity" and especially "The Moral Argument Against Calvinism"; not spiteful of orthodoxy because, at last, no longer bound to battle in orthodox terms.[7] But the wish may here

231

have fathered the fact, for there remain strong verbal warnings not to place this admirable poise too far beyond the reach of saintly obsession. "Antinomian" may be entirely too strong and simple a term for the style of Emerson's religious personality, but convinced exponent of the argument of the Spirit most certainly is not.

We've known for a while, for example, that Emerson's famous "Address" to the Divinity School was written with the lesson—perhaps even the texts—of the so-called Antinomian Controversy open before him. The problem, apparently, was to insist once again on an adequately "subjective" version of the Christian tradition without seeming to license the wayward motions of private whim. Was it by chance, therefore, that when he reasoned himself out of the Unitarian ministry six years earlier, his rhetoric appeared to recall the famous debates of 1636 and 1637? Seeking positive, that is, "historical" support for religious conviction is, he suggests, just exactly like bringing good deeds in to witness the presence of the Spirit: "operose," in a word; which is to say "worksy." The Puritan "Elders" had tried to convince John Cotton that his subtle theory of spiritual witness made the works of sanctification "no more an evidence than a Candle to the Sun." Cotton tried to resist their formulation, but it remains a strong and revealing moment in an important debate. And then, years later, in the privacy of his Journals, Emerson positively rejoiced in the charge, turning its hostile language into a triumphant credo. The Spirit is indeed its own evidence: "You don't get a candle to see the sun rise."[8]

And how in fact do we respond to the ambiguous example of the "Address"? Does it mark a clear and definitive going beyond the conceptual and rhetorical possibilities of puritanic Christianity? Or does its meaning significantly depend on the intellectual and generic context it agrees to inhabit? Bluntly taken, it is nothing less than a calculated personal apostasy, prepared for by the natural theologies of the eighteenth century and forcibly provoked by the deconstructive findings of the Higher Criticism. And yet, as it does not in fact "deny" Christ, Emerson might well have thought it merely did the reforming work of insisting again that this holy word must do more than re-identify the historical Jesus. And, in terms somewhat more social in their bearing, can we read the "application" of this consciously Christological sermon without recognizing one more Awakener's warning against "The Danger of an Unconverted Ministry"? Emerson is no ordinary "awakener," to be sure, but the line "From Chauncy to Emerson" disappears almost as soon as it is drawn.

Well past the moment of revival, moreover, the puritanic provocation continues. When the rhetoric of Emerson's more openly rebellious "Self-Reliance" recommends an intuitive, even instinctual self-trust to a life measured out in conformable behaviors, only the unwary will fail to notice that the argument comes to rest not with the ordinary human subject of liberal self-culture but in that "aboriginal Self, on which a universal reliance may be grounded" (268).[9] In fact one looks in vain, in this essay and elsewhere, for Emerson to reverse the Humean (and also, we may recall, the Edwardsian) teaching that the empirical self cannot be regarded as a substance. Further, and more particularly, when the essay goes on to suggest that a person may clear himself "in the *direct* or in the *reflex* way" (274), we suddenly realize that an ethics of "self-direction" is being discovered in, or translated out of, the familiar discourse of Puritan sainthood theory: "direct" assurance is the privileged sort (à la Taylor's Rank One) which follows from some experience of the Spirit as such; the other, the "reflex," is the sort which must be inferred from pious good wishes and well socialized moral actions. We have been listening, it turns out, to an Emersonian sermon on justification by faith—appropriately demystified, to be sure, but significantly less so than in the self-identified instance of William James' "Will to Believe."[10]

The problem is not only (as Jonathan Bishop has cogently argued) that the meaning of Emerson's thought, its strength and corresponding weakness, can be measured only in terms of its conversation and indeed its competition with the doctrines of Christianity;[11] or that the version of Christianity in question is decidedly an orthodox brand. It is also, importantly, that Emerson himself has set up the contest, and that more is involved than a canny attempt to borrow on the credit of certain terms of great religious currency. Content to stand or fall by his ability to make better use of the language of tradition than his ancestors had done, or the more "reverent" of peers were proving able to do, he asks his reader to judge if he has not seized the survivable sense of the venerable old words. Could piety itself mean more, he asks, without surrendering the duties of the intellect? Could criticism retain less without destroying the thing it was supposed to render more intelligible? Credulous, it would be, to go on repeating the received "translations" of Scripture, from one generation to the next, but faithless and unnecessary—if not impossible—to make the language of religion entirely new.

Nor is the strategy limited to the early works, before the lecturer and, finally, the essayist have had time to outgrow the idiom of the minister. One could argue, in fact, just the reverse—that Emerson's reverence for the language of orthodoxy increases with the gravity of the essays themselves. The declaration, from the throes of "Experience," that "all success and failure" are the issue of some "vital force supplied from the Eternal," speaks from a profound and continuing conviction that genuine inspiration is to no one's individual credit; and he evidently finds it not only churlish but false to the sources of his own learning not to identify, just here, a prime locus of "grace" (483). More technically still, when the tense and reciprocating logic of "Nominalist and Realist" finally declares the individual "justified in his individuality, as his nature is found to be immense" (586), Emerson is evidently offering his philosophic version of the prime doctrine of Pauline Christianity: individual human being is fallen as such; and it is redeemed—"justified"—only by its participation in the general nature of humanity, which the Christ of the "Address" had declared to be nothing other than Being come at last to moral consciousness. And, as if to provide the needful reminder that this theology implies submission to general law more surely than triumph over individual circumstances, Emerson offers a whole essay on the antinomies we discover within the competing languages of self-determination.

Beginning with the reminder that America had not *always* had "a bad name for superficialness," that "our Calvinists in the last generation" (944) knew the dignity of duty without the illusion of autonomy, and working his way through a most current version of the problem once identified as "Predestination and Human Exertions," "Fate" says what it can, in a roughly Kantian way, for the space which the experience of freedom inevitably occupies within the phenomenology of consciousness. But it rests its case in a conclusion which, as Stephen Whicher long since recognized, was made to recall the New Divinity's "willingness to be damned for the glory of God." We have the right, I suppose, not to be *impressed* by the refrain of Emerson's hymn to the "Beautiful Necessity," any more than by Edwards' reiterated invocations of "Being in General." But as a simple matter of literary history, what Puritan can outdo the ending of Emerson's "Fate" in the escalating competition to efface the selfish and affirm the sovereign?[12]

Followed out, this line of analysis will suggest that Emerson, in spite of all the learned have said about his formation within and continuing affinity for the moral culture of Unitarianism, is just as fairly describable—and perhaps more deeply intelligible—in terms of a discourse the Unitarians sought to subvert. Where they had been suspicious of the tropes of earlier tradition, anxious to omit those they could not reduce to reason, Emerson positively reveled in their poetic reapplication. More "liberal" than the Unitarians, he was also in an important sense less "rational." Rather than discarding, with Locke and his successors in the art of "supernatural rationalism," all formulas which enlightened men could not univocally apply, Emerson chose the "natural supernaturalist" path of seeing what intimations might yet be hiding in the "Barbarous and Sacred words" of orthodox tradition.[13] And in this we may risk calling him a Puritan in spite of himself.

But there are sharper and more painful cases of what we might mean by spite. Hawthorne, Melville, and Dickinson also count as instances of a religious intelligence not univocally persuaded by the terms which make its expression possible. At least as self-aware as Emerson, they are also, evidently, less assured of their relation to the language of orthodoxy. And more significantly, perhaps, their Puritanism appears, in different degrees, resentful of its own necessity.

With Emerson, it is largely a case of liberating the older religious language for application to the Soul whose salvation is secure in a structure more absolute than that of personal identity. The only "ambiguity" is the one implied in every form of natural supernaturalism: is the literal preparation entirely annulled in its metaphoric fulfillment?[14] Is the language of Puritan salvation merely a hint or clue to Emerson's own meta-religious formulations? Or does it actually partake in the mystery being celebrated? With the others the ambiguity runs deeper: not much given to the habits of historical figuralism, are they literary opportunists, merely? Or do their rehearsals of the classic anxieties of Puritanism indicate that they themselves deeply participate in the system it sought to deploy, despite the resistance, even the hatred they clearly have the historical distance to express? Are they not, somehow, Puritans in spite of their own spite?

Hawthorne, let us cautiously agree, presents the easiest case. Hawthorne the "moral historian," that is: the Perry Miller-like hero of a certain book on the early tales. From that venue we need to recall only that Hawthorne recreates Puritanism more noticeably than he inherits it; that his recreations count as history for all but the studiously pedantic or the hopelessly naïve, and that this creative distancing prevents us from reading characterization as spiritual biography.[15] So stated, the evidence surely supports some case for the importance of Puritanism—namely, that Hawthorne found Mather and Winthrop as fascinating as Bunyan and Milton, and that he had as keen a sense of the American Awakening as of European Romanticism.

Yet many of the tales will not let us off this easily. It is absolutely necessary to consider that "Young Goodman Brown" may be an historical rather than a personal inquiry into the wonders of the invisible world; that this account of initial presumption, penultimate despair, and terminal gloom appears to fill up a gap in the historical record and not to prosecute any case of Hawthorne's own; that Brown discovers what his term system predicts, not what Hawthorne believes. Still, the tale did have to be written: somebody in the nineteenth century had to be darkly curious enough to imagine that the "superstition" of spectral evidence might encode some fact about the projective nature of guilty thought. To suspect, that is to say, that the lore of witchcraft might be somehow true: less a benighted and inexplicable aberration to be happily and inevitably outgrown than a condition of mentality we have yet to fathom.

And, more disturbingly, not all the story's wicked sayings are equally dissolvable into remote history. We richly appreciate the irony by which the Devil of Salem Forest is made to parody the Saint of Geneva on the subject of depravity: "Evil is the nature of mankind…Welcome…to the communion of your race" (287): universal sin without elective grace, as some early commentators noticed.[16] And we readily follow the steps of presumptuous bad faith by which a Puritan postulant is led to the blasphemous declaration that "There is no good on earth; and sin is but a name." But what voice do we hear next, recounting Goodman Brown's rush to darkness, "with the instinct that guides mortal man to evil"? (283). The quasi-Calvinist Narrator surely is, himself, a character in our experience of the story, but he is all we have by way of authority; and, as he is the one who suggests that we might want to imagine the whole forest episode was only a dream, he cannot be written off as someone trapped in the folklore of the seventeenth century. The story may provide ways to situate, or even to counter, his gloomy moral prejudice; but it will not permit us to ignore the question altogether. Something there is that does not love the light.

A more enlightened narrator presides over Hawthorne's later redaction of the drama of faith and doubt. But neither his complacent good faith nor our own anxious feminism has been sufficient to convice all readers that there can be nothing *really* poisonous about Beatrice Rappaccini. And though the strategy and tactics of her fatal father sound like another parody of Calvin, and though we might yet think to blame some further father for the image of the poisoned plant at the center of the enclosed garden, the problem of narrative "distance" is more difficult than in "Goodman Brown," and the spirit of the parody is anger and fear rather than scorn and triumph. As if the rumor of a God who presides over a creation corrupt in root and branch were somewhat more than bizarre fantasy. As if an original sin were transmitted, in fact, as a rare form of venereal disease.[17]

Other examples are less melodramatic, but their tendency would be about the same: Hawthorne is far from wholeheartedly embracing the ideology he has studied to reconstruct, but he is not perfectly certain he can defeat its claim. Thus the conflict between Parson Hooper and his baffled parishioners perfectly epitomizes the moment, well into the eighteenth century, when a new round of revivals appeared to predict a new round of separations; but it leaves our sympathies somewhat baffled. When the confrontation becomes quite personal, the reader tends to side with Hooper's fiancee, who decides in the end not to consummate a marriage with this powerfully eccentric prophet. Before their interview ends, however, his symbolic indirection brings her sensible good humor to tears, perhaps to insight. And the impression persists that Hooper may know something worth remembering about the "true sight of sin."

So too in a later, more archly metaphorical approach to this same question. When a man tormented by private guilt begins to confront his more liberated townsmen with the issue of their own "Bosom Serpent," they preserve a needful decency of composure by committing this moral atavism to an asylum for the insane. Then, when this liberal diagnosis will not hold, the privileged female "other" appears to propose that love will cure this serpentine fantasy. But—even without the strategically unhappy sequel—the reader is left to suspect that neither psychologism nor sentiment will cure all known cases of conscience. And to wonder what these audience figures might make of the man who went actively searching for the "Unpardonable Sin": Rosina Emerson Peabody comes in to rescue Roderick Poe Very Hawthorne from the depression of his overlong exposure to Puritan Gloom, but evidently there are some Brands no one may pluck from the burning.

Closer to the literal, perhaps, Hawthorne's emendation of *The Pilgrim's Progress* famously insinuates that the "Moral Argument Against Calvinism" may have been an act of repression rather than of enlightenment. We can reassure ourselves that Hawthorne's redaction is largely a literary exercise, a sort of "reverent parody" of Bunyan, and that, unlike the hysterical protest registered by Timothy Dwight in "The Triumph of Infidelity," Hawthorne's resistance to Liberal Religion is chiefly a matter of tone—at least the old-time religion *sounded serious*.[18] Yet it appears that comfortable men, well adapted to the lifestyle of Vanity Fair, are still having their anxious moments. And, though utterly decorous and polite, this curious literary experiment finds its own way to remember guilt, and to preserve the intellectual baggage they used to call "sin." And what if salvation does come "at the sight of the cross" (824) and nowhere else? "Thank Heaven, it was a Dream" (824).

The Puritanism of *The Scarlet Letter* will scarcely summarize in a paragraph or two. Indeed it deserves to be an ongoing question in our scholarship: will we really be comfortable if the "New Americanists" succeed in proving that the implications of Hawthorne's tale are controlled by the political considerations set forth in "The Custom-House," even if these turn out to involve the dynamics of a political deal we love to find abhorrent? Or if the literary historians of the nineteenth century establish that Hester Prynne is chiefly a figure of Hawthorne's sin of "romance"? Or if the psychoanalysts show that Dimmesdale's sufferings chiefly express Hawthorne's own desire to be beaten? No one thinks Hester Prynne is offered as an "Antinomian" in full cry, but the example of Ann Hutchinson surely counts for something. For the idea of Hawthorne's heroine is heavily in debt to the rhetoric the Puritan establishment used to oppose its famous female rebel, so that she enters Hawthorne's novel—as if from another literary life—trailing clouds of theologically formulated gender bias. A-ccommodation, in the American style of Compromise, may be the term of Hester's "return," but the sexual hysteria of Puritan theology and social theory has been the *donnée* of her invention.[19]

Nor is Dimmesdale's career any less amply foreshadowed. Pathetically weak and outrageously irresponsible, this supposed model of regenerate experience tries to confess but cannot bring himself to the particular point: "Subtle but remorseful hypocrite," Hawthorne calls him, and the oxymoron is permitted to stand as epitome and *reductio* of the Puritans' special problem of assurance.

237

But Dimmesdale's story has an inside as well: his adultery is a fatal attraction only if he turns out to desire Hester more than God. On the verge of accepting the fact that he does—and running away to seize the day—he reverses himself and dies in a last-ditch attempt to confirm the opposite. The decently meta-doctrinal narrator declines to observe that Dimmesdale has had to make his soul female, in perfect submission to the formula of readiness to meet the heavenly Bridegroom, but clearly, and killingly, Dimmesdale has had to fight the widespread and long-lived, indeed the "essential" Puritan battle of loving the creature too much, in an act of idolatry of which adultery was the constant and inevitable figure.[20]

Perhaps Melville read and responded to Hawthorne's painful moral contrivance in just this way; for what else could so aptly have inspired Pierre Glendinning to express his decision to abandon the sweetheart of his youth as the choice of "Lucy or God"? The reader senses that the real choice ought to be "Lucy or Isabel," blond girl or brunette, homebody or femme fatale, even as Hawthorne himself is said to have been torn between the pale reality of Sophia Peabody and the rich oriental seductress of his recurrent fantasy; but the inflation of terms is not without its own interest. Perhaps Puritanism had made it easy to think about sex chiefly as a metaphor.

But *Pierre* is not the first neo-Puritan text Hawthorne inspired Melville to write, as a timely rereading of "Young Goodman Brown" (and other tales from the *Mosses*) released Melville from a mighty repression and seemed to sanction the "wicked book" of Ahab's Quarrel with Sovereignty.[21] Nor would it be the last, as witness the nameless narrator's timely reading of "Edwards on the Will" in "Bartleby the Scrivener." The reader who feels invited, or perhaps dared, by this single passing reference is rewarded by the very first chapter of the *Freedom*, where Edwards is struggling with Locke's brave attempt to make *prefer* mean something quite other than *will*, and to discover behind this semantic variance the magic entry into the domain of authentic human freedom. We *will* to do such-and-such, Locke argues, but we can always *prefer* to be doing something else, and it is this "preference," always in the negative, that we escape that otherwise unbreakable chain of causes called *motive*. And Bartleby may seem to prove Locke's more liberal case—willing less and less, suspending all attraction, and finding (perhaps) some rare spiritual freedom in an ever more generalized preference not. Yet the caveat remains quite strong: freedom is always a refusal, of the object of desire in the first analysis and of life itself at last; elsewhere they may call the goal *nirvana*, but in the puritanic West it looks a lot like death.[22] Perhaps we are *indeed* to choose the choices of Edwards.

Just less teasing is the cautious confrontation with the author of the *Magnalia Christi Americana* in "The Apple-Tree Table," whose uncanny interest in "Wonders," within and without the bounds of established science, will not be written off, in the usual manner, as the figure of beliefs which survive

Enlightenment in the form of Superstition. And the wearing encounters with the matter of depravity in "The Encantadas" and "Benito Cereno" will amply suggest that an older episteme is alive and ill. *The Confidence Man* may figure primarily as an agon of faith and evidence, in an epistemological line begun by "Young Goodman Brown." But its argument from fools and knaves tests the premises of liberal anthropology as fairly as the limits of rational interpretation; its "Metaphysics of Indian Hating" risks its argument about race by daring to confuse it with its belief about depravity; and the whole affair manages to center itself on a most unlikely riverboat discussion of "St. Augustine on *Original Sin*." And, whether anything further followed from that masquerade or not, the texts of the later years hardly suggest the invention of a totally new, post-Puritan persona.

The tireless but wearisome search for authentic Christian origins makes *Clarel* seem more "Victorian" than "Puritan," but the *Battle Pieces* have trouble interpreting the Civil War as anything but an irruption from "The unreserve of Ill" beneath the world's thin crust of civility, a grim slur on the Republican faith "that Man is naturally good." And the overdetermined drama of *Billy Budd* makes its realpolitical way amidst a series of Calvinist problems and specific allusions so unremittingly dense that they threaten always to become the subject of investigation rather than the idiom of explanation. Too much to consider, clearly, in this preface by way of conclusion. A few observations about *Moby-Dick* must stand for the suspicion that Melville's attention, once arrested by the evidence of various sorts of "depravity according to nature"— and of the published news of possible "election"—could scarcely tear itself away from the fascinated meditation of "man's final lore."[23]

About Ahab's case against the God who causes—even if only by "permitting" such a wide variety of evil, which it seems a sin to call merely "natural," there seems little ambiguity:

> "Look! See yon Albacore! who put it into him to chase and fang that flying fish? Where do murderers go, man! Who's to doom, when the judge himself is dragged to the bar?" (1375)[24]

Usually violent in his hatred of the world's violence, cruelty, or flat injustice, Ahab can also make the case more sentimentally; as when he puts his question to a sperm whale's severed head. How defend the case of "'the murdered mate when tossed by pirates from the midnight deck'"?

> "For hours he fell into the deeper midnight of their insatiable maw; and his murderers still sailed on unharmed—while swift lightnings shivered the neighboring ship that would have borne a husband to outstretched, longing arms."

And these facts, he feels, might make "an infidel of Abraham" (1126–7), the Father in Faith to all but every lonely Ishmael.

And in the universal (and climactic) case, the whale himself: "outrageous strength, with an inscrutable malice sinewing it" (967). Strength and inscrutability are, of course, the Calvinistic given: a God of power and might, well expressed in a Nature whose ways are not our ways. Malice is but the inference of a mind immune to the pious version of the argument from design, which pleases to dress the Law of our "terrific benefactor in a clean shirt and white neckcloth of a student in divinity";[25] and to the still more pious exception, the premise of "affliction," which loves to discern the outline of discipline in the body of pain. And in these cosmic terms, Melville clearly gives Ahab his full say, opposing the God he recognizes, but does not worship, as the fiery Father:

> "Come in thy lowest form of love, and I will kneel and kiss thee; but at thy highest, come as mere supernal power; and though thou launchest navies of full-freighted worlds, there's that in here that still remains indifferent." (1334)

And more, of course, to the same blasphemous purpose, as Ahab matches, burst for burst, the Father of lightning and of woe, raising the stakes of rebellion well beyond the usual limits of the house of Freud.

Then, as Ahab goes on to seek an unknown God, the "sweet mother" who lives beyond the terror of the material creation, we have had to learn, from a Gnostic source, a theology more subtly plural than the redundant masculism by which a Father generates a Son by self-knowledge, and then this putative pair produce a (genderless) third by loving their own nondifference. For here, as everywhere else in this most supply learned text, the morale of the local cult is being dragged to the bar of World Religion. Yet the local gloss remains cogent, for the spiteful Ahab appears to be echoing the modest Channing, who steeled his gentle Unitarian nerves to insist that our moral nature forbids us "to love a being who wants, or who fails to discover, moral excellency" or to "prostrate ourselves before mere power." And thus a strong line of criticism portrays Melville as torn between a vision of a depravity profound enough to warrant *any* scheme of salvation—or none at all—and the liberal evocation of a system adapted to a creature endowed with "many ennobling immunities which render him the most august animal in the world."[26]

Nor is it frivolous to imagine that Christian soteriology is also part of Melville's blasphemous yet not altogether dismissive protest. Ahab's name is a little less infamous in the lore of reprobation—his case a little more complicated, perhaps—than that of Pharoah, whose faithless heart God moved to "harden." But who in New England could innocently ignore the example of

"Ishmael," that bastard-outcast of the universe whom Paul makes, by contrast with the gracious Isaac, an allegory of our birth in sin, and whom Calvin reads as type and symbol of the mystery of predestination itself? Call him the man who *just missed* the Covenant. And small wonder if, early on at least, we hear him urging a reckless plunge into the "howling infinite" (906) in pretty much the language that first Calvin and then Thomas Shepard used to forbid any questioning of the divine decrees. One comes to wonder whether Melville himself knew the expression "Quarrel with God," which names, in the same Thomas Shepard, the soul's resentment of its status as mere clay in the hands of the Pauline "potter."[27]

One can claim, of course, that all this fury is no more than a second and less favored son's elaborately encoded way of crying out against a world that continued as it began, failing everywhere to satisfy the need for loving acceptance. And no doubt most readers will want to make *some* translation of the insistent Calvinist language—to read the theology of non-adoption, as we fondly say, "existentially."[28] But as the coding is very nearly as elaborate as the pain is keen, we seem entitled to pursue its own interest. And to wonder, perhaps, how the evidence of resistance and protest would be different if Melville had felt himself a "Castaway" of *God* as well an orphan of worldly existence?

A similar question may govern a cautious approach to some of the lost-soul poems of Emily Dickinson. As painful in their implication as the daring tropes of Ishmael, they seem more nearly to court the literal, yet in a very unusual way. Designed to epitomize and to parody the problem of Puritan sainthood, they not only deploy the ordinary spiritual opposition between hope and despair; they also evoke a sort of Calvinist contest, to see who suffers reprobation most. They are, that is to say, *very* literary.

Some attempts have been made, early and late, to assimilate certain testaments of nonacceptance to an ongoing and finally resolved narrative of Dickinson's own conversion experience. But the biographical evidence does not entirely support the idea of a finite process with a single happy result; and, more cogently perhaps, many of the poems themselves seem both more settled and strategically resentful than one might expect from statements set out to mark the beginnings of the mind's road to God. Not even the organizational force of the fascicles has been sufficient to make these poems surrender the power of their resistant little lives to the known laws of spiritual turning in New England.[29] Most of them know quite well the morphology of which they fail to become a part. And they say just this much, in a most knowing way. Which makes it very hard—here, as everywhere else in this canon of remarkably terse intensity—to make and maintain a plausible human story.

Eager for a premise, therefore, one comes to imagine the possibility that the youthful Dickinson may have played a wicked sort of game with Mary Lyon,

241

who had the care of souls at the Holyoke Female Seminary, allowing herself to be put, all but alone, into the category of those who seemed to have "no hope" of salvation. A piquant little satire, perhaps, from one who thought she knew better, like Hawthorne, whose "Sunday sickness" helped him elude the agents of Awakening at Bowdoin College. Or maybe just a way to get adult attention, or satisfy misplaced curiosity: play the lost soul, then, if that will please their passion to identify. And just so, her poems may be, all of them, entirely dramatic, masterpieces of a capability whose "negativity" is sometimes a matter of substance as well as of form. Their speaker, on this account, is not herself "but a supposed person," even as she warns us.[30] In the present case, a person regardful of religion and anxious to discern the evidences of Puritan sainthood, but sadly, or quizzically, or despondently, or bitterly unable to do so. Perhaps a number of persons, given all those moods.

But then this literary multiplication only generalizes the interest in the theme of reprobation. For there certainly is no dilution of the fateful quarrel. Only the sense that its true significance is less as a record of individual fact than as a problem widely diffused through a culture, which the historic sense could then and still can find poignant and instructive. Emily truly lost? Perhaps not, in spite of her poignant experimental sense. Others of her acquaintance lost or dreading that fateful fact? Evidently so, even if the acquaintance were merely literary.

Some of Dickinson's religious poems seem playful—"childlike," even—as the one which knows it won't "like Paradise − / Because it's Sunday − all the time" (#413): they'll want to "sivilize" her.[31] Or the one which dares God to climb "Over the fence" where "Strawberries − grow," forgetting, perhaps, in its anxiety of gender, that the Christ-ian God had once been himself "a Boy" (#251). Sometimes, to be sure, the unbuttoned playfulness is more apparent than real: boys may find the Bible "antique," its authors "faded"; but in preferring "Orpheus' Sermon" because it "captivated" and "did not condemn − " (#1545), the Dickinson speaker slights orthodoxy in terms used by the thirty-five-year-old author of the Divinity School "Address." And when (in #357) God's "Vicarious Courtship" of humanity is compared to the famous, and not very successful, representation of Miles Standish by John Alden, the sense of "archness" has grown "hyperbolic" indeed; for somebody here is supposed to know that although God and Christ are, famously, *homoiousian* (of the same substance), they are "Synonym" in some sentences only.[32]

Other of these reductive exercises seem bent on their own small spite from the outset—daring to thank the "Burglar! Banker − Father!" (#49) for the gift of repeated bereavement. Or, more technically, offering their speaker back to that "Heavenly Father" with apology for the "iniquity" framed by His own "candid" hand; apologizing, with irony more cruel than subtle, "For *thine* own Duplicity − " (#1461, Emphasis added). Or again, with the same refusal to accept the pious intent of the doctrine of original sin, asking God "That we may be forgiven" for a crime only "he is presumed to know"; and then adding, for full measure, the further fate which requires we "reprimand the Happiness/ That too competes with Heaven" (#1601).

And one or two poems, beginning in childish resentment, may actually earn their own bereft surprise. It sounds petulant to say "Of Course – I prayed – / And did God care?" And the image of the bird stamping her foot and crying "Give Me" seems to suggests a conscious evocation of the merely immature. But the mood continues, long enough to insist on itself; and, as the speaker makes clear that it was, after all, God's own self she sought, the nervous reader finds it hard to argue with the brutal conclusion of her preferring nonexistence to the "smart Misery" (#376) of a life beyond the reach of Grace. Here, as elsewhere, "I asked no other thing – / No other – was denied – " (#621). The Puritanism of the logic is perfect: God or nothing at all. The most which orthodoxy can object is that, as absence is no sign of its own continuance, the present application has been premature.[33] Yet the familiar advice, to wait, still, as long as it takes, sounds like it might be wasted on a speaker who says "I *shall* know why" I bear the scalding "Anguish" of rejection; "Christ will explain" it all, in the "fair schoolroom of the sky"—when, she implies, it is largely too late to matter. Childish impatience or adult undeception—madness or divinest sense—some repression has lifted: we're not supposed to talk that way.

Often, as in that last case, the poems have the sense of trying to respond to considered religious advice, such as the mature Christian Saint might offer the novice of Grace or otherwise perplexed poor Soul. We have tended to take quite straight the iterated poetic teaching that "Success is counted sweetest/ By those who ne'er succeed" (#67); and to learn too well the lesson of negativity—that it is better, finer, keener, somehow, "To learn the Transport by the Pain" (#167). But much of the *valeur* comes off this *via negativa* when we hear it thrown into the accents of indirect discourse: "Defeat- whets victory – they say – /...'Tis Beggars – Banquets – can define – / 'Tis Parching – vitalizes Wine – " (#313). *They say.* And the irony is particularly acute in a poem that tries—and fails—to persuade itself that *any* assurance of salvation would bring only a smug confidence or a blythe forgetful-ness of the lesson of need suffered in the long preparation:

> I should have been too saved – I see –
> Too rescued – Fear too dim to me
> That I could spell the Prayer
> I knew so perfect – yesterday –
> That Scalding One – Sabachthani –
> Recited fluent – here –

Saved in my own time, they say, I should have had the Good News without
the bad, "The Palm – without the Calvary." To suffer is to appreciate, the
longer the better.

Easy for *them* to say, implies a speaker who is actually quite sure she could
bear a little comfort, some small earnest of what they call a firm assurance. And
soon. For, as another poem has it, there's a limit to our ability to appreciate the
divine game of strategic withholding. He's hid "his rare life/ From our gross
eyes": that's fair. And, had we but world enough and time, this coyness were
just the thing to whet the sense of need:

> 'Tis an instant's play.
> 'Tis a fond Ambush –
> Just to make Bliss
> Earn her own surprise! (#338)

Yet the "glee" of God's little hide and seek might "glaze"/ In Death's – stiff –
stare." And the author of a "jest" that "crawled" this far might be hard to recognize as God.

Easy to recognize, however, though more by spiritual extrapolation than
textual imitation, is the profile of a seeker but not a finder of salvation on the
Puritan model. Fairly dramatized here—uniquely, to my knowledge—is the
noncooperating, indeed the resisting auditor of sermons and tracts on how to
read the signs of the work of the Spirit; or, if Edward Taylor's shameless but
friendly truth were told, how to make the ragged content of religious frustra-
tion count as "Faith." When the ministers write, they have and exercise the
happy power to frame their own objections; and happier still, to place them in
the mouths of sincere persons who need only to hear what they themselves
have to teach in order to realize the gracious truth of their own election. But
what if the preacher's words continued only words, without the power to call
or reassure? And what if some hapless hearer, unconverted but unwilling to
give up on the project, wrote up a version of her own lasting distress? Or, if
not, what if some agent, friendly or merely curious, took up the pen on her
behalf? Enriching, thereby, the literature of Puritanism in a way it might least
expect?

One poem even suggests that the locus of such distress is, as Taylor himself
made clear, nowhere but the Congregational Church. At the beginning of a
little allegory of Biblical farming, a "cautious" speaker "scans [her] little life,"
winnows "what would fade/ From what would last," and stores her hopeful
evidences in a "barn" we readily identify as memory or the hoarding heart.
Then, when she finds these treasures missing, "one winter morning," she wonders at once "Whether Deity's guiltless." But while we are waiting for her to

prosecute this most cruel but quintessentially Calvinist case of "temporary faith,"[34] the poem turns from God to her audience:

> How is it Hearts, with Thee?
> Art thou within the little Barn
> Love provided thee? (#178)

Taking its blasphemous charge of divine infidelity absolutely for granted, it changes the meaning of barn from human heart to Puritan meetinghouse, and challenges instead the evidences that let one into, or keep one out of, a Particular Church of visible saints. Dickinson is not Edward Taylor, of course, but we may recall that the terms of the Half-Way Covenant endured in the Connecticut Valley down to her own day, and that she alone, of her family and close friends, was never "gathered" into full communion.[35] Perhaps we should call *her* Ishmael—escaped alone, from morphology to form, to tell us just enough.

Someone's experience of missing salvation, yet coming entirely too close for comfort, is so tightly coiled into one poem that eight lines of sustained ironic understatement manage to snap out a blasphemy that makes Ahab's charges of God's loveless power seem bombastic and crude:

> To One denied to drink
> To tell what Water is
> Would be acuter, would it not
> Than letting Him surmise?

> To lead Him to the Well
> And let Him hear it drip
> Remind Him, would it not, somewhat
> Of His condemned lip? (#490)

The fate of Moses is in the poem, perhaps, drawing water from a stone in the desert yet never going on to slake his thirst in the Promised Land; of Christ on the cross too, if one insists, offered only the vinegar of a despair named "Sabachthani." And, along with many other Dickinson poems about hunger and thirst, this one may express a failure to nourish more subtle and acute than any holy or nervous anorexia can yet approach. For who knows better the quality of desire than someone left "to die of thirst – suspecting/ That Brooks in Meadows run"? (#167). Or one who only watches while, "Over and over, Like a Tune," the Sacrament of "Recollection plays"?—and while "Justified Processions" (#367) of saintly others all share the same spiritual food and drink?

But the present poem reads best as nothing more than a direct question put to John Calvin and his disciples, all of whom struggled—manfully, shall we say?—with the question of why the Good News of Salvation needed to be preached, with such a plainness and a power, to all, when only some would stand to profit. *Why* is it, again, that so many are called when so few are chosen? What—given the self-expressive end for which God created the universe—is the exact use of this "smart misery"? It seems a little cruel. And which of Calvin's studiously diologic preachers, we might wonder, could imagine the objection they all feared most in quite so nice a form? Was this hardness of heart? Or a case of conscience keener still? Were there, in fact, persons who knew they needed Grace to thrive, who belived, on life, that Grace was flowing round about, but never did quite happen in its way? Would William James himself know the "Varieties" well enough to name the once-born sick soul?[36]

But the most memorable instance of Dickinson's ironical Puritanism—her refusal to walk away from the system she seemed to know could never save her—comes in her longest and seemingly most personal poem. Perhaps it is only the uncustomary length which creates the impression of proper personality as, for once at least, the speaker offers a few of the words that surround the syntax. In any case, a supposed person declares and appears to rationalize her separation from a lover in terms that must seem very familiar to students of the American seventeenth century; yet in a tone too killing for that epoch to imagine.

> I cannot live with You –
> It would be Life –

Life, in fact, to me—when every Christian knows that "Life is over there – / Behind the Shelf" where the Sexton stores the vessels that serve the Sacrament: no Life, our text has said, unless we eat His flesh and drink His blood. I give you up, therefore, to avoid the cognitive dissonance which, in this culture at least, can count as nothing but idolatry.

Anne Bradstreet effectively dramatizes the strain of saying yes to the will of a sovereign God in the experience of losing not only her house but indeed all the earthly possessions stored there, assuring some stable sense of self-identity through the change from Old England to New. Fearful of the effect of some "Hellish breath" on the garden of his fruitful marriage, Edward Taylor watches in horror as, instead, a "glorious hand" comes "from glory" to "Crop" a share of the flower children growing there: "Grief o're doth flow," as well it might, "and nature fault would finde" could not the Saint find grace to find God's will his "Spell Charm, Joy, and Gem." Thomas Shepard watches himself watch a dying wife lose the comforting sense of his own last loving touch in

the hallucinated embrace of the Heavenly Bridegroom—learning to reorder
the hierarchy of his own loves as he learns to love her loving only Christ. And
Michael Wigglesworth was willing to carry this thought of weaned affections
beyond the pale of death where, at the Last Judgment, the Elect are well
resigned, as they must be, to the news of loved ones doomed to hell.[37] But
only Dickinson has the theologic nerve to imagine this deadly last act of
Augustinian piety as occurring in full life: I give you up now, because you
would, I know, entirely dominate the affective competition between creature
and creator.

Even now—after a brief aside to stop for the natural death—the speaker
can imagine the Judgment scene: in my eyes "Your Face/ Would put out Jesus'
– " in the contest of risen glory. Nor could any judge fail to notice that where
"You – served Heaven – …I could not – ":

> You saturated Sight –
> And I had no more Eyes
> For sordid excellence
> As Paradise.

Still, with a logic more strictly Calvinist than *The Day of Doom* itself, the call
of election might go either way: "And were you lost, I would be – " even
though my saintly name led all the rest.

> And were You – saved –
> And I – condemned to be
> Where You were not –
> That self – were Hell to me – (#640)

The odd syntax of the last line may signal the strain of literary competition as
well as spiritual discipline; yet neither Milton nor Marlowe quite knew how
to say "Your not-self am hell."

It has seemed tempting, in the days before the full emergence of "Sue" as
the principal player in the Dickinson love plot, to read this poem as a tortured
farewell to the Reverend Charles Wadsworth, departing the regions of the East
for his new post at the Calvary Church in San Francisco. So read, it becomes
entirely ironic, a bald laying out of an argument not deeply or originally her
own. The enhanced Puritan logic of the enforced separation is not hers but
his; she is the temptation his fearful faith must flee. She, once again, could *bear*
a little comfort; he alone bequeaths a life of "Prayer – / And that White
Sustenance – / Despair." The final effect of her most faithful yet unholy love,
on this reading, is that she ends up repeating a theology she only half accepts:
I admit it, I love you best and always will; therefore, it seems—on premises

always friendlier to your experience than to mine—we must part. Well, if you say so. But one of us may keep the door ajar.

To come this far, however, is to realize that the poem's drama is movable indeed. It might be ascribed, for example, to a certain Elizabeth, who finds she cannot marry Parson Hooper, but maintains a significant nearness of separation, loving the man, fearing his logic, and leaving the rest to some God beyond God. Or more poignantly, perhaps, to Hester Prynne, as she, long since willing to be damned with Dimmesdale, tries to imagine what he *could* be thinking, for seven tortured years, or cautiously triumphant in death. The problem and the passion of the poem would be the same if it had begun as a meditation on the implication of his dying question, "Is this not better than what we dreamed of in the forest?" (337). Or—as the narrator proves himself most equal to the Puritan demand—on the space between the graves, "as if the dust of the two sleepers had no right to mingle" (345).[38] Some loves die hard. So, where history watches, do some meanings.

But as they do not live everywhere, the field lies open for competing explanation. The urgency of Puritan problems in some important literature of the nineteenth century seems too remarkable to overlook, but one hastens to disown any attempt to generalize the lesson. Having learned that literary history is the very opposite of a totalizing operation, that individual comparisons and connections explain only what they do in fact explain, it will be entirely appropriate—and necessary, elsewhere—to ask what other influences compete, and how effectively, with the legacy or the imitation of Puritanism in the formation of writers associated with New England, by birth or by the elective affinity of tone.

First of all, as we began by conceding, it is not exclusively the "Puritan" habits of self-consciousness which permit the classic creed to become its own self-exacerbating subject. And agencies of challenge and change are no less describable than evidences of stubborn survival. Further, the list of neo-Puritans in the nineteenth century is certainly finite. Other writers, whose moral programs appear to rely on otherworldly sanction, might well be added to the present list: the logic of Stowe's abolitionism may imply a sort of "feminization" of the slave-holding sensibility, but it depends, even more radically, on the possibility of a conversion not much changed from the Puritan model; and when loving mother in Susan Warner's *Wide, Wide World* teaches her most loving daughter to imitate her own example, of loving Christ even more, one gets the feeling that the theology of Puritanism has found a perfect way to heighten and to redeem the morale of sentiment. But other writers resist addition: Frederick Douglass and Harriet Jacobs have found their way to the moral haven of the Northeast; but having observed, along the way, how the rhetoric of slavery to sin can dull the political faculty, they keep their religious views distinct from the neo-orthodoxy of the region.[39]

Nor is the traditional canon without its own curious cases. Why, for example, do writers in the "Transcendental" tradition after Emerson seem so much less determined—less anxious, it may be—to wrest their "original" meanings from the words of an orthodoxy which puritanic Spiritism seems to epitomize? Thoreau's obsessive desire for a life of utter simplicity seems recognizable as a generalized version of the Puritan impulse to clear the religious field of everything but God and the Soul; but it really is a "secular" wish, unchurched in tone as well as cosmic in extent. A similar liberation seems to mark the neo-Quakerism of Whitman. He invokes the Spirit, right enough, and books have been written to mark his place in the "antinomian" strain of American poetry, but Quaker tradition, Hicksite or otherwise, is far less precise than that which Cotton handed on to Edwards. And, though he sometimes supports the Puritan attempt to keep the Spirit from reducing to the individualized self, he seems satisfied—gleeful, even—to let its figure be sex. In the end, it appears, the task of defending the goodness of Being, against the puritanic slander of "mere" nature, seemed to overwhelm all other questions of value and even of distinction.[40]

The problem most surely entailed in the nature of the analysis itself, however, is one we have been sensing and skirting all along, as the figure of "Puritan Influences in American Literature" became personally complex as well as ideologically insistent: where, in the sharpest and most spiteful of cases, could all this pain of faith and loss be thought to occur? Is their evident representation properly "historical"—deliberately a comment upon or hypnotically a reproduction of the terms and conditions of a lapsed Puritan era? Or is it in fact "biographical," fairly assignable therefore to the real present of the nineteenth century?

If the locus is properly the seventeenth century, then it is as if the later writers were filling in a space that surely *should* have been occupied then but somehow, oddly, was not. For one looks in vain for evidence, there, that the powerful Puritan system of repression had begun to fail. Shepard really does come to love the fact that his wife loves Jesus more. Bradstreet hates the burning of her house, but teaches herself to call the aroma of that earthly love a "dunghill mist." Taylor loves his dying babes with an affection as truly weaned as one can without inhumanity imagine. And we would like the conclusion of *Day of Doom* better, perhaps, if it seemed at all aware of how our own, more sentimental generation might respond to the instruction to *stop* loving our loved ones the second the decree of their separation is read aloud. Perhaps all this protest is some version of what the nineteenth century thought the seventeenth century *should* have said: do *not* go gentle into that last good thought.

249

Except that, if the human power to resent decree had found its full expression there, the store of later writers were surely shorter by a theme.

Or, if the true setting is the nineteenth century, then our idea of a "neo-Puritanism" may concede entirely too much to the power of historical change. If Hawthorne, Melville, Dickinson are themselves simply "having" the problems they dramatize—along with Warner, Stowe, and many others who assumed the burden of "Faith in Fiction"—then crafted irony may lapse to piety or to pain.[41] On this model, liberalism does not gradually challenge and undermine orthodoxy; it merely provides an alternative which some people seem unable or unwilling to take. Some find real solace in the good old way. Others, less fortunate, simply refuse to walk away from the system which cannot save them; they cherish and revile it together.

Perhaps it is enough to decide that these puritanic dramas of nonsalvation by faith occur only "intertextually": suspending themselves somewhere between the authentic record of piety and the more studied but equally authentic provocation of resentment, they occupy the space not of invention but of critique. Enlightened, if historical, yet not fully liberated; entrapped, if biographical, yet left some room to turn around; belated in either case, they know themselves as "coming after" and "written in response." But that may be only another way of saying that they are the creation of the activity of literary history. Our own activity, of course, as none of this happens without readers who enjoy their own distance from and recreated interest in the instructive fiction of Puritanism. But it is based on an activity already being carried out by writers who, in the nineteenth century, found few subjects more consuming than the rise and fall of the faith which enabled the literature of original New England; whose writing is simply unthinkable apart from a pointed interest in the public doctrines and personal dilemmas of that historic creed.

Learning sometimes from the "classic" texts themselves, and sometimes from other, more material indices of inherited culture, a number of important writers of the American nineteenth century created a body of writings they knew to be no less post-Puritan than it was transatlantic. It was both of these, they knew, in spite of their own powerful wish to be original, in Emerson's meaning; or their recognition of themselves as "American," in some sense yet to be derived; or their inchoate wish *not* to be antebellum, as the logic of their age unfolded. And they might not thank us for trying to make their fate any less complex than it was.

NOTES

INTRODUCTION

[1]See H. Aram Veeser ed., *The New Historicism* (New York: Routledge, 1989); Brook Thomas, *The New Historicism* (Princeton: Princeton University Press, 1991), esp. pp. 24–50; and Louis Montrose, "New Historicisms," in Stephen Greenblatt and Giles Gunn, ed., *Redrawing the Boundaries* (New York: MLA of America, 1992), pp. 392–418. For an inspired attempt to redeem the premise of "false consciousness," see Fredric Jameson, *The Political Unconscious* (Ithaca: Cornell University Press, 1981); for a spirited resistance to that attempt, see Frederick Crews, *Skeptical Engagements* (New York: Oxford University Press, 1986), pp. 137–58.

[2]For Foucault's extended definition of "discourse," see the A.M.S. Smith translation of *The Archeology of Knowledge* (New York: Harper Colophon Books, 1976), esp. pp. 21–39. For the correlative dismissal of "the author function," see "What Is An Author?" in *Language, Counter-Memory, Practice*, trans. Donald F. Bouchard and Sherry Simon (Ithaca: Cornell University Press, 1977), pp. 113–38.

[3]Surviving reviews which accused it of attempting to infer a social history from the intellectual, the second volume of Miller's study of religious mentality in New

England stands as a specifying defense of the cultural being of religion; see *The New England Mind: From Colony to Province* (Cambridge: Harvard University Press, 1953). For resistance to the social model in which silent political motive is made to embarrass religious discourse, see Miller, "From the Covenant to the Revival," in *Nature's Nation* (Cambridge: Harvard University Press, 1967), pp. 90–120; and Alan Heimert, *Religion and the American Mind* (Cambridge: Harvard University Press, 1966), esp. pp. 1–24.

[4]The best way to approach the Bercovitch *oeuvre* as deriving from the project of Miller is through *The American Jeremiad* (Madison: University of Wisconsin Press, 1978), esp. pp. 3–30. For the best presentation of significant differences from Miller, see *The Rites of Assent* (New York: Routledge, 1993), esp. pp. 1–89.

[5]For a systematic account of the discipline of American Literature as a set of attitudes and expectations, rather than a specified set of texts, see David R. Shumway, *Creating American Civilization* (Minneapolis: University of Minnesota Press, 1994), esp. pp. 1–24, 123–47.

[6]The general history of "American Studies"—as an experiment in realigning the academic disciplines and in mixing the methods of the human sciences—remains to be written; but for a lively set of field-reports on its evident commitment to comment back upon various aspects of American Culture, see the following general estimates: Henry Nash Smith, "Can American Studies Develop a Method?" *American Quarterly*, 9 (1957), 197–208; Robert E. Spiller, "Unity and Diversity in the Study of American Culture," *American Quarterly* 25 (1973), 611–18; Cecil F. Tate, *The Search for a Method in American Studies* (Minneapolis: University of Minnesota Press, 1973); Jay Mechling, Robert Meredith, and David Wilson, "American Culture Studies," *American Quarterly*, 25 (1973), 363–89; Robert Sklar, "The Problem of an American Studies 'Philosophy,'" *American Quarterly*, 27 (1975), 245–62; John G. Blair, "Structuralism, American Studies, and the Humanities," *American Quarterly*, 30 (1978), 261–81; Gene Wise, "'Paradigm Dramas' in American Studies," *American Quarterly*, 31 (1979), 293–337; Various Contributors, "Some Voices in and Around American Studies," *American Quarterly*, 31 (1979), 338–406; Linda K. Kerber, "Diversity and the Transformation of American Studies," *American Quarterly*, 41 (1989), 415–31; Robert F. Berkhofer, Jr., "A New Context for a New American Studies?" *American Quarterly*, 41 (1989), 588–613; Allen F. Davis, "The Politics of American Studies," *American Quarterly*, 42 (1990), 353–74; Martha Banta, "Working the Levees," *American Quarterly*, 43 (1991), 375–91; Philip Fisher, Introduction to *The New American Studies* (Berkeley: University of California Press, 1991), pp. vii–xxii; and Donald E. Pease, "New Americanists," in Pease, ed., *Revisionary Interventions into the Americanist Canon* (Durham: Duke University Press, 1994), pp. 1–37. For an urbane sense of disappointment at the failure of all this cultural good will, see Gerald Graff, "The Promise of American Literary Studies," in *Professing Literature* (Chicago: University of Chicago Press, 1987), pp. 209–25.

[7]For a critical review of the succession of formalisms which have tempted criticism in the Academy, see Frank Lentricchia, *After The New Criticism* (Chicago: University of Chicago Press, 1980).

[8]In *Literary Into Cultural Studies* (London: Routledge, 1991), Antony Easthope epitomizes the recent "paradigm shift" in English Studies as the contrast between the "oligarchic" views of F.R. Leavis and Terry Eagleton's more "democratic" understanding of "'literature' as a name which people give…to certain kinds of writing within a whole field of what Michel Foucault has called 'discursive practices'" (p. 4). The political contrast is sharp indeed, but the continuity appears in the common assumption that texts do important cultural work. More generally, I.A. Richards and William Empson are commonly (dis)credited with the invention of the New Criticism—theorized, afterwards, by Americans from Cleanth Brooks and Austin Warren to Murray Krieger; yet it remains true that Richards and Empson went right on with their culture-based crit-

icism of the British Romantics and, in Empson's emphatic case, of "Milton's God"; and that neither wrote anything like Brooks' *Well Wrought Urn*, that elegant summa of criticism turned to find its texts beyond the sea. For the place of the New Criticism in the history of American critical practice, see William E. Cain, *The Crisis in Criticism* (Baltimore: Johns Hopkins University, 1984), pp. 85–121; and Vincent B. Leitch, *American Literary Criticism from the 30s to the 80s* (New York: Columbia University Press, 1988), pp. 24–59.

[9]To be sure, one might trace a growing sense of "literary" consciousness in Americanist criticism from the avowed liberalism of V.L. Parrington's *Main Currents in American Thought* (1927–31), to the divided emphasis on democracy and organicism of F.O. Matthiessen's *American Renaissance* (1941), to the Cassirer-ist interest in symbolic form of Charles Feidelson's *Symbolism and American Literature* (1953); but even Feidelson's all-but-postmodern study is anchored in culture by his chapter on "An American Tradition" of allegory and symbolism. Similarly, one could rank the social methodologies of Henry Nash Smith's *Virgin Land* (1950), R.W.B. Lewis' *American Adam* (1955), and Leo Marx's *Machine in the Garden* (1964); but one may also regard these "myth-symbol" ventures more specified and self-conscious experiments in understanding the way texts say culture.

[10]For the cultural emphasis of critics outside the University in the founding years of the professional study of American literature, see Kermit Vanderbilt, *American Literature and the Academy* (Philadelphia: University of Pennsylvania Press, 1986), pp. 185–219; and cp. Shumway, *Creating*, pp. 61–95.

[11]The reference is to the first chapter of Lawrence's influential *Studies in Classic American Literature* (1923), the original (magazine) version of which begins as follows: "It is natural that we should regard American literature as a small branch or province of English literature. None the less there is another view to be taken"; see Armin Arnold, ed., *The Symbolic Meaning* (London: Centaur Press, 1962), pp. 16–31.

[12]Less insistant today, as Professors of American literature (their shame well clothed in the robes of Multiculturalism) are coming to be more generously received in Departments of English, the old so-literary knowingness persists, oddly but with a vengeance, in the rhetoric of William R. Spengemann, that Americanist *Malgré Lui*, who still knows how to recognize any "literature" worthy of the name; see *A New World of Words* (New Haven: Yale University Press, 1994), pp. 1–50; and "E Pluribus Minimum," *Early American Literature*, 29 (1994), 276–94.

253

[13]While we await some definitive account of the lapse of the "the literary"—whose episteme it was the prime achievement of the New Criticism to identify and to define as such—everyone must make their own story. For me, it began, belatedly, with the appearance one day in the Cornell Bookstore of a new book by Leslie Fiedler: *What Was Literature?* (New York: Simon and Schuster, 1982); and it continues as I notice the magical ease with which Easthope accounts for the process of first "Constructing" and then "Dissolving" the "Literary Object" (*Cultural Studies*, pp. 3–42). More specifically, it may be observed that literature has everywhere been collapsing back into something else: for linguists like Tzvetan Todoroff, the collapse is back into language; for Derrida, into something called "writing"; for de Man, into the endless turnings of the tropes of rhetoric; for Foucault, into discourse; for Marxists, into the materials of production; for garden-variety multiculturalists, into the identity record of competing social groups; et cetera, for all of which I spare the reader a footnote to this footnote. Finally, though, "the literary" also suffers fatally from the more inclusive attack on "the esthetic"; for an account of their rise, together, in the pseudo-theology of the eighteenth century, see M.H. Abrams, "Art-as-Such: The Sociology of Modern Aesthetics," and "From Addison to Kant: Modern Aesthetics and the Exemplary Art," in *Doing Things with Texts* (New York: Norton, 1989), pp. 135–87. And for their present embattled state, see Pierre Bourdieu, *Distinction: A Social Critique of the Judgement of Taste*, Richard Nice, trans.

(Cambridge: Harvard University Press, 1984); and Terry Eagleton, *The Ideology of the Aesthetic* (London: Basil Blackwell, 1990).

[14]One speaks from experience within an English Department that "went over" to theory and also with reference to Gerald Graff's argument that theory is needed to center departments otherwise tending to greater and greater (pseudo-scientific) specialization; see *Professing Literature*, esp. pp. 1–15.

[15]For example: the Department of English at the University of California, Riverside, whose political reorientation in the 1990s is just less spectacular than theoretical self-invention of the UC, Irvine Department several decades earlier.

[16]Critics favoring the *Narrative* are likely to argue that this shorter, simpler work makes a more immediate impact than the more mannered and "literary" text of *My Bondage*; see David Leverenz, *Manhood and the American Renaissance* (Ithaca: Cornell University Press, 1989), pp. 108–34. Clearly, however, the later version shows Douglass following his own lead rather than enacting the project of William Lloyd Garrison; see William L. Andrews, *To Tell a Free Story* (Urbana: University of Illinois, 1986), pp. 214–39.

[17]Neglected areas of American literature, before the so-called American Renaissance, may have even more to gain from a radical opening of the canon. And yet, as the lengthening of Art into Culture does not by itself elongate either Life or the academic term, decisions of curriculum and syllabus will still have to be made. Somebody might always begin with works which reflect or estimate culture most adequately, or intelligently, or "best"; and that way, always, lies "literature."

[18]Such appears to be the default position of William C. Spengemann; see *A Mirror for Americanists* (Hanover, NH: University Press of New England, 1989), esp. pp. 115–66. See also Peter Carafiol, *The American Ideal* (New York: Oxford University Press, 1991); and Gregory S. Jay, *America the Scrivener* (Ithaca: Cornell University Press, 1990).

[19]Miller's representation of Thomas Hooker's preparationism is entirely adequate, both in his two-volume *The Puritans*, edited with Thomas H. Johnson (Rpt. New York: Harper and Row, 1963), Vol. 1, pp. 290–314, and in his one-volume *The American Puritans* (Garden City, NY: Anchor Books, 1956), pp. 152–71. But neither anthology is adequate to the accomplishments of Shepard, and both fail to represent Cotton's precise theological emphasis; the longer version cuts off the text of *Christ The Fountain of Life* just before Cotton makes his slighting remarks about "sanctification," and the shorter version presents him, confusingly, as an arch-theorist of social calling. In *The Puritans in America* (Cambridge: Harvard University Press, 1985), Alan Heimert and Andrew Delbanco provide extremely professional introductions to *all* their selections—which then turn out to be too brief to do any independent (literary) work of their own. And Volume One of *The Heath Anthology of American Literature*, Paul Lauter, Gen. Ed. (Lexington, MA: D.C. Heath, Second Edition, 1994) represents the culture of New England in-migration with selections from Winthrop, Bradford, Williams and Bradstreet, but with no sample of the Puritan sermon.

[20]For the text of "Cotton's Rejoinder"—which weaves the questions and objections of "the Elders" and the theological insights already set out in his own sermon sequence on "The Covenant of Grace," together, into a luminous account of what Protestants *must* hold, as against the semi-reformed theology of the Counter-Reformation—see David D. Hall, ed., *The Antinomian Controversy, 1636–1638* (Middletown, CT: Wesleyan University Press, 1968), pp. 70–151.

[21]John Seelye, *Prophetic Waters* (New York: Oxford University Press, 1977), p. 343.

[22]Assisting the cultural work done by the contents and the introductions of the anthology itself, its Publishers are happy to furnish, as a sort of guide to the perplexed, a regular *Heath Anthology of American Literature Newsletter*, which recently featured,

under the general heading of "Teaching the American Literatures, part 4," a "Forum in Teaching Early American Writings, part 1: The Uses of the Spanish Imperial Past in the Early 'American' Classroom"; this material competes in busy self-importance with various publications of the MLA; e.g., Greenblatt and Gunn, *Redrawing the Boundaries*, esp. pp. 209–31; and A. LaVonne Brown Ruoff and Jerry W. Ward, Jr., ed., *Redefining American Literary History* (New York: MLA of America, 1990), pp. 9–34.

23The older Taylor essay, excluded here for reasons of space, appeared in *American Literature*, 39 (1967), 298–314.

24Several years before his resignation sermon explained that "no subject has been more fruitful of controversy than the Lord's Supper," Emerson had set out his debt to Solomon Stoddard: "I believe the whole end and aim of this ordinance is nothing but this, *to make those who partake of it better*." Of old, he argues, "All who named the Lord's name partook of his supper. And so should we now." See *The Complete Sermons of Ralph Waldo Emerson* (Columbia: University of Missouri Press), Vol. 4 (1992), p. 185; and Vol. 2 (1990), pp. 58–9.

25In Miller's famous formulation, Edwards was "one of America's five or six major artists, who happened to work with ideas instead of with poems or novels"; see page two of the Foreward to *Jonathan Edwards* (New York: William Sloane Associates, 1949). For Miller's most extended treatment of Edwards as poet, see the Introduction to his edition of *Images or Shadows of Divine Things* (New Haven: Yale University Press, 1948), pp. 1–41.

26For Miller's view of Edwards as a sort of frontier version of Samuel Richardson, see *Edwards*, pp. 133–63. And on the general topic of Edwards' "literariness," see Wilson H. Kimnach, "The Literary Techniques of Jonathan Edwards," unpub. Ph.D. Dissertation, University of Pennsylvania, 1971.

27Thus Henry F. May formulates the first proposition agreed upon by all the speakers at a widely interdisciplinary conference on Edwards; see "Jonathan Edwards and America," in Nathan O. Hatch and Harry S. Stout, ed., *Jonathan Edwards and the American Experience* (New York: Oxford University Press, 1988), p. 30. For the inspiration of this minimalism, see Richard Bushman, "Jonathan Edwards As Great Man," *Soundings*, 52 (1969), 15–46.

28See Spengemann, "Minimum," pp. 293–4.

29For Hume's suave deconstruction of the "substantial" self, see Section V and VI of Part IV of Book I of *A Treatise of Human Nature*; in the Penguin Classic (Ernest C. Mossner, ed.), pp. 280–311. Derrida's attack on the "philosopheme of the subject" is more diffuse, but see (for example) "The Voice That Keeps Silence," in *Speech and Phenomena*, David B. Allison and Newton Garver, trans. (Evanston: Northwestern University Press, 1973), pp. 70–87; "Cogito and the History of Madness" and "Violence and Metaphysics," in *Writing and Difference*, Alan Bass, trans. (Chicago: University of Chicago Press, 1978), pp. 31–63, 79–153; and "White Mythology," in *Margins of Philosophy*, Alan Bass, trans. (Chicago: University of Chicago Press, 1982), pp. 207–71.

30The weakness of Harold Bloom's model of literary history for Americanist Criticism—its insistence on discovering Strong Poets behind all Strong Poets—appears most clearly in *A Map of Misreading* (New York: Oxford University Press, 1975) where the author can identify no significant precursors for Emerson.

31For purposes of Hawthorne criticism, at least, the arch New Historicist is Sacvan Bercovitch, whose several essays on the "consensual" politics of *The Scarlet Letter* are gathered as *The Office of "The Scarlet Letter"* (Baltimore: Johns Hopkins University Press, 1991); Bercovitch's methods are suitably advertised in "*The New Historicism* and *The Scarlet Letter*," in Ross C. Murfin, ed., *The Scarlet Letter* (Boston: Bedford Books, 1991), pp. 330–58. And see also Jonathan Arac, "The Politics of *The Scarlet Letter*," in Sacvan

Bercovitch and Myra Jehlen, ed., *Ideology and Classic American Literature* (Cambridge: Cambridge University Press, 1986), pp. 247–66; and Donald Pease, *Visionary Compacts* (Madison: University of Wisconsin Press, 1987), pp. 81–107.

[32]For a (quasi-Emersonian) account of identity, personal or corporate, as a function of the inevitable if various activity of "strong evaluation," see Charles Taylor, *The Sources of the Self* (Cambridge: Harvard University Press, 1989), esp. pp. 3–107.

[33]Religionist criticisms of Miller must repress the beginning of his account; see *The New England Mind: The Seventeenth Century* (Cambridge: Harvard University Press, 1939), pp. 3–63.

CHAPTER ONE

[1]Thus is William Ellery Channing's "Moral Argument Against Calvinism" (1820) already advertised in his "Unitarian Christianity" (1819); see David Robinson, ed., *Selected Writings* (New York: Paulist Press, 1985), p. 90. For the Congregational practice of the public profession of saving faith, see Edmund S. Morgan, *Visible Saints* (Ithaca: Cornell University Press, 1963); and Patricia Caldwell, *The Puritan Conversion Narrative* (Cambridge: Cambridge University Press, 1983), esp. pp. 45–116.

[2]See my own essay, "Gods Determinations Touching Half-Way Membership," *American Literature*, 39 (1967), 298–314. For the tendency of that essay to localize and specify subsequent readings of GD, see Jeffrey Hammond, *Sinful Self, Saintly Self* (Athens: University of Georgia Press, 1993), pp. 267–68; and for an able and comprehensive review of GD criticism, see Hammond's *Edward Taylor: Fifty Years of Criticism* (Columbia, SC: Camden House, 1993), esp. pp. 13–14, 36–37, 44–48, 84–86, 104–106, 127–29.

[3]For citations of the text of GD, here and elsewhere in this essay, see Donald E. Stanford, ed., *The Poems of Edward Taylor* (New Haven: Yale University Press, 1960).

[4]The initial correction to my 1967 reading of GD was offered by J. Daniel Patterson, "GD: The Occasion, The Audience, and Taylor's Hope for New England," *Early American Literature*, 22 (1987), 63–81. See also Michael Schuldiner, *Gifts and Works* (Macon, GA: Mercer University Press, 1991), pp. 111–20; and Thomas M. Davis, *A Reading of Edward Taylor* (Newark: University of Delaware Press, 1992), pp. 20–47.

[5]The expectation of a threefold analysis is set out in "The Frowardness of the Elect" where, after Grace wins some Souls, the remnant "divide into two rancks/ And this way one, and that the other prancks" (402). Patterson and Schuldiner also notice that there is in fact only a *twofold* distinction; see "Taylor's Hope," p. 67; and *Gifts*, pp. 113–15.

[6]In his sermon sequence on "The New Covenant" Cotton parodies Hooker's endless preparation as teaching, essentially: 'blessed are those that hunger and thirst for they shall be hungry and thirsty'; see Phyllis and Nicholas Jones, ed., *Salvation in New England* (Austin: University of Texas Press, 1977), pp. 52–54. Less officially, Ann Hutchinson said of Hooker that she "liked not his spirit," and Nathaniel Ward observed that Hooker's preparationism made men "better Christians before they are in Christ than many are afterwards." Still, no one actually accused Thomas Hooker of doing it all in the name of Justice.

[7]Significantly, Taylor's two (and not three) styles of assurance correspond pretty well to those identified, briefly, by Michael McGiffert in the Introduction to his modern edition of Thomas Shepard's *Autobiography*, and at greater length by Janice Knight; see McGiffert, ed., *God's Plot* (Amherst: University of Massachusetts Press, 1972), pp. 3–29; and Knight, *Orthodoxies in Massachusetts* (Cambridge: Harvard University Press, 1994).

[8]For the paradoxical mixing of Devil and Conscience under the aspect of Justice, see John Gatta, *Gracious Laughter* (Columbia: University of Missouri Press, 1989), pp. 118–33.

⁹Hutchinson was undone not by anything she said or implied about Grace vs. Law, but by her appeal to "an immediate revelation" from "the voice of [God's] own spirit to my soul"; see David D. Hall, ed., *The Antinomian Controversy, 1636–1638* (Middletown, CT: Wesleyan University Press, 1968), p. 337.

¹⁰For the "purpose" of this unpublished yet audience-oriented poem, see my "Occasion and Audience"; and cp. Patterson, "Taylor's Hope," esp. pp. 74–81.

¹¹McGiffert, Introduction to *God's Plot*, p. 19. Everywhere upbeat about assurance, Schuldiner thinks that Ranks Two and Three have received "initial testimony from Christ" earlier. Possibly, but only with typic indistinction—and certainly not in the place he indicates; see *Gifts*, pp. 114–15.

¹²See *Edward Taylor* (New York: Twayne, 1961), p. 164.

¹³Since Perry Miller made Solomon Stoddard's policy of "open communion" a major issue in the drama of latter-day Puritanism—*The New England Mind: Colony to Province* (Cambridge: Harvard University Press, 1953), pp. 209–87—studies of his thought and influence have proliferated; see, for example, Robert G. Pope, *The Half-Way Covenant* (Princeton: Princeton University Press, 1969), pp. 251–58; James P. Walsh, "Solomon Stoddard's Open Communion," *New England Quarterly*, 43 (1970), 97–114; E. Brooks Holifield, "Intellectual Sources of Stoddardeanism," *New England Quarterly*, 45 (1972), 373–92, and *The Covenant Sealed* (New Haven: Yale University Press, 1974), pp. 193–224; Paul R. Lucas, "'An Appeal to the Learned': The Mind of Solomon Stoddard," *William and Mary Quarterly*, 30 (1973), 257–92; and Ralph J. Coffman, *Solomon Stoddard* (Boston: Twayne Publishers, 1978). For the beginnings of our understanding of Taylor's battle with Stoddard, see Donald Stanford, "Edward Taylor and the Lord's Supper," *American Literature*, 27 (1955), 172–78; and Norman Grabo, "The Poet to the Pope," *American Literature*, 32 (1960), 197–201 and "Edward Taylor and the Lord's Supper," *Boston Public Library Quarterly*, 12 (1960), 22–36. For a full review of the Taylor-Stoddard dialogue, see the Introduction to the Thomas M. and Virginia L. Davis edition of *Edward Taylor vs. Solomon Stoddard* (Boston: Twayne Publishers, 1981), pp. 1–57.

257

¹⁴For a conscientious verdict against *any* test for "saving faith," see Morgan, *Visible Saints*, pp. 139–52.

¹⁵For the astonishment of the Preparationists in the face of Cotton's contention that sanctification is evidence only in conjunction with a "faithful" experience of justification itself, see "The Elders Reply," in Hall, ed., *Controversy*, p. 67.

¹⁶In the impatient (and somewhat imprecise) account of Karl Keller, "The soul of the saint is left to carry on a long series of dialogues with itself over the…desirability of conversion, and Taylor comes in as long-winded, but gentle, admonishing minister"; see *The Example of Edward Taylor* (Amherst: University of Massachusetts Press, 1975), p. 135.

¹⁷As Taylor's "Dialogue between Justice and Mercy" seems written with its parodic eye on the heavenly debate of Book Three of *Paradise Lost*, so does "The Joy of Church Fellowship rightly attended" dispute the implication of *Pilgrim's Progress* that the way to heaven is a lonely and "pedestrian" affair.

¹⁸The scornful formula is that of Thomas Shepard; see McGiffert, ed., *God's Plot*, p. 67.

¹⁹For the relevance of Hooker's *Poor Doubting Christian*, see John Gatta, "Edward Taylor and Thomas Hooker," *Notre Dame English Journal*, 12 (1979), 1–13; also *Laughter*, pp. 119–22. For more general accounts of Taylor and Hooker (and preparation), see Stephen Fender, "Edward Taylor and 'The Application of Redemption,'" *Modern Language Review*, 59 (1964), 331–34; David L. Parker, "Edward Taylor's Preparationism," *Early American Literature*, 11 (1976/7), 259–78; and George Sebouhian, "Conversion

Morphology and the Structure of GD," *Early American Literature*, 16 (1981/2), 226–40. And for the similar preparation systems of Hooker and Shepard, see Norman Pettit, *The Heart Prepared* (New Haven: Yale University Press, 1966), pp. 86–114; and Knight, *Orthodoxies*, 96–100 and *passim*.

[20]For the flowering of the *anxious* norm, see Knight, *Orthodoxies*, pp. 88–108. And for the argument that, one way or another, many New England churchmembers did indeed achieve assurance, see Schuldiner, *Gifts*, esp. pp. 1–13, 61–105.

[21]See Cotton, *Covenant*, in Jones, ed., *Salvation*, pp. 52–53; also Cotton, *A Brief Exposition…upon the Whole Book of Canticles* (rpt. New York: Arno Press, 1972), pp. 4–5; and *Jonathan Edwards*, in John E. Smith, ed., *Treatise Concerning Religious Affections* (New Haven: Yale University Press, 1959), p. 205. For Cotton's revisions of his *Brief Exposition* in the interest of *personal* application, see Jeffrey Hammond, "The Bride in Redemptive Time," *New England Quarterly*, 56 (1983), 78–102.

[22]At issue in the controversies that follow the practical failure of the Half-Way Covenant is the Biblical warrant for requiring professions (or other tests) of saving faith; see the documents in Davis, *Taylor vs. Stoddard*, esp. Stoddard's "Arguments for the Proposition" (pp. 67–82), and Taylor's "Animadversions," (pp. 87–128); and compare the case between Increase Mather, *The Order of the Gospel* (Boston, 1700) and Stoddard, *The Doctrine of the Instituted Churches* (London, 1700), both contained in *Increase Mather vs. Solomon Stoddard* (New York: Arno Press, 1972).

[23]Except for supporting the inference that they decided to go for Hutchinson *instead*, the sources are silent on what compromise The Elders may have reached with Cotton; possibly he agreed not to devalue Sanctification altogether, and they came to see his point about not accepting Sanctification as the first and only evidence. From the side of Cotton, John Norton's *Orthodox Evangelist* (London, 1654) is an explicit attempt at damage control; see Pettit, *Heart*, pp. 177–84; James W. Jones, *The Shattered Synthesis* (New Haven: Yale University Press, 1973), pp. 3–31; and Knight, *Orthodoxies*, pp. 123–28. It also appears that very much of Shepard's *Ten Virgins* is—like Winthrop's famous "little speech" of 1645—an explicit attempt to win the language of love and the figures of sex back to the conservative side: the bride *obeys*.

[24]The modern reprint of Hooker's *Application of Redemption* (New York: Arno Press, 1972), contains only Books I through VIII of this *magnum opus*; Books IX and X—from which Perry Miller drew his anthology selections—must be read in rare book rooms or in microform. For the matter of the absent Book XI—on the Soul's union with Christ—see "The Soules Ingrafting into Christ," in Everett H. Emerson, ed., *Redemption: Three Sermons* (Gainesville, FL: Scholars' Facsimiles, 1956), pp. 101–08.

[25]In *The Sound Believer*—Shepard's most fully balanced account of the *ordo salutis*—Preparation gets more than three times as much attention as do the explicitly gracious stages of Justification, Reconciliation, Adoption, Sanctification, Audience, and Glorification; see *The Works of Thomas Shepard* (rpt. Boston: Doctrinal Tract and Book Society, 1953), Vol. I, pp. 115–237 and 237–74. The work then returns to the *practice* of Sanctification (pp. 274–84), but is cut short by the religious authorities in England; when Shepard takes up the topic again, in New England, in the midst of the Hutchinson controversy, the result is the massive *Parable of the Ten Virgins*, which stresses that as professed Christians wait for the Second Coming, their Sanctification is yet another form of Preparation; see *Works*, II, 13–635; and for an epitome of this emphasis, see Jones, *Salvation*, pp. 133–41.

[26]Perhaps it might be said of the Saint—as well as of "The Poet"—that "The man is only half himself, the other half is his expression." Such might be the moral of Caldwell's account of the "Origins" of the practice of professing conversion (*Conversion Narrative*, pp. 45–80). And of Edwards' report on the "Surprising Conversions" of 1733–34, which makes good on Taylor's "hope": his Congregation broke out not only

in "singing [God's] praises" but in making their "open explicit profession of Christianity," even though such was "not the custom here," in the house that Stoddard built; see C.C. Goen, ed., *The Great Awakening* (New Haven: Yale University Press, 1972), pp. 151, 157. For a reading of Emerson's relation to Taylor and to Sainthood, see Elisa New, *The Regenerate Lyric* (Cambridge: Cambridge University Press, 1993), pp. 1–55.

[27]For the practice of "reverent parody," see Gatta, *Laughter*, pp. 14–20; cp. Michael Clark, "The Honeyed Knot of Puritan Aesthetics," in Peter White, ed., *Puritan Poets and Poetics* (University Park: Pennsylvania State University Press, 1985), esp. pp. 75–78; and William J. Scheick, "The Necessity of Language," in *Design in Puritan American Literature* (Lexington: The University Press of Kentucky, 1992), esp. pp. 19–29.

[28]For a detailed account of how, when, and why Taylor's focus gradually "narrowed," see Davis, *A Reading*, esp. pp. 68–132.

[29]In the established theory of "meditation," a concerned person moves from a "notional" relation to some religious question to a more "affective" grasp and settled love; see Louis L. Martz, *The Poetry of Meditation* (rev. ed., New Haven: Yale University Press, 1962), pp. 25–70; also Martz's Forward to Stanford, ed., *Poems*, pp. xiii–xxxvii; and Grabo, *Taylor*, pp. 59–66. On my account, Taylor often affronts this program by presenting, at the outset, a paradox too surprising to resolve.

[30]At issue is the venerable but always astonishing orthodoxy of "substitutionary atonement"—according to which Christ, being God, can perform a sacrifice of infinite worth, but being man as well, can enact a "representative" deed on our behalf; for its Anselmian invention, see Jaroslav Pelikan, *The Christian Tradition*, Vol. 3 (Chicago: University of Chicago Press, 1978), pp. 106 ff.

[31]For the foundation and discipline of Taylor's own Church, see Thomas M. and Virginia L. Davis, ed., *Edward Taylor's "Church Records" and Related Sermons* (Boston: Twayne Publishers, 1981), esp. pp. xi–xl, 97–158.

[32]After repeated encounters with Canticles in—I. 23 and II. 19, 62–65, 69, 79, 83–86, 96–98—Taylor takes it up systematically, at the end of his career, in II. 115–153, 155–165. For commentary, see Karen Rowe, "Sacred or Profane?: Edward Taylor's Meditations on Canticles," *Modern Philology*, 72 (1974), 123–38; Keller, *Example*, pp. 207–20; Ivy Schweitzer, *The Work of Self-Representation* (Chapel Hill: University of North Carolina Press, 1991), pp. 98–123; Davis, *Reading*, pp. 169–98; and Hammond, "A Puritan *Ars Moriendi*," *Early American Literature*, 17 (1982/83), 191–214; also "Approaching the Garden," *Studies in Puritan American Spirituality*, 1 (1990), 65–76; and *Sinful Self*, pp. 225–35.

[33]Of the critics who look closely at the opening of Taylor's *Meditations*, only Davis thinks to problematize their arrangement (*Reading*, pp. 48–60), and no one emphasizes the gap that opens between I.3 and "The Experience": for example, Gatta, *Laughter*, pp. 141–51; and Schweitzer, *Self-Representation*, pp. 93–100.

[34]In the footnote of Donald Stanford, "Johnson suggests that Taylor uses mammulary throughout the poem to refer to the olfactory system, but there is no evidence for a meaning other than the normal 'nipples' or 'breasts'" (*Poems*, p. 7). More helpful comment is offered by Michael Schuldiner, "Taylor's 'Problematic' Imagery," *Early American Literature*, 13 (1978), 92–101.

[35]For Edwards' insistence on the "sensation" of salvation, see "A Divine and Supernatural Light," in Clarence H. Faust and Thomas H. Johnson, ed., *Jonathan Edwards* (New York: Hill and Wang, 1935), pp. 106–08; and his discussion of the first of the "Distinguishing Signs," in Smith, ed., *Affections*, pp. 205–15.

[36]Gatta passes over Meditation I.3, but the case is another of "The Ludicrous Trials of the Doubting Soul" (*Laughter*, pp. 118 ff.)

[37]At issue in Taylor's baffled will-to-assurance is a hint of Stoddard's claim that New England policy will produce not "Days of Comfort" but "Days of Torment" (*Instituted Churches*, p. 22.)

[38]By the account of *The Application of Redemption*, God employs a "a holy kind of violence" which will "either pluck you from your evil wayes, or…will pul you al in pieces" (VIII, 349, 363). As Ivy Schweitzer notices, "Taylor's *Meditations* abound with the violence necessary to wean fallen men from the sin of self-reliance" (*Self-Representation*, p. 103.)

[39]No simple reading of the biographical experience behind Taylor's first few *Meditations* can withstand Davis' account of their text; see *Reading*, pp. 48–68. For speculation on the range of fiction and/or the use of persona in these poems, see William J. Scheick, *The Will and the Word* (Athens: University of Georgia Press, 1974), pp. 150–68; Karl Keller, "Edward Taylor, The Acting Poet," in White, ed., *Puritan Poets*, pp. 185–97; Michael Clark, "The Subject of the Text in Early American Literature," *Early American Literature*, 20 (1985), 120–30; and Jeffrey Hammond, "Who Is Edward Taylor?" *American Poetry* 7:3 (1990), 2–19; also *Sinful Self*, pp. 186–212.

[40]For a multiform account of Calvin on assurance, see Schuldiner, *Gifts*, pp. 15–34; also R.T. Kendall, *Calvin and English Calvinism* (Oxford: Oxford University Press, 1979), pp. 25–28.

[41]Just so may some off-brand mysticism unite Taylor with a "Song" his reading of Canticles could no way predict.

[42]For the nearly literal insistence on the presence of "light" in a wide variety of mystical experiences, see Evelyn Underhill, *Mysticism* (New York: E.P. Dutton, 1955), pp. 232–65. For a useful review of the question of mystical experience in the *Meditations*, see Gatta, *Laughter*, pp. 142–51.

[43]On Taylor's "Super-Angelic Anthropology," see Gatta, "Little Lower Than God," *Harvard Theological Review*, 75 (1982), 361–68.

[44]In Gatta's admirable formula, "The almost selfish desire for ecstatic transport…must be restrained by a recognition that he has 'thy Pleasant Pleasant Presence had'" in all the ordinary churchly ways (*Laughter*, p. 144).

[45]If Whitman's "Song," then (a priori) the "Nature" chapter of Emerson's *Nature*.

[46]Though Taylor treats Solomon as a personal type of Christ—with the standard warning that, read any way but typically, "the Canticles" is nothing but "an amorous Love Song"—he treats the "spouse" as the Church rather than the Saint and makes no comment on roses and ointments; see Charles W. Mignon, ed., *Upon the Types of the Old Testament* (Lincoln: University of Nebraska Press, 1989), Vol. I, p. 244. For the sources of Taylor's Canticles lore, see Rowe, "Sacred or Profane," esp. pp. 124–30; and on the roses of Meditation I.4, see Davis, *Reading*, pp. 54–57.

[47]Prudence Steiner reminds us that moral warnings about the proper use of the Song of Songs go back to the very "Synod of Javneh, which met in A.D. 90 to establish the canon of the Jewish Bible"; see "A Garden of Spices in New England," in Morton Bloomfield, ed., *Allegory, Myth, and Symbol* (Cambridge: Harvard University Press, 1981), p. 229.

[48]For an extended comparison of "Emily Dickinson and Edward Taylor," see Karl Keller, *The Only Kangaroo Among the Beauty* (Baltimore: Johns Hopkins University Press, 1979), pp. 38–66.

[49]Thus Hawthorne puts the case of Melville in the 1850s; see Randall Stewart, ed., *The English Note-Books* (New York: MLA of America, 1941), pp. 432–33.

[50]Keenly aware that there are at least two "selves" involved in Taylor's tireless/tiresome attempt to say himself in the Langauge of Canaan, and anxious to affirm that

"Taylor usually passes the test of spiritual vision that the Bible offered him," Hammond (*Sinful Self*, p. 217) seems to miss the fact that there is more than one test.

[51]In the formula of Roy Harvey Pearce: Puritan meditation "was a matter not of disciplining oneself into knowledge of God…but of being lucky enough to catch a sudden glimpse of that knowledge as God might make it mainfest"; see *The Continuity of American Poetry* (Princeton: Princeton University Press, 1961), p. 43.

[52]Honoring Luther's famous paradox of *simul sanctus, simul peccator*, Antinomians and other purists typically insist that the Christian merely puts on the righteousness of Christ, like a robe, to cover his essential and enduring sinfulness; or, in another idiom, that this "imputed" righteousness never becomes "inherent" in the human moral subject.

[53]In Davis' account of the First Series of *Meditations*, the interest remains high through a climax at I.39 and 40 (*Reading*, pp. 106–26). My attention gives out sooner.

[54]The totalizing ambition is that of Schuldiner (*Gifts*, p. vii); for his reading of *Meditations* I.1–41, in terms of Calvin's morphology of assurance, see "The Christian Hero and the Classical Journey," *Huntington Library Quarterly*, 49 (1986), 113–32.

[55]Standing above the spiritual-biography interest of Davis and Hammond, and the generic (carnivalesque) approach of Gatta, Karen Rowe proposes the rare pleasure of mastering the technology of the types; see *Saint and Singer* (Cambridge: Cambridge University Press, 1986) esp. pp. 229–76.

[56]Still captivated by the elan of Taylor's narrative, I see no purpose in repeating that "*Gods Determinations* is an uneven poem," with some "pedestrian lines" and a "shaky development"; or that it owes much of its importance to its place in "the emergence" of the poet of the *Meditations*; see Davis, *Reading*, pp. 32–47. For a more relevant critique, see Carol M. Bensick, "Preaching to the Choir," *Early American Literature*, 28 (1993), 133–47.

261

CHAPTER TWO

[1]The question of Edwards' "modernity" eventually generated its own casebook: John Opie, *Jonathan Edwards and the Enlightenment* (Lexington, MA: Heath, 1969). For the initial reminder of Edwards' Medievalism, see Vincent Tomas, "The Modernity of Jonathan Edwards," *New England Quarterly*, 25 (1952), 60–84. The most effective placement of Edwards in his contemporaneous context is Norman Fiering, *Jonathan Edwards's Moral Thought and Its British Context* (Chapel Hill, University of North Carolina Press, 1981).

[2]For Miller's continuing power to serve as point of departure, see the opening of Sang Hyun Lee's *Philosophical Theology of Jonathan Edwards* (Princeton: Princeton University Press, 1988): "My contention…is that Edwards was actually more radically 'modern' than Miller himself might have realized" (p. 3). Another recent study inspired by Miller protests the tendency to allow Edwards to lapse back into his sources; see Robert W. Jenson, *America's Theologian* (Oxford: Oxford University Press, 1988), pp. 197–198.

[3]Thus Tomas quotes H.A. Wolfson, somewhat too gleefully, back against Perry Miller ("Modernity," 70).

[4]See *Aquinas On Mind* (London: Routledge, 1993), pp. 1–13.

[5]One understands Jenson's evangelical tendency to scoff at the problem: "Certainly, if to be Christian is by definition to be medieval, Edwards was medieval—and so what?" (*Theologian*, p. 197); but criticism needs to keep track of the difference between premise and argument.

^{6}Edwards' basic text on the problem of "Reason and Revelation" is "The Insufficiency of Reason as a Substitute for Revelation," which constitutes Chapter VII of his *Miscellaneous Observations on Important Theological Subjects*; it appears in Volume VII of the Sereno Dwight edition of *The Works of President Edwards*, 10 Vols. (New York: Converse, 1829). For discussion, see Tomas, "Modernity"; and Claude A. Smith, "Jonathan Edwards and the 'Way of Ideas,'" *Harvard Theological Review*, 59 (1966), 153–173. Other relevant texts would be the sermon on "Christian Knowledge" (Dwight, *Works*, VI) and that portion of the *Miscellanies* edited by Harvey Townsend under the title "Mysteries"; see *The Philosophy of Jonathan Edwards* (Eugene: University of Oregon Press, 1955), pp. 210–35. For the Medieval comparison, see Etienne Gilson, *Reason and Revelation in the Middle Ages* (New York: Scribners, 1938). And for Aquinas' definition of the "science" of the rational study of Scripture, see the *Summa Theologica*, Part I, Question 1, on "The Nature and Domain of Sacred Doctrine."

^{7}The theological limitations of Miller's study of Edwards have been obvious to all. Douglas Elwood's *Philosophical Theology of Jonathan Edwards* (New York: Columbia University Press, 1960) has a promising title but actually makes Edwards more rationalistic than Miller; and A.O. Aldridge's *Jonathan Edwards* (New York: Washington Square Press, 1964) is an outright philosophical account. The classic attempt to right this uneven balance by treating Edwards as a "Calvinist theologian" is Conrad Cherry's *The Theology of Jonathan Edwards* (New York: Doubleday, 1966), which passes over the specific problem of rational analysis and faith. Subsequent studies tended to be partial to some aspect of Edwards' thought. See, for example, Clyde A. Holbrook, *The Ethics of Jonathan Edwards* (Ann Arbor: University of Michigan Press, 1973). Roland Delattre's schematic study—*Beauty and Sensibility in the Thought of Jonathan Edwards* (New Haven: Yale University Press, 1968)—constructs a special plea for the "help" Edwards can give us in "Aesthetics and Theological Ethics." Studies which appear to follow the "interdisciplinary" manner of the 1979 version of this essay are David Laurence, "Jonathan Edwards, John Locke, and the Canon of Experience," *Early American Literature*, 15 (1980), 107–23; Bruce Kuklick, *Churchmen and Philosophers* (New Haven: Yale University Press, 1985), pp. 27–42; Clyde A. Holbrook, *Jonathan Edwards* (Lewisburg: Bucknell University Press, 1987), esp. pp. 33–54; and James Hoopes, *Consciousness in New England* (Baltimore: Johns Hopkins University Press, 1989), pp. 64–94. From among recent studies, Jenson's "Recommendation" (*Theologian*) sponsors an Edwardsian Christianity identified with his own; Lee's re-vision of the Elwood project (*Philosophical Theology*) uses Edwards to press a philosophical program of "habit" and "relation"; and Michael Jinkins reviews Edwards' later treatises from the standpoint of a "Foundational-Coherentist Approach"; see "'The Being of Beings': Jonathan Edwards' Understanding of God," *Scottish Journal of Theology*, 46 (1993), 161–90.

^{8}At the moment of this revision, Volume 13 of *The Works of Jonathan Edwards* (New Haven: Yale University Press, 1994) contains only The *"Miscellanies," a-500*. Volume 10 of the Yale Works provides *Sermons and Discourses, 1720–1723* (1992).

^{9}The character of Edwards' primary audience is brilliantly evoked by Perry Miller; see *Jonathan Edwards* (New York: Sloane, 1949), esp. pp. 3–28, 101–63.

^{10}Miller, *Edwards*, p. 276. Tomas accepts the formula but denies that Miller himself knows the "secret" ("Modernity," p. 82). Miller's remark is cited with full approval by Clyde A. Holbrook in his "Editor's Introduction" to the *Original Sin* (New Haven: Yale University Press, 1970, p. 101; and Jenson is still fussing with the issue in 1988 (*Theologian*, pp. vii-viii).

^{11}*The Puritan Mind* (New York: Holt, 1930), pp. 136–41. For the latter-day account of Edwards' philosophical origins, see Wallace E. Anderson, "Editor's Introduction" to Volume 6 of *The Works of Jonathan Edwards: Scientific and Philosophical Writings* (New Haven: Yale University Press, 1980), esp. pp. 52–136.

¹²Impatient with an old argument about the influence of Berkeley, Miller sets aside the problem of idealism almost totally, calling it a "stratagem" (*Edwards*, p. 62). His uneasiness about idealism is shared by a number of later commentators: Loren Baritz, *City on a Hill* (New York: Wiley, 1964), pp. 47–90; Claude A. Smith, "Edwards and the 'Way of Ideas'"; George Rupp, "The 'Idealism' of Jonathan Edwards," *Harvard Theological Review*, 62 (1969), 209–26. Even Wallace Anderson was once somewhat wary of the "idealist" label; see "Immaterialism in Jonathan Edwards' Early Philosophical Notes," *Journal of the History of Ideas*, 25 (1964), 181–200.

¹³For Schneider's other important treatment of Edwards, see *A History of American Philosophy* (New York: Columbia University Press, 1946), pp. 11–18.

¹⁴Miller emphasizes Edwards' assertion that we can continue to speak, properly, "in the old way" (*Edwards*, p. 63), but fails to point out that Berkeley makes exactly the same disclaimer; and that Edwards himself goes on to say we may speak of atoms and motions even though "all this does not exist anywhere perfectly but in the divine mind"; see "The Mind," in Townsend, *Philosophy*, p. 39; cp. *Philosophical Writings*, pp. 353–54. The older school of "idealist" critics would include G.P. Fisher, "*The Philosophy of Jonathan Edwards*," *Discussions in History and Theology* (New York: Scribners, 1880); A.V.G. Allen, *Jonathan Edwards* (Boston: Houghton Mifflin, 1891); E.C. Smyth, "Jonathan Edwards' Idealism," *American Journal of Theology*, 1 (1897), 950–64; H.N. Gardiner, "The Early Idealism of Jonathan Edwards," *Philosophical Review*, 9 (1900), 573–96; J.E. Woodbridge, "The Philosophy of Jonathan Edwards," *Exercises Commemorating the Two-Hundredth Anniversary of the Birth of Jonathan Edwards* (Andover, 1904); I. Woodbridge Riley, *American Philosophy: The Early Schools* (New York: Dodd, Mead, 1907); Townsend, *Philosophy*; Elwood, *Philosophical Theology*; Leon Howard, ed., *"The Mind" of Jonathan Edwards* (Berkeley: University of California Press, 1963); and Paul Conkin, *Puritans and Pragmatists* (Bloomington: Indiana University Press; 1968). Latter-day sponsors of this now established reading include Kuklick, *Churchman*; Holbrook, *Edwards*; Jenson, *Theologian*; and Hoopes, *Consciousness*.

¹⁵This specific correlation, which will turn up at the climax of the *Original Sin*, is first made in a "Corollary" to a "Proposition" about atoms in the essay "Of Being." Edwards here identifies "body" with "solidity," "solidity" with "resistance," and "resistance" with divine "power"; he proceeds to observe that, strictly speaking, "there is no proper substance but God himself," so that He is very aptly called the "*ens entium*"; then, extending his idealistic reduction to "motion" as well, he concludes: "How truly then is it in Him that we live, move, and have our being"; see Townsend, *Philosophy*, pp. 17–18; and cp. *Philosophical Writings*, pp. 215–16.

¹⁶See Miller, *Edwards*, pp. 71–99; and cp. Fiering, who notes the possibility of regarding Edwards as essentially a philosopher of causality (*Moral Thought*, p. 284). For more orthodox readings of Edwards on "Justification," see Thomas A. Schafer, "Jonathan Edwards and Justification by Faith," *Church History*, 20 (1951), 55–67; and Cherry, *Theology*, pp. 90–106. The suggestion about the relevance of Malebranche—fashionable since the work of Fiering, but alien to Miller, Schafer, and Cherry—was a commonplace among earlier critics: see, for example, F.H. Foster, *A Genetic History of New England Theology* (Chicago: University of Chicago Press, 1907), pp. 47–81.

¹⁷See Louis Bouyer, *The Spirit and Forms of Protestantism* (New York: World, 1954), pp. 136–65.

¹⁸For the centrality of the "Divine and Supernatural Light," see Miller, *Edwards*, pp. 43–68. For the influence of the Cambridge Platonists, see Emily Stipes Watts, "Jonathan Edwards and the Cambridge Platonists," Doctoral Thesis, University of Illinois, 1963); and Mason Lowance, "Jonathan Edwards and the Platonists," *Studies in Puritan American Spirituality*, 2 (1992), 129–52. The basic studies of Edwards and Lockean epistemology are Miller, *Edwards*, pp. 52–67; E.H. Davidson, "From Locke to Edwards," *Journal of the*

History of Ideas, 24 (1963), pp. 355–72; Anderson, *Philosophical Writings*, esp. pp. 16–26; and Laurence, "Canon of Experience."

[19]The principal attempts to modify our sense of the primacy of Locke, in favor of an established Puritan epistemology, are Cherry, *Theology*, pp. 12–24, John E. Smith, "Editor's Introduction" to *A Treatise Concerning Religious Affections* (New Haven: Yale University Press, 1959), pp. 52–73; and James Hoopes, "Jonathan Edwards's Religious Psychology," *Journal of American History*, 69 (1983), 849–65. The passage cited in Locke is Book II, chap. 1 and 2 (supplemented by related matter in Book III, chap. 4); for the comparable portion of the "Supernatural Light," see John E. Smith, Harry S. Stout, and Kenneth P. Minkema ed., *A Jonathan Edwards Reader* (New Haven: Yale University Press, 1995), pp. 110–11.

[20]The idea that God's communication of Himself can only be "ideal" is the main theme of Edwards' "The Mind"; see, for example, Townsend, *Philosophy*, pp. 32, 36–41; 42–44, 52; cp. *Philosophical Writings*, pp. 344, 350–55, 356–59; 368–9. Edwards' answer to Locke's dogmatically maintained belief in some occult "substratum" of material substance (in spite of his own suggestive theory of "power") is the burden of Par. 61 of "The Mind," (Townsend, pp. 60–63; cp. *Philosophical Writings*, pp. 376–80). For Edwards' association of Plato with the empiricist way of ideas, see Par. 40 (Townsend, pp. 42–44; cp. *Philosophical Writings*, pp. 356–59). For resistance to this line of reading, see Stephen R. Yarbrough, "Jonathan Edwards on Rhetorical Authority," *Journal of the History of Ideas*, 47 (1986), pp. 395–408.

[21]"The Mind," Par. 34 (Townsend, p. 39; cp. *Philosophical Writings*, p. 354). The passage follows Edwards' disclaimer about continuing to speak "in the old way."

[22]"The Mind" (Townsend, pp. 33, 48; cp. *Philosophical Writings*, pp. 345, 364).

[23]For endorsement of this "Metaphysical Idealism Interpreted as Religious Conversion," see Hoopes, *Consciousness*, pp. 69–75.

[24]"A Faithful Narrative," in C.C. Goen, ed., *The Great Awakening* (New Haven: Yale University Press, 1972), pp. 199–205.

[25]"Faithful Narrative," pp. 191–99.

[26]*Some Thoughts Concerning the Revival of Religion in New England*, in Goen, ed., *Awakening*, pp. 331–47.

[27]Once the basis of his precocious promise as boy-scientist, Edwards' famous "Spider Letter"—"almost certainly addressed to Judge Paul Dudley, Fellow of the Royal Society"—actually dates from October, 1723; see *Philosophical Writings*, p. 147.

[28]See Miller, *Edwards*, pp. 44–51, and *passim*.

[29]For a reading of the *Religious Affections* which stresses the convertability of its argument about "The presence of the divine Spirit" into the less problematic one about the "nature of true religion," see Smith, *Affections*, pp. 1–51.

[30]*Affections*, pp. 205–12.

[31]*Affections*, pp. 197–205.

[32]The closest Edwards comes to awkward questions about the "mechanics" of sensation in an idealist system is to reject as improper (and faintly silly) the temptation to press the notion that the senses and the brain are essentially ideas; see "The Mind," Par. 35, 40, 51 (Townsend, pp. 40–41, 42–44, 52; and cp. *Philosophical Writings*, pp. 355, 356–57, 368–69).

[33]Smith, *Affections*, pp. 205–6. And compare "A Divine and Supernatural Light" (Smith, et al., ed, *Reader*, pp. 110–15.)

[34]For Edwards' simplification of faculty psychology, see Miller, *Edwards*, pp. 181 ff.; Paul Ramsey, "Editor's Introduction," *Freedom of the Will* (New Haven: Yale University Press, 1957), pp. 47–65; Smith, *Affections*, pp. 12–18; Cherry, *Theology*, pp. 12–24; and Delattre, *Beauty and Sensibility*, pp. 1–11, 41–44.

[35]"The Mind," Par. 34 (Townsend, p. 39; cp. *Philosophical Writings*, p. 354.) Elsewhere Edwards calls this insight—Perry Miller fashion—"the secret": "that which truly is the substance of all bodies is the infinitely exact and precise and perfectly stable idea in God's mind together with his stable will that the same shall gradually be communicated to us" (Townsend, Par. 13, p. 32; cp. *Philosophical Writings*, p. 344).

[36]"The Mind" (Townsend, Par. 34, p. 40; cp. *Philosophical Writings*, pp. 354–55.

[37]It is precisely the similarities with Emerson which cause one to suspect that Edwards' redundantly "theistic" language may be self-consciously metaphoric.

[38]The possibility of some proto-pantheism in Edwards is one of the famous suggestions of Perry Miller's influential essay "From Edwards to Emerson," *New England Quarterly*, 13 (1940), 589–617. A similar possibility is elaborated by Douglas J. Elwood: what Edwards needed, he argues, is some panentheistic "third way," with the advantages of both traditional pantheism (Immanence) and traditional theism (Transcendence), which would, thereby, place the Calvinist doctrines of sovereignty on a firm metaphysical basis (*Philosophical Theology*, pp. 12–64). The suggestion was treated "cautiously" by Anderson ("Immaterialism," p. 190), and was sharply attacked by Robert C. Whittemore in "Jonathan Edwards and The Theology of the Sixth Way," *Church History*, 35 (1966), 60–75. One reviewer has concluded that Elwood's book "lacks both seriousness and conviction" and that Edwards is far better described as a Christian Neoplatonist than as a panentheist; see Everett Emerson, "Jonathan Edwards," in Rees and Harbert, ed., *Fifteen American Authors* (Madison: University of Wisconsin Press, 1971), p. 177. And R.C. De Prospo has devoted an energetic and sophisticated book to the language in which Edwards seeks to resist the "humanist" implications of a Spinozan or Emersonian pantheism; see *Theism in the Discourse of Jonathan Edwards* (Newark: University of Delaware Press, 1985), esp. pp. 9–56, 184–238. By my lights, however, Elwood's third chapter—"Beyond Theism"—remains a serious and challenging statement, and recent critics (Holbrook, Jenson, and especially Lee) are right to press in that direction. In and out of so many words Edwards repeatedly stresses that "speaking most strictly, there is no proper substance but God himself" and that this universal proposition includes "the substance of the soul" ("Miscellanies," #267, Townsend, p. 78). In Edwards the premise that in God "we live, move, and have our being" is more than a "cliche" (Whittemore, "Sixth Way," p. 63); and the question of Neoplatonism is beside the point. Which is: whether Edwards does indeed develop a special philosophical idiom, the rationale of which is to support Scripture's absolutist definition of God, with an emphasis unique among "modern" Christian thinkers; whether the tendency of this system is to rationalize Calvin in a way his latter-day scholasticism himself would have thought "pantheistic"; and whether he pressed his arguments not toward the deification but toward the abolition of Man.

[39]For the Christian/Philosopher argument as it once flourished in Catholic Universities, see Anton C. Pegis, *Christian Philosophy and Academic Freedom* (Milwaukee: Bruce, 1955); Jacques Maritain, *An Essay in Christian Philosophy* (New York: Philosophical Library, 1955); and Maurice Nedoncelle, *Existe-t-il une Philosophie Chretienne?*, trans. by Illtyd Trethowain, O.S.B. as *Is There a Christian Philosophy?* (New York: Hawthorne, 1960).

[40]For resistance to Miller's claim of the purely scientific character of "Part One" of the *Original Sin* (*Edwards*, pp. 266 ff.), see Holbrook, "Editor's Introduction," *Original Sin*, pp. 27–41.

[41]Ramsey, *Freedom*, p. 16. For Conrad Wright's less forgiving view, see *The Beginnings of Unitarianism in America* (Boston: Starr King, 1955), pp. 91–114.

[42]Noticing Edwards' title-page invocation of St. Paul and his concluding vindication of Calvinist divinity, Allen C. Guelzo calls the assumed "secularism" of the *Freedom* "only a means of justifying the theological a priori of Calvinism"; see *Edwards on the Will* (Middletown, CT: Wesleyan University Press, 1989), p. 40.

[43]For the sake of agreeing with Locke's basic sense of "liberty" as the capacity of a human agent and not of a "faculty," Edwards permits himself certain cautious use of the word "power" in *The Freedom* (see pp. 137–38, 163, 171–72, 175, 204); and similarly in "The Mind" and the "Miscellanies" (see Townsend, pp. 38, 155–65). But everywhere he makes it clear that this power is one of execution and not of origination. Even in a rare passage on man's "likeness to God," Edwards stresses that the "soul of man" has the "power of motion" rather than of self-determination; and the passage ends with this curiously constrained formula: "If there be anything amongst all the beings that flow from [the] first principle of all things, that bears any sort of resemblance to it or has anything of a shadow of likeness to it, spirits or minds bid abundantly the fairest for it" ("Miscellanies," #383, Townsend, p. 81). Carefully protected in all of this is that sort of "bare" power which, as Locke implied (Book II, Chap. 23), is all we really know of substance.

[44]It is probably correct to argue that beauty is for Edwards, "the first principle of being" (Delattre, *Beauty and Sensibility*, pp. 27–41); see also Lee, *Philosophical Theology*, pp. 176–81. But this should not obscure the fact that Edwards' primary speculations are—in the "ontological" manner of Anselm and Descartes—about the idea of Being Itself.

[45]See Jinkins, "Understanding of God," pp. 171–77.

[46]*The Nature of True Virtue*, in Paul Ramsey, ed., *The Works of Jonathan Edwards*, Volume 8: *Ethical Writings* (New Haven: Yale University Press, 1989), p. 571.

[47]*Virtue*, p. 564.

[48]Holbrook, *Original Sin*, p. 405. Further references are given in the text.

[49]See H. Shelton Smith, *Changing Conceptions of Original Sin* (New York: Scribners, 1955), pp. 1–35. Also relevant is Conrad Wright's contention that it is Adam and not Will which really divides Edwards from his liberal opponents; see *Beginnings of Unitarianism*, pp. 59–114.

[50]"Of Being" (Townsend, p. 1; cp. *Philosophical Writings*, p. 202.) For Edwards' "rationalist" beginnings, see Anderson, "Editor's Introduction," *Philosophical Writings*, pp. 53–75; Fiering, *Moral Thought*, pp. 33–45; also "The Rationalist Foundations of Jonathan Edwards's Metaphysics," in Nathan Hatch and Harry S. Stout, ed., *Jonathan Edwards and the American Experience* (Oxford: Oxford University Press, 1988), pp. 73–101; and Jinkins, "Understanding of God," esp. pp. 164–71.

[51]If there is one subject on which Edwards' tendency towards Anselmian-Cartesian "ontologistic" rationalism makes itself clearer than any other, it is that of the Trinity: Edwards' speculations touch not only its internal structure or "procession" but also its relation to the economy of redemption; and he treats both cases as very largely affairs of deductive reasoning. See his "Observations Concerning the Scripture Oeconomy of the Trinity, and the Covenant of Redemption" and his "Essay on the Trinity," in Paul Helm, ed., *Jonathan Edwards' Treatise on Grace and Other Posthumously Published Writings* (Cambridge: James Clarke, 1971). For commentary, see De Prospo, *Theism*, pp. 96–102; Jenson, *Theologian*, pp. 91–122 and *passim*; and Lee, *Philosophical Theology*, pp. 185–95.

⁵²The word is that of Holbrook (*Original Sin*, p. 34), as he summarizes Edwards' view of his opponents' position. For a vigorous defense of the truth of that view, see Joseph Haroutunian, *Piety vs. Moralism* (New York: Holt, 1932), esp. pp. 15–42; and cp. Jenson, *Theologian*, pp. 150–68, 197–98.

⁵³For the liberal theory of the relation between Scripture and Reason ("supernatural rationalism"), see Wright, *Beginnings of Unitarianism*, pp. 135–60.

⁵⁴The "classic" view remains compelling: the covenant idiom is basically rationalist and not voluntarist; see Perry Miller, "The Marrow of Puritan Divinity," rpt. in *Errand into the Wilderness* (Cambridge: Harvard University Press, 1956), pp. 48–98. The problematical relation of covenant language to the original style of "Calvinism" remains unchanged, even if Calvin himself turns to covenant explanations; see Everett H. Emerson, "Calvin and Covenant Theology," *Church History*, 25 (1956), 136–44.

⁵⁵Besides Miller (*Edwards*, p. 274), see George P. Fisher, "The Augustinian and the Federal Theories of *Original Sin* Compared," *New Englander*, 27 (1868), 507–8; and Holbrook, *Original Sin*, p. 50.

⁵⁶For the travails of Puritan "Federalism," see Fisher, "Augustinian and Federal Theories"; Miller, "Marrow," and *The New England Mind: The Seventeenth Century* (Cambridge: Harvard Press, 1939), pp. 365–97; Smith, *Changing Conceptions*, pp. 1–9; and Holbrook, *Original Sin*, pp. 1–16.

⁵⁷Anderson, "Immaterialism," pp. 181–200.

⁵⁸On the one hand see Williston Walker, *Ten New England Leaders* (New York: Silver, Burdette, 1901), p. 257; Smith, *Changing Conceptions*, pp. 35–36; and especially Tomas, "Modernity," pp. 82–84. On the other, Miller, *Edwards*, pp. 278–79—supported by Holbrook, *Original Sin*, p. 101; and more recently by Jenson, *Theologian*, pp. 144–52.

⁵⁹"The Mind," Par. 34, (Townsend, p. 39; cp. *Philosophical Writings*, pp. 353–54).

⁶⁰Explicit application of idealism to the theory of identity is not lacking in "The Mind": "the Most High could, if he saw fit, cause there to be another being who should begin to exist in some distant part of the universe, with the same ideas I now have after the manner of memory" (Townsend, p. 68; cp. *Philosophical Writings*, p. 386). And see David Lyttle, "Jonathan Edwards on Personal Identity," *Early American Literature*, 7 (1972), 163–71.

⁶¹Quoted from H.T. Kerr, ed., *A Compend of the Institutes of the Christian Religion* (Philadelphia: Westminster, 1964), p. 132.

⁶²For Edwards' anticipation of arguments that would show up in the so-called Miracles Controversy, see the Fifth Sign of Part III of the *Religious Affections* (Smith, ed., pp. 291–311).

⁶³Although Edwards sometimes speaks, conventionally, of spiritual entities as more (or more nearly) real than the supposed material ones, one passage (at least) from the "Miscellanies" makes it clear that the human soul could not escape his pervasive and all-explaining theory of total, instantaneous, powerful, and direct re-creation at every moment. Edwards is arguing that "the mere exertion of a new thought is a certain proof of a God." Here, he suggests, is a new thing, needing a cause. Where might that cause be located? "Not in antecedent thoughts, for they are vanished and gone…If we say 'tis the substance of the soul, if we mean that there is some substance besides that thought that brings that thought forth, if it be God, I acknowledge" (Townsend, p. 78; cp. Schafer, *The "Miscellanies, a-500*, p. 373). Otherwise, nonsense. Apart from God's all-creative power, the soul of man is exactly as insubstantial as the moon.

⁶⁴In my view it is Edwards (and not Karl Barth) who completes and epitomizes the Protestant tendency to refer all being and all good in man directly and entirely to God. As Louis Bouyer has argued, both classical Protestantism and some forms of neo-ortho-

doxy make it seem "as if man could only belong to [God] in ceasing to have a distinct existence" (Bouyer, *Spirit and Forms*, p. 151); the explanation, he argues, lies in Protestant piety's chosen philosophical style—a "radical empiricism, reducing all being to what is perceived, which empties out, with the idea of substance, all possibility of real relations between beings, as well as the stable substance of any of them" (ibid., p. 153). This may be a sectarian view, but no less friendly a commentator than Thomas Schafer wonders that Edwards "never seems to have been aware of [the] potential objection" that his system "leaves God finally alone, talking to a reflection of himself in a mirror" ("Editor's Introduction," *The "Miscellanies," a-500*, p. 49); nor will all readers feel reassured by Jenson's reminder that this lonely conversation is essentially intra-Trinitarian (*Theologian*, pp. 91–110). To me it seems obvious that Edwards' eclectic and omnivorous idealism—begun in the style of ontologism, and fostered by an immaterialism out of Newton and the empiricism of Locke read in a radical (Berkeleyan) way—constitutes a sort of inevitable *terminus ad quem* and *ne plus ultra* in the (Protestant) metaphysics of sovereignty.

[65]Quoted from Smith et al., *Reader*, p. 283.

[66]"Of the Prejudices of the Imagination" (Townsend, p. 2).

[67]The earlier version of this essay suggested that in some ways Edgar Poe (not Emerson) might be Edwards' true intellectual child, especially as Poe's *Eureka* reveals a scientific inspiration similar to that which Edwards took from Newton and as they share a similar sense of God's cosmic "plot." Both invoke gravity as a figure of cosmic unity or "consent," and both seem to have seen that, given "atoms" as the building blocks of matter, matter and spirit are really indistinguishable as "power"; both evince a strong neoplatonic drive toward the mathematical One as source, end, and explanation of all reality; and both locate salvation in some magical ("Ligeian") experience of grace, only *after* which does earthly analogy make sense. For discussion of these suggestions, see Joan Dayan, *Fables of Mind* (Oxford: Oxford University Press, 1987), pp. 15–22, 45–48, 155–57, 173–74 and *passim*.

[68]Whittemore suggests that the that category of Becoming "has no part whatsoever in the Edwardsian ontology" ("Sixth Way," p. 70). And Christian Enthusiasts may wish to reconsider whether, given Edwards' metaphysics, anything "real" happened when "God became man."

CODA

[1]For the revisionist work in question, see Norman Fiering, *Jonathan Edwards's Moral Thought and Its British Context* (Chapel Hill: University of North Carolina Press, 1981); Wallace E. Anderson, "Editor's Introduction" to Volume 6 of *The Works of Jonathan Edwards: Scientific and Philosophical Writings* (New Haven: Yale University Press, 1980), esp. pp. 37–53; and Peter Gay, *A Loss of Mastery* (Berkeley: University of California Press, 1966). For effective correction of Miller's sense of Puritan typology, see Sacvan Bercovitch, "Typology in Puritan New England," *American Quarterly*, 19 (1967), 166–91.

[2]For the heart of Miller's "postmodern" appreciation of Edwards, see *Jonathan Edwards* (New York: William Sloane Associates, 1949), pp. 71–99, 235–63. And see Stephen H. Daniel, *The Philosophy of Jonathan Edwards* (Bloomington: Indiana University Press, 1994).

[3]Edward's *Diary* is quoted from John E. Smith, Harry S. Stout, and Kenneth P. Minkema, ed., *A Jonathan Edwards Reader* (New Haven: Yale University Press, 1995), p. 266.

[4]The standard account of piety's invention of guilty subjectivity is Sacvan Bercovitch, *The Puritan Origins of the American Self* (New Haven: Yale University Press,

1975) pp. 1–34. If the present analysis is correct, James Hoopes verges on overstatement in asserting that "Edwards's position amounted to a compromise with the consciousness concept"; see *Consciousness in New England* (Baltimore: Johns Hopkins University Press, 1989), p. 65.

[5]Though the crucial definitions which determine Edwards' philosophy of "will" are all included in the five sections of Part I, the burden of his argument against installing "the will" as agent or principal of the self is carried in Part Two, Section 4, "Whether Volition Can Arise Without a Cause, Through the Activity of the Nature of the Soul," and Part Four, Section 2, "The Falseness and Inconsistence of [a certain] Metaphysical Notion of Action and Agency." For the argument that Edwards' "will" is not precisely a "faculty," see Miller, *Edwards*, pp. 251–63; Paul Ramsey, "Editor's Introduction" to Volume 1 of *The Works of Jonathan Edwards: Freedom of the Will* (New Haven: Yale University Press, 1957), pp. 48–49; and especially Allen C. Guelzo, *Edwards on the Will* (Middletown, CT: Wesleyan University Press, 1989), pp. 33–35, 72–83.

[6]"Of Being," quoted from Harvey G. Townsend, ed., *The Philosophy of Jonathan Edwards* (Eugene: University of Oregon Press, 1955), p. 17. Ses also Anderson, ed., *Scientific Writings*, p. 215.

[7]"Miscellanies," quoted from Townsend, *Philosophy*, p. 78. See also Thomas A. Schafer, ed., Volume 13 of the Yale *Works of Jonathan Edwards: The "Miscellanies," a-500* (1994), p. 373.

[8]Because Ishmael says it is "Jove" (and not Jehova) who cannot lay a glove on his soul, one infers that he continues to express himself in Platonese; see Merton M. Sealts, Jr., "Melville and the Platonic Tradition," in *Pursuing Melville, 1940–1980* (Madison: University of Wisconsin Press, 1982), pp. 300–05.

[9]Recent scholarship has moved the date at which Edwards wrote the idealism of his "Notes" on "The Mind" and "Natural Science" from his undergraduate to his graduate years at Yale, but the jury is still out on the "influence" of Berkeley; see Anderson, "Editor's Introduction," *Scientific Writings*, pp. 36, 123–24. Emerson, by contrast, revels in the memory of his "boyhood" contact with the "Berkleian philosophy" (which may have come from Edwards); see Ralph L. Rusk, *The Letters of Ralph Waldo Emerson*, Volume 2 (New York: Columbia University Press, 1939), p. 385.

[10]See Schafer, "Editor's Introduction," *Works*, Vol. 13, "Miscellanies", p. 49. Other recent accounts which support (though they do not cite) the conclusions of my 1979 article are Bruce Kuklick, *Churchmen and Philosophers* (New Haven: Yale University Press, 1985), esp. pp. 39–42; Robert W. Jenson, *America's Theologian* (Oxford: Oxford University Press, 1988), esp. pp. 23–34; and Hoopes, *Consciousness*, pp. 64–94.

[11]If one reads Aristotle as a naïve realist, the "substance" of his *Logic* will amount to somewhat more than a "predicable"; but because, even in the *Metaphysics*, substance is always linked the to correlative notion of "accident," its meaning is more like "real enough to have qualities" rather than "real in itself."

[12]See Hoopes, *Consciousness*, p. 69.

[13]See Louis E. Loeb, *From Descartes to Hume* (Ithaca: Cornell University Press, 1981), esp. pp. 25–110.

[14]See Loeb, pp. 143–48; 205–10; 244–47.

[15]Edwards might stand out even in an account of worldwide systems of thought—as one of the few thinkers in the West to press philosophical insight to the limit of religious conviction. For the account of Edwards in various versions of the American context, see Herbert W. Schneider, *A History of American Philosophy* (New York: Columbia University Press 1946, 1963), pp. 11–26, 199–207, 531–33; William A. Clebsch, *American Religious Thought* (Chicago: University of Chicago Press, 1973), pp. 11–68; Paul K. Conkin, *Puritans and Pragmatists* (Bloomington: Indiana University Press, 1976),

pp. 39–72; Elizabeth Flower and Murray Murphey, *A History of Philosophy in America* (New York: G.P. Putnam, 1977), Vol. I, pp. 137–202; Hans Oberdiek, "Jonathan Edwards," in Marcus G. Singer, ed., *American Philosophy* (Cambridge: Cambridge University Press, 1985), pp. 191–214; and Kuklick, *Churchmen*, pp. 27–42.

[16]Internalizing the critical position in question, Jenson's Jeremiad on Edwards and the lost soul of America argues that "'Substance' is a God-concept" (*America's Theologian*, p. 26.) For a sample of the Postmodern reading of Edwards, see Richard De Prospo, *Theism in the Discourse of Jonathan Edwards* (Newark: University of Delaware Press, 1985). And for the beginnings of a post-substance account—in terms of "habit" and "relation"—see Sang Hyun Lee, *The Philosophical Theology of Jonathan Edwards* (Princeton: Princeton University Press, 1988), esp. pp. 3–114.

[17]For Derrida's admission that, in spite of all objections, philosophy still finds it hard to do without *some* notion of the self, see his interview with Jean-Luc Nancy: "'Eating Well,' or the Calculation of the Subject," in Eduardo Cadava, Peter Connor, and Jean-Luc Nancy, ed., *Who Comes After the Subject?* (New York: Routledge, 1991), pp. 96–119. For a theological approach to the philosophy of "Differance," see Mark C. Taylor's "Introduction" to *Deconstruction in Context* (Chicago: University of Chicago Press, 1986), pp. 1–34.

[18]Quoted from Smith, Stout, Minkema, ed., *Reader*, pp. 95–6.

CHAPTER THREE

[1]For Emerson's "metaphysical" interest, see Norman A. Brittin, "Emerson and the Metaphysical Poets," *American Literature*, 8 (1936), 1–21; F.O. Matthiessen, *American Renaissance* (New York: Oxford University Press, 1941), pp. 100–114; and Hyatt H. Waggoner, *Emerson as Poet* (Princeton: Princeton University Press, 1974), pp. 115–26. The best treatment of Emerson's specific relation to Herbert is R.A. Yoder, "Toward the 'Titmouse Dimension': The Development of Emerson's Poetic Style," *PMLA*, 87 (1972), 255–70; also *Emerson and the Orphic Poet in America* (Berkeley: University of California Press, 1978), pp. 80–88; for a skeptical account of the importance of this influence, see Alice Hall Petry, "Emerson's Debt to Herbert," in Edmund Miller and Robert DiYanni, ed., *Like Season'd Timber: New Essays on George Herbert* (New York: Peter Lang, 1987), pp. 297–315. And for Harold Bloom's psycho-poetic theory of the "precursor," see *The Anxiety of Influence* (New York: Oxford University Press, 1973), esp. pp. 5–16.

[2]The citations of "Quotation and Originality" come from *The Complete Works of Ralph Waldo Emerson* (W), Edward Emerson, ed. (Boston: Houghton Mifflin Co., 1903–1904), Vol. VIII, pp. 178, 179, 187–188, 192, 200–201. For the critical analysis in question, see Julie Ellison, *Emerson's Romantic Style* (Princeton: Princeton University Press, 1984), pp. 141–153.

[3]In the place of a possible discussion of Emerson's own precursors, Bloom offers instead a chapter called "Emerson and Influence," providing not an account of actual influence but a theory of its possible resistance; see *A Map of Misreading* (New York: Oxford University Press, 1975), pp. 160–176.

[4]*Romantic Style*, pp. 61–84.

[5]On Christianity's "cultic" fallacy of ascribing every truth to the life and teaching of Jesus, see Emerson's revolutionary meditation for October 1, 1832: *The Journals and Miscellaneous Notebooks of Ralph Waldo Emerson* (JMN), Alfred Ferguson, ed. (Cambridge: The Belknap Press of Harvard University, 1964), Vol. IV, p.45. And for Emerson's Divinity School "Address" as a contest of language with Jesus, see Jonathan Bishop, "Emerson and Christianity," *Renascence*, 38 (1986), 183–200.

[6]Cf. Bloom, *Agon: Towards a Theory of Revisionism* (New York: Oxford University Press, 1982), pp. 145–48.

[7]The crucial sections of *English Traits* are Chapter I ("First Visit to England"), which works up the ironies latent in the 1833 meetings with Coleridge, Carlyle, and Wordsworth (cp. JMN, IV, 219–25, 408–11); Chapter XIV ("Literature"), which registers the rise and fall of the platonic influence on British literature; Chapter XVI ("Stonehenge"), which tries hard to confer dignity on Carlyle; and Chapter XVII ("Personal"), which ends by giving Wordsworth his (neoplatonic) due.

[8]JMN, IV, 87. Together with Luther and Fox, Milton stands forth as a figure of prophetic authority in Emerson's (1835) lectures on "Biography"; see *The Early Lectures of Ralph Waldo Emerson* (EL), Stephen E. Whicher and Robert E. Spiller, eds. (Cambridge: The Belknap Press of Harvard University, 1959), Vol. I, pp. 118–82. None of these religious personalities endures to join the company of Emerson's (1850) more secular list of *Representative Men* (Plato, Swedenborg, Montaigne, Shakespeare, Napoleon, Goethe).

[9]JMN, IV, 287. For Ellison's not quite biographical "plot summary," see *Romantic Style*, pp. 77–84.

[10]The text of Nature—incorporating that of Herbert—is cited from *The Collected Works of Ralph Waldo Emerson* (CW), Robert E. Spiller and Alfred E. Ferguson, eds. (Cambridge: The Belknap Press of Harvard University, 1971), Vol. I, pp. 40–41.

[11]*Nature*, p. 11.

[12]Matthiessen long ago noticed Emerson's truncation of Herbert's poem, but he mentions the omission of only the final stanza, not of the poem's first two stanzas as well. In his relatively un-anxious reading, "Emerson broke off the quotation at just the point where he and Thoreau unconsciously parted company with the metaphysical strain" (*Renaissance*, p. 108). For Emerson's early remarks on "organic unity," see the early lectures on "The Naturalist" (EL, I, 73–74) and "Shakspear" (EL, I, 317–18); and cp. JMN, IV, 291.

[13]The text of Herbert's "Man" unquoted by Emerson is cited from F.E. Hutchinson, ed., *The Works of George Herbert* (London: Oxford University Press, 1941), pp. 90–92.

271

[14]As Barbara Packer suggests, at the outset of *Emerson's Fall* (New York: Continuum, 1982), none of Emerson's various post-Christian fables has any place for the personalizing notions of "sin or disobedience" (p. x); all appear to be, rather, inevitable or "structural."

[15]*Nature*, p. 41.

[16]*Nature*, pp. 44–45. My sense of the context of Emerson's demythologic confidence comes from M.H. Abrams, *Natural Supernaturalism* (New York: W.W. Norton, 1971), esp. pp. 17–70. For the myth of Orpheus in Emerson, see Yoder, *Orphic Poet*, pp. 3–30.

[17]Emerson's nontheistic definition of prayer is clear in his first Unitarian sermon: "Pray Without Ceasing" (July, 1826) openly declares that in the "only proper sense" prayers are the "momentary desires, that come without impediment, without fear, into the soul, and bear testimony at each instant to its shifting character"; see A.C. McGiffert, ed., *Young Emerson Speaks* (Port Washington, NY: Kennikat Press, 1968), pp. 4–5.

[18]Emerson and "the language of persons" remains a vital and neglected topic. *Nature* grandly recognizes some creative entity which "man in all ages and countries" names "the FATHER" (CW, I, 19). Yet the Divinity School "Address" staunchly opposes "the soul" to the "noxious exaggeration" of the personal (CW, I, 82). And the sermons move close to the same radical point: the decision to "drop all personification" comes casually enough in "Religion and Society" (Oct., 1833); but as early as "Astronomy" (May, 1832) Emerson was ascribing the entire, elaborated orthodoxy of the atonement to the

tendency of "infant religion" to impute divinity to "the person of man"; see McGiffert, *Young Emerson*, pp. 194, 173–75.

[19]See Gay Wilson Allen, *Waldo Emerson* (New York: Viking Press, 1981), pp. 165–78.

[20]Except for his spelling of "defenses," Whicher's text is identical with that of W, IX, 359. For Whicher's commentary, see *Selections from Ralph Waldo Emerson* (Boston: Houghton Mifflin Co., 1957), p. 500. For Emerson's identification of "grace" as one of those "Barbarous & Sacred words, to which we must still return, whenever we would speak an ecstatic & universal sense," see JMN, VIII, 74–75.

[21]Whicher, *Selections*, p. 11; cp. JMN, IV, 47–48. For the passages from "Self-Reliance," see CW, II, 30.

[22]Cf. Yvor Winters, *In Defense of Reason* (Denver, CO: Alan Swallow, 1937), p. 587.

[23]*Works*, pp. 45–46.

[24]For the bibliographical history of "Grace," see Ralph H. Orth (et al.), ed., *The Poetry Notebooks of Ralph Waldo Emerson* (Columbia, MO: University of Missouri Press, 1986), pp. 805–06. The editors of this volume also summarize the (antique) controversy over the date of composition of "Grace," in relation to various possible "sources"— Samson Reed's article on "External Restraint" (in the *New Jerusalem Magazine*), or Milton (inside the front cover of whose *Works* the poem was first drafted), or Herbert's "Sinne" (first read in Coleridge's *Aids to Reflection*).

[25]Quoted from Edward Emerson's note to "Grace," in W, IX, 510.

[26]See "Quotation and Originality," W, VIII, 192. For the text of "Grace" in the Transcendentalists' posthumous tribute to Margaret Fuller, see *Memoirs of Margaret Fuller Ossoli* (Boston: Phillips, Sampson and Co., 1852), Vol. II, p. 117.

[27]For the example of a criticism trying to prove that "Sinne" is similar enough to "Grace" to be its "source," see Brittin, "Metaphysical Poets," pp. 9–11; Matthiessen, *Renaissance* pp. 108–09; and John C. Broderick, "The Date and Source of Emerson's 'Grace,'" *Modern Language Notes*, 73 (1958), 91–95.

[28]The evidence of the Journals overwhelmingly supports the critical consensus that "Emerson always placed Herbert in the first rank of poets" (Yoder, *Orphic Poet*, p. 80). From the moment in 1831 when Emerson first makes the remark on "my friend Herbert's diction that his thought has that heat as actually to fuse the words so that language is wholly flexible in his hands" (JMN, III, 284; and cp. EL, I, 350), he never ceases to praise Herbert's gift for inspired utterance. He also admires, repeatedly, some of Herbert's renditions of the "moral sublime"—e.g., the final couplet of "Affliction, I": "Ah, my dear God! though I am clean forgot,/ Let me not love thee, if I love thee not" (see JMN, IV, 255; and cp. EL, I, 352; JMN, VI, 230; JMN, XIV, 277). Further, Emerson continues to stress Herbert's platonic anticipations of both science and Emersonian "analogy"; he even appropriates Herbert to his own "later" doctrine of Nature, as when he declares it "mystically true" that "Herbs gladly cure our flesh because that they/ Find their acquaintance there" (see JMN, IX, 278; and cp. W, IV, 11–12). Above all, perhaps, he treasures Herbert as exemplar of some "fragrant piety which is almost departed out of the world" (JMN, V, 144–45; and cp. JMN, XII, 110; EL, II, 97). Yet there is another response as well—as when Emerson acerbically reflects that "We all know why Jesus serves men so well for a deity; why pure and sublime souls like A Kempis & Herbert can expend their genius & heart so lavishly on his name & history & feel no check"; it is, he thinks, "for the same reason that Swedenborg's mythus is so coherent & vital & true to those who dwell within, so arrogant or limitary to those without" (JMN, VII, 409–410). And he will, at last, dismiss Herbert with the same charge he earlier used to damn Swedenborg: his genius is, in a word, "Jewish" (JMN, XV, 151). Evidently it is some sense of Herbert's "simple" failure to outgrow "the myth" that surfaces in the poetic confrontations.

²⁹See Jonathan Bishop, *Emerson on the Soul* (Cambridge: Harvard University Press, 1964), pp. 86–92; and Joel Porte, *Representative Man* (New York: Oxford University Press, 1979), pp. 114–33.

³⁰The text of Herbert's "The Collar"—all but unquoted in Emerson's "Address"—is cited from Hutchinson, *Works*, pp. 153–54. (It is not to be supposed that Herbert considered wearing a "Roman collar"; yet the "Catholic" symbol survives—as do many of Herbert's "Anglican" ones, in the Puritan poetry of Edward Taylor.)

³¹The old controversy over the dating of "Grace" is, potentially, at least, an argument about whether resignation from the ministry (Sept., 1832) or the inviting spectacle of European manners was Emerson's first great temptation. Yet the crucial point is that Emerson's real "plunge" is 1838—when his "Address" makes aggressively public a logic entirely worked out in private by 1832.

³²In declaring that all religious institutions are subordinate to a "faith" which "has for its object simply to make men good and wise" (W, XI, 21), "The Lord's Supper" effectively subsumes the explicitly Stoddardean logic of "A Feast of Remembrance" (1829): no one is to be barred from a rite designed "to make those who partake of it better" (*Young Emerson*, p. 58). For Herbert's view of the Lord's Supper—for him, the Eucharist—see Jeanne Clayton Hunter, "'With Winges of Faith': Herbert's Communion Poems," *Journal of Religion*, 62 (1982), 57–71.

³³For Whitman's original celebration of Emerson's natural sacrament, see "Song of Myself," in Malcolm Cowley, ed., *Leaves of Grass: The Original Edition* (New York: Viking Press, 1959), pp. 42–43. For the quotations from Emerson's "Address," see CW, I, 76. (Italics in both quotations are added.)

³⁴Cf. Emerson's "Bacchus" (W, IX, 126).

³⁵In Herbert's (British) English "corn" means primarily "grain" or seed"; then, by specification, "Wheat, rye, or barley"; and then, by poetic transubstantiation, "bread"; hence the communion reference in both texts. The different sense of the literal in American English provides a clear signal of Emerson's allusive intent.

273

³⁶See Carl F. Strauch, "The Year of Emerson's Poetic Maturity: 1834," *Philological Quarterly*, 34 (1955), 353–77; and Yoder, *Orphic Poet*, pp. 77–88.

³⁷The text of "Each and All" is cited from W, IX, 4–6.

³⁸Reproduced here is Jonathan Bishop's original (and still impressive) argument about Emerson's radically Romantic "connection between the organic and the moral" (*Soul*, p. 91).

³⁹*Works*, pp. 85–86.

⁴⁰For the explicit pairing of Herbert's (Christian) question and Fichte's (Transcendentalist) answer, see *Memoirs*, Vol. I, p. 143.

⁴¹*Works*, p. 111.

⁴²For the mixture of moods leading up to Emerson's "Address," see Porte, *Representative Man*, pp. 91–113.

⁴³CW, I, 93. Emerson's terms appear to predict a Teacher who would fuse the discoveries of Wordsworth and Coleridge with the analyses of Kant's three critiques.

⁴⁴CW, I, 81. For Emerson's sense of the generic incompatibility of prophecy and rational argumentation, see his (October, 8, 1838) letter to Henry Ware, Jr.; in Whicher, *Selections*, pp. 116–17.

⁴⁵After the fact, Emerson's survey of the "European scene," seemed merely to have "confirmed me in my convictions"—chiefly by convincing his competitive sense that "Landor, Coleridge, Carlyle, Wordsworth" were all "deficient—in insight into religious

truth. They have no idea of that species of moral truth which I call the first philosophy" (JMN, IV, 78–79). For a fuller survey of Emerson's motives and insights, see Allen, *Waldo*, pp. 195–219 .

[46]W, IX, 6.

[47]See Strauch, "Year of Maturity," pp. 353–57; cp.Yoder, *Orphic Poet*, pp. 84–85. And for Emerson's own ("later") definition of Nature as "a work of ecstasy," see "The Method of Nature" (CW, I, 120–137).

[48]As Emerson competes with Jesus on one scale (Bishop, "Emerson and Christianity"), with his own father on another (Porte, *Representative Man*, pp. 99–104), and with Barzillai Frost on yet a third (Conrad Wright, *The Liberal Christians*, Boston: Beacon Press, 1970, pp. 41–61), it may yet be worth studying the anxiety of his response to the man he once nominated as "our bishop."

[49]See *A Priest to the Temple, Or, The Country Parson*, in *Works*, pp. 224–90. For a characterization of the un-Emersonian side of Herbert, see Rosemond Tuve, "George Herbert and Caritas," *Journal of the Warburg Courtnald Institutes*," 22 (1959), 303–31.

[50]JMN, X, 28. For the personal element in Emerson's "slander" of the preaching of the Unitarian Association, see Wright, *Liberal Christians*, pp. 41–46. For his sense of the conflict "between preaching and pastoring"—and his uneasy competition with Henry Ware, Jr.—see David Robinson, *Apostle of Culture* (Philadelphia: University of Pennsylvania Press, 1982), pp. 30–68.

[51]JMN, V, 471.

CHAPTER FOUR

[1]My composite of this "unstable" Emerson draws particularly on Robert Lee Francis, "The Architectonics of Emerson's *Nature*," *American Quarterly*, 19 (1967), 39–52; Lawrence Buell, *Literary Transcendentalism* (Ithaca: Cornell University Press, 1973), esp. pp. 21–187; B.L. Packer, *Emerson's Fall* (New York: Continuum, 1982); and Julie Ellison, *Emerson's Romantic Style* (Princeton: Princeton University Press, 1984). For recent samples of the more confidently "philosophical" approach, see the various efforts of Stanley Cavell, especially those contained in *The Senses of Walden* (San Francisco: North Point Press, 1981) and *In Quest of the Ordinary* (Chicago: University of Chicago Press, 1988); also David Van Leer, *Emerson's Epistemology* (Cambridge: Cambridge University Press, 1986); and (applying Cavell, resisting Van Leer) Russell B. Goodman, *American Philosophy and the Romantic Tradition* (Cambridge: Cambridge University Press, 1990), pp. 1–57.

[2]See, for example, Catherine Albanese, "The Kinetic Revolution," *New England Quarterly*, 48 (1975), 319–40; Daniel B. Shea, "Emerson and the American Metamorphosis," in David Levin, ed., *Emerson—Prophecy, Metamorphosis, and Influence* (New York: Columbia University Press, 1975), pp. 29–56; Harold Bloom, "The Freshness of Transformation," in Levin, *Prophecy*, pp. 129–48; Donald Pease, "Emerson, Nature, and the Sovereignty of Influence, *Boundary 2*, 8 (1980), 43–74; Joseph Kronik, "Emerson and the Question of Reading/Writing," *Genre*, 14 (1981), 363–81; Leonard Neufeldt, *The House of Emerson* (Lincoln: University of Nebraska Press, 1982), esp. pp. 41–71; David L. Smith, "Emerson and Deconstruction," *Soundings*, 67 (1984), 379–98; and Lawrence Buell, *New England Literary Culture* (Cambridge: Cambridge University Press, 1986), esp. pp. 76–77, 162–63, 420, 438–39.

[3]Quotations from Emerson's published works—cited in the text by volume and page number only—are taken from *The Collected Works of Ralph Waldo Emerson*, ed. Alfred R. Ferguson, et al., 5 Vols. to date (Cambridge: The Belknap Press of Harvard University, 1971–1994), when the appropriate volume is available; otherwise, citation is from *The Complete Works of Ralph Waldo Emerson*, ed. Edward W. Emerson, 12 Vols.

(Boston: Houghton Mifflin, 1903–1904); cited hereafter (in the text) as W. (N.B.: quotations from the Divinity School "Address" are cited, from Vol. I of the Belknap Edition, by page number only.)

[4]For Norton's "rage," see Perry Miller, *The Transcendentalists* (Cambridge: Harvard University Press, 1950), p. 193. For a review of the reasons advanced to explain why the response to Emerson's "Address" was so drastic, see Mary Kupiec Cayton, *Emerson's Emergence* (Chapel Hill: University of North Carolina Press, 1989), pp. 169–81. And for reviews of Emerson and the "Miracles Controversy," see Miller, *Transcendentalists*, pp. 186–200; William R. Hutchison, *The Transcendentalist Ministers* (New Haven: Yale University Press, 1959), pp. 52–97; and David Robinson, *Apostle of Culture* (Philadelphia: University of Pennsylvania Press, 1982), pp. 123–37.

[5]See Ralph L. Rusk, ed., *The Letters of Ralph Waldo Emerson*, Vol. II (New York: Columbia University Press, 1939), pp. 166–67.

[6]The basis of a "psychoanalytic" reading of the "Address" is laid by Conrad Wright's seminal chapter on "Emerson, Barzillai Frost, and the Divinity School Address," in *The Liberal Christians* (Boston: Beacon Press, 1970), pp. 41–61. The argument is given a specifically "oedipal" turn by Joel Porte, in *Representative Man* (New York: Oxford University Press, 1979), pp. 91–113. And it is ably summarized, elaborated, and criticized by Van Leer, in *Epistemology*, pp. 72–74, 235–36. A recent "analytic" essay by David Leverenz focuses primarily on "Experience" (and omits philosophical considerations altogether); see *Manhood and the American Renaissance* (Ithaca: Cornell University Press, 1989), pp. 42–71. Something of the same is true of Eric Cheyfitz, *The Trans-Parent* (Baltimore: Johns Hopkins University Press, 1981), which in any case devotes only a couple of pages to Emerson's "Address." Evelyn Barish's psychobiography—*Emerson: The Roots of Prophecy* (Princeton: Princeton University Press, 1989)—provides a better balance between rational thought and nervous symptom, but it follows Emerson only to 1833.

[7]Wright (*Liberal Christians*) and Robinson (*Apostle*) have well identified the issue of Emerson's debt to Unitarianism, despite his own gestures of denial. But it was Yvor Winters who long ago suspected that Emerson's flirtation with Romantic irrationalism was made all but safe by "an audience which, like himself, had been [utterly] conditioned by two hundred years of Calvinist discipline"; see *In Defense of Reason* (Denver: Alan Swallow, 1937), pp. 578–588.

[8]For the shock value of Emerson's opening, see Jonathan Bishop, *Emerson on the Soul* (Cambridge: Harvard University Press, 1964), pp. 86–92. And for a recent reading of the "Address" which begins with the Unitarian appetite for poetry, see David M. Robinson, "Poetry, Personality, and the Divinity School Address," *Harvard Theological Review*, 82 (1989), 185–99.

[9]Emerson's 1829 sermon on Psalms 74:16–17, titled "Summer" by A.C. McGiffert (*Young Emerson Speaks*, Boston, Houghton Mifflin, 1938), is henceforth known as Sermon XXXIX; see Albert J. von Frank, ed., *The Complete Sermons of Ralph Waldo Emerson*, Vol. 1 (Columbia: University of Missouri Press, 1989), pp. 296–300. For the presence of "Romantic" elements within Unitarianism, see Daniel Walker Howe, *The Unitarian Conscience* (Cambridge: Harvard University Press, 1970), pp. 113–20; 197–201; and also Andrew Delbanco, *William Ellery Channing* (Cambridge: Harvard University Press, 1981), pp. 154–79.

[10]*The Correspondence of Emerson and Carlyle*, Joseph Slater, ed. (New York: Columbia University Press, 1964), p. 191.

[11]Recent discussions of Emerson's practice of preaching include Teresa Toulouse, *The Art of Prophesying* (Athens: University of Georgia Press, 1987), pp. 143–75; Wesley T. Mott, *"The Strains of Eloquence": Emerson and His Sermons* (University Park: The

Pennsylvania State University Press, 1989), esp. pp. 79–112; and David M. Robinson, "Historical Introduction" to von Frank, ed., *Complete Sermons*, I, 1–32.

[12]Quotations from Emerson's Journals are hereafter cited, in the text, as JMN, volume, page: the reference is to *The Journals and Miscellaneous Notebooks of Ralph Waldo Emerson*, ed. William Gilman et al. (Cambridge: The Belknap Press of Harvard University, 1960–1982).

[13]The argument here follows Porte, *Representative*, p. 91–104. See also Amy Schrager Lang, *Prophetic Woman* (Berkeley: University of California Press, 1987), pp. 111–16.

[14]Emerson's "Address" is often labled as (yet another) Jeremiad; a better model, perhaps—for its "negative" portion, at least—is Gilbert Tennent's classic (1740) protest on behalf of souls "who have no other but Pharisee Shepherds"; see Alan Heimert and Perry Miller, ed., *The Great Awakening* (New York: Bobbs Merrill, 1967), pp. 71–99. For the revival context of Tennent's sermon, see Edwin Scott Gaustad, *The Great Awakening in New England* (New York: Harper and Row, 1957), pp. 32–36. And for the conflicting images of the Awakening in circulation, see Joseph Conforti, "Edwardsians, Unitarians, and the Memory of the Great Awakening," in Conrad Edrick Wright, ed., *American Unitarianism, 1805–1865* (Boston: Massachusetts Historical Society and Northeastern University Press, 1989), pp. 31–52.

[15]In the formulation of Philip F. Gura, the Unitarians "championed an empirical, rational reading of the Bible," while the Trinitarians "defended a more orthodox reading...by adopting a figurative view of its language"; see *The Wisdom of Words* (Middletown: Wesleyan University Press, 1981), p. 18. For an elaboration of such a view—placing Emerson somehow, oddly, closer to "orthodoxy"—see Richard A. Grusin, *Transcendentalist Hermeneutics* (Durham: Duke University Press, 1991), esp. pp. 64–72. And for a brief but authoritative discussion of Emerson's relation to German biblical criticism, see Barbara Packer, "Origin and Authority: Emerson and the Higher Criticism," in Sacvan Bercovitch, ed., *Reconstructing American Literary History* (Cambridge: Harvard University Press, 1986), pp. 67–92. Also, more recently, Elisabeth Hurth, "'The Last Impiety of Criticism'" ESQ, 40 (1994), 319–52; and Robert D. Richardson, *Emerson: The Mind on Fire* (Berkeley: University of California Press, 1995), pp. 41–59.

[16]See Jonathan Bishop, "Emerson and Christianity," *Renascence*, 38 (1986), 183–200. Bishop localizes the "Christian" import of the "anxiety" identified by Bloom and Ellison.

[17]As Emerson declared in favor of "preserving all those religious writings which were in their origin poetic, ecstatic expressions which the first user of did not know what he said" (JMN, VIII, 74), so he had a surprising confidence in his own ability to "translate" all such "barbarous and sacred words" (JMN, VIII, 75). Thus, while the whole of a Calvinist minister's sermon might be "literally false, it is really true; only he speaks Parables which I translate as he goes" (JMN, IV, 320). Or, as regards "Luther's creed," Emerson had "only to translate a few of the leading phrases into their equivalent verities." The modern interpreter—as doubtful of Reason as he is of Revelation—can only envy Emerson's sense of possessing "the everlasting advantage of truth" (JMN, IV, 352).

[18]Wesley T. Mott treats the 1827 sermon which McGiffert titled "Christ Crucified" as a somewhat sentimentalized version of the Unitarian genre Lawrence Buell defined as "biblical fiction"; but its dramatic invitation to return in imagination "to the sad Alcedama, to the field of blood" is not its only distinguishing mark. Beginning with Solomon's reminder that "mourning" is better than "feasting," it wishes to eschew the available "abundance of smooth & pleasant speculation on the agreeable topics"; and it reminds its self-consciously liberal audience that "as we are baptized into suffering," so the emblem of the Christian faith is "not a crown but a cross." See Mott, "'Christ

Crucified': Christology, Identity, and Emerson's Sermon No. 5," in Joel Myerson, ed., *Emerson Centenary Essays*, (Carbondale: Southern Illinois University Press, 1982), pp. 17–40. The text in question is now available as Sermon V, *Complete Sermons*, I, 85–92; and for Mott's enlarged reading, see *Strains*, pp. 9–33. For the "literary" setting, see Buell, *Literary Transcendentalism*, pp. 105–10. And for an account of Emerson's (Unitarian) Christology, see Susan L. Roberson, *Emerson in His Sermons* (Columbia: University of Missouri Press, 1995), pp. 178–92.

[19]For *Nature* as the "text" of the "Address," see Bishop, *Soul*, p. 87; cp. Van Leer, *Epistemology*, pp. 86–90. And for a competing sense of Biblical texts "embedded in the opening of the Divinity School Address," see Porte, *Representative*, p. 126.

[20]The distinction between the "person" of the historical Jesus and the "office" of the divine Christ is (of course) a staple of Trinitarian and Incarnationalist theology. And in Sermon XCV, on II Cor. 5.10, delivered fourteen times between Nov., 1830 and Mar., 1837, Emerson patiently explains that "the writers of the epistles" frequently use "the name of Christ" to mean something quite different from "the *bodily person* of Jesus."

[21]The other Biblical texts in question are Mark 1.9–11, Luke 3.21–22, and John 1.29–34. For Emerson's (limited) interest in the "parallel" texts of Scripture, see Karen Kalinevitch, "Turning From the Orthodox," in Joel Myerson, ed., *Studies in the American Renaissance* (Charlottesville: University of Virginia Press, 1986), pp. 69–112.

[22]For a comparable moment in Emerson's comparative mythology, see "The Sphinx": once named by a "poet," "she melted into a purple cloud."

[23]In Sermon XXI (August 17, 1828) Emerson had pronounced that there was "no need of curious metaphysics" to support our knowledge of virtue: "We are men…[and] we do not remember the time in the early dawn of our faculties when we first learned the alphabet of moral distinctions." Yet we can hardly escape the sense of a metaphysics lurking, thus early, when he goes on to suggest that "the perception of good and evil we feel is intwisted with life. We may almost say, we exist to make that distinction" (*Complete Sermons*, p. 191.)

[24]More likely to conjure with "Rational" than with "Moral," Channing yet rests his case against the "orthodoxy" of New England on its supposedly immoral tendency and on the correlative power of "liberal religion" to restore Christianity's pure moral essence; see "Unitarian Christianity," in *The Works of William Ellery Channing* (Boston: American Unitarian Association, 1903), Vol. III, esp. pp. 82–87; "The Moral Argument Against Calvinism," Vol. I, esp. pp. 223–33; and "Unitarian Christianity Most Favorable to Piety," Vol. III, esp. pp. 191–200. For the Unitarian context of Channing's argument, see Howe, *Conscience*, 93–120.

[25]See JMN, VII, 112: "It is plain from all the noise that there is Atheism somewhere. The only question is now, Which is the Atheist?"

[26]See my own "Better Mode of Evidence: The Transcendental Problem of Faith and Spirit," *ESQ*, 54 (1969), 12–22. For Mott's instructive account of Emerson and Channing, with special emphasis on the problem of "Evidences," see *Strains*, pp. 53–78.

[27]"The Evidences of Revealed Religion," *Works*, Vol. III, pp. 122–23, 126–28, 135.

[28]See McGiffert, ed., *Young Emerson,* pp. 91, 95, 124, 184, 186; and, for Sermon LXXVI, cp. *Complete Sermons*, II, 361, 364.

[29]First to propose the importance of Thomas Clarkson's *Portraiture of Quakerism* to the logic of Emerson's resignation was Mary C. Turpie, "A Quaker Source for Emerson's Sermon on the Lord's Supper," *New England Quarterly*, 17 (1944), 95–101. Noting a pattern of Quaker reading, John McAleer contends that "without question [Emerson's] apostasy was being carried out under Quaker auspices"; see *Ralph Waldo Emerson: Days of Encounter* (Boston: Little, Brown, 1984), p. 120. A broader (though somewhat simplistic) account of Emerson and the Quaker question is Yukio Irie,

Emerson and Quakerism (Tokyo: Kenyusha, 1968). More relevant (though indirectly) is Geoffrey Nuttall, *The Holy Spirit in Puritan Faith and Experience* (London: Oxford University Press, 1946): in Nuttall's terms, Emerson would appear as yet another post-Reformation thinker insisting that the Spirit not be absorbed into Christ (let alone the historical Jesus). Also apt is Mott's conclusion that "the habits of thought that led Emerson to resign his pulpit owe less to Antinomian antiformalism than to orthodox Puritan concepts of the Spirit" (*Strains*, p. 143).

[30]See (one version of) Sermon LXXVI, in *Complete Sermons*, II, p. 364. Thus Emerson insists that the Christic "office" is, identically, "the utterance of [the] truth" of the soul's moral self-constitution. Channing clings not only to miracles but also (it appears) to the orthodox sense that there must be *some* connection between the sacrificial death and "the remission of sins"; see "Unitarian Christianity," *Works*, Vol. III, pp. 88–89.

[31]For an account stressing Emerson's recognition that "it is only through the moral teachings of Jesus and his apostles that mankind has learned to free itself from a purely formal religion," see Grusin, *Hermeneutics*, pp. 9–54.

[32]Much has been written on Emerson's debt to Coleridge's distinction between Understanding and Reason, which Emerson characterized (in 1834) as "philosophy itself"; see Kenneth Walter Cameron, *Emerson the Essayist* (Raleigh, NC: Thistle Press, 1945), Vol. I, pp. 191–94; and, for recent examples, Peter Carafiol, *Transcendent Reason* (Tallahassee: University Presses of Florida, 1987), pp. 108–14; and Kenneth Marc Harris, "Reason and Understanding Reconsidered," *Essays in Literature*, 13 (1986), 263–81. Equally instructive (and more bracing) would be a consideration of the account Emerson gives of his odd personal encounter with Coleridge in 1833 (JMN, IV, 407–08, 409–12)—which becomes the basis of the absolutely devastating portrait in *English Traits*.

[33]See Channing, *Works*, Vol. III, pp. 82–85.

[34]Cf. Porte, *Representative*, pp. 102–04.

[35]As Mott has ably shown, Unitarian unrest with miracles and other external evidences *alone* goes back at least as far as the sermons of Joseph Buckminster; yet he also suggests that, as an interpretative community, the Unitarians refused to abandon them altogether (see *Strains*, pp. 54–61).

[36]For the seventeenth-century locus of sun and candle, see David D. Hall, ed., *The Antinomian Controversy, 1636–1638* (Middletown: Wesleyan University Press, 1968), pp. 67–68, 104–05.

[37]See Channing, "Unitarian Christianity Most Favorable," *Works*, Vol. III, pp. 170–78.

[38]For a discussion of Emerson's early fascination with the character of Jesus—and of his final rejection in *Representative Men*—see Mott, *Strains*, 15–29. In one sense Jesus is replaced by *all six* of Emerson's "Representative Men": when the singular "New Adam" lost his unique atoning function, Emerson saw at once his partialness as a model of "personality" or variable human achievement.

[39]Albert von Frank has suggested—in a most helpful reading of this paper—that Emerson's congregation was given, between 1830 and 1832, a full and fair chance to accept conversion from Unitarianism to Transcendentalism, which they of course declined.

[40]Mott (*Strains*, p. 1) begins his valuable study of Emerson's sermons with the observation of Elizabeth Palmer Peabody: "Mr. Emerson was always pre-eminently the preacher to his generation and future ones, but as much—if not more—out of the pulpit as in it; faithful unto the end to his early chosen profession and the vows of his youth" ("Emerson as Preacher," in F.B. Sanborn, ed., *The Genius and Character of*

Emerson (Boston: Houghton, Mifflin, 1898), p. 146.) And, in the same spirit, he titles his last chapter "Preacher Out of the Pulpit." A form of this claim also animates the work of David Robinson: Emerson's "new vocation of lecturer was really a version of his own concept of the Christian ministry" (*Apostle*, p. 3).

[41]In the preliminary formulation of Wesley T. Mott: "For too long…Emersonians eager to start with the exuberant addresses and essays of the late 1830s have been satisfied with the notion that nothing in Emerson's career as a minister became him like the leaving it"; see "From Natural Religion to Transcendentalism: An Edition of Emerson's Sermon No. 43," *Studies in the American Renaissance*, p. 2. For similar gestures, see *Strains*, pp. 1–10; Robinson, "Introductory Historical Essay," pp. 1–3; and Grusin, *Hermeneutics*, pp. 9–14.

[42]See JMN,V, 154; and cp.VI, 266.Yet Charles' "Christianity"—posthumously transcribed into Emerson's own Journal (VI, 265–67)—does not everywhere appear altogether sentimental, as when he wonders "whether the Cross is an idea in the divine mind" (V, 135); or whether God has thrown "this Collective Humanity into the form of the painful Cross" (VI, 265). It is just possible that Charles (or his memory) may have served as a "traditional" influence on Emerson in somewhat the same way as his Aunt Mary Moody.

[43]Van Leer makes a subtle case for Emerson's deployment of a Kantian ("logical") notion of selfhood in *Nature* (*Epistemology*, pp. 52–54); yet the language of self-positing is noticeably absent there. And further, it is the very emptiness of such a notion—along with its supplementary ("psychological") sense of "pain"—that Emerson exposes in "Experience," where he holds "hard" to the "capital virtue of self-trust" in morals (III, 46). And in "Montaigne," similarly, it is the "moral sense" which alone "makes Skepticism impossible" (IV, 103).

[44]Too much can easily be made of Carlyle's aboriginal prediction of *Nature* as "Foundation and Groundplan" of whatever it had "been given [Emerson] to build"; see Joseph Slater, ed., *The Correspondence of Emerson and Carlyle* (New York: Columbia University Press, 1964), p. 157. Not only do Emerson's "Early Lectures"—particularly those of 1836–37 ("The Philosophy of History") and 1837–38 ("Human Culture")—introduce a more useful sense of Emerson's peculiar "form," the series of connected essays, but also (as I am arguing here) the marked tendency of Emerson's early thought and life-experience is perfected in the naturalized scripture of the "Address" more clearly than in the idealized philosophy of *Nature*.Whatever may be true of the more famous case of Kant, Emerson did Metaphysics chiefly to enable Morals.

[45]Somewhat in the spirit of Yvor Winters, Quentin Anderson speaks for the cautious modern distrust of Emerson's moral tendency: his "audience" represented "antinomian man, gathered into the antinomian congregation"; see *The Imperial Self* (New York: Knopf, 1971), p. 46. For a careful and soberly doctrinal refutation of the "antinomian" charge, see Wesley T. Mott, "Emerson and Antinomianism:The Legacy of the Sermons," *American Literature*, 50 (1978), 369–397 (and cp. *Strains*, pp. 144–67). For a more overtly political answer, see Amy Schrager Lang, "'The Age of the First Person Singular': Emerson and Antinomianism," *ESQ*, 29 (1983), 171–83. More apt is Bishop's observation that though, for Emerson, "the Mind…occupies the place of God," still "this absolute possibility belongs to the sense of duty"; Emerson is thus "a moral, not a rational, idealist"; see "Emerson and Christianity," p. 188.

[46]Cf. Bishop, "Emerson and Christianity," pp. 187–88. For friendlier accounts—of the interpretative *necessity* of Emerson's creative quotation of Jesus—see Grusin, *Hermeneutics*, pp. 22–24; and Robinson, "Poetry," pp. 187–88.

[47]Bishop, *Soul*, p. 91.

[48]See Perry Miller, *The New England Mind: The Seventeenth Century* (New York: Macmillan Co., 1939), pp. 280–99. And cp. Babette May Levy, *Preaching in the First Half*

Century of New England History (New York: Russell and Russell, 1967), pp. 81–97; Lawrence Buell, "The Unitarian Movement and the Art of Preaching in Nineteenth Century America," *American Quarterly*, 24 (1972), esp. pp. 179–82; Buell, *Literary Transcendentalism*, pp. 104–06, 115–20; Robinson, *Apostle*, pp. 48–68; and Toulouse, *Prophesying, passim*.

[49]See Channing, "Unitarian Christianity," *Works*, Vol. III, pp. 60–65. For the development of a moderate rationalism among the Liberals, see Conrad Wright, *The Beginnings of Unitarianism in America* (Boston: Starr King Press, 1955), pp. 135–60; also his "Rational Religion in Eighteenth-Century America," in *Liberal Christians*, pp. 1–21.

[50]Unlike Wright's "supernatural rationalism," the (Carlylesque) "natural supernaturalism" of M.H. Abrams is not offered specifically as a Biblical hermeneutic. Yet Abrams' formulation—that "characteristic concepts and patterns of Romantic philosophy and literature are a displaced and reconstituted theology"—seems to bear the implication; see *Natural Supernaturalism* (New York: W.W. Norton, 1971), pp. 65–70. What the "example of Emerson" suggests, I think, is the logic by which Liberal interpretation became Romantic displacement.

[51]Colacurcio, "Better Mode," p. 15. But for an account of idealistic (and therefore "subsumptive") forces at work within Unitarianism itself, see Daniel Walker Howe, "The Cambridge Platonists of Old England and the Cambridge Platonists of New England, in Wright, ed., *American Unitarianism*, pp. 87–119.

[52]For the "intellectual history" of the Dudleian sequence, see Perry Miller, "The Insecurity of Nature," in *Nature's Nation* (Cambridge: Harvard University Press, 1967), pp. 121–33. When Channing's Dudleian Lecture of 1821—"The Evidences of Revealed Religion"—refers to "Paley's inestimable work," the title in question is certainly the scripture-oriented *View of the Evidences of Christianity* (1794); yet a modern editor glosses the reference as Paley's later work of natural theology, *Evidences of the Existence and Attributes of the Deity Collected from the Appearances of Nature* (1802); see Irving H. Bartlett, *William Ellery Channing: Unitarian Christianity and Other Essays* (New York: Bobbs-Merrill, 1957), p. 81. The bibliographical confusion may have more than pedantic significance: unless we have a clear sense of the history and usage of the two coordinate but discrete polemic projects of post-Enlightenment Christianity, it will be impossible to sense the pressure of the logic by which Emerson forces their conflation into one.

[53]Miller, "Insecurity," p. 129.

[54]Bishop is hasty, I believe, in associating Fichte with the "'strong' misreading of Kant" according to which "the unlimited subject is regularly understood in cognitive terms" ("Christianity," p. 188); for Fichte is unambiguous in his ("Emersonian") assertion that "only through this medium of the moral law do I behold *myself*"; see Johann Gottlieb Fichte, *Science of Knowledge*, ed. and trans. Peter Heath and John Lachs (Cambridge: Cambridge University Press, 1982), p. 41.

[55]On the purely philosophical side, as a number of commentators have managed to suggest, Emerson's deepest problem is with Hume: not so much with miracles as with the radical (deconstructive) skepticism about the reality of the self; see Barish, *Emerson*, esp. pp. 108–15; John Michael, *Emerson and Skepticism* (Baltimore: Johns Hopkins University Press, 1988), pp. 33–65; B.L. Packer, *Fall*, pp. 156–62; and ultimately, Stephen Whicher, *Freedom and Fate* (Philadelphia: University of Pennsylvania Press, 1953), pp. 10–16.

[56]See "Experience" (III, 42). Emerson's point seems to be that "modernism" is marked by the discovery of "subjectivity"—which it was Kant's revolutionary task to systematize, but which had been well divined in "the discovery of Jesus" that "God must be thought within, not without" (JMN, V, 5).

[57]For the entirely "tautological" character of Emerson's theory of virtue, see Van Leer, *Epistemology*, pp. 90–93. Kant's "categorical imperative," by contrast, offers at least a minimum of moral content: "Act as if the maxim of your action were to become through your will a Universal Law of Nature." Thus, though Kant is far from implying that "concrete rules of conduct can be deduced" from his prime imperative, it nevertheless serves "as a criterion for judging the morality of concrete principles of conduct." And, significantly, Kant eventually provides an altogether "humanistic" translation of his abstract formula: "So act as to treat humanity…as an end, and never merely as a means." See Frederic Copleston, S.J., *A History of Philosophy*, Vol. 6, Pt. II (Garden City: Image Books, 1964), pp. 116–20. So far as Emerson goes on to provide content for his own imperative—in "Self-Reliance," for example—he sounds at least as much like Fichte: "Act so that you could consider the maxims of your willing as eternal laws for yourself"; see "Some Lectures Concerning the Scholar's Vocation," in Ernst Behler, ed., *Philosophy of German Idealism* (New York: Continuum, 1987), p. 6. Thus Emerson's theory of an ineluctably moral subjectivity continued to defer the problem an 1831 sermon (CIV) had as good as named "Self and Others."

[58]See Joel Porte, *Emerson and Thoreau* (Middletown: Wesleyan University Press, 1965), pp. 68–92. What Porte's evidence really shows is that Emerson had mastered the jargon of England better than that of Germany. Yet a more substantive point is also cogent: as "the moral" remains emphatic in Kant, Jacobi, and Fichte, so the anticipations of Kant's revolutionary ethic extend back through Price, the Scottish Common-Sense School, Hutcheson (if not Shaftesbury), the Cambridge Platonists, all the way to the "Puritan" notion of "experimental" faith.

[59]For a fuller account of Emerson's resistance to the idea of a "personal" God, see the previous chapter. And for an endorsement of Ware's (opposing) position, see Robinson, "Poetry," 193–96.

[60]The roots of Emerson's (1841) essay "Compensation" go back at least as far as Sermon IV (June 17, 1827). For a sympathetic reading of this maligned but "integrally important essay," see Gertrude Reif Hughes, *Emerson's Demanding Optimism* (Baton Rouge: Louisiana State University Press, 1984), pp. 96–100; and cp. Barish, *Emerson*, pp. 155–56. One might also propose that this master-idea of Emerson functioned as a not quite ironic answer to the master-idea of (Charles') Christianity: "Sacrifice" might indeed be "written on the plan of the world by the Christian exposition" (JMN, VI, 265): to gain one's life one had only to lose it.

[61]The standard analysis of the form and approximate content of the Puritan "Jeremiad" in America is Perry Miller, *The New England Mind: From Colony to Province* (Cambridge: Harvard University Press, 1953), pp. 3–39. For a powerful revisionist argument—stressing the power of the hopeful upturn, and significantly including Emerson himself—see Sacvan Bercovitch, *The Puritan Origins of the American Self* (New Haven: Yale University Press, 1975), esp. pp. 136–86; and cp. *The American Jeremiad* (Madison: University of Wisconsin Press, 1978). For a specifically Jeremiad intention in the "Address," see Carol Johnston, "The Underlying Structure of the Divinity School Address: Emerson as Jeremiah," in Joel Myerson, ed., *Studies in the American Renaissance* (Charlottesville: University of Virginia Press, 1980), pp. 41–49; and cp. Porte, *Representative*, pp. 120–33.

[62]Bishop thinks that "Emerson somewhat disingenuously calls for a 'new Teacher,'" and that "the role of the Baptist adopted here seems a transparent mask"; see "Emerson and Christianity," p. 187. That Emerson means to claim for himself a prophetic role theoretically coequal with Jesus seems clear; but he is far from declaring himself the One Man who shall perfect and abolish his own renovated Christology. Nor is he sanguine enough to imagine that his own efforts—here or in *Nature*—have done the intellectual work of showing how German metaphysics might be reconciled with English Romantic poetry.

281

[63]No doubt the remaining Protestant sacraments suffered, in New England, from some "Puritan" determination to go "as far as mortals could go in removing intermediaries between God and man"; see Perry Miller, *Seventeenth Century*, p. 45. And no doubt this tendency provoked, in time, a "sacramental renaissance"; see E. Brooks Holifield, *The Covenant Sealed* (New Haven: Yale University Press, 1974), pp. 197–230. Constant throughout this history, however, and possibly growing since the Awakening, is the clear sense of the preacher's role as the apt "second cause" in the ordinary "application of redemption."

[64]For the Wordsworthian basis of Emerson's theory of poetic speech in the "Address," see Stephen Railton, "'Assume an Identity of Sentiment': Rhetoric and Audience in Emerson's "Divinity School Address,"'" in Jack Salzman, ed., *Prospects*, Vol. 9 (Cambridge: Cambridge University Press, 1984), pp. 31–47. Construing the evidence as un-anxiously as possible, Railton ably argues that Emerson "goes to considerable lengths to preclude dissent, to create a context for agreement" (40).

[65]Acts 2.1–4. It could not have escaped Emerson's notice that prophetic activity begins among the disciples of Jesus only after a period of gloom at Jesus' literal disappearance.

[66]See Hutchison, *Ministers*, pp. 99–136.

[67]Bishop calls Emerson's Jesus an "oddly epicene version of the figure of whom we can also read in the New Testament"; see "Emerson and Christianity," p. 191. For a more approving view—of the *necessity* of Emerson's translation of Jesus into the terms of beauty and emotion—see Robinson, "Poetry," 190–93. A larger version of this same issue would involve the attempt to keep distinct two questions a present consensus seems in danger of conflating: one can agree with Robinson, Mott, Grusin and others that Emerson was molded by his ministry and that his evolution from Unitarianism was perfectly gradual without at the same time accepting the implication that he is, in the outcome, more Unitarian than anything else. This latter view puts Emerson "in some danger of disappearing back into his contexts" (Bishop, "Emerson and Christianity," p. 183).

[68]See Bishop, "Emerson and Christianity," p. 184. And for the argument that the *students* are the prime audience of the "Address," see Barish, *Emerson*, pp. 145–46.

[69]Bishop, p. 184; and cp. Mary Worden Edrich, "The Rhetoric of Apostasy," *Texas Studies in Literature and Language*, 8 (1967), 547–60.

[70]For a reading of the "Address" so determinedly philosophical as to suggest that "history and biography may be the wrong places to start," see Van Leer, *Epistemology*, pp. 77–99.

CHAPTER FIVE

[1]All quotations from *The Scarlet Letter* (SL), identified by page numbers in the text, refer to the Centenary Edition, Vol. 1 (Columbus: Ohio State University Press, 1962).

[2]See, particularly, Hyatt H. Waggoner's *Hawthorne* (Cambridge: Harvard University Press, 1955), pp. 118–50; and Roy R. Male's "From the Innermost Germ," *Journal of English Literary History*, 20 (1953), 218–36.

[3]The critic must be alert for tones of mock self-condescension in Hawthorne. In a famous letter to Longfellow (4 June 1837) Hawthorne calls his "studious life" at Salem a "desultory" one; but when he complains that his reading has not brought him "the fruits of study," he may well be remembering that it is Longfellow who is Professor of Modern Languages in Harvard University and not "the obscurest man of letters in America"; see the Centenary Edition of Hawthorne's *Letters, 1813–1843*, (Columbus: Ohio State University, 1984), pp. 251–53.

⁴I explore these historical relationships, among others, in *The Province of Piety* (Cambridge: Harvard University Press, 1984), pp. 160–202, 283–385. For the "dating" of SL, see Charles Ryskamp, "The New England Sources of SL," *American Literature*, 31 (1959), 257–72; and for speculation about the meaning of those dates, see the next essay in this collection, particularly footnote #17.

⁵Focusing on the implications of "Hester's Return," Sacvan Bercovitch has shown a generation of Hawthorne scholars how to read SL in relation to a whole network of American political issues of the 1840s and 50s; see *The Office of SL* (Baltimore: Johns Hopkins University Press, 1991), esp. pp 1–31. For other "contemporaneous" interpretations, see Jonathan Arac, "The Politics of SL," in Sacvan Bercovitch and Myra Jehlen, ed., *Ideology and Classic American Literature* (Cambridge: Cambridge University Press, 1986), pp. 247–66; Donald Pease, *Visionary Compacts* (Madison: University of Wisconsin Press, 1987), pp. 81–107; and Larry J. Reynolds, *European Revolutions and the American Literary Renaissance* (New Haven: Yale University Press, 1988), pp. 79–96.

⁶I have assumed a basic familiarity with the career and heresies, spoken and alleged, of Ann Hutchinson. A full study of her "influence," at least indirect, leads virtually everywhere in the seventeenth century. The following items seem most relevant: for primary sources beyond those demonstrably read by Hawthorne—Winthrop's *Journal*, Edward Johnson's *Wonder-Working Providence of Sion's Saviour*, Cotton Mather's *Magnalia Christi Americana*, and Thomas Hutchinson's *History of Massachusetts Bay*—consult Charles Francis Adams' collection of material on *Antinomianism in the Colony of Massachusetts Bay, 1636–1638*, published as Volume 21 of the *Publications of the Prince Society* (Boston, 1894) and David D. Hall, ed., *The Antinomian Controversy, 1636–1638* (Middletown: Wesleyan University Press, 1968). This last may contain some sources which Hawthorne could not have seen; but both contain the crucial transcripts of her two "trials" as well as Winthrop's *Short Story of the Rise, Reign, and Ruine of the Antinomians, Familists, and Libertines* (1644). For scholarly commentary on the meaning of Mrs. Hutchinson's ideas and career, several older works continue to seem indispensable: Emery Battis, *Saints and Sectaries* (Chapel Hill: University of North Carolina Press, 1962) and Larzer Ziff, *The Career of John Cotton* (Princeton: Princeton University Press, 1962); and Jesper Rosenmeier, "New England's Perfection," *William and Mary Quarterly*, 27 (1970), 435–59. Also useful is Part Two of C.F. Adams' *Three Episodes in Massachusetts History*, 2 vols. (Boston, 1893). Of the many works which have appeared since the original (1972) publication of this essay, the most relevant would be Lyle Koehler, "The Case of the American Jezebels," *William and Mary Quarterly*, 31 (1974), 55–78; Patricia Caldwell, "The Antinomian Language Controversy," *Harvard Theological Review*, 69 (1976), 345–67; William K.B. Stoever, *'A Faire and Easie Way to Heaven'* (Middletown: Wesleyan University Press, 1978), esp. pp. 21–57; Amy Schrager Lang, *Prophetic Woman* (Berkeley: University of California Press, 1987), esp. pp. 1–71. And for a brief account of the relationship at issue, see Sarah I. Davis, "Another View of Hester and the Antinomians," *Studies in American Fiction*, 12 (1984), 189–98.

⁷"Mrs. Hutchinson" first appeared in the *Salem Gazette* for 7 December 1830. As the Centenary text had not appeared at this essay's first publication, quotations are taken from the "Riverside Edition" of Hawthorne's *Works*, Vol. 12 (Boston: Houghton Mifflin, 1882–83).

⁸The harshest modern judgment is that of Perry Miller: "Cotton tried to adhere to the Protestant line until his colleagues forced him to recognize that he, for all his great position, would be sacrificed along with Mistress Hutchinson unless he yielded. As many another man in a similar predicament, Cotton bent"; see *The New England Mind: From Colony to Province* (Cambridge, Harvard University Press, 1953), pp. 59–60. For a view which emphasizes Cotton's naïveté, see Ziff, *Cotton*, pp. 106–48.

⁹For an account of the undesultory scholarship behind *The Scarlet Letter*, see Ryskamp, "Sources."

[10]Some of the facts in this paragraph have been noticed by other Hawthorne critics, but they have not pressed the Cotton-Dimmesdale implication. Besides Ryskamp, see Austin Warren's "Introduction" to SL (New York: Rinehart, 1947). The most direct anticipation of my theme is Larzer Ziff's brief observation that "The literary ancestor of [Hester Prynne] is Anne Hutchinson, about whom he had written one of his earliest published pieces"; see "The Artist and Puritanism," in Roy Harvey Pearce, ed., *Hawthorne Centenary Essays* (Columbus: Ohio State University Press, 1964), p. 262.

[11]In "spirit" this essay derives from the suggestion by Roy Harvey Pearce that Hawthorne criticism has "tended to rush on, identifying and collocating his symbols and their forms, and then pursuing them out of space—out of time, too often beyond the consciousness of those whose life in art they make possible" ("Romance and the Study of History," in *Centenary Essays*, Columbus: Ohio State University Press, 1964), p. 221. I have not tried to reread all SL criticism in preparing this essay, nor to cite specific debts at every point. I should, however, acknowledge the special influence of Austin Warren, "SL: A Literary Exercise in Moral Theology," *Southern Review*, 1 (1965), 22–45; and E.W. Baughman, "Public Confessions and SL," *New England Quarterly*, 40 (1967), 532–50.

[12]Hawthorne's remark about the "damned mob" is made, from abroad, in an 1855 letter to William Ticknor. The very next letter to Ticknor, which contains an altogether less dismissive estimate—of women writers who "throw off the restraints of decency, and come before the public naked, as it were"—may also be relevant to the sex-and-freedom theme of "Mrs. Hutchinson" and *The Scarlet Letter*; see the Centenary *Letters, 1853–1856*, 304, 307–08.

[13]The earlier form is in Chapter V: "Here, she said to herself, had been the scene of her guilt, and here should be the scene of her earthly punishment." The change from "punishment" to "penitence" is obviously significant in *somebody's* interpretative scheme. Also noteworthy: the earlier explanation suggests that "doubtless" Hester has a "secret" reason for remaining (80).

284

[14]See Francis E. Kearns, "Margaret Fuller as a Model for Hester Prynne," *Jahrbuch Für Amerikastudien*, 10 (1965), 161–97.

[15]*Saints and Sectaries*, p. 6.

[16]The standard account of the way Puritan theory made the visible church nearly identical with the invisible is Edmund S. Morgan, *Visible Saints* (rpt. Ithaca: Cornell University Press, 1965). A strong sense of the process seems implied everywhere in Hawthorne's writings about the Puritans; and, indeed, one could scarcely read Mather's *Magnalia* without grasping that it was in the Huchinson affair that the mystified public achieved precedence, in the Puritan world, over the mystical private.

[17]This point is made very effectively by Nina Baym—in spite of a logically inconclusive argument about the lack of meaningful Puritan categories in *The Scarlet Letter*; see "Passion and Authority in SL," *New England Quarterly*, 43 (1970), pp. 209–30.

[18]See *Province*, pp. 160–202.

[19]The larger quotation is from Battis (p. 287); he, in turn, is quoting from Gertrude Huehns, *Antinomianism in English History* (London: Cresset Press, 1951).

[20]Rufus Jones, *The Quakers in the American Colonies* (rpt. New York: Norton, 1966), p. 26. See also Geoffrey Nuttall, *The Holy Spirit in Puritan Faith and Experience* (London: Oxford University Press, 1946). Nuttall treats early Quakerism as a "limit" of one sort of Puritan logic and experience; though he does not argue the case, one cannot help being struck by the prominence of women in his accounts of early Quaker prophecy.

[21]Thomas Hutchinson's three-volume *History of Massachusetts Bay* probably provided Hawthorne with his most judicious account of the Hutchinson affair; certainly it

was useful in providing the transcript of Mrs. Hutchinson before the General Court at Newtown in November, 1637—where she gave a far better account of herself than would appear from Winthrop's *Short Story*. But the account given by *this* Hutchinson contains no hint of sexual language. For Hawthorne's reading of Hutchinson, Mather, Johnson, and Winthrop, see Marion L. Kesselring, *Hawthorne's Reading* (New York: New York Public Library, 1949); and see Colacurcio, *Province*, pp. 71–78.

[22]I quote from a nineteenth-century edition: *Magnalia Christi Americana* (Hartford: Silas Andrus and Son, 1855), II, 516.

[23]The heresy-bastard conceit is also in Thomas Weld's "Preface" to Winthrop's *Short Story* (reprinted in both Adams and Hall; see note 6); the *Short Story* is, in turn, the main source of Mather's account. It seems likely that Hawthorne saw Winthrop's book independently.

[24]*Magnalia*, II, 518. Probably this is only Mather's pedantry at work, re-translating from Revelations. In Winthrop's *Short Story* Cotton says "make and maintain a lye" (Hall, *Antinomian Controversy*, p. 307).

[25]Quoted from Hall, *Antinomian Controversy*, pp. 315–316 and p. 267. Hawthorne would have found all he needed in the "Appendix" to Thomas Hutchinson's second volume; see *History* (rpt., Cambridge: Harvard University Press, 1936), II, 366–91, esp. 368–69.

[26]*Wonder-Working Providence of Sion's Saviour*, ed. Franklin L. Jameson (New York: Barnes and Noble, 1910), p. 134. Note also that Winthrop, besides his relentless pursuit of "monstrous" evidences against both Ann Hutchinson and Mary Dyer, does not overlook instances of irregular sexual practice resulting from Hutchinsonian principles; see his *Journal*, ed. James Kendall Hosmer, 2 Vols. (New York: Barnes and Noble, 1908), esp. II, 28.

[27]The three formulations are, respectively, those of Baym, "Passion and Authority"; Feidelson, "SL," in *Centenary Essays*; and Warren, "Literary Exercise."

285

[28]The "pragmatic" (or moral) argument against Calvinism runs backwards from Henry Bamford Parkes' essay "The Puritan Heresy," in *The Pragmatic Test* (San Francisco: Colt Press, 1941) to William Ellery Channing, at least, and probably to Jonathan Mayhew.

[29]See Baughman, "Public Confession," esp. pp. 533–37.

[30]Though John Winthrop is only a background figure in SL, his moral presence is strongly felt. It is surely the famous "Little Speech" of this most energetic opponent of Ann Hutchinson that Hawthorne had in mind when he wrote in "Main-street" that what the Puritans "called Liberty" was very much "like an iron cage" (III, 449). In fact, it is Winthrop's doctrine of liberty as holy obedience which sinews the clerical doctrines of visible sanctity, preparation, and sanctification, to make the Puritan world the massive and unitary legal construct Hawthorne represents it to be in the opening pages of SL. Hawthorne gives us that world as of the 1640s: one could argue that rigidification was not complete by that point and that Hawthorne is really describing a later stage of development, when "one generation had bequeathed…the counterfeit of its religious ardor to the next" (III, 460); see E.H. Davidson, "The Question of History in SL," *Emerson Society Quarterly*, 25 (1951), 2–3. But one could also argue that, though Hawthorne does indeed "encapsulate" a long historical sequence into the moments of its beginning, he clearly intends to point us to the banishment of Ann Hutchinson (1636–1638) as the crucial defeat of "spiritism" in the Puritan world.

[31]The autonomy of the spiritual self, along with the coordinate subjection of the outward man to civil authority, is the lesson Hawthorne learned from the career of Roger Williams—of whom Hawthorne seems a true disciple; see *Province*, pp. 221–51.

[32]For a reading of the adultery/idolatry question in SL, see Margaret Olafson Thickstun, *Fictions of the Feminine* (Ithaca: Cornell University Press, 1987), pp. 132–56. And for recent readings of Hawthorne's construction of gender apart from the matter of Ann Hutchinson, see Mary Suzanne Schriber, *Gender and the Writer's Imagination* (Lexington: University of Kentucky Press, 1987), pp. 45–85; Andrew Schreiber, "Public Force, Private Sentiment," ATQ, 2 (1988), 285–99; and Emily Miller Budick, "Hester's Skepticism, Hawthorne's Faith," *New Literary History*, 22 (1991), pp. 199–211.

[33]Conveniently, one might look at *The Diary of Michael Wigglesworth*, ed. Edmund Morgan (New York: Harper, 1956) for a sense of the painful doubts experienced, for a time, at least, by the already encovenanted saints. If Solomon Stoddard is to be believed—that Puritan theory had turned Communion Sundays into "days of torment"—then some version of Dimmesdale's problem was widespread indeed.

[34]Quoted from Hall, *Antinomian Controversy*, pp. 65–66. The document in question is "The Elders Reply"—to the answers Cotton had given to sixteen questions addressed to him by those same "Elders."

[35]From "Mr. Cotton's Rejoynder," quoted in Hall, p. 88.

[36]"Rejoynder," in Hall, pp. 88–89. I do not suppose that Hawthorne had seen this document. Somewhere, however, he did acquire a first-hand familiarity with Cotton's works, or with those of some Puritan writers who introduced the problem of justification without perfect sanctification. For an epistemological account of the question of hypocrisy in SL, see Kenneth Marc Harris, *Hypocrisy and Self-Deception in Hawthorne's Fiction* (Charlottesville: University of Virginia Press, 1988) pp. 46–88.

[37]See Miller, *Colony to Province*, pp. 79–80.

[38]*The Doctrine of the Saints' Infirmities* (London, 1638), pp. 36–38. John F.H. New has interpreted the passage in question to mean, simply, that adultery is a cardinal example of a sin which disproves covenant status; see *Anglican and Puritan* (Stanford: Stanford University Press, 1964), p. 93. The serious critic of SL will be rewarded by a reading of Preston's treatise, especially the first sermon. His call for a lifelong struggle against "infirmities" forms an appropriate background to Dimmesdale's weakening after seven years; and his clear statement that "a sin committed simply with deliberation cannot be an infirmity" seems to supply the ironic context for Hawthorne's comment on Dimmesdale's state just after he has lost the struggle: "he had yielded himself with deliberate choice, as he had never done before, to what he knew was deadly sin" (222).

[39]For the outline of a reply to Bercovitch's sense of "Hester's Return" as a form of "Compromise," see Charles Swann, *Nathaniel Hawthorne: Tradition and Revolution* (Cambridge: Cambridge University Press, 1991) pp. 75–95.

CHAPTER SIX

[1]The standard "source study" of *The Scarlet Letter* (SL) is Charles Ryskamp, "The New England Sources of SL," *American Literature*, 31 (1959), 257–72. Its final, modest claim is for "a firm dependence upon certain New England histories for the background of SL" (p. 271).

[2]See my own "Footsteps of Ann Hutchinson," appearing here as Chapter Five, pp. 177–204.

[3]For the three issues in question see, respectively, Ryskamp, "Sources," pp. 260–61, 267; Ernest W. Baughman, "Public Confession and SL," *New England Quarterly*, 40 (1967), 532–50; and Michael Davitt Bell, *Hawthorne and the Historical Romance of New England* (Princeton: Princeton University Press, 1971), pp. 135–37.

[4]Arguing against the relevance of Puritanism to much of America's classic literature, William C. Spengemann concedes Winthrop as an "apparent" source of SL but writes

off the pursuit of such matters as "a harmless provincialism"; see his "Review Essay," *Early American Literature*, 16 (1981), 184–85. Arrogance aside, it may yet appear, however, that Winthrop is more nearly Hawthorne's vital subject than his necessary source. For a more political enactment of this possibility, see Lauren Berlant, *The Anatomy of National Fantasy* (Chicago: University of Chicago Press, 1991), esp. pp. 70–95, 128–34.

[5]This study cautiously proposes that one take seriously the suggestion of the first chapter of SL—that its historical world should indeed be regarded as some projected "Utopia of human virtue and happiness" (47). An analysis of Hawthorne's reduction of utopian pretense to local ideology might base itself on Fredric Jameson's "Dialectic of Utopia and Ideology," in *The Political Unconscious* (Ithaca: Cornell University Press, 1981), pp. 281–99.

[6]Though three years of real or "maturational" time have elapsed when Hester is called from her needle to appear before Governor Bellingham, the "fictional" time is brief indeed. This successful manipulation of dramatic or psychic time contributes to the novel's brilliant compression and marks Hawthorne's narrative advance over his longer tales, e.g., "The Gentle Boy"; see my own *Province of Piety* (Cambridge: Harvard University Press, 1984), esp. pp. 179–81.

[7]For the "worthy" observation on the puritanic sensitivities of mice, see *Winthrop's Journal: "History of New England,"* J.K. Hosmer, ed. (New York: Scribners, 1908), Vol. II, p. 18.

[8]Ryskamp, "Sources," p. 265. For Morison's discussion of the transformation of the Massachusetts "charter" into a workable "constitution"—including his account of "the cause celebre of Goody Sherman and her stray sow"—see *Builders of the Bay Colony* (Boston: Houghton Mifflin, 1930), pp. 83–94; and cp. George Lee Haskins, *Law and Authority in Early Massachusetts* (New York: Macmillan, 1960), esp. pp. 9–65; and Edwin Powers, *Crime and Punishment in Early Massachusetts* (Boston: Beacon Press, 1966), esp. pp. 45–99.

[9]For Winthrop's original account of the stray sow, see *Journal*, II, 64–66; for the political aftermath, *Journal*, II, 211–17. Dating the action of SL has proved simple enough: Pearl is seven years old by the end of the story, which the text itself marks as 1649 by its mention of the death of Governor Winthrop; it thus begins in 1642 and, as the narrative declares, "in this month of June" (48); see Ryskamp, "Sources," pp. 259–61.

287

[10]Winthrop, *Journal*, I, 305.

[11]Robert Emmet Wall, Jr., *Massachusetts Bay: The Crucial Decade, 1640–1650* (New Haven: Yale University Press, 1972), esp. pp. 41–92.

[12]Ryskamp, "Sources," pp. 260, 267–68; and cp. Bell, *Romance*, pp. 135–36.

[13]For the view that Hawthorne's recent political experiences figure largely in the dramatic action of SL itself, see James R. Mellow, *Nathaniel Hawthorne in His Times* (Boston: Houghton Mifflin, 1980), esp. pp. 292–308; and, more radically, Stephen Nissenbaum, "Introduction," *The Scarlet Letter and Selected Writings* (New York: Modern Library, 1984), esp. pp. xix-xxxvi.

[14]*Journal*, II, 43–44; the entry is for Nov. 8, 1642. For a brief review of the (sparsely preserved) facts of Bellingham's life, see the article of Henry P. Stearns in the *Dictionary of American Biography*, Allen Johnson, ed. (New York: Scribners, 1927), Vol. II, pp. 166–67; and cp. James Savage, *A Geneological Dictionary of the First Settlers of New England* (Boston: Little, Brown, 1860), pp. 161–62.

[15]The editorial remark is that of Hosmer: see Winthrop, *Journal*, II, 44. See also John Gorham Palfrey, *The History of New England* (London: Longmans, 1849), Vol. I, pp. 611–12.

[16]The references are, respectively, *The Bourgeois Experience: Victoria to Freud* (New York: Oxford, 1984); and *The History of Sexuality*, Robert Hurley, trans. (New York: Vintage, 1980). For the argument that Hawthorne's Puritans *already* typify this "bourgeois" world, see Charles Feidelson, Jr., "*The Scarlet Letter*," in Roy Harvey Pearce, ed., *Hawthorne Centenary Essays* (Columbus: Ohio State University Press, 1964), pp. 31–77.

[17]Granting the specific 1642–49 setting of SL, a few critics have thought to ask "why just then?" But the answers have largely centered on events in England. H. Bruce Franklin neatly evokes the situations of Bellingham and Winthrop, but turns quickly to the context of the English Civil War; see his "Introduction" to *The Scarlet Letter and Other Writings by Nathaniel Hawthorne* (Philadelphia: J.B. Lippincott, 1967), pp. 13–17. And see also Frederick Newberry, "Tradition and Disinheritance in *The Scarlet Letter*," *ESQ*, 23 (1977), 1–26.

[18]For the expurgated materials, see the James Savage edition of John Winthrop, *The History of New England from 1630 to 1649* (Boston: Phelps and Farnham, 1825–1826), Vol. II, pp. 45–50. For Hawthorne's knowledge of this edition, see Marion L. Kesselring, *Hawthorne's Reading* (New York: New York Public Library, 1949), p. 64.

[19]Winthrop, *Journal* (Hosmer, ed.), II, 38.

[20]Winthrop, *Journal* (Savage, ed.), II, 46.

[21]It is virtually impossible, of course, that Hawthorne could have seen the Bradford text itself, since it had disappeared from (private) circulation since the Revolution and did not see print until 1856. Nor, significantly, do any of the historians who loyally retell parts of his story (often *verbatim*) include any mention of the "wickedness" that totally preoccupied his attention in 1642. Yet his own account powerfully reinforces the impression created by Winthrop—of a whole godly nation frightfully astounded by an unseemly return of the repressed; and the "answers" he includes indelibly reinscribe the painful terms of the Bellingham questionnaire as described by Winthrop. To read Bradford into the record is thus merely to authenticate Hawthorne's primary intuition. For the history of the text in question, see Samuel Eliot Morison's "Introduction" to William Bradford, *Of Plymouth Plantation* (New York: Knopf, 1952), pp. xxvii–xxxii. For Bradford's (interwoven) account of "wickedness" at both Plymouth and Massachusetts Bay, see pp. 316–22; and for the answers the Plymouth Elders made to Bellingham, pp. 404–413.

[22]See Winthrop, *Journal* (Savage, ed.), p. 47; and cp. Bradford, *Plymouth*, pp. 404, 407, 408–12. In fairness, it should be pointed out that, though the defendants in question escaped with severe whippings, confinements, and social brandings, the case eventually forced a clear definition of "rape" and a declaration that it would be, in the future, a capital offense—despite the lack of warrant from Scripture; see Haskins, *Law and Authority*, pp. 116, 150–51; and cp. Powers, *Crime and Punishment*, pp. 264–68.

[23]Winthrop, *Journal* (Savage, ed.), p. 47; and Bradford, *Plymouth*, p. 318.

[24]It should go without saying that Hawthorne had noticed the case of "one Mary Latham," put to death for her adultery (with James Britton), but only after this "once proper young woman" taunted the husband of her loveless marriage as "old rogue and cockold"; see Winthrop, *Journal* (Hosmer, ed.), II, 161–63.

[25]The quotation is from Faulkner's "Delta Autumn." For a brief selection of John Winthrop's letters to and from his (third) wife, Margaret, see Perry Miller and Thomas H. Johnson, ed., *The Puritans* (New York: Harper and Row, 1963), Vol. II, pp. 465–571; as the editors remark, these letters "reveal certain depths of the Puritan spirit and the nature of conjugal affection in Puritan households" (p. 464).

[26]See John Cotton, *A Brief Exposition…Upon the Whole Book of Canticles* (London: Ralph Smith, 1755), esp. pp. 4–8; this rare edition has been reprinted, in facsimile, as a

volume of the Research Library of Americana (New York: Arno Press, 1972). For the sexual implication of Cotton in SL, see Chapter Five, pp. 197–202.

[27]Cotton's "standard catechism for New England children" bore the title: *Spiritual Milk for Boston Babes In Either England, Drawn out of the Breasts of Both Testaments*; see David Leverenz, *The Language of Puritan Feeling* (New Brunswick: Rutgers University Press, 1980), p. 2. Leverenz's (psychoanalytic) study amply documents the Puritans' widespread use of sexual language for a variety of "higher" concerns; and see Ivy Schweitzer, *The Work of Self-Representation* (Chapel Hill: University of North Carolina Press, 1991), esp. pp. 1–39. On the crucial question of "weaned affections," see Perry Miller, *The New England Mind: The Seventeenth Century* (Cambridge: Harvard University Press, 1939), pp. 35–63; and Edmund S. Morgan, *The Puritan Family* (New York: Harper and Row, 1966), pp. 29–86.

[28]Chapter Five, pp. 182–91.

[29]For an unhysterical modern account of the Puritans actual difficulties with sexuality—beneath both their coarseness and their metaphoric enthusiasm—see Philip Greven, *The Protestant Temperament* (New York: Alfred A. Knopf, 1977), esp. pp. 62–73, 124–48. A more forgiving view is advanced by Robert Daly, *God's Altar* (Berkeley: University of California Press, 1978), esp. pp. 26–27.

[30]Chapter Five, pp. 200–202.

[31]As I have argued elsewhere, Hester's habit of looking, fearfully, day after day, into Pearl's "expanding nature," constantly expecting "to detect some dark and wild peculiarity" (90) is plainly an echo of the Puritans' ascription of Ann Hutchinson's "monster birth" to her heresies; see Chapter Five, pp. 189–90.

[32]"Structural" analysis of SL always points to the definitive importance of the three "scaffold scenes," at precisely the beginning, middle, and end of the novel's drama. Such an approach must always privilege Dimmesdale: when (and why) *will* he eventually get up where he belongs, in the naked light of day? See Leland Schubert, *Hawthorne the Artist* (Chapel Hill: University of North Carolina Press, 1944), pp. 137–38.

289

[33]Winthrop, *Journal* (Hosmer, ed.), II, 83–84.

[34]Ironically, Dimmesdale decides to run away with Hester the very day he discovers she still has a living husband. The point was first seized (somewhat moralistically) by Robert F. Haugh, "The Second Secret in SL," *College English*, 17 (1956), 269–71.

[35]Winthrop, *Journal* (Hosmer, ed.), II, 238–39.

[36]Such is the verdict on Puritan "liberty" in Hawthorne's sketch called "Mainstreet," published the year before SL, and alluded to in "The Custom House": "How like an iron cage was that which they called Liberty!" See the Centenary Edition of *The Snow Image and Uncollected Tales* (Columbus: Ohio State University Press, 1974), p. 58. The *allusion*, as Q.D. Leavis pointed out, is almost certainly to the place in *The Pilgrim's Progress* where "Christian is shown a man in an iron cage as an awful example of what a true Christian should never be"; see "Hawthorne as Poet," rpt. in A.N. Kaul, ed., *Hawthorne: A Collection of Critical Studies* (Englewood Cliffs, NJ: Prentice Hall, 1966), p. 35. The *reference*, however, is just as surely to Winthrop's representative and famous "little speech." For an extended consideration of Winthrop's political thought, see Loren Baritz, "Political Theology," in *City On A Hill* (New York: John Wiley and Sons, 1964), pp. 3–45; and cp. G.L. Mosse, *The Holy Pretense* (New York: Howard Fertig, 1968), pp. 88–106.

[37]Conveniently, the case of Thomas Shepard may be added to those of the semi-antinomian John Cotton, the Canticles-inspired Edward Taylor, and the decidedly female Anne Bradstreet to suggest that Puritan men and women thought of their souls alike, allegorically, as female: Shepard's conversion clearly involved his accepting Christ as "Husband"; see his *Autobiography*, edited by Michael McGiffert as *God's Plot*

(Amherst: University of Massachusetts Press, 1974), p. 45. For the generality of the phenomenon, see "Brides of Christ" in Greven, *Protestant Temperament*, pp. 124–48; and Schweitzer, *Self-Representation*, pp. 20–35. For the view that Dimmesdale makes the better bride than Hester, see Margaret Olofson Thickstun, *Fictions of the Feminine* (Ithaca: Cornell University Press, 1988), pp. 132–57. And, on the other side of the literal, for the Puritans' "liberal" divorce policy, see Emil Oberholzer, *Delinquent Saints* (New York: Columbia University Press, 1956), pp. 117–18.

[38]For the relevant "blasphemy" of Emily Dickinson, see "I cannot live with you," in Thomas H. Johnson, ed., *Final Harvest* (Boston: Little, Brown, 1961), pp. 162–64.

[39]See Franklin, *SL and Other Writings*, p. 15.

[40]John Winthrop, "Model of Christian Charity," *Collections of the Massachusetts Historical Society*, 3rd Series, Vol. VII, 1838, p. 42. For the "true" identity of the Puritan self, see Sacvan Bercovitch, *The Puritan Origins of the American Self* (New Haven: Yale University Press, 1975), esp. pp. 1–34. And for Lawrence's moral of America, see *Studies in Classic American Literature* (rpt. Garden City, NY: Doubleday, 1951), pp. 11–18.

[41]Winthrop, "Model"; quoted from the corrected text of Edmund S. Morgan, ed., *Puritan Political Ideas* (Indianapolis: Bobbs-Merrill, 1965), pp. 87–88. For Hawthorne's knowledge of the 1838 version (cited above), see Colacurcio, *Piety*, pp. 237, 597.

[42]See Perry Miller, ed., *The Puritans* (Garden City, NY: Doubleday, 1956), p. 90.

[43]Both of Miller's widely used anthologies truncate Winthrop's "Model" badly, eliding both its theology and its sexual metaphors, and thus stressing instead its arch-conservative theory of social hierarchy; see, for example, Miller and Johnson, *Puritans*, pp. 195–202. This simplified version of the original "vision" tends to reinforce the decidedly partial view of Winthrop as altogether secular and "lawyerly"; see Vernon L. Parrington, *Main Currents in American Thought* (New York: Harcourt, Brace, 1927), pp. 38–50; and cp. Darrett B. Rutman, *Winthrop's Boston* (Chapel Hill: University of North Carolina Press, 1965), esp. pp. 19–21.

[44]Winthrop, *Journal* (Hosmer, ed.), II, 239.

[45]David Leverenz rightly denies that Hawthorne ultimately "reduces Hester's radical perceptions to her sexuality," but his psycho-sexual reading fails (in my view) to identify the metaphorical (theological) burden of that sexuality; see "Mrs. Hawthorne's Headache: Reading *The Scarlet Letter*," *Nineteenth-Century Fiction*, 37 (1983), 552–75. For the larger novelistic traditions in question, see Judith Armstrong, *The Novel of Adultery* (London: Macmillan Press, 1976); Tony Tanner, *Adultery in the Novel* (Baltimore: Johns Hopkins University Press, 1979); and, more philosophically, Rene Girard, *Deceit, Desire, and the Novel*, Yvonne Freccero, trans. (Baltimore: Johns Hopkins University Press, 1965).

[46]The infamous formula of *Paradise Lost*—"Hee for God only, shee for God in him" (Book IV, line 299)—clearly implies that woman's "natural" sex role makes her theologic submission seem natural as well. The logic of SL would seem to question that implication.

[47]Although Melville's literary response to Hawthorne is the most famous such case in all of American literary history, the influence of SL has been remarkably difficult to detect. Restoring the emphasis on metaphoric sexuality makes its link to *Pierre* (1852) seem obvious and powerful. It may also indicate that Melville read Dimmesdale as a precursor of the sort of "feminization" which appears to have marked the nineteenth century; see Ann Douglas, *The Feminization of American Culture* (New York: Alfred A. Knopf, 1977), esp. pp. 80–117, 294–96, 309–13. It is also imaginable that, granting a certain theological slippage, Dimmesdale's death-by-allegory predicts the sexual attenuation of Quentin Compson.

CHAPTER SEVEN

¹For the small debate in question, see William C. Spengemann's "Review Essay" (of Emory Elliott's *Puritan Influences in American Literature*) in *Early American Literature*, 16 (1981), 175–86; Elliott's letter "To the Editor" and Spengemann's "Reply" appear in Volume 17 (1982), 97–99. See also the various essays in Spengemann's *A Mirror for Americanists* (Hanover, NH: University Press of New England, 1989).

²See Lawrence Buell, *New England Literary Culture* (Cambridge: Cambridge University Press, 1986), esp. pp. 38–55, 175–81.

³In addition to the always quoted verdicts on Unitarianism as "corpse-cold" and full of "pale negations," Emerson's other formulas include "empty" (V, 145), "boyish" (V, 416), not "poetic" (V, 471), "cold, barren, & odious" (VI, 40), without "vision" (VI, 232), and like an "icehouse"; quoted from *Journals and Miscellaneous Notebooks* (JMN), William H. Gilman et al, ed., (Cambridge: Harvard University Press, 1960–1982).

⁴Buell, quoting Herbert, in "*Moby-Dick* as a Sacred Text," in Richard H. Brodhead, ed., *New Essays on "Moby-Dick"* (Cambridge: Cambridge University Press, 1986), p. 68. For Herbert's views in full, see "Calvinist Earthquake: '*Moby-Dick*' and Religious Tradition," in Brodhead, *New Essays*, pp. 109–40; and, more largely, in "*Moby-Dick" and Calvinism* (New Brunswick: Rutgers University Press, 1977).

⁵Lawrance Thompson's discussion of Melville's rhetorical strategies is debatable enough, but his account of Melville as protesting victim of a latter-day Calvinist culture remains classic; see *Melville's Quarrel With God* (Princeton: Princeton University Press, 1952), esp. pp. 4–6.

⁶The formula is Perry Miller's—responding to accounts of the religious rhetoric of the American Revolution as "propeganda"; see *Nature's Nation* (Cambridge: Harvard University Press, 1967), p. 99.

⁷For the outlines of a "Unitarian" Emerson, see Conrad Wright, "Emerson, Barzillai Frost, and The Divinity School Address," in *The Liberal Christians* (Boston: Beacon Press, 1970), pp. 41–61; and David Robinson, *Apostle of Culture* (Philadelphia: University of Pennsylvania, 1982), esp. pp. 7–68.

⁸JMN, IV, 45. For the earlier, conservative use of the formula, see "The Elders' Reply," in David D. Hall, ed., *The Antinomiam Controversy* (Middletown, CT: Wesleyan University Press, 1968), p. 67. And for Emerson's reference to the Antinomian moment, see Joel Porte, *Representative Man* (New York: Oxford University Press, 1979), pp. 98–104.

⁹Quotations of Emerson's published works are taken from The Library of America *Emerson: Essays and Lectures* (1983).

¹⁰For the neo-Calvinist problem of direct and reflex assurance, see R.T. Kendall, *Calvin and English Calvinism to 1649* (Oxford: Oxford University Press, 1979), esp. pp. 25, 33–4, 107–09. After beginning his "Will to Believe" with a humorous reference to "the difference between justification and sanctification," William James identifies his own lecture as "something like a sermon on justification by faith," though more properly "an essay in justification of faith" (457); quoted from The Library of America *Writings 1878–1899* (1992).

¹¹"Emerson and Christianity," *Renascence*, 38 (1986), 183–200; see also Donald L. Gelpi, S.J., *Endless Seeker* (Lanham, MD: University Press of America, 1991), esp. pp. 3–66.

¹²In the memorable formulation of Stephen Whicher, there is, in the logic of "Fate," "more than a suggestion…of the 'consistent Calvinist' 'Are you willing to be damned for the glory of God?'"; see *Freedom and Fate* (Philadelphia: University of Pennsylvania, 1953), p. 140.

¹³JMN,VIII, 75. For the logic of "supernatural rationalism," see Conrad Wright, *The Beginnings of Unitarianism in New England* (Boston: Starr King Press, 1955), pp. 135–60; and "Rational Religion in Eighteenth-Century America," in *The Liberal Christians*, pp. 1–21.

¹⁴For the history of the ambiguity by which Romantic writers recouperate the language of Christian mystery, see M.H. Abrams, *Natural Supernaturalism* (New York: W.W. Norton, 1971); esp. pp. 17–70, 253–313.

¹⁵So runs the general argument of my own *Province of Piety* (Cambridge: Harvard University Press, 1984), esp. pp. 5–36.

¹⁶For the classic case of Hawthorne as *more* than Calvinist on the question of sin, see Austin Warren's "Introduction" to The American Writers Series *Hawthorne* (New York: American Book Co., 1934), pp. xix-xl. For an updated version, see Agnes McNeill Donohue, *Hawthorne: Calvin's Ironic Stepchild* (Kent: Kent State University Press, 1985). Quotations from Hawthorne's published works are taken from The Library of America *Hawthorne: Tales and Sketches* (1982).

¹⁷For the Calvinism of "Rappaccini's Daughter," see William H. Shurr, *Rappaccini's Children* (Lexington: University of Kentucky Press, 1981), pp. 1–4. Serious work on the tale's "medical" theology begins with Carol M. Bensick, *La Nouvelle Beatrice* (New Brunswick: Rutgers University Press, 1985), esp. pp. 113–137.

¹⁸For the problem of "Smooth" divinity in Hawthorne and Dwight, see my own "Cosmopolitan and Provincial," *Studies in the Novel*, 23 (1991), esp. pp. 4–7. A similar problem of doctrine vs. tone arises from the passage in "The Old Manse" which contrasts the "warmth" of puritanic publications with a "frigidity of the modern productions" that seems "characteristic and inherent" (1137).

¹⁹Thus my (small) dissent from the political reading of Sacvan Bercovitch; see *The Office of "The Scarlet Letter"* (Baltimore: Johns Hopkins University, 1991). For the other readings in question, see Jonathan Arac, "The Politics of *The Scarlet Letter*," in Sacvan Bercovitch and Myra Jehlen, ed., *Ideology and Classic American Literature* (Cambridge: Cambridge University Press, 1986), pp. 247–66; Nina Baym, *The Shape of Hawthorne's Career* (Ithaca: Cornell University Press, 1976), pp. 123–51; and David Leverenz, *Manhood and the American Renaissance* (Ithaca: Cornell University Press, 1989), pp. 259–78.

²⁰For the question of adultery and idolatry in *The Scarlet Letter*, see Chapter Six; and Margaret Olofson Thickstun, *Fictions of the Feminine* (Ithaca: Cornell University Press, 1988), pp. 132–56. Quotations from *The Scarlet Letter* are taken from the Library of America *Hawthorne: Novels* (1983).

²¹The famous review ("Hawthorne and His Mosses") and also the letters to Hawthorne all indicate that what Melville got from Hawthorne was less a store of ideas than a certain "sanction"—for the project of writing with the sort of religious seriousness that insists the Devil have his due. The "wickedness" of *Moby-Dick* resides, accordingly, in its (Humean) implication that One God cannot be both "sovereign," in Edwards' sense, and also "guiltless" in that of Dickinson.

²²My reading of "Bartleby the Scrivener" draws on Allan Moore Emery, "The Alternatives of Melville's 'Bartleby,'" *Nineteenth-Century Fiction*, 31 (1976), pp. 170–87; and Daniel Stemple and Bruce Stillians, "'Bartleby the Scrivener': A Parable of Pessimism," *Nineteenth-Century Fiction*, 27 (1972), pp. 268–82. For the Edwardsian provocation, see Paul Ramsey, ed., *The Works of Jonathan Edwards*, Volume 1: *Freedom of the Will* (New Haven: Yale University Press, 1957), pp. 137–40.

²³Quotations from *Battle Pieces* are taken from *Collected Poems* (Chicago: Hendricks House, 1947), pp. 102, 57, 94.

[24]Quotations from *Moby-Dick* are taken from The Library of America *Melville: Redburn, White-Jacket, Moby-Dick* (1983).

[25]The subversive formula is from Emerson's "Fate" (946).

[26]The text of William Ellery Channing's "Moral Argument Against Calvinism" is amply and aptly quoted in Herbert's *"Moby-Dick" and Calvinism*, pp. 40–41, 75–77, 80, 89–91, 111, 131, 147, 155. The evocation of man as "most august animal" is the work of John Wise, standing at the head of liberal anthropology in New England; quoted from Perry Miller's selections of his *Vindication of the Government of New England Churches*, in *The American Puritans* (New York: Columbia University Press, 1982), p. 127.

[27]For the imagery by which Calvin and his disciples forbid the enterprise of Ahab, see Thomas Werge, "*Moby-Dick* and the Calvinist Tradition," *Studies in the Novel*, 1 (1969), 484–506. Shepard's denial of man's right "to quarrel with God" occurs in defense of His sovereign right to withhold assurance from the soul in the preparatory state of "humiliation"; see *The Sound Believer*, in *The Works of Thomas Shepard* (Boston: Doctrinal Tract and Book Society, 1853), Vol. I, p. 186.

[28]For more personal readings of the plight of Ishmael and Ahab, see Edwin H. Miller, *Melville* (New York: George Braziller, Inc., 1975), pp. 192–219; and Leverenz, *Manhood*, pp. 279–306.

[29]For the argument that some of the fascicles reveal "the pattern of Calvinist conversion narrative," see Diane Gabrielsen Scholl, "Emily Dickinson's Conversion Narratives: A Study of the Fascicles," *Studies in Puritan American Spirituality*, 1 (1990), 202–24; for an older form of the argument, without the emphasis on the fascicles, see William R. Sherwood, *Circumference and Circumstance* (New York: Columbia University Press, 1968), esp. pp. 137–79. More generalized studies of Dickinson's Calvinism are Ronald Lanyi, "'My faith that dark adores-': Calvinist Theology in in the Poetry of Emily Dickinson," *Arizona Quarterly*, 32 (1976), 264–78; and Jane Donahue Eberwein, "'Graphicer for Grace': Emily Dickinson's Calvinist Language," *Studies in Puritan American Spirituality*, 1 (1990), 170–201.

293

[30]Dickinson's warning about the fictive nature of her speaker, widely unheeded in this post-New Critical age, is offered in a letter of July, 1862 to T.W. Higginson (#268); see Thomas H. Johnson, ed., *The Letters of Emily Dickinson* (Cambridge: Harvard University Press, 1958), Vol. II, pp. 411–12. For Hawthorne's references to his avoidance of religious agencies and services, see the *Letters 1813–1843*, which appears as Vol. XV of the Centenary *Works of Nathaniel Hawthorne* (Columbus: Ohio State University Press, 1984), pp. 159–90.

[31]Quotations from Dickinson's poetry are taken from Thomas H. Johnson's one-volume *Complete Poems of Emily Dickinson* (Boston: Little Brown, 1957); identification is by poem number only.

[32]Clearly—as Dickinson could hardly not know—the problem of "same name" is, in orthodox theology, a perilous matter indeed: "Christ" (as distinguished from "Jesus") always implies Godhood; but "God" need not specify the "Son" or "Second Person" but some other "hypostasis" altogether.

[33]The belief that Reprobates (almost) never know themselves as such appears to enter the tradition of Puritan casuistry with the (not quite certain) teaching of William Ames: "it is seldom or never shown ordinarily to anyone before the end of this life that God will not make him a partaker in grace and glory"; see *The Marrow of Theology*, John Dykstra Eusden, trans. (Boston: Pilgrim Press, 1968), p. 249. For Calvin's more famous teaching on God's "blinding" of the Reprobate, see *Institutes of the Christian Religion*, Henry Beveridge, trans. (Grand Rapids: Eerdman's Publishing Co., rpt., 1972), Vol. II, p. 252.

[34]The latter-day Calvinist problem of "temporary faith"—distinct from the Arminian belief that saving grace can be won but then lost—is the running issue of Kendall's *Calvin*; see esp. pp. 6–7, 21–25, 64–75, 94–99, 106–07, 115–16, 121–24, 130–35, 143–45, and 154–59.

[35]For a convenient summary of the relation of the Dickinson circle to the Congregational Church, see Thomas H. Johnson, *Emily Dickinson: An Interpretative Biography* (Cambridge: Harvard University Press, 1955), esp. pp. 3–20. For an account of Dickinson's "unrealized but constructible" relationship with Edward Taylor, see Karl Keller, *The Only Kangaroo Among the Beauty* (Baltimore: Johns Hopkins University Press, 1979), pp. 38–66.

[36]James' master distinction—between the "once-born," who appear not to require anything like conversion, and the "twice-born sick-soul," who sorely need and happily find just that thing—may well elide the most interesting case: the soul sufficiently sick of its sin or self to long for divine translation, but unable, for an indefinite stretch of psychological time, to confess the experience or prospect of that prime spiritual fact; see *Varieties of Religious Experience* (Library of America, 1992), esp. pp. 77–154. For Calvin's theory of preaching to the Reprobate, see *Institutes*, Vol. II, p. 241.

[37]The texts in question are, respectively, Bradstreet's "Upon the Burning of Our House," Taylor's "Upon Wedlock and the Death of Children," Shepard's "Autobiography," (see Michael McGiffert, ed., *God's Plot*, [University of Massachusetts Press, 1972], pp. 70–71), and Wigglesworth's *Day of Doom*, stanzas 189–200.

[38]For the flourishing and the eclipse of the Reverend Charles Wadsworth in Dickinson's life and poetic career, see Johnson, *Dickinson*, esp. pp. 69–102; Richard B. Sewall, *The Life of Emily Dickinson* (New York: Farrar, Straus and Giroux, 1974), esp. pp. 444–62; William Shurr, *The Marriage of Emily Dickinson* (Lexington: University of Kentucky Press, 1983), esp. pp. 142–70; Cynthia Griffin Wolff, *Emily Dickinson* (New York: Alfred A. Knopf, 1986), esp. pp. 388–90; and Judith Farr, *The Passion of Emily Dickinson* (Cambridge: Harvard University Press, 1992), esp. pp. 28–29.

[39]For the problems a former slave might have with the orthodox idea of the "slavery" of sin, see, David Van Leer, "Reading Slavery: The Anxiety of Gender in Douglass's *Narrative*," in Eric J. Sundquist, ed., *Frederick Douglass: New Literary and Historical Essays* (Cambridge: Cambridge University Press, 1990), pp. 118–40.

[40]The heart of Whitman's "Natural Quakerism"—analogous with "Wordsworth's Natural Methodism," perhaps—is a founding conviction of the undiminished fullness of the creative and sustaining Spirit in all times and places; its classic locus, the answer to "what the talkers were talking" in the third section of *Song of Myself*: "There never was any more inception [or anything else] than there is now"; quoted from the Library of America *Whitman: Poetry and Prose* (1982), p. 190.

[41]For an account of the way Calvinist and Liberal might express themselves in a literature less indirect and ironic, see David S. Reynolds, *Faith in Fiction* (Cambridge: Harvard University Press, 1981), pp. 73–122.

INDEX

Adams, Henry, 116

Battis, Emery, 184

Bellingham, Richard: discussed 211-17

Bercovitch, Sacvan, 3, 16, 229; on Puritan Jeremiad, 14

Berkeley, George, 75, 102, 105; and idealism of Edwards, 103, 104

Beverley, Robert, 14, 17; History of the Present State of Virginia, 16

Bishop, Jonathan, 138, 174-75, 233

Bloom, Harold, 121

Bradford, William, 17, 217; Of Plymouth Plantation, 11

Bradstreet, Anne, 246, 249

Brownson, Oerestes, 173

Buell, Lawrence, 230; account of Moby-Dick, 230

Bunyan, John, 235, 237

Byrd, William, 14, 17

Cabeza de Vaca, Alvar Nuñez, 17

Calvin, John, 236, 246

Carlyle, Thomas, 111; and Ralph Waldo Emerson, 134

Cartier, Jacques, 15

Channing, Ellery, 173

Channing, William Ellery, 145, 147-48, 150, 152, 154, 161, 163, 176; "The Moral Argument Against Calvinism," 151, 231; "Unitarian Christianity," 151, 231; and Jonathan Edwards, 150; Dudleian Address, 146

Channing, William Henry, 118, 119, 144

Chauncy, Charles, 72, 73, 151, 232

Child, Lydia Maria, 10

Coleridge, Samuel Taylor, 111, 150, 164; and Ralph Waldo Emerson, 146

Columbus, Christopher, 15, 17

Cotton Jr., John: adultery of, 182

Cotton, John, 2, 13, 35, 36, 38, 39, 40, 41, 166, 218, 225, 232, 249; and John Preston, 202; association with character of Dimmesdale, 180, 181, 192, 196; Rejoinder, 14; difference from the Antinomians, 198

Delbanco, Andrew, 13

Derrida, Jacques, 108

Descartes, Rene, 97, 136

Dickinson, Emily: discussed 241-48; 223, 231; and the Puritan past, 25

Donne, John, 90

Douglass, Frederick, 9, 248; My Bondage and My Freedom, 9

Dwight, Timothy: "The Triumph of Infidelity," 237

Dyer, Mary, 178, 187

Eagleton, Terry, 4

Edwards, Jonathan: discussed 61-108; 2, 3, 11, 14, 19, 35, 39, 111, 128, 130, 136, 138, 146, 150, 160, 229, 233, 249; affective theory of will, 73; and Berkeley, 66, 75, 102-4; and Chauncy, 72-3; and Edward Taylor, 19, 24, 68; and Emerson, 21; and Hume, 67; and John Donne, 90; and John Locke, 238; and John Taylor, 85; and Kierkegaard, 95; and Locke, 66, 68, 74, 75; and Luther's Bondage of the Will, 80; and Malebranche, 67, 106; and Newton, 66, 67, 75; and panentheism, 70; and Thomas Shepard, 68; and William James, 62; as "last medieval," 93; as Christian Philosopher, 62; idealism, 21, 65; influence on Melville, 238; modernity of, 61; on Arminians, 64; pastoral context of philosphy, 65; works: Divine and Supernatural Light, 80;

Essay Concerning Human Understanding, 68; Faithful Narrative, 70; Freedom of the Will, 63, 65, 72, 77, 78, 79, 80, 87, 95, 101, 107, 238; God Alone, 97; Miscellanies, 19; Narrative of Surprising Conversions, 66; Nature of True Virtue, 20-1, 63, 77-8, 81, 94-5, 100, 102, 107; Personal Narrative, 19, 72, 96; "Sinners in the Hands of an Angry God," 19, 108; Thoughts Concerning the Revival, 71; Treatise Concerning Religious Affections, 21, 66, 72, 75, 77, 80, 94

Ellison, Julie, 110-11

Emerson, Ellen, 116

Emerson, Ralph Waldo: discussed 109-128 and 129-176 and 231-35; 13, 21, 35, 89, 229, 249-50; and Andrews Norton, 131, 145; and Antinomianism, 135; and Charles Chauncy, 232; and Edward Taylor, 116, 166; and Fichte, 125-26; and Henry Ware Jr., 131; and Imanuel Kant, 165; and Jeremy Taylor, 127; and the figure of Jesus, 138; and John Cotton, 166; and Jonathan Edwards, 111, 130; and Margaret Fuller Ossoli, 118; and Mary Moody (aunt), 122; and Nathaniel Hawthorne, 24, 131; and Ripley, 135, 147; and Solomon Stoddard, 121; and the Puritan past, 25; and Thomas Jefferson, 155; and Walt Whitman, 121; and William Ellery Channing, 145-47, 169; and William Henry Channing, 118; works: "Circles," 130; "Each and All," 123, 125; "Early Lectures," 161; "Experience," 157, 194; "Fate," 234; "Grace," 117, 118; "Human Culture," 155, 158; "Quotation and Originality," 110, 111; "Science," 155, "Self-Reliance," 117, 130, 232; "The American Scholar," 130, 155-56; "The Authority of Jesus," 147; "The Geniune Man," 148; "The Lord's

Supper," 110, 158; "The Philosophy of History," 131; "The Poet," 130; "The Problem," 126; Divinity School Address, 119, 125-27, 232; Divinity School Address as sermon, 134; English Traits, 111; Essays, First Series, 155; letter to Carlyle, 134; Nature, 110, 114, 116, 120, 130, 133, 136, 155-56, 161, 176; reading of Scripture, 143; Representative Men, 111, 154; sermons, 116, 156

Endicott, John, 186

Fichte, Johann Gottlieb, 124, 126, 136, 157

Finney, Charles Grandison, 214

Foucault, Michel, 2, 213, 221

Fox, 111

Franklin, Benjamin, 11, 96, 107

Freud, Sigmund, 98

Frost, Barzillai, 132, 135, 150, 176

Fuller Ossoli, Margaret, 118-19; and the character of Hester Prynne, 184

Gay, Peter, 213

Goethe, 111

Grabo, Norman, 33

Hakluyt, Richard, 15

Hawthorne, Nathaniel: discussed 177-204 and 205-228 and 231-38, 250; and Ann Hutchinson, 237; and Ralph Waldo Emerson, 24; and the Puritan past, 25; and women writers, 182; as "Americanist," 22; works: "Main Street," 178; "Mrs. Hutchinson," 180, 185; "Rappaccini's Daughter," 236; "The Bosom Serpent," 236; "The Custom House," 131, 237; "The Gentle Boy," 178, 187, 188; "The Minister's Black Veil," 178, 195, 203, 236; "Young Goodman Brown," 178, 195, 203, 235, 236, 238; Grandfather's Chair, 178, 185; The Blithedale Romance, 10; The Scarlet Letter, discussed 177-204 and 205-228, 10, 22, 237

Hawthorne, Sophia, 186

Hedge, Frederick Henry, 164, 173

Heimert, Alan, 13

Herbert, George: discussed 109-128; "The Collar," 119, 120, 123, 125, 127; "Vanitie," 124; The Country Parson, 127

Herbert, T. Walter: account of Moby-Dick, 230

Herder, Johann Gottfried, 139

Hooker, Thomas, 2, 13, 36, 38, 40, 41; Application of Redemption, 40; preparation, 13

Hoopes, James, 105

Hume, David, 67, 107, 144, 146, 233

Hutchinson, Ann, 136, 218, 237

Irving, Washington, 15

Jacobs, Harriet, 9, 248

James, William, 62, 98; "Will to Believe", 233

Jefferson, Thomas, 110, 155

Johnson, Edward: as source for The Scarlet Letter, 188, 190; on Ann Hutchinson, 191

Kant, Imanuel, 165

Lawrence, D.H., 6, 178, 224

Leavis, F.R., 4

Lewis, C.S., 4

Lewis, R.W.B., 5

Locke, John, 64, 66, 68, 74-5, 97, 107

Luther, Martin, 111, 175; Bondage of the Will, 80

Lyon, Mary: and Emily Dickinson, 241

Malebranche, Nicholas, 67, 106

Marlowe, Christopher, 247

Marx, Leo, 5

Mather, Cotton, 11, 14, 204, 235; as pretext, 206; as source for The Scarlet Letter, 188, 189, 190; Magnalia Christi Americana, 14, 16, 238; The Christian Philosopher, 14

Matthiessen, F.O., 3

Melville, Herman: discussed 237-250; 227, 234; "Bartleby the Scrivener," 238; "quarrel with God," 231; and Cotton Mather, 238, 239; and Jonathan Edwards, 238; and the

Puritan past, 25; Moby-Dick, 10; Pierre, 238

Miller, Perry, 3, 13, 16, 25, 66, 67, 72, 93, 97, 98, 99, 164, 208, 229, 230, 235; and Edwards' "modernity," 61, 62; and Jonathan Edwards, 19; on Puritan Jeremiad, 14

Milton, John, 59, 110-11, 127, 166, 235, 247; and Emerson, 114; as pretext, 206

Montaigne, Michel de, 111

Moody, Mary, 122

Morison, Samuel Eliot, 209

Morton, Thomas, 12

Mott, Wesley T., 146

Newton, Isaac, 66-7, 75, 97

Norton, Andrews, 133, 145-46, 150, 152; "The Latest Form of Infidelity," 131

Noyes, John Humphrey, 214, 223

Paine, Thomas, 144, 175

Paley, William, 152, 163

Parker, Theodore, 173

Peters, Hugh, 186

Philadelphia, 15, 17

Plato, 111

Porte, Joel, 120

Preston, John: and the character of Dimmesdale, 202

Quakers, 187-88

Ripley, George, 135, 144, 147, 173

Robinson, David, 132

Rowlandson, Mary, 14

Schleiermacher, Friedrich, 139

Schneider, Herbert, 72

Sedgwick, Catharine Maria, 10

Seelye, John, 15

Sewall, Samuel, 14

Shakespeare, William, 111; as pretext, 206

Shepard, Thomas, 38, 40-1, 68, 225, 249; and Anne Hutchinson, 12; and Thomas Shepard III, 12; Autobiography, 12; sanctification, 13

Smith, Henry Nash, 5

Smith, John, 12, 14-15, 17; as historian, 16

Snow, Caleb, 206-7

Spengemann, William, 21

Stoddard, Solomon, 36, 39, 42, 122; and Emerson, 121

Stowe, Harriet Beecher, 9, 250; Uncle Tom's Cabin, 10

Strauss, David Friedrich, 139

Swedenborg, Emanuel, 98, 111

Taylor, Edward: discussed 27-60; 2, 3, 11, 64, 68, 96, 114, 116, 166, 201, 218, 233, 244, 245, 246, 249; and Calvin, 39; and Emerson's Poet, 42; and John Cotton, 38, 39; and Jonathan Edwards, 24, 35, 39; and Milton, 59; and open communion, 34; and Puritan doctrine, 19; and Solomon Stoddard, 19, 36, 39; and the Congregational Church, 37; and Thomas Hooker, 38; and Thomas Shepard, 38; and visible sainthood, 27; vs. Cotton's opposition to works, 38; compared to John Cotton, 35; ; Gods Determinations, 18; on conversion, 28; Preparatory Mediations, 14

Taylor, Jeremy: and Ralph Waldo Emerson, 127

Taylor, John, 85

The Dial, 118

Thoreau, Henry David, 173, 221; and Frederick Douglass, 9; Walden, 9

Very, Jones, 174

Ward, Nathaniel, 186

Ware Jr., Henry, 132-33, 135, 150, 176; "The Personality of the Deity," 131

Warner, Susan, 10, 248, 250

Whicher, Stephen, 116, 234

Whitman, Walt, 112, 174, 249

Wigglesworth, Michael, 2, 247, 249

Williams, Raymond, 4

Williams, Roger, 222

Wilson, John, 181

Winters, Yvor, 117, 132-33

Winthrop, John: discussed 205-228; 178, 235; "Model of Christian Charity", 207, 221; and Ann Hutchinson, 13; and Roger Williams, 13; as source for The Scarlet Letter, 182, 188, 190,

206; Journal, 13, 206; "Model of
Christian Charity", 13; relationship to
American Studies, 206; Short Story,
192

Woolman, John, 11, 107

Wordsworth, William, 111; and Emerson,
114

Wright, Conrad, 132